Line on Fire

This book offers much more than a mere clinical analysis of the nature and causes of ceasefire violations in J&K, and how they impact India–Pakistan escalation dynamics. What makes the book distinct and different from the majority of such publications is that, in addition to formulating the key issues, the author applies certain theoretical models to explain India–Pakistan escalation dynamics. A valid point the author makes is that viewing the escalating conflict between the two countries as mere 'mindless' violence is trivializing the conflict. Instead the author relies on the 'conflict-spiral' model to convincingly argue that in 'hyper-nationalist' settings—such as the India–Pakistan rivalry—rational calculations and neatly built scenarios cannot explain escalation. It would be tantamount to ignoring several aspects, apart from the 'fog of war', namely, autonomous military factors, the overhang of repeated ceasefire violations, and the existence of organizational subcultures. All these are of critical importance, in addition to continuing cross-border terror attacks.

The author has carried out interviews with a large number of serving and retired Indian and Pakistani military officers, together with field visits to both sides of the Line of Control. He has made use of fresh data sets, and brought a strategic insight into the nature of the India–Pakistan conflict and escalation dynamics. The book is, hence, not merely a valuable addition to the existing literature on the India–Pakistan conflict, but a compelling read for anyone interested in gaining a deeper understanding of one of the longest conflicts in the world.

—M.K. Narayanan, Former National Security Advisor (2005–2010), Government of India; Former Governor, West Bengal

A very useful addition to the scholarly literature on India–Pakistan relations on a hitherto little researched but most important contemporary topic. Happymon Jacob's *Line on Fire* analyses India–Pakistan ceasefire violations between 2003 and 2017 and makes a strong empirical and theoretical case for their significance in India–Pakistan crisis escalation dynamics. With almost 2,000 ceasefire violations since 2011, the potential for their escalation into conventional and even nuclear war must be a general concern, particularly in the present state of India–Pakistan relations. Analysing how and why ceasefire violations take place, Jacob also suggests policies to overcome the ad hocism that he thinks has so far characterised management of the border by both sides. A significant contribution to our understanding of a complex issue.

—Shivshankar Menon, Former National Security Advisor (2010–2014), Government of India; Former Foreign Secretary, Government of India

To me the greatest value of this book is in it bringing to light an eminently readable conversation between two protagonists who otherwise refuse to talk to each other! While it endorses a crying need for peace at an unfortunate dividing line, I imagine readers on both sides will be scrambling to understand the 'enemy' mind through the words and actions recorded herein. Happymon provides a rare insight through his unique good fortune in seeing it from both sides, first hand. There are ideas here for the Indian and Pakistani leadership to finally end the suffering, and to make the next 70 years unlike the previous seventy.

—Lt Gen. (Retd) Tariq Waseem Ghazi, Former Defence Secretary,
Government of Pakistan

Happymon Jacob shines much-needed light on an extremely important risk to the security and well-being of India and Pakistan. Through extensive original research, including scores of interviews with well-placed sources, he corrects the often simplistic assumptions of what drives the use of force by India and Pakistan in Jammu and Kashmir. Autonomous local military interests and decisions, paired with uneven attention and direction from political leaders on both sides, cause and enable ceasefire violations to occur even when there are no clear provocations. The result is a greater potential for escalation—intentional or otherwise—that has not been adequately understood and could spiral out of control. There is much here for decision-makers, scholars, and commentators who will shape the future of war or peace between India and Pakistan.

—George Perkovich, Vice President, Carnegie Endowment for
International Peace, Washington, DC

This book is essential reading for anyone who wants to understand the dynamics of the fraught relationship between India and Pakistan. The author provides very sophisticated new insights into the relationship and explains why it is so dangerous.

—Bruce Riedel, Senior Fellow and Director, Brookings Intelligence
Project, Brookings Institution, Washington, DC

THE OXFORD INTERNATIONAL RELATIONS IN SOUTH ASIA SERIES

SERIES EDITORS
Sumit Ganguly and E. Sridharan

After a long period of relative isolation during the Cold War years, contemporary South Asia has grown immensely in its significance in the global political and economic order. This ascendancy has two key dimensions. First, the emergence of India as a potential economic and political power that follows its acquisition of nuclear weapons and its fitful embrace of economic liberalization. Second, the persistent instability along India's borders continues to undermine any attempts at achieving political harmony in the region: fellow nuclear-armed state Pakistan is beset with chronic domestic political upheavals; Afghanistan is paralysed and trapped with internecine warfare and weak political institutions; Sri Lanka is confronted by an uncertain future with a disenchanted Tamil minority; Nepal is caught in a vortex of political and legal uncertainty as it forges a new constitution; and Bangladesh is overwhelmed by a tumultuous political climate.

India's rising position as an important player in global economic and political affairs warrants extra-regional and international attention. The rapidly evolving strategic role and importance of South Asia in the world demands focused analyses of foreign and security policies within and towards the region. The present series addresses these concerns. It consists of original, theoretically grounded, empirically rich, timely, and topical volumes oriented towards contemporary and future developments in one of the most populous and diverse corners of the world.

Sumit Ganguly is professor of political science and holds the Rabindranath Tagore Chair in Indian Cultures and Civilizations, Indiana University, Bloomington, USA.

E. Sridharan is academic director, University of Pennsylvania Institute for the Advanced Study of India, New Delhi.

THE OXFORD INTERNATIONAL RELATIONS IN SOUTH ASIA SERIES

Line on Fire

Ceasefire Violations and India–Pakistan
Escalation Dynamics

Happymon Jacob

OXFORD
UNIVERSITY PRESS

OXFORD
UNIVERSITY PRESS

Oxford University Press is a department of the University of Oxford.
It furthers the University's objective of excellence in research, scholarship,
and education by publishing worldwide. Oxford is a registered trademark of
Oxford University Press in the UK and in certain other countries.

Published in India by
Oxford University Press
2/11 Ground Floor, Ansari Road, Daryaganj, New Delhi 110 002, India

ISBN-13 (print edition): 978-0-19-948989-3
ISBN-10 (print edition): 0-19-948989-0

ISBN-13 (eBook): 978-0-19-909547-6
ISBN-10 (eBook): 0-19-909547-7

Typeset in Adobe Jenson Pro 10.5/13
by The Graphics Solution, New Delhi 110 092
Printed in India by Nutech Print Services India

Contents

Tables, Figures, and Cases

Tables

Figures

Cases

Abbreviations

ACR	annual confidential report
AGPL	Actual Ground Position Line
AK	Azad Kashmir
AMF	autonomous military factor
AOR	area of responsibility
BAT	Border Action Team
BGRs	Border Ground Rules
BJP	Bharatiya Janta Party
BOP	border outpost
BMD	ballistic missile defence
BSF	Border Security Force
C&C	command and control (C&C)
CBMs	confidence-building measures
CFA	ceasefire agreement
CFL	Ceasefire Line
CFV	ceasefire violation
CI	counter-insurgency
CO	Commanding Officer
COAS	chief of the army staff
DG	director general
DGMO	director-general of military operations
DIG	deputy inspector general
FCNA	Force Command Northern Areas (Pakistan)
GHQ	General Headquarters (Pakistan)
GOC	general officer commanding
GOC-in-C	general officer commanding-in-chief
GRsA	Ground Rules Agreement
HLM	hotline message
HQ	headquarters

IAF	Indian Air Force
IB	International Border
IED	improvised explosive device
IG	inspector general
ISI	Inter-Services Intelligence
ISPR	Inter Services Public Relations (Pakistan)
J&K	Jammu and Kashmir
JCO	junior commissioned officer
JeM	Jaish-e-Mohammed
JNU	Jawaharlal Nehru University
LAC	Line of Actual Control
LeT	Lashkar-e-Taiba
LoC	Line of Control
MAC	Multi Agency Centre
MEA	Ministry of External Affairs
MFA	Ministry of Foreign Affairs
MHA	Ministry of Home Affairs
MI/MO	military intelligence/military operations
MLI	Maratha Light Infantry
MOD	Ministry of Defence
NDTV	New Delhi Television
NIA	National Investigative Agency (India)
NLI	Northern Light Infantry
NSA	National Security Advisor
OP	observation post
PASCOM	Pakistan Army Strategic Communications
PATCOM	Pakistan Army Tactical Communication
PIA	Pakistan International Airlines
PIB	Press Information Bureau
POK	Pakistan Occupied Kashmir
RR	Rashtriya Rifles
SBH	secretary border management
SC	Security Council
SCO	Shanghai Cooperation Organization
SCP	Simultaneous Coordinated Patrolling
SOP	standard operating procedure
SSG	special services group
TNW	tactical nuclear weapon

UAV	unmanned aerial vehicle
UPA	United Progressive Alliance
USIP	United States Institute of Peace
UN	United Nations
UNCIP	United Nations Commission for India and Pakistan
UNGA	United Nations General Assembly
UNMOGIP	United Nations Military Observer Group in India and Pakistan
UNSC	United Nations Security Council
US	United States
WB	Working Boundary

Foreword

Lt Gen. (Retd) Harcharanjit Singh Panag,
Former General Officer Commanding in Chief
Northern Command and Central Command, Indian Army
Chandigarh, 29 May 2018

Line on Fire, written by Happymon Jacob, could not have been timed better to prove his conclusion that the conflict waging along the unsettled border between the Indian state of Jammu and Kashmir (J&K) and Pakistan can lead to higher rungs of escalation between the two nuclear weapon-armed states. The line in question is the Ceasefire Line (CFL) based on the Karachi Agreement, 1949, which was converted into the Line of Control (LoC) following the Simla Agreement, 1972, which is the line that runs between the actual positions held at the end of the 1971 war. Barring short spells, the line has always been on fire due to its very nature, as a result of the absolutist claims of both the states and a host of other factors, including the fourth-generation war or proxy war being waged by Pakistan in J&K with a spillover into the hinterland of India.

Sample the headlines/news reports of *The Tribune* dated 23 May and 24 May 2018 referring to the firing along the 201 km of plain portion of the line between J&K and Punjab, Pakistan, treated as International Boundary (IB) by India and Working Boundary (WB) by Pakistan.

'Shelling Spreads along Entire IB: BSF [Border Security Force] Jawan among 20 Hurt as 90 of 120 Jammu Villages Hit'[1]

'5 killed, 90,000 Displaced along IB: Pak targets 80 BSF Posts, 3 Jawans among 40 Hurt'[2]

---

[1] Amit Khajuria, 'Shelling Spreads along Entire IB', *Tribune*, 23 May 2018, https://www.tribuneindia.com/news/jammu-kashmir/shelling-spreads-along-entire-ib/593607.html, accessed on 25 May 2018.

[2] Amit Khajuria and Arteev Sharma, '5 Killed, 90,000 Displaced along IB', *Tribune*, 24 May 2018, https://www.tribuneindia.com/news/jammu-kashmir/5-killed-90-000-displaced-along-ib/594110.html, accessed on 25 May 2018.

Similar headlines must be appearing in Pakistani newspapers. In fact, the situation along the rest of the LoC is even worse. Both sides, of course, claim that they are responding to unprovoked firing. Indian generals are on record saying that LoC warfare is being utilized to compel Pakistan to stop the proxy war in J&K. The Pakistan Army's spokesperson is on record saying that they are deliberately targeting the villages along the WB based on demographic factors in response to the Indian Army doing so across the LoC.

Let alone the bloody past, the present situation itself highlights the justification for this book and its principal argument that ceasefire violations (CFVs) are intrinsically linked to the escalation ladder and may lead to a war between India and Pakistan.

Having spent 10 years on this 'Line on Fire', from the rank of 2/Lt to an army commander when the entire 1,125 km less the IB/WB in J&K was under my command, I must confess that we viewed the issue as a military management problem to be handled based on the political and operational environment. Our actions were focused on quid pro quo response to incidents triggered by a host of complex factors and unilateral retribution for perpetrating the proxy war, the direct and indirect support for which comes through the LoC.

Happymon Jacob in the *Line on Fire* seeks to explain the causes of CFVs, the under-analysed link between the CFVs and crisis escalation between India and Pakistan, and the dangers of CFV-linked escalation under nuclear conditions. In doing so, the book nuances the existing notions about the escalatory dynamics between the two South Asian nuclear rivals. Moreover, it establishes a significant relationship between CFVs and India–Pakistan escalation dynamics. In short, this book de-mythifies the popular notions regarding the causes of CFVs in J&K and India–Pakistan escalation dynamics. The book further explains CFVs using the concept of 'autonomous military factors' (AMFs).

Happymon has eminently succeeded in the objectives set out for his book. His definition of escalation itself is very interesting. 'A sudden intensification of political, military, and diplomatic tensions between countries in a general atmosphere of adversarial relations that may or may not lead to a war.' It helps us to view escalation occurring in a not-so-tightly-controlled atmosphere, but as a result of AMFs. Having had the benefit of visiting the LoC from both sides and interviewing a host of military and paramilitary personalities of both sides, the role of AMFs has been brilliantly analysed. This, in my view, has been his original and singular contribution. He proves that the politicians have, by default in India and due to the supremacy of the military in Pakistan, allowed the AMFs along the LoC to become the main cause of escalation of crisis. From personality traits of commanders, reputations of units, moral ascendency, psychology of soldiers, military vendetta, compellence to stop infiltration, and mere accidents, the AMFs have been analysed threadbare.

I have a major disagreement with the author with respect to his conclusion that the proxy war is not a major reason for the CFVs. In my experience, the opposite is true. Before the proxy war began, the CFVs were more manageable and the guidelines of the Karachi Agreement were generally adhered to. Post 1989, the perception on the Indian side is that the Pakistan Army manning the LoC connives and facilitates the movement of terrorists and material support for the proxy war. Hence, it must be deterred through unprecedented retribution and compellence. More so when the nuclear deterrent forecloses the option of a full-scale war. The CFVs have thus become part of the operational strategy. This strategy also has political sanction since mid-2014. The LoC, both on and across, has thus become the main arena for retributory punishment by fire and small-scale operations below the threshold of war. Pakistan responds with quid pro quo. This can always spiral into a major escalation and even lead to a J&K-centric limited war.

The author also recommends a solution in the form of a formal agreement to manage the LoC, along with better military-to-military contact and communications. One could not agree with him more as similar measures along the Line of Actual Control (LAC) have prevented even a single shot being fired, barring one stray incident since 1967.

I have read the research papers, articles, and books written by Happymon Jacob over the last two decades and have personally known him for a couple of years. Outstanding knowledge, thorough research, endearing communication skills, and a very affable personality is how I would like to sum up my impression of him. One may not agree with all that has been concluded by Happymon, but I have no hesitation in saying that had this research been available to me during my service on the LoC, I would have handled the situation with greater finesse.

Line on Fire is an extremely well-researched book with the author having the benefit of field visits and interviews with relevant civil and military personalities from both sides of the border, apart from his research and immense knowledge. The book is a must for all military and academic libraries of India and Pakistan and a must for the commanders serving on the 'Line on Fire'.

Foreword

Lt Gen. (Retd) Waheed Arshad
Former Chief of General Staff
Pakistan Army
Lahore, 19 May 2018

I met Happymon Jacob in the track-two circuit some years back during one of the meetings of the Ottawa Dialogue, a forum dedicated to discussing issues of conflict between Pakistan and India. It was a pleasant surprise to find his views unfettered by the systemic shackles of fixation that are often on display whenever there is a discussion between interlocutors from Pakistan and India on our mutual issues of conflict, specially Kashmir. Jacob follows an approach that is objective, tinged with new ideas, and questions entrenched views and mindset with deep logic and realism. His book *Line on Fire* is a reflection of all that and, in many ways, a seminal and path-breaking endeavour on a subject that is not only sensitive but also emotional. Typically, Jacob has tackled it with his customary depth of analysis, challenging conventional wisdom and providing great food for thought. When Jacob told me about his book, which was a follow-up to an earlier project on the same subject he was doing for the United States Institute of Peace (USIP), I was struck by the fact that he had not visited Pakistan and our side of the LoC and had almost finished his work! On my enquiry, it was revealed that after trying for more than a year, he had lost hope of visiting the LoC on the Pakistani side. I promised to assist him and was able to get his visit through with support from General Headquarters (GHQ). I dare say his trip to Pakistan provided him with a very different perspective, one which helped him in refining his outlook and views.

Despite the fact that the book is about the LoC, the real issue of conflict between Pakistan and India is Kashmir and not the LoC and WB. These are just the outcome and manifestation of the unresolved and festering issue. The dynamics of the LoC have evolved since 1972 when it came into being, and in many ways, the events happening along it reflect the evolution of the dynamics of Kashmir and how both the countries approach it. From the relatively quiet period of the 1970s and the 1980s, the situation changed drastically with the eruption of the Kashmir Freedom Movement in 1989. Since that time, life along the LoC has been defined by periods of intense disturbance of the 1990s free-for-all environment, marked by daily fire exchanges of all kinds of weapons and small-level tactical actions. All that again changed in November 2003 when Pakistan announced a unilateral ceasefire, which India followed, as a prelude to the rejuvenation of the bilateral dialogue for resolution of issues of conflict. This led to a period of relative calm till 2012, when suddenly the dynamics changed due to political reasons and the understanding of ceasefire practically broke down. The year 2017 was the bloodiest year, with almost 2000 violations and scores of deaths, mostly civilians.

In many ways, the time was ripe for someone to take a deeper look at the issue of ceasefire, its breakdown, and the dynamics of escalation. No one was better suited to do it than Happymon Jacob. In doing so, he has analysed important aspects within the framework of the overarching issue of Kashmir. He has studied the reasons for the breakdown of the ceasefire and challenged entrenched views in both countries through a realistic ground view. Post 2003, ceasefire understanding has led to greater control of the troops' actions along the LoC and WB to avoid escalation, but then again political reasons have led to the ceasefire practically breaking down last year. Discussion of the dynamics of escalation is another key area dissected by him. It is important to note that the political stances of both countries in regard to Kashmir and the ensuing conflict find their practical manifestation in the events along the LoC. India accuses Pakistan of CFVs to help movement of non-state actors in support of the Freedom Movement, while Pakistan accuses India of violating ceasefire and of escalation to divert from the domestic and international concerns about the events inside Indian-occupied Kashmir, externalizing it. Be that as it may, the opposing politics and resultant CFVs lead to escalation that, in an environment of conflict, may escalate further vertically and laterally leading to unintended consequences. The domestic environment in both countries gets shaped through media hype and nationalistic jingoism, which impacts national decision-making. In such an environment, even conflict stability becomes a problem, let alone conflict management or a move towards resolution.

Another important aspect regarding the dynamics of the LoC is that, contrary to the common perception of most people, there is no formal ceasefire agreement (CFA) between Pakistan and India that binds them to a greater degree of responsibility. Jacob's book provides a broad-spectrum understanding of the dynamics of the LoC, which should assist decision-makers in both countries to agree to formalize the ceasefire agreement while broadening its scope and dimensions. It would be a positive, confidence-building measure and augur well for stability and progress on bilateral dialogue. Jacob has been part of the team of track-two Ottawa Dialogue which prepared a comprehensive paper on 'Management of Ceasefire' along the LoC and WB. The paper has been shared with relevant decision-making authorities in both countries.

For anyone who wants to have an objective understanding of the environment of ceasefire along the LoC and how it influences the climate of conflict overshadowing Pakistan and India, the book is a must-read.

Acknowledgements

The idea for this book germinated in the many closed-door track-two dialogues I have been part of over the past one and a half decades under the aegis of the Chaophraya Dialogue, Pugwash Conferences on Science and World Affairs, the Ottawa Dialogue, the International Institute of Strategic Studies, and several others. I have never been part of the government. So, for an academic like me, track-two discussions are as close as one can get to the decision-making circles, often with a better view of things than those in the government, given that track-two interlocutors often speak frankly under the Chatham House rule. Moreover, one stands to gain a great deal when former officials from the rival sides interact in track-two settings and jointly search for solutions to their bilateral problems, albeit after retirement.

Threadbare discussions on CFVs and escalation dynamics as well as insights shared by senior military commanders from India and Pakistan convinced me of the need to dig deeper and undertake a systematic book-length study on the subject. The popular and even scholarly understanding of CFVs and escalation dynamics, I thought, was skewed in that it seemed to typically view CFVs as an effect of the escalation or part of it, almost never as a cause. This had to be problematized. Moreover, there was also a general sense that CFVs do not matter in the larger higher order conflict dynamics between the two nuclear rivals—both India and Pakistan, and their militaries and people were learning to live with the constant firing on the dividing lines in J&K. It was becoming business as usual. This dangerous sense of comfort also had to be disturbed.

These elementary thoughts first translated into a long paper that I wrote for the USIP. The paper, entitled 'Ceasefire Violations in Jammu and Kashmir', was well received and so I decided to expand it into a book.

It took me over two years to carry out the field visits in India and Pakistan, create fresh data sets on CFVs and escalation, conduct over 80 interviews with serving and retired officers, and finally write and rewrite the book. None of this would have been possible without the help and encouragement of several individuals and institutions.

My brilliant doctoral student and research associate, Tanvi Kulkarni, was always a call away. She helped me with the data collection, interviews, and field work, and had a solution whenever this project encountered a problem, practical or intellectual. Thank you, Tanvi. Muhammad Faisal helped with data collection and interviews in Pakistan. Amanat Boparai created all the graphs and charts used in the book. Aditi Razdan and Manu Sharma also pitched in with research and data.

This work would have been seriously inadequate had it not been for the field work I managed to do despite the heavy odds. I thank the BSF officials who organized my field visits to Jammu, Punjab, Rajasthan, and Gujarat; Northern Command of the Indian Army, and Lt Gen. (Retd) D.S. Hooda in particular, for helping me with field visits in Kashmir; and finally, the Pakistan army for the field visits to the Pakistani side of the LoC, and to the GHQ, Rawalpindi. I thank Lt Gen. (Retd) Tariq Waseem Ghazi, Lt Gen. (Retd) Aditya Singh, Lt Gen. (Retd) Waheed Arshad, and Aditya Mishra of the BSF for facilitating my visits to the India–Pakistan border areas.

Several of my colleagues at Jawaharlal Nehru University (JNU), New Delhi, India in particular, Rajesh Rajagopalan, have contributed in significant ways to my understanding of national security and foreign policy. Rajesh has been my sounding board for ideas.

I am grateful to Moeed Yusuf for encouraging me to write a paper for USIP on CFVs, and Sumit Ganguly for encouraging me to publish this book as part of the Oxford University Press series, International Relations in South Asia co-edited by E. Sridharan and him.

After I completed my data collection, field work, and interviews, it was important for me to get away from New Delhi to have some much-needed 'writer's solitude'. I went on a sabbatical from JNU to join the Institute of Advanced Studies at the Central European University, Budapest, Hungary as a senior global challenges fellow for over six months, and a few months at Berlin's Global Public Policy Institute.

I could not have asked for a better place to write my book than the beautiful, historical city of Budapest. I am grateful to Nadia Al-Bagdadi, Éva Gönczi, Agnes Forgo, Sanjay Kumar, Anup Sam Nainan, Garima

Mohan, and Maria Rybakova for their warm hospitality, friendship, and advice while I was writing the book.

I wish to thank the following scholars for their comments on the earlier drafts of the book: Rajesh Rajagopalan at JNU; Anit Mukherjee and Rajesh Basrur at the Rajaratnam School of International Studies, Singapore; Fahd Humayun at Yale University, New Haven, Conneticut; Toby Dalton and Frédéric Grare at the Carnegie Endowment for International Peace; Michael Krepon at the Stimson Center; Moeed Yusuf at USIP; Sadia Tasleem at the Quaid-i-Azam University; Sumit Ganguly at the Indiana University; T.V. Paul at the McGill University; Feroz Khan at the Naval Postgraduate School; Jack Gill at the Near East South Asia Centre; and the two anonymous reviewers. This book is in a much better shape today thanks to their sound advice.

I am grateful to the former national security advisors of India, M.K. Narayanan and Shivshankar Menon, and George Perkovich of the Carnegie Endowment for International Peace for writing short, thoughtful blurbs for the book. I also thank Lt Gen. (Retd) H.S. Panag of the Indian Army and Lt Gen. (Retd) Waheed Arshad of the Pakistan army for writing the forewords for the book.

I wish to thank Peter Jones and Nicole Waintraub of the Ottawa Dialogue and Paolo Cotta-Ramusino of the Pugwash Conferences on Science and World Affairs for making me a part of their outstanding and highly effective track-two initiatives on South Asia.

The team ot Oxford University Press deserves my gratitude for keeping me on track with the delivery of the book, and Gaurav Saini for providing the cover illustration for the book.

Finally, I thank all those serving officers and soldiers of the Indian and Pakistani armies and the BSF for hosting me in their mess halls, barracks, and bunkers, and answering my often irritating and persistent questions.

I dedicate this book to Siddhartha, and the men and women in uniform.

1   Introduction

Operation Kabaddi—2001[1]

IN THE EARLY SUMMER OF 2001, the Indian Army was making meticulous preparations to carry out a highly classified operation across the LoC in J&K. Code-named Kabaddi, the operation would, when carried out, alter the geography of the LoC, the line agreed upon by India and Pakistan at Simla in 1972 after the Bangladesh War of Independence. Around 25–30 Pakistani army posts from the Batalik sector of the Ladakh region of J&K right down to Chamb-Jaurian in the Jammu sector were earmarked by the Indian Army's Northern Command for capture: around one–two posts per brigade. They were to be captured in a surprise operation judiciously divided into multiple phases, overrunning the Pakistani defences. It had to be a limited operation—no one wanted a full-scale war with Pakistan.

The general outlines of the audacious operation, codenamed Kabaddi,[2] were drawn up in June 2001 in a meeting among the newly appointed general officer commanding-in-chief (GOC-in-C), Northern Command of the Indian Army, Lt Gen. Rostum K. Nanavatty, Lt Gen. Gurbaksh

[1] The account of Operation Kabaddi is based on the interviews provided by two senior retired officers of the Indian Army: Interview with Lt Gen. Rustom K. Nanavatty, Northern Army Commander, February 2001 to May 2003, 6 December 2017, New Delhi; and Interview with Lt Gen. H.S. Panag, Army Commander, Central and Northern, 3 March 2017, Bangkok. Clarifications were sought from the two officers on several occasions thereafter via email and text messages.

[2] The Indian Army's operation in Kanjarkot during the 1965 India–Pakistan war is also called 'Operation Kabaddi'.

Singh Sihota, the director general of military operations (DGMO) of the Indian Army, and the then Indian army chief Gen. Sundararajan Padmanabhan at the office of the chief of the army staff (COAS) in New Delhi. It was an unusually long meeting for the three senior officers of the Indian Army in which Gen. Nanavatty and Gen. Sihota appraised their chief, Padmanabhan, of the situation on the LoC and the increasing terrorist infiltration into J&K. They had to do something to radically change the payoff structure for Pakistan, Gen. Nanavatty argued. Gen. Padmanabhan agreed and gave the go ahead to make preparations for Operation Kabaddi.

Gen. Nanavatty returned to his headquarters (HQ) in Udhampur, in the foothills of the Shivalik ranges in J&K, with a three-month preparation time from his chief to get his command ready for Operation Kabaddi. Gen. Padmanabhan told Gen. Nanavatty to expect orders to carry out the operation to arrive in due course.

The top-secret operation, which continues to remain undisclosed to the public, was to be carried out at the brigade level and below so as not to cross any dangerous threshold in a nuclearized environment. Operation Kabaddi would include a wide spectrum of evolving punitive operations such as the execution of deliberate fire assaults to destroy military and terrorist points, and area targets across the LoC; ambushes and raids across the LOC; and company, battalion, and brigade-sized deliberate offensive attacks to capture objectives of tactical importance across the LoC that would improve the Indian Army's counter-insurgency (CI) posture. However, according to Gen. Nanavatty, 'it was not a single, coordinated operation to commence on a prescribed date. There was no mathematical distribution of tasks to formations and units.' They were planned to take place in several phases based on various operational contingencies. There was a great flexibility built into Gen. Nanavatty's operational plans to deal with contingencies and Pakistani responses to a surprise attack by India.

It was to be a purely army operation—the Indian Air Force (IAF) was neither notified nor integrated into the operational plans. However, as the preparations progressed, Gen. Nanavatty did suggest to Gen. Sihota that the IAF be brought into the picture to effectively carry out the mission.

The underlying strategic rationale behind the top-secret plan was to ease the pressure from the Pakistan-sponsored insurgency in J&K which was showing no respite despite the several military gains made by India through the 1990s. Home-grown insurgency was dying out, but infiltration from Pakistan continued unabated. The Indian Army wanted to bring an end to it, or demonstrate to the Pakistan Army the costs of aiding infiltration into J&K.

The execution of Operation Kabaddi was to take place on or after 1 September 2001. In the words of Gen. Nanavatty, 'We were required to be ready to execute operations as planned on orders any time on or after 1 September 2001. But there were no "start" and "finish" dates.'

There is no clarity on whether Operation Kabaddi had political approval from the Vajpayee government in New Delhi. The two officers who were extensively interviewed to get an understanding of the 2001 operation, Gen. Nanavatty, the then Northern Army commander, and Lt Gen. H.S. Panag, who was a brigade commander under Nanavatty, could not confirm whether the plan had political clearance from Defence Minister George Fernandes, Defence Minister Jaswant Singh (who took over from Fernandes in March 2001), or Prime Minister Atal Bihari Vajpayee. Gen. Panag talked about discussions with Gen. Nanavatty. The latter recalled his discussions with the then army chief Gen. Padmanabhan. When Gen. Padmanabhan, who lives in Chennai after retirement, was contacted by the author, he said that due to his advanced age, he did not recall the specifics of the operation or whether such an operation had political clearance. On whether there was political clearance, Gen. Nanavatty responded that 'only army HQ can answer the question as to whether the planned operations had the sanction of the government. As far as Northern Command was concerned we had the approval of army HQ.'

The rationale for this large-scale offensive operation had its origin in the previous year. The year 2000 had witnessed several small-scale and successful operations of this kind. During the previous year, local units of the army, with the tacit understanding and green signal from the army's higher ups, had 'adopted a calibrated offensive action across' the LoC 'to sanitise areas of infiltration' on the Pakistani side.[3] In an article written in 2014, military analyst Pravin Sawhney wrote rather candidly about several minor operations that were carried out during those months.

> For example, on 22 January 2000, fighting in the Chhamb sector left 16 Pakistani soldiers dead. While both sides blamed one another, the

[3] Pravin Sawhney, 'At the Crossroad', *Force Newsmagazine.com*, 26 January 2014, http://forcenewsmagazine.blogspot.de/2014/01/at-crossroad.html, last accessed on 21 September 2017.

truth was that Indian troops, in strength, attacked a Pakistani post and overran it. Similar instances occurred in Akhnoor, Mendhar, Kotli, Naushera and Pallanwala between January and August 2000.[4]

So the planners, in a sense, only had to repeat the smaller operations on a larger scale.

The success of the previous year's minor operations and the success of the Kargil War in 1999 under nuclear conditions had emboldened the Indian Army. Moreover, the then defence minister George Fernandes was a fan of the Indian Army's limited war doctrine. The army's recently retired chief V. P. Malik had spoken about it at length and become one of its proponents in later years.

Gen. Nanavatty personally oversaw the preparations, going from brigade to brigade along the LoC to discuss the minute details of the plan with his brigade commanders. Operational plans were shared down to the brigade commanders' level who were told to be ready for an assault, when the time came.

Three posts were selected from the Batalik sector, where Gen. Panag was posted during those days. Gen. Panag was a brigade commander then and he was in charge of carrying out the operation on three Pakistani posts. Gen. Panag recalls Nanavatty flying into the former's brigade HQ to decide the objectives and details of the operation. The general and the brigadier then went up to the LoC on the Indian side and the army commander was shown the three posts that were marked out to be captured. Panag's brigade was holding around 70 km of frontage of the LOC, so the objectives were spread out but he was confident of capturing them when the orders came. Nanavatty approved the plan before returning to his Command HQ.

Reserve battalions were pulled back from CI duties inside Kashmir, and were trained to carry out the mission and were kept on operational alert. The planners were aware that such an offensive land grab operation would not go unanswered by the Pakistani side: they were prepared to absorb the Pakistani response, most importantly by anticipating it.

To the chief architect of the operations, the Northern Army commander, the plan of action was crystal clear: battalion and brigade-size operations would involve crossing the LoC, capturing ground and posts by forcibly dislodging Pakistani soldiers, and holding the captured

---

[4] Sawhney, 'At the Crossroad'.

positions. What would the Indian Army do with the captured territory and posts across the LoC? The chief was unambiguous that there would be no withdrawal of forces from the captured posts, unless the central government intervened and issued clear and direct orders for a pull-back. The thinking behind that was that the captured posts would improve the Indian Army's defensive posture at the LoC both in the operational sense as well as to deter infiltrators. In Gen. Nanavatty's words: 'Offensive operations constituted attacks at brigade, battalion and company level to capture objectives and ground of tactical importance that would improve our defensive and CI posture. We intended to hold ground that was captured unless ordered by the government to the contrary.'

In early September, Gen. Sihota, the DGMO, rang up Gen. Nanavatty from the army HQ in New Delhi and asked, 'Are you ready? Are your plans ready?' The Northern Army Commander responded, 'We are ready since the 1st of September'. The plans were in place, material preparations were complete and the men were ready to strike—all they needed was the order from the chief.

The order never came. The choice of September 2001 to carry out the mission turned out to be fateful.

Just when everything was in place and the plan was to go forward, the terror attacks on the twin towers in New York took place. 9/11 changed everything, including the geopolitics in South Asia thanks partly to changing United States (US) calculations vis-à-vis Pakistan. Perhaps there was a small window of opportunity to carry out the operation immediately after 9/11 when Pakistan had not yet been drafted as an American ally in its war against terror. That window was never taken.

Prior to September 2001, there were several occasions when the opportunity had arisen for the operation to be carried out at the sectoral levels but those opportunities were also not taken by the army leadership.

Gen. Nanavatty recommended that Operation Kabaddi be put on hold.

> The DGMO enquired whether, in the altered circumstances, we should launch offensive operations as planned if the opportunity were to present itself. I remember saying that to my mind the timing was not right. With the world, including Pakistan, seemingly united in its anti-terror stance, any unilateral military action by us against Pakistan would be viewed unfavourbly by the international community and be seen as taking advantage of the situation to settle scores on the side

lines. I did not recommend the launch of offensive operations until the situation became clearer.

Operation Kabaddi was finally called off.

Following the September 2001 attacks in New York, the Indian Parliament was attacked in December that year. A new operation, Operation PARAKRAM, was prepared in the wake of the terror attack on the Indian Parliament on 13 December 2001. The attack led to a major military standoff between India and Pakistan that lasted several months, but no attacks were carried out against Pakistan.

In October that year, after the operation was called off, defence analyst Manvendra Singh discussed in an article he wrote for *India Today*[5] an imaginary scenario of India launching military strikes across the LoC to take out terror camps. Written by a former officer of the army whose father Jaswant Singh was the defence minister when the operation was called off, the scenarios looked strikingly similar to what was planned.

Had Operation Kabaddi gone ahead as planned, how would things have played out between the two sides? Were there other operations of a similar kind along the India–Pakistan border in J&K and what have been their impact?

Pakistan's Kargil Misadventure

Pakistan's Kargil operations in the spring of 1999 in the Kargil–Dras sector of J&K are too well known to merit recollection here. Let us briefly recall the salient features to compare it to India's aborted cross-LoC operation of 2001. Pakistan's intrusion into the posts vacated by the Indian Army during the winter months was an essentially opportunistic one. There was a general understanding, though not an agreement, that during the winter months, the two sides would withdraw to less harsh terrain and return and reoccupy the posts once the winter snow melted. In 1999, the Pakistan Army under Gen. Pervez Musharraf broke the pattern. Musharraf and his coterie of army officers had other plans for the winter.

---

[5] Manvendra Singh, 'The War Begins', *Indiatoday.in*, 29 October 2001, http://indiatoday.intoday.in/story/an-imaginary-scenario-of-india-launching-military-strikes-at-pakistan-run-terror-camps/1/231558.html, last accessed on 21 September 2017.

Posts and territory vacated by the Indian Army were easy to occupy and the new occupants came dressed as 'Kashmiri freedom fighters', except they were regular Pakistani army soldiers. The strategic objective was to cut off the Srinagar–Leh National Highway 1A.

As retired Indian brigadier Gurmeet Kanwal argues:

> In the Dras, Mushko Valley and Kaksar sectors, the military aim was to sever the Srinagar–Leh National Highway (NH) 1A to isolate Kargil district and cut India's lifeline to Leh with a view to eventually choking supplies and reinforcements to Indian troops at Saltoro Ridge across the Siachen Glacier. Failing the full achievement of this aim during the summer months of 1999, the Pakistan Army hoped to establish a 'firm base', occupied by regular soldiers, from which traffic on the Srinagar–Leh highway could be disrupted at several places by trained mercenaries within one day's return march.[6]

Pakistan's Force Command Northern Areas (FCNA) and the Northern Light Infantry (NLI) were given the primary responsibility to carry out the operation.

Kargil was different from the earlier India–Pakistan skirmishes along the LoC in several ways. A Rand report, for instance, argues that the Kargil conflict was different. 'First, both sides used regular forces in combat. Second, the conflict involved struggles over territory. Third, the scale of military operations was substantially different in that widespread use of heavy artillery and air power was witnessed during the conflict.'

The Pakistani adventure was detected by the Indian side by early May 1999, which reacted strongly, to the utter surprise of the Pakistani side. From early May to late May, a forceful eviction process was carried out by the Indian Army. On 26 May, the IAF came to the aid of the army. IAF launched air-to-ground strikes using fifth-generation aircrafts.[7] As the tide turned in favour of India through June and early July, Prime Minister Nawaz Sharif had a meeting with President Bill Clinton in the first week of July in Washington, following which Pakistan offered to withdraw its forces. The Indian and Pakistani DGMOs talked over the

---

[6] Gurmeet Kanwal, 'Pakistan's Strategic Blunder at Kargil', *CLAWS Journal* 1 (Summer 2009): 55, available at http://www.claws.in/images/journals_doc/1400824835Gurmeet%20Kanwal%20CJ%20SSummer%202009.pdf, last accessed on 15 September 2017.

[7] Kanwal, 'Pakistan's Strategic Blunder at Kargil', 59.

phone on the night of 10 July and met the following day and the Pakistani troop withdrawal began. Thus, the limited war came to an end. This was a limited conflict for intents and purposes. There was no spread of hostilities to other sectors; there was no crossing of the LoC; there was no war termination agreement like the previous wars of 1947–8, 1965, and 1971–2; and Pakistan did not even acknowledge that its regular forces were fighting in Kargil.

There is no clarity on whether the political leadership in Pakistan was aware of the preparations for the Kargil operation by the Pakistan Army. Nawaz Sharif has reportedly denied any knowledge of it, while Gen. Musharraf insists that everyone was on board. Gen. Tariq Ghazi of the Pakistan Army thinks that there may be some truth in both assertions.[8] According to him, the key question that has never been answered is 'who knew what, when'. Two participants of a briefing that Musharraf gave Nawaz Sharif sometime in late March 1999, four or five months after Kargil had been launched, are reported to have confided that Sharif egged the army chief (Musharraf) on by flippantly saying—'General Sahib, Srinagar *kub pahunchen ge?!*' ('General, when will you reach Srinagar?!') Ghazi does not think this was Musharraf blustering as this was also told to him by another person present in the meeting.

Ghazi thinks that the Kargil operation was initiated as a series of limited tactical actions that normally would not require prior political authorization. But, spurred on by the local and personal ambitions of a very small coterie who did not foresee battlefield dynamics, this limited objective ballooned into an unintended and unplanned strategic provocation, something the military leadership suddenly found as being untenable. It is possible that the political leadership came into the picture at this stage, and without an understanding of the gravity of the situation, endorsed further actions.[9] The lack of discussion of Kargil in Pakistan (especially during the Musharraf years) points to a suspicion that it may have been viewed in some circles as an embarrassing episode, Ghazi argues.

---

[8] Interview with Gen. Tariq Ghazi, 6 March 2018, Bangkok.

[9] Several accounts point to the fact that Sharif was told the details of the operations only after they were initiated. See, for instance, John H. Gill, 'Military Operations in the Kargil Conflict', in *Asymmetric Warfare in South Asia: The Causes and Consequences of the Kargil Conflict*, ed. Peter R. Lavoy (New Delhi: Cambridge University Press, 2009), 95.

Several other Pakistani generals seem to agree with this view. President Pervez Musharraf's former colleague, Lt Gen. (Retd) Jamshed Gulzar Kiani, once stated: 'I am not sure from where he (Sharif) came to know, but it wasn't through the army and the Kargil operation was kept secret from Nawaz Sharif.'[10] Sartaj Aziz, a minister in Sharif's cabinet, also confirms this in his book.[11]

There is also academic scholarship that supports the view that this was not meant to be a large-scale operation. Feroz Khan, Peter Lavoy, and Christopher Clary argue that 'the Pakistan army perceived the Kargil incursion as a tactical operation to create a local advantage that also might have broader benefits, such as improving the morale of the army, enhancing the military's position in domestic politics, and increasing bargaining power for negotiations with India.'[12]

Lavoy further shows how local military decisions can sometimes go beyond brief, something that we often hear of when discussing CFVs in Kashmir. 'The rugged NLI soldiers penetrated the LoC and set up several posts along the originally identified watersheds without detection. The operation then "grew bigger than planned" when they were authorised to push even further into Indian territory.'[13] Moeed Yusuf points out in his new book that 'Pakistan had hoped to apply the finders keepers rule to these unattended heights.'[14]

It is possible then to argue that Kargil was a medium-sized, limited-aims operation conceived of and carried out by the Pakistani army leadership (without political go-ahead) that eventually went out of its control.

[10] Test Sharma, 'Musharraf Planned Kargil, Nawaz Didn't Know: Ex-Pak Gen', *News18*, 3 June 2008, available at https://www.news18.com/news/india/musharraf-planned-kargil-nawaz-didnt-know-ex-pak-gen-290441.html, last accessed on 15 September 2017.

[11] Sartaj Aziz, *Between Dreams and Realities: Some Milestones in Pakistan's History* (Karachi: Oxford University Press, 2009).

[12] Feroz Hassan Khan, Peter R. Lavoy, and Christopher Clary, 'Pakistan's Motivations and Calculations for the Kargil Conflict' in *Asymmetric Warfare in South Asia: The Causes and Consequences of the Kargil Conflict*, ed. Peter R. Lavoy (New Delhi: Cambridge University Press, 2009), 86.

[13] Aziz, *Between Dreams and Realities*, 177.

[14] Moeed Yusuf, *Brokering Peace in Nuclear Environments U.S. Crisis Management in South Asia* (Stanford: Stanford University Press, 2018).

Operation Kabaddi and the Kargil Conflict: A Brief Comparison

In light of the discussion on the aborted operation of 2001, that is Operation Kabaddi, and the Kargil adventure by the Pakistan Army, the question we must ask is this: Was the Indian Army's aborted operation any different from the Kargil operation of 1999? There are indeed several striking similarities and differences between the two operations. As a matter of fact, when asked 'How was the 2001 operation different from the Kargil operation by Pakistan?' Gen. Nanavatty responded, 'Not very different.'

Let us start with a striking dissimilarity. The Kargil campaign, by most accounts, was a purely opportunistic land grab operation to occupy the temporarily vacated posts of the Indian Army. It was well planned and equally well executed by the Pakistan Army under Gen. Musharraf, but it was a 'back-door operation' and did not require the forceful dislodging of Indian troops from their positions. Indeed, the Pakistan Army would have been able to cause troubles for the Indian forces in J&K had their operation been a successful one. But it failed. On the other hand, the aborted Indian operation of 2001 was hardly an opportunistic one. It was an aggressive operation that aimed to bring to bear the sheer numerical and material superiority of the Indian Army on carrying out an aggressive military campaign to capture territory and posts held by the Pakistan Army across the LoC.

Secondly, both the operations were aimed at capturing, occupying, and keeping the land for military advantages. Capturing 25–30 Pakistani army posts would reduce the infiltration and dampen the spirits of the Pakistan Army, the Indian side reasoned. Capturing Indian posts and adjacent territories would, as Gurmeet Kanwal argues, isolate the Kargil district and cut India's lifeline to Leh, which would have adverse implications for Indian supplies and reinforcements to its troops at Saltoro Ridge across the Siachen Glacier, Pakistan had calculated. Pakistan had a political aim as well—to flag the Kashmir issue internationally. In short, both were land grab operations: one miserably failed, and the other was never carried out.

Thirdly, both the Kargil operation and the 2001 campaign were carried out in the general backdrop of nuclear weapons. It is often argued that Pakistan's Kargil misadventure was a dangerous one, especially because it came immediately after the two sides tested their nuclear devices a year earlier. Pakistan attempted to take advantage of the general deterrence stability provided by nuclear weapons to carry out a shallow military operation. The argument also meant that Kargil destabilized the subcontinent under nuclear conditions. Let us look at the 2001 military operation by India using the same analytical lens. Logically, it could be said that just like Kargil, the 2001 operation was also planned, though not carried out, under the same nuclear umbrella. However, the Indian side was not taking advantage of the stability provided by nuclear weapons as they had anticipated a firm Pakistani response. But that does not take away from the fact that this was a gamble in the dangerous nuclear environment.

Finally, what was the nature of the political concurrence available to the respective armies for carrying out these operations? Available evidence shows that the Pakistani prime minister and the political dispensation there were unaware of the Pakistan Army's move to capture Indian territories until the actual occupation. There is no clarity about the Indian case. What we can safely state is this: the Indian Army had made operations plans to capture the Pakistani posts but would not have carried them out without the political concurrence of the civilian government in New Delhi, given the enormity of the operation. However, several Indian Army officers interviewed for this book have unambiguously stated that several small-scale operations, including land grab operations, have taken place in the past without explicit permission from the civilian government in New Delhi. Such operations are regularly planned and carried out at the army's command, divisional, and brigade levels. However, an operation such as the one in 2001 would never have been carried out without explicit political permission from the Indian prime minister.

The aforementioned discussion comparing the differences and similarities between the 2001 operation and the Pakistan Army's Kargil campaign throws up several insights. One, land grab operations by either side along the LoC in J&K is nothing new (as argued in the later parts of this book). Two, Kargil can be seen as a major land grab operation that escalated, to the dismay of the Pakistani army planners, when the Indian Army struck back with full force and determination to dislodge the intruding troops. The operation planned by the Indian military in 2001 was no different from the Kargil operation in scale, intent, and employment. If anything, as pointed out earlier, unlike the Kargil operation of the Pakistan Army that was opportunistic in nature, operation Kabaddi was meant to be an aggressive operation.

Thirdly, the Indian decision to prepare a plan to capture Pakistani posts across the LoC was a direct result of incessant firing that was happening between the two sides, and infiltration into J&K. In other words, land grab operations of varying intensity are planned, and sometimes carried out, in order to gain varying levels of advantage on the LoC. Some of them are carried out without explicit permission from the central decision-makers, and some with permission. Four, cross-LoC operations are often not planned and directed by the central decision-makers but are dictated by the tactical requirements on the front lines of the India–Pakistan border in J&K.

Finally, what the aforementioned narrative also highlights is the ability of CFVs/cross-border firing to lead to cross-border operations, triggering crisis escalation between the two rivals. The 2001 operation, which if carried out would have escalated, was triggered by the incessant firing along the LoC.

Several questions remain: What would have happened if New Delhi had decided in September 2001 to go ahead with operation Kabaddi to capture 25–30 Pakistani army posts? Would it have escalated? What implications would it have had for nuclear stability in the subcontinent?

Fast forward to 2018. The LoC and the IB (as India refers to it) or WB (as Pakistan refers to it) between India and Pakistan in the disputed state of J&K has in recent years witnessed repeated violations of the CFA of 2003. According to Pakistani official sources (including the Ministry of Defence [MoD], National Assembly, and Inter Services Public Relations [ISPR]), 1,390 CFVs have taken place since 2011. Indian official records (from the Indian MoD and Ministry of Home Affairs [MHA]) claim that there have been 1,948 CFVs.

***

What This Book Is About

This book seeks to explain the causes of CFVs, the little-analysed link between CFVs and crisis escalation between the two sides, and the dangers of CFV-linked escalation under nuclear conditions. In doing so, the book further nuances the existing notions about the escalatory dynamics between the two South Asian nuclear rivals. Moreover, it establishes a significant relationship between CFVs and India–Pakistan escalation dynamics. In short, this book offers to de-mythify popular notions about the causes of CFVs in J&K and India–Pakistan escalation dynamics. The book further explains CFVs using the concept of AMFs.

LoC and the IB/WB between India and Pakistan in J&K have witnessed repeated CFVs over the past many years. Indeed, with the new low in the relations between India and Pakistan, CFVs have gone up exponentially. These CFVs have the potential to not only begin a crisis but also escalate an ongoing crisis. Indeed, barring the terror attack on Mumbai in 2008 and more recently in Uri in September 2016, CFVs have arguably been the single-most prominent trigger of tensions and crisis escalation between New Delhi and Islamabad in the past decade. In other words, CFVs could lead to crisis escalation between the two countries even in the absence of other triggers. To make things worse, in the event of such violations, political leadership on either side often engages in high-pitched rhetoric, some of which even have nuclear undertones.

Causes of CFVs

What causes CFVs? India offers a uni-causal explanation: the 2003 ceasefire is violated by the Pakistani side to provide covering fire to terrorists infiltrating into the Indian side of J&K. Pakistan, on the other hand, blames India of engaging in unprovoked firing targeted at civilian population. Publicly available data show these two as the most-cited reasons for CFVs.

However, new data sets used in this book and the interviews conducted with serving and retired military officers on the Indian and Pakistani sides tell a very different story. CFVs have multiple causes, sometimes hereto unknown and/or neglected, most of which have not been recognized adequately and hence not taken up by the two governments for resolution.

This book is premised on the assumption that wrong diagnosis by India and Pakistan regarding the causes of CFVs and the linkage between CFVs and escalation dynamics have led to the adoption of wrong policies by the two governments to deal with the recurrent violations of the ceasefire and the consequent building up of bilateral tensions. Wrong diagnosis is a result of an inadequate understanding of the causes of CFVs. This book offers a set of alternative explanations on why the India–Pakistan ceasefire is so prone to breaking down.

The focus in India on terrorist infiltration has led to policies aimed at preventing terrorism but have not addressed the other more important causes that lead to CFVs. Put differently, even if terrorist infiltration ceases to exist, CFVs could potentially continue to take place, leading to an escalation of tensions between the two sides. In any case, during periods of bilateral tension, CFVs tend to rise even in the absence of terrorist attacks. The Pakistani argument about unprovoked firing at civilians also does not address the alternative explanations examined in this book. Hence, policymaking on escalation control in South Asia has been suboptimal and misleading due to the wrong diagnosis of CFVs.

CFVs and Escalation Dynamics

The second major aim of this book is to carry out an in-depth empirical examination of the link between CFVs and escalation dynamics between India and Pakistan. Literature and arguments on the escalation dynamics between India and Pakistan usually revolve around major terrorist incidents. That is, it is widely held that escalation is triggered by terrorist violence. While this study does not dispute the significance of terrorist incidents (such as the attacks on Mumbai in 2008 or the Uri army camp in 2016) in explaining escalation dynamics, it argues that CFVs are a major source of political, military, and diplomatic escalation between the two countries.

Using empirical data on escalation and CFVs from 2002 to 2017, this book examines the linkage between CFVs and escalation and concludes that there exists a strong relationship between CFVs on the India–Pakistan border in J&K and crisis escalation between the two countries. In doing so, this book examines eight cases wherein CFVs triggered crisis escalation between India and Pakistan. The eight cases presented in this book examined three types of cases: one, where CFVs lead to crisis escalation; two, where CFVs contribute to worsening an ongoing crisis and thereby spiking the escalatory ladder; and three, where conventional military escalation gets played out on the front lines in the form of CFVs, either because it is nearly impossible to go to war and so focus gets shifted to the border, or because firing on the border, however severe, is not viewed as risky.

While the aforementioned arguments might sound obvious to many, it needs to be examined in detail using empirical evidence, mainly because the academic literature on South Asian escalation dynamics seems to by and large ignore the crucial links between CFVs and escalation.

Misplaced Optimism

There also seems to be a strongly held belief among policymakers in India and Pakistan that CFVs only constitute acceptable levels of lower-order violence and that they would not matter in the larger scheme of India–Pakistan balance or regional stability in the subcontinent. Put differently, there seems to be a belief that escalation can be managed at the top, so the respective central leaderships could afford to let things boil a bit at lower levels. An associated belief is that given the existence of general nuclear stability, CFV-linked violence would not escalate to higher levels. This mistaken sense of optimism about the inability of CFVs to escalate to higher levels may have been true in an era when what happened on the border remained there without any serious spillover effect on the larger political and diplomatic relationship between the two countries.

Today, however, things have changed radically thanks to the increased levels of hyper-nationalism and the role of the independent and empowered media on both sides, which unfailingly convey to the citizens of the two countries what takes place on the border often with undesirable hyperboles, exaggeration, and half-truths. Domestic audiences then demand retribution, which democratic governments find difficult to ignore. In short, what happens on the LoC and IB does not stay there anymore—they have implications for the larger bilateral politico-diplomatic relations and strategic balance. Moreover, when CFVs and terrorist violence occur simultaneously or sequentially, their escalatory potential increases manifold.

That said, the proactive media environment in the two countries is not the only reason why we should be concerned about the escalatory potential of CFVs, but more so because, in the past, CFVs have demonstrated their ability to cause escalation or to add to an ongoing escalation.

The next chapter (Chapter 2) of the book, 'Conceptualizing Escalation Dynamics in South Asia', recaptures some of the existing arguments in the theoretical literature as well as in the literature on South Asia on what causes crisis escalation between states, in particular between India and Pakistan.

Why This Book?

The idea for this book germinated in the many closed-door track-two discussions I have been part of over the past one and a half decades. Discussions on CFVs and escalation, and insights shared by senior military commanders from India and Pakistan convinced me of the need to dig deeper and undertake a systematic book-length study on the subject.

Much of the conventional military escalation between India and Pakistan gets played out on the front lines in the form of CFVs, either because it is nearly impossible to go to war and so focus gets shifted to the border, or because firing on the border, however severe, is not viewed as risky. What this means is that a lot more than we usually understand happens on the border and a lot gets subsumed under the term 'CFVs'. Thus, there should be a lot more focus on CFVs than is normally accorded.

This book then aims to do three new things: (*i*) examine a number of hitherto unexplored causes for the CFVs in J&K; (*ii*) challenge the existing wisdom in the academic literature and policy circles on crisis escalation in South Asia; and, (*iii*) offer an overview of the historical evolution of the India–Pakistan border in J&K.

This book also uses several primary data sets and over 80 in-depth interviews with practitioners to understand the triggers for CFVs and then show the linkages between CFVs and crisis escalation between India and Pakistan. This book is also a result of extensive field visits to both, the Indian and Pakistani sides of the LoC.

Rationale for the Choice of the Period under Study

The period from 2003 to 2017 is selected for the study as it was in 2003 that a ceasefire was agreed to by the two sides. There were two CFAs before the 2003 one: The 1949 Karachi Agreement, which established the CFL, and the 1972 Simla Agreement, which set up the LoC. However, they were both war termination agreements. The 2003 CFA is different in the sense that it was agreed to when firing between the two sides was happening in a 'free for all' manner. So the 2003 agreement attempted to put in place 'an understanding' between the two sides that the cross-border firing in J&K should be avoided. The proposed study specifically looks at how and why this agreement broke down from time to time.

The Two Puzzles

I began this work with two puzzles and the book is, in a sense, an attempt to explain those puzzles. The first puzzle is that despite sustained bilateral political and diplomatic attempts to reduce tensions between India and Pakistan, CFVs continue to take place. Let us consider an example. When CFVs were spiking in September 2013, Prime Ministers Nawaz Sharif and Manmohan Singh met in New York on 29 September on the sidelines of the United Nations General Assembly (UNGA) meeting and agreed to ask senior military officers to find 'effective means' of restoring the 2003 ceasefire in Kashmir. Although the situation was temporarily de-escalated, the meeting of the prime ministers and the agreement to get the senior military officials to talk to each other did not put an end to the crisis. Within days of their meeting, a fresh spell of CFVs were reported from Krishna Ghati and Mendhar sectors from 2 October to 5 October with both Indian and Pakistani sides accusing each other of violating the CFA. Here's a more recent example. During the CFVs of July 2015, a temporary halt in the firing was achieved when, on 10 July, Prime Ministers Sharif and, this time, Narendra Modi, met on the sidelines of the Shanghai Cooperation Organization (SCO) Summit in Ufa and agreed to resume bilateral dialogue. Soon after their agreement, CFVs resumed with even more vigour, and the two sides blamed each other for the resumption.

If CFVs are politically sanctioned by either New Delhi or Islamabad, we should expect them to stop when political authorities desire so. But they do not always stop. Sometimes CFVs begin, and end, for no obvious reason. How does one explain that? One might be tempted to explain that away by arguing that Pakistan's military does not listen to its political leadership and, hence, the violations. But if one were to establish that argument, it would also have to be established that the Pakistan Army is the chief instigator of CFVs, a claim not sustained by the findings of this book. This book argues that local military factors significantly contribute to CFVs, and that explains why CFVs often do not sit well with the positive political dynamics between the two countries. There is at times an incongruence between local military factors and larger political developments.

This is not to say that CFVs are never a result of central political decisions. Often enough, firing on the J&K borders is a decision taken by New Delhi or Rawalpindi. This book also discusses those instances. However, the reason why there should be focus on local-level military factors is twofold: one, the existing literature on the causes of CFVs largely ignores local factors; two, this has important policy implications. If local military factors are not seen as contributing to escalation dynamics, they could lead to inadvertent escalation since they do have an impact on the escalation process, in any case.

The second puzzle is that though it is widely believed that terror attacks are the major cause of Indo-Pak escalation, political, military, and diplomatic escalation has taken place between India and Pakistan even in the absence of terror attacks.[15] If terror incidents alone explain escalation dynamics, how does one explain escalation in the absence of terror strikes? A great deal of the data presented in this book and, in particular, the eight cases of escalation examined in Chapter 6 show that escalation is caused by CFVs, and not terror attacks. Moreover, just as sometimes terror attacks have not led to escalation, so have CFVs.

Central Arguments of the Book

I make five arguments in this book. CFVs are generally not planned or directed by higher military or political authorities but are instead driven by the dynamics on the front lines of the India–Pakistan border. AMFs, a concept that is explained in the next chapter, are a major trigger for CFVs between India and Pakistan. The prominence of AMFs is directly proportional to the abdication of responsibility by the political establishment in resolving the border standoffs and conflicts between the two sides. Even more worryingly, central decision-makers have empowered the respective militaries to take matters into their hands in dealing with the situation on the J&K borders.

There are three scenarios with regard to the relationship between central political/military leaderships and the prominence of AMFs. When central political/military leaderships assert themselves against border violence, AMFs tend to lose prominence, reducing CFVs; when there is ambiguous signalling from the central leaderships about how they wish to

---

[15] There is a difference between terror attacks and infiltration attempts by terrorists. The former sometimes lead to CFVs but the latter, by themselves, have not led to any major CFVs.

deal with the situation on the borders, AMFs have maximum autonomy, leading to high levels of CFVs; thirdly, when the central leaderships are desirous of upping the ante, the AMFs may not have much prominence, even though there would be high levels of CFVs. In short, the rise and fall of CFVs on the J&K border between India and Pakistan is to a great extent a result of the dynamic relationship between central political/ military leaderships and AMFs.

Two, the 2003 CFA tends to hold when the two sides engage in a dialogue process on key disputes. During those phases, AMFs have little or no influence. During times of bilateral tension, however, the CFA tends to break down and CFVs become routine. It is during such phases that local factors tend to have a dramatic influence on CFVs.

Three, CFVs, prominently caused by AMFs, contribute to India–Pakistan escalation dynamics in a significant manner. Conventional wisdom suggests that terror attacks are the primary cause of India–Pakistan escalation. However, evidence shows that political, diplomatic, and military tensions between the two adversaries have occurred due to CFVs even when there have been no terror attacks. More importantly, the combined effect of terror attacks and CFVs have the potential to increase the escalatory effect exponentially.

Four, in the nuclearized India–Pakistan rivalry, crisis escalation is often a result of lower-level conflicts, adversarial interaction between forces in tactical environments on the contested border in J&K, and their unpredictable impact on higher-level military and or political relationship. That is, it would be wrong to assume that crisis escalation would only be a product of decisions made by central actors in a rational, calculated manner.

Finally, adhocism in managing the border has historically been a key factor behind border tensions between India and Pakistan. In that sense, unsettled borders, among other factors, have played a major role in escalating tensions between the two sides.

Note on Sources and Methods

For a study of this kind, both contemporary and involving military strategy and national security, secondary material is not particularly helpful, nor are primary archival sources readily available. Parts of the book that deal with the historical aspects of the India–Pakistan border have extensively used a large number of historical documents, bilateral agreements, official correspondence, statements in the Parliament/National Assembly, reports on bilateral discussions, United Nations (UN) resolutions, official reports, and minutes of meetings, among others. And yet, for the purposes of this book, the primary material can only tell a partial story. Therefore, I began looking beyond the ready-made material, both primary and secondary.

Data Sets

The first stop was to get data on CFVs and escalation. There is no systematic official data on CFVs available in the public domain in India or Pakistan, let alone data specifying the causes behind CFVs and the locations where CFVs take place. CFVs are reported in India and in Pakistan by the security forces through set channels to the concerned government departments, the MoD and the MHA in the case of India. Aggregate numbers of yearly CFVs are often released by the two governments without indicating the specific places or when, why, and how they occurred. While the United Nations Military Observer Group in India and Pakistan (UNMOGIP) reports CFVs to the UN HQ, this information is not shared publicly. In any case, the Indian side has not been reporting the CFVs to UNMOGIP since 1972, after the Simla Agreement. Therefore, the UNMOGIP data would only include 'alleged' CFVs reported by Pakistan as investigations into alleged CFVs stopped a long time ago.

To overcome this lack of meaningful data, two new data sets (separately, for India and for Pakistan) were created by listing all the CFVs reported in open sources in India and Pakistan, from 2002 to 2017. Open sources primarily include print media reports and digital media reports (newspapers, mostly English-language national dailies and, in some cases, even non-Indian and non-Pakistani press reports). Media reports usually include the date, location, and, in some cases, the cause of the CFVs and casualties as indicated by the security officials. However, it should be noted that not all CFVs get reported in the press, since press reporting of CFVs is bound to be lower than the actual occurrences of violations, the number of CFVs listed in the book's data sets is significantly lower than the number of CFVs accounted for in the official records. However, data sets presented in this book are able to provide a chronological record of the CFVs from 2002 to 2016 and are helpful in understanding the patterns, the locations, and the major causes of CFVs between India and Pakistan.

A second set of data sets on escalation between India and Pakistan between 2002 and 2017 was also created. Two separate, one each for India and Pakistan, data sets of major, moderate, and minor escalation events in political, diplomatic, and military domains between India and Pakistan during the period from 2002 to 2017 were also compiled. Escalation in three domains was analysed, that is, political, military, and diplomatic, in order to juxtapose the CFV data with the escalation data. Chapter 6 discusses these data sets in more detail.

Field Visits

The second challenge was to get access to the border areas as I was convinced that this study would be incomplete without an extensive field visit to the LoC and IB/WB. As is to be expected, civilians were not allowed to travel freely to the border areas on the Indian side, let alone travel to the Pakistani side of the LoC or WB. I then approached the Northern Army commander who graciously offered to host me for a week in Kashmir's border (LoC) with Pakistan. After completing a visit to the LoC in May 2016, I got in touch with the senior officers of the BSF in New Delhi, who offered to take me on a border visit from Jammu to Gujarat through Punjab and Rajasthan. My researcher in Pakistan, M. Faisal, chipped in by conducting initial interviews with several serving army officers and diplomats in Islamabad and Rawalpindi.

I then approached the Pakistan Army for accessing their side of the LoC. After over a year of waiting, the invitation to visit the Pakistani side of the LoC came in the first week of December 2017. The field visit consisted of visits to the HQ of the Pakistan Army's 12 Division in Murree, HQ of 1-Azad Kashmir (AK)[16] brigade in Muzaffarabad, HQ of 2-AK Brigade in Rawalakot, and the General HQ of the Pakistan Army in Rawalpindi.

But there is only so much that data and field visits can offer a researcher in a sensitive geopolitical setting such as Kashmir. There is a significant gap between what 'dry' data and 'sanitized' field visits can offer, and what really happens on the front lines. In-service military personnel,

---

[16] AK is referred to as 'Pakistan Occupied Kashmir (POK)' by India, and AK brigades of the Pakistan Army are referred to by India as 'POK brigades'.

both from the army and the BSF, can only tell you so much due to official constraints and operational reasons and that is the nature of the beast. This was a major gap that I realized as I researched more. I then decided to overcome this challenge by reaching out to senior retired generals of the Indian and Pakistani armies, and the BSF and the Rangers. And that has made all the difference to this book.

Excavating Oral History

In over two years or so, I, along with my team of researchers, managed to interview over 80 officials (most of them from the Indian and Pakistani militaries). In order to select potential interviewees, I used a stratified, snowballing, and purposive sampling method. Purposive sampling as opposed to random sampling was used because we knew who was in charge of which sector/command at which point of time; so we knew who to approach, not that we always managed to get through to whom we wanted.

A great deal of snowball sampling was used because of access problems—once you get referred to a senior general by a contemporary, access problems tend to disappear. There was also a constant attempt at process tracing—to use several interviews to trace back to the origins of events, operations, and the run-up to them. Needless to say, one has to be cautious about contamination—there was the potential for censored responses, interviewer effects on the interviewee, location of the interview (for example, an active duty officer being interviewed on the LoC versus freewheeling discussion at a dinner table with a senior retired officer), and so on.

Conscious efforts were made to 'triangulate' the findings—by double/triple-checking facts with other interviewees so as to increase generalizability. I also tried to increase generalizability by looking at different regions, using different data sets, and approaching several 'competing' organizations.

Interview style also determines the kind of answers you get. It may sound blasphemous to a researcher, but that's the reality. Answers often depend on your questions and how you ask them. I adopted a semi-structured, freewheeling, open-ended, semi-directive interview method. I avoided, as far as possible, carrying a printed set of questions, which tends to make the interviewee conscious and cautious. I often, though not always, let the interviewee direct me. I encouraged them to wander, give anecdotes, and be reflective. Open-ended questions have the virtue of allowing the interviewees to tell you what is relevant and important rather than being restricted by the preconceived notions of what is significant.[17] As Jeffrey Berry puts it, I was using 'the interview for what it is.'[18]

Such interviews can provide information you were not aware of and thus were not looking for. As a result, several freewheeling interviews threw up unexpected findings and information. Needless to say, directive interviews are required when you need specific information and details.

It may be useful to mention here some of the challenges that I faced during the field work and interviews. One of the challenges I faced was that I knew that I was on a 'guided' and 'sanitized' field visit while I was traveling with the armed forces and was only seeing what I was supposed to see and hearing what I was supposed to hear. I had to overcome this by being an informed and inquisitive interviewer and a good listener. Secondly, during interviews, one is often confronted with the horror of the 'party line', wherein interviewees stick to the formal official narrative. However, the 'party line' often tends to change when engaged in in-depth conversations or given counter explanations of their seniors. In any case, the party line becomes more prominent during directive interviews. Finally, I also had to be careful about the interviewee's privacy and his official obligations. For instance, I avoided using information I gathered from several interviews as I thought that doing so could do more harm to them than good to my research.

A final thought on the insights I gathered from the field visit. There exists a disconcerting level of compartmentalization of expertise and domain knowledge in the government. Government, contrary to what many people would assume, is not an omniscient monolith, and as a result, one agency/department often does not know about the work/role of the others, and they hardly ever talk to each other. Inter-agency coordination is often an exercise in dodging questions and hiding facts. Each agency/force/department works in its own silo, jealously guarding its interests and domain knowledge, and unwilling to share it with anyone else. The lessons from the age-old Indian parable of the blind men and the elephant readily

---

[17] Jeffrey M. Berry, 'Validity and Reliability Issues in Elite Interviewing', *Political Science and Politics* 35, no. 4 (December 2002): 680.

[18] Berry, 'Validity and Reliability Issues in Elite Interviewing', 680.

springs to mind here. The job of a serious researcher then is to break the interdepartmental/agency/force barrier and get a comprehensive picture.

Interviews with retired military officials have been recorded and transcribed. Interviews with serving Indian and Pakistani officials have not been recorded but contemporaneous notes were made during discussions with them, which are used in the study without taking the names of the interviewees. They are identified as Officer 1, Officer 2, and so on with the date and venue of the interview. Interviews with serving and retired diplomats and other officials as well as my own observations from the month-long visit to India's border with Pakistan were also used in the study.

Format of the Book

The book is divided into seven chapters including the introductory and concluding chapters. Chapter 2 entitled 'Conceptualizing Escalation Dynamics in South Asia' serves as a theoretical and conceptual basis of the book. The chapter discusses the classical views on escalation, followed by an analysis of the various debates on India–Pakistan escalation dynamics. The chapter thereafter examines the traditional understanding of the India–Pakistan escalation ladder. The chapter concludes by highlighting the missing link in the India–Pakistan escalation ladder, that is, the potency of CFVs to trigger bilateral escalation.

Chapter 3 entitled '(Mis)managing the Border: A History of Practices and Mechanisms' builds on the previous chapter and examines the management of the India–Pakistan border in J&K. Following a brief discussion on the various terminologies used in the context of the India–Pakistan border, the first section discusses the early role played by the UN monitoring group in helping the management of the India–Pakistan borders in J&K as well as the occasional, though minor, reworking of the border that took place in the 1950s and 1960s. Section two will discuss the various border management practices and mechanisms used by India and Pakistan in managing the IB and LoC. This chapter provides the much-needed technical knowledge to understand the occurrence of CFVs that happen on the LoC and IB in J&K.

The fourth chapter entitled 'Lull Before the Storm: The 2003 Ceasefire Agreement and After' offers a historical and statistical analysis of CFVs in J&K to put them in proper perspective before attempting to, in the fifth chapter, explain why they occur. The chapter is divided into two broad sections. Section one focuses on the occurrence of CFVs prior to 2003 when the current CFA was signed and explain the immediate background to the CFA of 2003. Section two analyses the various data sets on CFVs, including the one my team of researchers put together, and draws conclusions regarding the locations, causes, and various other related factors relating to CFVs. This section also discusses how CFVs are counted, how they spread horizontally and vertically, and the existing explanations for the occurrence of CFVs.

Chapter 5, a rather longish one, entitled 'Military Gamesmanship and Moral Ascendency: Explaining Ceasefire Violations', unearths several hitherto unexamined causes behind CFVs in J&K. While the focus of the chapter is to explain the triggers for the CFVs from 2003 onwards, several of these causative explanations pre-date 2003 especially the 1990s, when the firing between the two forces were at a high, or as many officers describe it as 'a free for all era'. After a brief discussion on the concepts used in this chapter and explanation of the research methods adopted, this chapter examines the causes of CFVs in two subsections: political factors and AMFs.

The sixth chapter entitled 'Ceasefire Violations and Crisis Escalation: Analysing the Data' argues that there is an empirically evident linkage between CFVs in J&K and India–Pakistan escalation dynamics. The chapter offers quantitative evidence to show how CFVs and escalation dynamics are interconnected. Escalation data as well as CFV data for 15 years, from 2002 to 2016, are presented for this purpose. The final section also picks out eight cases from the data set to show the linkage between CFVs in J&K and India–Pakistan crisis escalation.

The final chapter reflects on the theoretical and practical implications of the arguments made in this book. The first part of the chapter discusses the various theoretical implications of the book. The chapter thereafter discusses the policy implications of the findings in the book as well as offers policy recommendations to reduce CFVs and control India–Pakistan crisis escalation.

2 Conceptualizing Escalation Dynamics in South Asia

WHAT ARE THE TRIGGERS FOR CRISIS escalation between India and Pakistan? How is escalation conceptualized in the Cold War literature? How has the scholarly literature on South Asia discussed escalation dynamics between India and Pakistan? Does the literature sufficiently explain the origins and dynamics of Indo-Pak escalation? This chapter aims to conceptualize escalation dynamics with special reference to India–Pakistan relations. In doing so, it challenges the existing arguments and conceptualization on the sources of India–Pakistan crisis dynamics and escalation.

The chapter will first discuss the classical views on escalation, followed by an analysis on the various debates on India–Pakistan escalation dynamics. The chapter will then examine the traditional understanding of the India–Pakistan escalation ladder. The chapter will conclude by highlighting the missing link in the India–Pakistan escalation ladder, that is, the potency of CFVs to trigger bilateral escalation.

Classical Views on Escalation Dynamics

The Cold War literature on escalation has had a strong influence on the South Asian thinking on crisis escalation, which necessitates a brief survey of the notions, definitions, models, and strategies, among others, of escalation, as understood in the Cold War literature before we undertake the discussion on the South Asian debates on escalation.

This discussion draws from the huge body of literature on escalation that was generated during the Cold War years. Even though the analytical focus of the Cold War writings was the management of superpower dynamics and nuclear deterrence,[1] they provide useful insights for examining the escalation dynamics between India and Pakistan.

Most of these studies analysed the concept of escalation from the point of view of bargaining with the adversary. From Thomas Schelling's point of view, for instance, escalation can be used to convince the adversary to withdraw from the contest by exploiting his fear of disaster.[2] As Lisa J. Carlson puts it, according to the classical Cold War thinkers, 'because both actors are engaged in demonstrating their superior ability to tolerate these risks, escalation is conceptualized as a game of competitive risk taking'.[3]

There is another important strand of literature that seeks to understand inadvertent escalation in the context of the causes of escalation, a body of literature that is very pertinent to our discussion here. Organizational theory approaches highlight how escalatory behaviour is inbuilt in certain organizational structures such as those of militaries.[4] The key limitation of such approaches is that they tend to treat organizations as monoliths. Jeffrey Legro improves upon the organizational literature to argue that there is a need to look closely at the specific organizational cultures, as opposed to a generalist treatment of organizational structures, to better appreciate the causes of inadvertent escalation.[5] This insight

---

[1] Some of the key writings that have examined the Cold War escalation dynamics included Barry R. Posen, *Inadvertent Escalation: Conventional War and Nuclear Risks* (Ithaca, NY: Cornell University Press, 1991); Bernard Brodie, *Escalation and the Nuclear Option* (Princeton, NJ: Princeton University Press, 1966); Ole R. Holsti, *Crisis, Escalation, War* (Montreal: McGill-Queens University Press, 1972); Thomas C. Schelling, *The Strategy of Conflict* (Cambridge, MA: Harvard University Press, 1960); Richard Smoke, *War: Controlling Escalation* (Cambridge, MA: Harvard University Press, 1977); Michael Brecher, *Crises in World Politics: Theory and Reality* (Oxford: Pergamon Press, 1993); Herman Kahn, *On Escalation: Metaphors and Scenarios* (New York: Praeger, 1965).

[2] Schelling, *The Strategy of Conflict*.

[3] Lisa J. Carlson, 'A Theory of Escalation and International Conflict', *The Journal of Conflict Resolution* 39, no. 3 (September, 1995): 513.

[4] Barry Posen, *The Sources of Military Doctrine: France, Britain, and Germany between the World Wars* (Ithaca: Cornell University Press, 1984); Graham T. Allison, *Essence of Decision: Explaining the Cuban Missile Crisis* (Boston: Little, Brown and Company, 1971).

[5] Jeffrey W. Legro, 'Military Culture and Inadvertent Escalation in World War II', *International Security* 18, no. 4 (Spring 1994): 108–42.

would be helpful to understand how organizational cultures of the Indian and Pakistani armies (and other border-guarding organizations) trigger and sustain escalation.

Important insights for this chapter are also drawn from literature that focuses on conflict behaviour and escalation dynamics.[6] This specific strand of literature emphasizes the importance of understanding the psychological dynamics behind escalation.

Defining Escalation

What is escalation? Scholar Richard Smoke defines escalation as an 'action that crosses a saliency which defines the current limits of a war, and that occurs in a context where the actor cannot know the full consequences of his action, including particularly how this action and the opponent's potential reaction(s) may interact to generate a situation likely to induce new actions that will cross still more saliences'.[7] Put differently, escalation is the process by which the previous limits of a war are crossed and new ones established'.[8]

Smoke further discusses two images of escalation, namely actor images and phenomenal images. The former 'presents escalation as being a unilateral act of specifiable individuals and institutions, an independent and conscious decision to commit a certain kind of action and deliberate execution of that decision'. The latter, phenomenal image, on the other hand, views escalation as a 'natural phenomenon of war, a process that seems to get started keep going on its own, partially outside the control of any participant'.[9] As we shall see going forward, much of the Cold War literature seems to be persuaded by the actor model of escalation.

Smoke's 'phenomenal image' deserves closer attention as it is useful for understanding the concept of AMFs used in this book, a concept that is defined later in this chapter. According to Smoke, the phenomenal model 'includes the concept that escalation tends to happen automatically in war; that it is almost a kind of force; that this tendency or force is

---

[6] See, for instance, Dean Pruitt and Jeffrey Z. Rubin, *Social Conflict: Escalation, Stalemate, and Settlement* (New York: Random House, 1994).

[7] Smoke, *War: Controlling Escalation*, 35.

[8] Smoke, *War: Controlling Escalation*, 17.

[9] Smoke, *War: Controlling Escalation*, 21.

constantly present; and that it may get out of control, and indeed is likely to do so'.[10]

Smoke also makes a useful distinction between reciprocal escalation— 'one belligerent escalates to achieve an advantage, whereupon the opponent counter-escalates in reply'—and 'cyclical-sequence escalation'—which he defines as a situation wherein 'an original escalation triggers a reaction, which in turn leads to a counter-reaction, and so on, with no clear, necessary, or definite end to the cycle'. Smoke offers a cogent definition of escalation when he writes that escalation is 'a step of any size that crosses a saliency'.[11]

Smoke's 'cyclical-sequence escalation' when combined with the 'phenomenal image' is particularly significant in understanding how escalation occurs in protracted conflicts such as in the India–Pakistan context, where several layers of conflicts and their accumulated memories continue to foster constant friction on the India–Pakistan borders.

Pruitt and Rubin also refer to the cyclical nature of escalation when they define escalation as 'the result of a conflict spiral (a form of vicious cycle) in which each party reacts contentiously to the other party's contentious action'.[12]

Herman Kahn, in his landmark book *On Escalation*, explaining the inherent logic of escalation in a game-theoretic manner, writes:

> In many situations it will be clear that if the increase in effort were not matched and thus resulted in victory, the costs of the increased effort would be low in relation to the benefits of victory. Therefore, the fear that the other side may react, indeed overreact, is most likely to deter escalation, and not the undesirability or costs of the escalation itself. It is because of this that the 'competition in risk-taking' and resolve take place.[13]

Kahn's writings on escalation go on to construct a very complex 44-rung escalation ladder, starting from a no-war situation up to nuclear war.

Michael Brecher broadens the definition of escalation by specifying the three different phases of escalation: (*i*) 'change from embryonic to full-scale crisis; in terms of stress, from low to peak stress'; (*ii*) 'change from

---

[10] Smoke, *War: Controlling Escalation*, 21
[11] Smoke, *War: Controlling Escalation*, 32.
[12] Pruitt and Rubin, *Social Conflict*, 68.
[13] Kahn, *On Escalation*, 3.

non-violent to violent crisis'; and (*iii*) 'change from no/low violence to severe violence'.[14]

Cold War literature also contains useful discussions on the various models of escalation. In the 'aggressor-defender model', Pruitt and Rubin argue, the aggressor and defender have divergent goals.[15] The former escalates to fulfil his goals and the defender merely defends, and the escalation goes on 'until the aggressor either wins or gives up trying'.[16] The second model they discuss is the 'conflict spiral', in which 'escalation results from a vicious cycle of action and reaction. Party's contentious tactics encourages a contentious response from other, which contributes to further contentious behaviour from Party, completing the cycle and starting it on its next iteration.'[17]

As Pruitt and Rubin correctly point out:

> [Conflict spirals] produce escalation of tactics when, as is often the case, each reaction is more severe and intense than the action it follows. They also contribute to the perpetuation of tactical escalation—that is, to the fact that heavy tactics continue to be used on both sides once they are first employed. If I hit you, you will often hit me back, which leads me to hit you again, and so on.[18]

The third model Pruitt and Rubin discuss is the 'structural change' model, which is defined as 'conflict, and the tactics used to pursue it, produce residues in the form of changes in the parties and communities to which the parties belong. The residues then encourage further contentious behaviour, at an equal or still more escalated level, and diminish efforts at conflict resolution. This escalated conflict is both antecedent and consequent of structural changes.'[19]

For our purposes, the conflict spiral model is a useful one that seems to convey the 'unending' nature of escalation, often the original provocation/escalation remaining intractable. The 'conflict spiral' model, akin to Smoke's cyclical-sequence escalation model, provides insights

---

[14] Brecher, *Crises in World Politics*, 130.
[15] Pruitt and Rubin, *Social Conflict*, 89.
[16] Pruitt and Rubin, *Social Conflict*, 90.
[17] Pruitt and Rubin, *Social Conflict*, 90.
[18] Pruitt and Rubin, *Social Conflict*, 90.
[19] Pruitt and Rubin, *Social Conflict*, 92.

into explaining what often looks to outsiders as 'mindless violence' on the India–Pakistan border in J&K.

There is also a considerable amount of literature on escalation that underlines the argument that escalation is a tool used by states to get leverage during bargaining with the adversary.[20] Lisa Carlson explains the bargaining model in the following words:

> The bargaining process is initiated by one or both actors to reconcile their positions on some issue in dispute. Actors begin the bargaining process by articulate their proposals for a negotiated solution, which can be either accepted or rejected by the opposing player. If one side accepts the terms for agreement, then actors receive the benefit they associate with the proposed outcome. If an offer is rejected, then the bargaining process continues and neither player receives any benefits until one of the sides concedes to a demand. The problem facing both actors is to provide the opponent with an incentive to make concessions. Actors can create that incentive by making it costly for the opponent to persist in rejecting demands.... Escalation is one way that actors can make bargain costly.[21]

Another important debate in the escalation literature is between the 'conflict strategists' and psychological approaches. Conflict strategists, notably Thomas Schelling and Herman Kahn, among others, Russel Leng argues,

> view escalation as a manageable process that provides state decision makers with better understanding of the structure of the crisis.... Thus, the escalation occurring in a militarized crisis allows the parties to determine the bilateral balance of power without resorting to war. The dispute, of course, can escalate to war if at least one of the parties is overly optimistic when it comes to estimating its bargaining power.[22]

In other words, writings by the conflict strategists tend to convey that escalation is something that can be calibrated and controlled as per the requirement of the hour.

---

[20] See: Schelling, *The Strategy of Conflict*; Kahn, *On Escalation*; and Glenn H Snyder, 'Crisis Bargaining', in *International Crises: Insights from Behavioural Research*, ed. Charles F. Hermann (New York: Free Press, 1972).

[21] Carlson, 'A Theory of Escalation and International Conflict', 515.

[22] Russell J. Leng, 'Competing Perspectives and Empirical Evidence', *International Studies Review* 6, no. 4 (December 2004): 56.

Psychological approaches, propounded by Rubin and Pruitt, Robert Osgood, Robert Jervis, Ole Holsti, among others, see escalation as a 'self-reinforcing process'.[23] They argue, according to Leng, 'that the escalation process and its outcome are less a function of the dispute structure than of the degree of aggressive behaviour exhibited during the dispute. States, they argue, do not necessarily behave according to a rational calculation of interests and capabilities. Parties are likely to respond in a hostile manner to any threats to their independence or freedom of act.'[24]

Escalation, in other words, is not merely a product of rational calculations and neatly built scenarios. There is a lot more that happens at several levels during an escalation, some of which could potentially trump rational behaviour or may not be sanctioned by rational calculations. In hyper-nationalist settings such as the India–Pakistan rivalry, rational calculation alone will not be sufficient in explaining crisis escalation—cultural factors such as nationalism, memories, prestige, and so on would be some of the other helpful explanatory variables.

It is important to throw a little more light on the arguments made by Thomas Schelling, who has been one of the Cold War's foremost thinkers on escalation. Schelling's analysis of escalation forms part of the bedrock assumptions about rational state actors engaging in a bargaining process during conflicts—bargaining and communicating through moves and actions.

For Schelling, 'where a war is beginning and each side, faced with a potentially chaotic situation, is searching for a set of limits that both can agree on', they communicate limits, red lines, and expectation through their deeds.[25] Schelling's analysis is of great importance when analysing limited wars and escalation. The Kargil War of 1999 is a classic example. By limiting the war to the sector where Pakistan had intruded even though it would mean more casualties, New Delhi was sending a message to Pakistan that it was merely interested in dislodging aggression and no more.

Strategies of Escalation

Herman Kahn discusses several kinds of strategies states adopt while engaged in an escalatory situation. In particular, Kahn talks about two

[23] Leng, 'Competing Perspectives and Empirical Evidence', 51.
[24] Leng, 'Competing Perspectives and Empirical Evidence', 55.
[25] Schelling, *Strategy of Conflict*.

classes of strategies—'agreed battle', which is 'waged in order to gain an advantage', and the other class 'uses the risks or threat of escalation and eruption from this agreed battle'. He elaborates the second class:

> Users of the second class of strategies can deliberately try to eschew the ultimate eruption threat by establishing a fixed limit on how high they will go. This limit can be kept secret, in which case one side may run the risk of a full-scale pre-emptive eruption by the other side; or it can be announced in advance, with varying degrees of solemnity and credibility.[26]

In this context, Kahn also discusses the 'brinkmanship model' and the game of 'chicken'—brinkmanship when played by two sides becomes the game of chicken.[27]

Why Does Escalation Happen?

Sometimes escalation is a product of the desire to hurt the other side. Vasquez refers to the self-perpetuating manner in which traditional rivals tend to continue with their conflicts: 'Rivals are more concerned with hurting the other side than maximizing their own value satisfaction. For this reason they will tend to oppose the position taken by a rival on any issue. Rivals tend to link all issues on the agenda into one grand overarching issue.'[28] From this point of view, escalation is a natural consequence of a pre-exiting and protracted conflict.

Moreover, the argument about hurting the other rather than benefiting oneself is an important insight—the border 'battles' waged by the Indian and Pakistani militaries invariably involve casualties for both sides and yet 'being more concerned with hurting the other side'[29] ensures the continuity of such battles. Karen Rasler and William Thompson support this argument and show how sustained rivalries can encourage

---

[26] Kahn, *On Escalation*, 7.

[27] Kahn, *On Escalation*, 7.

[28] John A. Vasquez, *The War Puzzle* (Cambridge: Cambridge University Press, 1993), 311.

[29] Happymon Jacob, 'The Strategy of Conflict', *Hindu*, 16 March 2018, available at http://www.thehindu.com/opinion/lead/the-strategy-of-conflict/article23264085.ece?homepage=true, last accessed on 20 March 2018.

escalation when they say that 'rivalry can trump or overwhelm constraints on crisis escalation.'[30]

On other occasions, escalation is merely about taking advantage against a strategy of calculated moves. William Kaufman pointed out way back in 1956 that belligerents in a conflict are constantly looking out for an advantage that has a potential to lead to escalation: 'Because of its competitive character war places a heavy premium upon the attainment of an advantage, however fleeting; and this in turn invites imitation. As the belligerents strive to gain a comparative advantage, the conflict undergoes an expansion.'[31] This means that, unresolved conflicts have an inherent tendency to escalate.

Then there are occasions where escalation needs to be viewed as the product of a conflict vicious cycle which, as the psychological models pointed out earlier, tend to produce crisis escalation without any clear rationale. Viewing escalation as a desire to hurt the other side or to take advantage is rooted in the rational calculus model, but they can also be viewed as part of the phenomenal or cyclical models.

Inadvertent Escalation

Escalation is not always intended by central rational actors, civilian or military, but is often a result of military factors in conflict zones, front lines, and theatres of conflict. Barry Posen, for instance, argues that 'offensive military actions can cause, or require, hostile contact between strategic and conventional forces.... This problem is hard to avoid because military organizations have a proclivity for offensive operations and because they generally resist civilian intervention in any operational planning.'[32]

Military planners tend to seek autonomy from civilian leaders or even surreptitiously make autonomous war plans. Posen writes:

> Military organizations, like all large organizations, tend to seek autonomy from outside influences. Thus, in peacetime, civilians are

[30] Karen A. Rasler and William R. Thompson, 'Contested Territory, Strategic Rivalries, and Crisis Escalation', *International Studies Quarterly* 50, no. 1 (March 2006): 146.

[31] William Kaufman, 'Limited War', in *Military Policy and National Security*, ed. William Kaufman (Princeton, NJ: Princeton University Press, 1956).

[32] Barry R. Posen, 'Inadvertent Nuclear War?: Escalation and NATO's Northern Flank', *International Security* 7, no. 2 (Fall 1982): 28–54.

seldom exposed to the intricacies of military planning, and, in wartime, when civilian intervention in the details of military policy is much more likely, soldiers often interpret policymakers' injunctions in ways that allow them maximum operational discretion. There are many historical examples which demonstrate military evasion of civilian control over military operations. During the Cuban Missile Crisis, the U.S. Navy ran its blockade according to its traditional methods, disregarding President Kennedy's instructions. Historically, offensive action, which requires complicated, detailed, expert planning, has been a way for militaries to evade civilian control. Under current conditions, this pattern suggests that American civilian policymakers may have the least influence over the most escalatory operations.[33]

Several interviews conducted for this study, as discussed in the later chapters, particularly in Chapter 5, indicate how local or even mid-level commanders of the Indian and Pakistani militaries often take things into their own hands due to perceived operational requirements or as personal initiatives. Such decisions by the local commanders more often involve the use of force. Recall the aborted cross-LoC operation of 2001 discussed in Chapter one. Much of the planning is likely to have gone ahead without clearance from the political bosses, though the actual operation would not have gone ahead without political clearance. While politicians and bureaucrats think of negotiations and violence-free political strategies, policy initiatives for the militaries could more often than not involve violence.

Posen also refers to what is widely believed to be a proximate cause for escalation in battlefields, the issue of the fog of war:

> Inadvertent escalation may also result from the extreme difficulty of gathering and understanding the most relevant information about a war in progress and using it to control and orchestrate the war. Not only might this difficulty help to cause inadvertent escalation, but it may exacerbate potentially escalatory situations created by offensive operations or by the indistinguishability of offensive and defensive acts.[34]

This argument could also be used to better understand how tactical local military activity, which might be passed off by the local commanders

---

[33] Posen, 'Inadvertent Nuclear War?'.

[34] Posen, 'Inadvertent Nuclear War?'.

as routine, could lead to higher-order military violence due to misunderstanding, inadequate comprehension of the impact of such activities, and lack of proper communication to the higher political authorities.

Once an instance of escalation begins, there are several different layers of complication, most important of which is on the battlefield itself. And some of the unintended incidents on the ground could potentially cause unwanted escalation. Further adding to such dilemmas, politicians often 'abdicate' their responsibility and give 'complete autonomy and a free hand' to the military to carry out operations, something one often comes across in the Indian context.[35]

In further explaining the link between military autonomy and escalation, Jeffrey Legro argues:

> While traditional organizational theory emphasizes the importance of formal structure in causing uniform military behaviour, a cultural approach contends that differences in belief can lead to dissimilar actions. Military organizational cultures not only influence what types of accidents might occur, but more importantly, what the implications of those incidents will be for escalation. In short, organizational culture leads to dynamics in use and restraint that are not predicted by the randomness of friction, the security dilemma, or traditional organization theory.[36]

Legro's argument is not an un-nuanced argument that military organizations by their very nature are prone to kinetic action, hence triggering crisis escalation, but that it is important to analyse the specific cultures of military organizations in order to understand how the specificities of certain military organizations could trigger or encourage or even constrain escalation: 'My contention is not that militaries always tend to foster escalation, as traditional organization theory would suggest.

---

[35] Rajat Pandit, 'Government Gives Army Free Hand to Avenge Pakistan's Mutilation Act: Sources', *Times of India*, 2 May 2007, available at http://timesofindia.indiatimes.com/india/government-gives-army-free-hand-to-avenge-pakistans-mutilation-act-sources/articleshow/58464264.cms, last accessed on 15 May 2017.

[36] Legro, 'Military Culture and Inadvertent Escalation in World War II', 110.

Rather, the point is that the armed forces, depending on their culture, can either reinforce restraint or instigate escalation.'[37]

The findings of this book broadly agree with Legro's postulation that beliefs and cultural practices matter. And yet, military cultural arguments tend to be silent on 'tactical innovation' done by forces on the ground without express political directions or bureaucratic oversight. Such innovation may not even be part of the larger belief system or the culture of the force as a whole but are developed over the years as standard operating procedures (SOPs) to be adopted in a particular context to guide operational effectiveness. SOPs developed for tactical operational environments need not flow from the overall culture of guidance of the military organization as a whole. For instance, while it is generally believed that Indian military is a defensive force, its behaviour in the tactical theatres on the LoC with Pakistan tells a different story.

Moreover, Legro does not discuss the possibility of subcultures within the military organizations. Legro's argument does not account for such tactical planning or innovation but aims to explain organizational autonomy and discretion. To that extent, I disagree with Legro.

In other words, the argument here is that in order to understand how militaries behave in terms of the use of force or restraint, besides focusing on the specific organizational cultures, it is also important to examine the AMFs and organizational subcultures that are in play in tactical environments.

The Rational/Unitary Actor Bias and Escalation Dynamics

One of the things that the above-mentioned discussion makes clear is that there exists a dominant rational actor bias in the literature on escalation. Conflict strategists, notably Schelling and Kahn, among others, clearly indicate escalation as the result of careful military planning and strategic bargaining. Consequent to the rational actor model is the belief that escalation can be carefully orchestrated, made to seem irrational, and yet be controlled (Schelling's references, for instance, to the utility of appearing to be unpredictable, irrational, and out of control while not

---

[37] Legro, 'Military Culture and Inadvertent Escalation in World War II', 111.

being so). That war and escalation is a game that centralized, rational decision-makers can control is the essential belief here.

There are alternative models (such as the psychological model) and explanations (Smoke's 'phenomenal' model as opposed to the 'actor' model) that point to a non-rational actor explanation for escalation. Both rational actor model and the alternative explanations, however, seem to focus excessively on conventional war situations, with not much focus on sub-conventional scenarios wherein tactical level and unforeseen military factors in 'no-war-no-peace' situations prompt escalation to higher levels.

Second, there also seems to be a bias towards viewing militaries, even when using explanations from military organizations[38] and military culture,[39] as a unitary entity in the context of escalation. What is being missed out here is the possibility of lower commands of the military forces innovating and taking tactical action 'on their own' for meeting tactical objectives without explicit sanction or knowledge of the higher commands.

A Working Definition of Escalation

This book uses an improved definition of escalation. I find Smoke's definition—'escalation is the process by which the previous limits of a war are crossed and new ones established'—to be useful for understanding the topic under study. However, most of the definitions of escalation, including that of Smoke, as described previously, view escalation in the context of war whereas it is important to discuss escalation in contexts where there is no outbreak of war but a serious rise in tensions between adversaries that may or may not lead to war.

For instance, in the wake of the terror attack on Mumbai on 26 November 2008, bilateral tensions between India and Pakistan rose rapidly to disturbing levels but there was no war. Yet another example is the 2001–2 crisis: after the Indian Parliament was attacked in December 2001, India made preparations for war, as did Pakistan in response, but there was no war. In both these cases, there was a great deal of escalation despite the absence of a war.

Similarly, there were several instances of bilateral crisis between India and Pakistan in the past none of which led to a war between the two sides. And yet several of them were serious crises.

---

[38] Posen, 'Inadvertent Nuclear War?'.
[39] Legro, 'Military Culture and Inadvertent Escalation in World War II'.

In other words, it is wrong to look at escalation purely in the context of an all-out war or even a limited conventional war. Crisis escalation below that threshold is a possibility and that's the possibility this book highlights.

Second, while mainstream definitions of escalation view it primarily from a military point of view, this book discusses escalation from three standpoints: military, diplomatic, and political. The rationale is straightforward: diplomatic and political escalation between adversaries who are located in a general atmosphere of military tension can lead to military escalation. Put differently, military escalation is not merely a function of military tensions but of diplomatic and political as well.

For the purposes of this study, I will define escalation as a *sudden intensification of political, military, and diplomatic tensions between countries in a general atmosphere of adversarial relations that may or may not lead to a war.*

Debates on India–Pakistan Escalation Dynamics

This section will examine the literature on the debates on escalation dynamics in the India–Pakistan context: the causes of crisis, conflict, and escalation between India and Pakistan. The objective of such an analysis is to show that the findings of this book differ from the dominant literature on Indo-Pak escalation dynamics.

There is a decent amount of literature on what prompts nuclear escalation in South Asia. There is, for instance, a great deal of writing on the stability–instability paradox and the nuclear angle, which examines the linkages between lower-level violence and nuclear stability.[40] Stimson

[40] See, for instance, Sumit Ganguly, 'Conflict and Crisis in South and Southwest Asia', in *The International Dimensions of Internal Conflict*, ed. Michael E. Brown (Cambridge, MA: MIT Press, 1996); P.R. Chari, 'Nuclear Restraint, Nuclear Risk Reduction, and the Stability/Instability Paradox in South Asia', in *The Stability/Instability Paradox: Nuclear Weapons and Brinkmanship in South Asia*, ed. Michael Krepon and Chris Gagne (Washington, DC: Henry L. Stimson Center, 2001); David J. Karl, 'Lessons for Proliferation Scholarship in South Asia: The Buddha Smiles Again', *Asian Survey* 41, no. 6 (November/December 2001), 1002–1022; Sumit Ganguly, 'Indo-Pakistani Nuclear Issues and the Stability/Instability Paradox', *Studies in Conflict and Terrorism* 18, no. 4 (October–December 1995), 325–334; Jeffrey W. Knopf, 'Recasting the

Center's 2004 book *Escalation Control and the Nuclear Option in South Asia* contains several contributions on various conventional scenarios that can lead up to nuclear confrontation and their escalation potential.[41]

Vipin Narang's analysis of escalation in South Asia considers terror attacks against India by Pakistan-based terror organizations to be the trigger for nuclear escalation.[42] Moeed Yusuf, one of the foremost Pakistani analysts on South Asia, in his new book *Brokering Peace in Nuclear Environments*,[43] considers India–Pakistan crisis escalation as something that begins with terror strikes against the Indian targets leading to retaliation by the Indian side.[44] Likewise, Michael Krepon has discussed the role of non-state actors in the context of crisis escalation in South Asia, but not the impact of CFVs on escalation.[45]

Several of Indian-American scholar Sumit Ganguly's outstanding contributions over the years to the South Asian literature on escalation and crisis focus on the Kashmir dispute and terrorism, but not on

Optimism-Pessimism Debate', *Security Studies* 12, no. 1 (Autumn 2002), 41-96; Paul Kapur, 'India and Pakistan's Unstable Peace: Why Nuclear South Asia Is Not Like Cold War Europe', *International Security* 30, no. 2 (Fall 2005): 127–52; Scott Sagan, ed., *Inside Nuclear South Asia* (Stanford, CA: Stanford University Press, 2009).

[41] Michael Krepon, Rodney W. Jones, and Ziad Haider, eds. *Escalation Control and the Nuclear Option in South Asia* (Washington, DC: Henry L. Stimson Center, 2004).

[42] See: Vipin Narang, 'Posturing for Peace?: Pakistan's Nuclear Postures and South Asian Stability', *International Security* 34, no. 3, (Winter 2009/10): 38–78, available at http://www.belfercenter.org/sites/default/files/legacy/files/Narang.pdf, last accessed on 2 March 2017.

[43] Moeed Yusuf, *Brokering Peace in Nuclear Environments: U.S. Crisis Management in South Asia* (Stanford, CA: Stanford University Press, 2018).

[44] Moeed Yusuf, 'An India–Pakistan Crisis: Should We Care?', *War on the Rocks*, 29 November 2016, available at https://warontherocks.com/2016/11/an-indian-pakistan-crisis-should-we-care/, last accessed on 15 July 2017.

[45] Michael Krepon, 'The Stability-Instability Paradox, Misperception and Escalation Control in South Asia', Stimson Center, May 2003, available at https://www.stimson.org/sites/default/files/file-attachments/stability-instability-paradox-south-asia.pdf, last accessed on 4 September 2016.

CFVs.[46] In a recent much-acclaimed book, Ganguly identifies Pakistan's greed and its use of terror groups as the key trigger for crisis in the region.[47] His argument implies that escalation is triggered by rational actors for strategic purposes.

Bruce Riedel in his book *Avoiding Armageddon*, which focuses on the causes of escalation and tensions between India and Pakistan, argues that 'another small war or another big terrorist attack, like Kargil or Mumbai, could spiral out of control all too easily, precipitating disaster'.[48] George Perkovich and Toby Dalton, in an insightful recent book on India–Pakistan crises, focus on the escalatory potential of terrorism and how to incentivize Pakistan to clamp down on it as terror has the potential, as demonstrated by past experience, to escalate tensions between the two sides. This is yet another example of 'rational actor-centric model' of escalation.[49]

Former practitioners have also tended to follow similar analytical paths, of not acknowledging the role of CFVs in the Indo-Pak bilateral crises. Shivshankar Menon, India's former national security advisor and foreign secretary, in his book *Choices*, argues that terror strikes are the starting point for a bilateral crisis without making any references to CFVs.[50]

Asymmetric Warfare in South Asia, an edited volume by Peter Lavoy, a former US State Department official, makes a welcome departure. In a prominent contribution to our understanding of the Kargil War of 1999, Khan, Lavoy, and Clary show how internal dynamics within Pakistan and Pakistan's India policy are linked, and how historical memories of war can influence the current behaviour of military forces. Examining the causes of Pakistan Army's Kargil intrusion, they focus on military subculture and institutional memory.

---

[46] Sumit Ganguly, 'Nuclear Stability in South Asia', *International Security* 33, no. 2 (Fall 2008): 45–70.

[47] Sumit Ganguly, *Deadly Impasse: Indo-Pakistani Relations at the Dawn of a New Century* (Cambridge: Cambridge University Press, 2016).

[48] Bruce Reidel, *Avoiding Armageddon: America, India, and Pakistan to the Brink and Back* (Washington, DC: Brooking Institution Press, 2013), 185.

[49] George Perkovich and Toby Dalton, *Not War Not Peace: Motivating Pakistan to Prevent Cross-Border Terrorism* (New York: Oxford University Press, 2016).

[50] Shivshankar Menon, *Choices: Inside the Making of India's Foreign Policy* (New Delhi: Penguin Random House India, 2016).

They write:

The 10 Corps and FCNA were particularly embarrassed by the loss of Siachen Glacier, which was undemarcated and unoccupied until 1984 when India launched Operation Meghdoot to capture it.... Officers posted to FCNA are quickly socialised to remember the past and at all cost defend their area of responsibility. They would rather be reprimanded for over-aggressiveness, than leave a perceived vulnerability unprotected. This tendency was given even more latitude in an area where the terrain does not allow for the clear demarcation of boundaries. Finally, the FCNA had an institutional memory of success in the Kargil area. Kargil had been a pivotal battlefield in past Indo-Pakistani conflicts. The grandfathers of current Northern Light Infantry (NLI) forces had taken part in successful operations to capture Kargil, Dras and the Zojila Pass.[51]

They bring out yet another important aspect of why escalation occurs between the two sides. Although they are discussing this in the context of Kargil, this is of great significance to the arguments made in this book—how tactical operations can go out of hand and lead to further escalation. They argue: 'The Pakistan Army perceived the Kargil incursion as a tactical operation to create a local advantage that also might have broader benefits, such as improving the morale of the army, enhancing the military's position in domestic politics, and increasing bargaining power for negotiations with India.'[52]

In another chapter in the same book, Lavoy shows how local military decisions can sometimes go beyond brief, something that we often hear of when discussing CFVs in Kashmir: 'The rugged NLI soldiers penetrated across the LoC and set up several posts along the originally identified watersheds without detection. The operation "grew bigger than planned" when they were authorised to push even further into Indian territory.'[53]

Escalation under Nuclear Overhang

There is also a good deal of literature on limited war under nuclear overhang. Indian decision-makers also fancy the possibility of limited

[51] Peter Lavoy, ed., *Asymmetric Warfare in South Asia: The Causes and Consequences of the Kargil Conflict* (Cambridge: Cambridge University Press, 2009), 67.

[52] Lavoy, *Asymmetric Warfare in South Asia*, 86.

[53] Lavoy, *Asymmetric Warfare in South Asia*, 177.

conventional wars under the nuclear overhang. Indian civilian analysts and even policymakers seem to think limited wars are a viable method of responding to Pakistan's Kargil-like aggression and the use of non-state actors against India.[54] That said, it is important to clarify that, from an official Indian standpoint, there is no Cold Start doctrine in existence. Moreover, a 2010 diplomatic cable from the US ambassador in India to Washington, leaked by Wikileaks, states that the Cold Start doctrine 'is a mixture of myth and reality'.[55] Be that as it may, there is an increasing 'talk in the town' about the utility of limited war, especially after the 'success' of the surgical strikes carried out by the Indian Army in September 2016.

While the Indian political establishment (especially the Bhartiya Janata Party [BJP]) seemed to have exaggerated the outcomes of the surgical strikes, the Indian Army and the Ministry of External Affairs (MEA) were more modest in their claims. Indian Army's DGMO stated that the 'Indian Army had conducted "surgical strikes" on sites "along" the Line of Control (LoC)'. India's foreign secretary stated that 'target specific, limited-calibre, counter-terrorist operations have taken place in the past as well'.

While the surgical strikes have not enhanced India's military options in a fundamental sense, they have indeed altered the Indo-Pak strategic calculus in significant ways: (*i*) it has reduced the reputational costs for the political establishment in New Delhi, which had found itself in a bind on how to respond to Pakistan in the wake of terror strikes, especially when popular emotions run high; (*ii*) Pakistan might find it difficult to respond to future Indian surgical strikes in a tit-for-tat manner due to conventional force inferiority; hence, the denial from the Pakistani side that the surgical strikes ever took place; and (*iii*) given that Pakistan has refused to acknowledge or respond to the strikes, the potential nuclear retaliation by Pakistan at least in the J&K borders could be ruled out.

[54] V.P. Malik, 'Limited War and Escalation Control—I', *Institute of Peace and Conflict Studies*, 30 November 2004, available at http://www.ipcs.org/ article/nuclear/limited-war-and-escalation-control-i-1570.html, last accessed on 17 July 2017.

[55] 'US Embassy Cables: India "Unlikely" to Deploy Cold Start against Pakistan', *The Guardian*, 16 February 2010, available at http://www.theguardian. com/world/us-embassy-cables-documents/248971, last accessed on 17 July 2017.

Put differently, the surgical strikes seem to have put the burden of choosing to escalate squarely on Pakistan. Responding in kind would mean initiating escalation, whereas not responding would mean accepting the new status quo dictated by New Delhi. On the other hand, the more interesting question to be asked is whether the new status quo has modified Pakistan's sub-conventional behaviour in India's favour. Evidence suggests that it has not. Moreover, should New Delhi decide to continue with this strategy in future, would it be able to ensure that it takes place well below Pakistan's red lines (even if they are not nuclear red lines)? So far there are no clear answers to any of these questions.[56]

From a regional stability point of view, the surgical strikes do not seem to have had much of an adverse impact. The fact that Pakistan neither acknowledged the attacks nor responded in kind shows that the general deterrence between the South Asian nuclear rivals remains intact. The lesson is straightforward: while it may be easy to talk about nuclear use and threaten nuclear retaliation, as Pakistan has consistently done, it is, however, not easy to translate such talk into action. In that sense, one could argue that the surgical strikes have called Pakistan's nuclear bluff.[57]

The Traditional Understanding of India–Pakistan Escalation Ladder[58]

Let us now briefly consider the rungs of a potential escalation ladder in the India–Pakistan context to fully appreciate the traditional explanation for how escalation dynamics operates in South Asia. Once we discuss the traditional explanation for crisis escalation in the subcontinent, we will positively complicate the argument by including CFVs in the mix.

As discussed previously, literature on South Asian escalation dynamics puts a great amount of premium on anti-India terror strikes as a

---

[56] Grateful to Deep Jyoti Barman for discussing this point with me.

[57] Happymon Jacob, 'Diary of a Very Long Year', *Hindu*, 26 September 2017.

[58] Material in this section draws from Happymon Jacob, 'The India–Pakistan Nuclear Dyad Strategic Stability and Cross-Domain Deterrence', in *The End of Strategic Stability? Nuclear Weapons and the Challenge of Regional Rivalries*, Lawrence Rubin and Adam N. Stulberg, eds. 203–29 (Washington, DC: Georgetown University Press, 2018).

key source of escalation. A typical example in the Indo-Pak context would be the Indian threat to use conventional forces against Pakistan in the event of a sub-conventional (read terror strike by Pakistan-based/ supported terror organizations) provocation by Pakistan to which Pakistan threatens to respond with nuclear weapons. Let us look at these steps in some detail.

Sub-Conventional Aggression

Pakistan is a revisionist state uneasy with the balance of power and status quo in the region. Pakistan's rivalry with India stems from its quest for wresting Kashmir from India, as well as from the hurt and humiliation it suffered when India helped in the creation of Bangladesh, carving out Pakistan's eastern part. This has prompted Pakistan to adopt ways and means to disrupt the region's status quo and decline to accept the regional order, which it thinks is dictated by New Delhi. This has led to the use of non-state, sub-conventional actors against India, especially in the northern Indian state of J&K. At the lowest level of the ladder then is the use of sub-conventional (terrorist) actors by the Pakistani state to destabilize Kashmir. When confronted with non-state actors such as the Lashkar-e-Taiba (LeT), India is befuddled and is at a loss as to how to respond. For Pakistan, sponsoring terrorism in Kashmir is a cheap strategy that allows plausible deniability to compel India to make concessions on Kashmir.[59]

New Delhi is unable to respond to Pakistan in the same domain, as it does not feel comfortable in doing so, nor does it think such a strategy useful. Despite the Pakistani argument about India fomenting terrorism on Pakistani soil, there is little evidence to suggest that India has been directly or indirectly carrying out terrorism in Pakistan.[60] Hence,

[59] '"Freedom Fighters" Fighting in Kashmir, Not Terrorists, Says Musharraf', *Dawn*, 9 December 2015, available at http://www.dawn.com/ news/1225049, last accessed on 18 July 2017; also see: 'Every Claim of India About 26/11 Backed By Man Who Headed Pak Probe', NDTV, 4 August 2015, available at http://www.ndtv.com/india-news/mumbai-attacks-launched-from-pakistan-soil-says-former-pak-investigator-in-article-1203702, last accessed on 18 July 2017.

[60] Pakistan has often argued that India has been interfering in its Balochistan province (and supporting the anti-Pakistan activities there) through Afghanistan but it has never presented any evidence to back up this

the dilemma—resulting from an unwillingness, on the one hand, to respond to Pakistan's use of terrorism with non-state actors, and setting a bad precedent by not responding to such Pakistani attacks for fear of nuclear escalation, on the other[61]—has been a source of distress for New Delhi and the leadership considers it to be costly both domestically and internationally. On at least two occasions, New Delhi actively considered conventional retaliation to terrorist attacks by Pakistan-based (and allegedly Pakistani-supported) terror groups: the December 2001 attack on the Indian Parliament and the 2008 Mumbai terror attacks. Yet, ultimately, India demonstrated restraint.[62] Indian reluctance probably comes from a fear of potential Pakistani early nuclear use. If so, Pakistan has succeeded in deterring Indian conventional aggression using nuclear threats even though Pakistan cannot be sure of such an Indian response each and every time. And yet there has been considerable thinking within India on how to carry out a limited conventional strike against Pakistan to retaliate against terror attacks, which would constitute a shift to a higher domain.

'Cold Start'

This thinking has led to the new, but unofficial, Cold Start doctrine of the Indian Army (the phrase that is more in circulation today is 'pro-active operations'). Using the potential of the conventional Cold Start strategy, New Delhi hopes to counter provocation in the sub-conventional domain. Cold Start enables the Indian forces to carry out quick, shallow, offensive operations against Pakistan without crossing the latter's nuclear red lines

---

allegation. See: 'US Snubs Pakistan's Bogus Complaint about Indian Inter-ference in Balochistan', *Times of India*, 22 October 2015, available at http://timesofindia.indiatimes.com/india/US-snubs-Pakistans-bogus-complaint-about-Indian-interference-in-Balochistan/articleshow/49489193.cms, last accessed on 19 July 2017.

[61] For more on this, see: Toby Dalton and George Perkovich, 'India's Nuclear Options and Escalation Dominance', *Carnegie Endowment for International Peace*, 19 May 2016, available at http://carnegieendowment.org/2016/05/19/india-s-nuclear-options-and-escalation-dominance/iydh, last accessed on 20 July 2017.

[62] For more on this, see: Menon, *Choices*.

so as to dismantle the terrorist infrastructure on the Pakistani side as well as to carve out some territory for negotiating purposes.[63]

On the other hand, India's Cold Start strategy is designed to be below the nuclear threshold, and therefore need not be ruinous for strategic stability, even as Pakistan considers it to be a serious threat to strategic stability. While for New Delhi, Cold Start is merely making the covert conflict overt and official, it crosses a major threshold for Islamabad. Indian strategists reason that Pakistan would not be able to defeat India at the conventional level due to the latter's conventional superiority, and may not even use nuclear weapons against it, as that would be breaking a very strong normative barrier. While for India, Cold Start is a way of defending against sub-conventional aggression, for Pakistan it is an offensive strategy.

Cold Start is also referred to as limited war under the nuclear umbrella. A former army chief who led the Indian Army during the Kargil conflict with Pakistan has gone on record to argue that limited wars under the nuclear umbrella are indeed a viable method of responding to Pakistan's Kargil-like aggression and the use of non-state actors against India.[64]

Yet, there is also a lot of scepticism about India's Cold Start strategy. It has been argued that the doctrine is nothing but 'hot air' as it does not have New Delhi's political backing and nor is it considered a serious war-fighting strategy by the Indian Army.[65] While such scepticism may or may not be well-founded, the fact is that some Pakistani war planners might believe India is serious about 'Cold Start'. As a result, Pakistan has responded by lowering its nuclear threshold[66] on its nuclear weapons as a counter-strategy.[67] Pakistan may contemplate deploying Nasr in times

---

[63] For an assessment of the Cold Start strategy, see: Walter C. Ladwig III, 'A Cold Start for Hot Wars? The Indian Army's New Limited War Doctrine', *International Security* 32, no. 3 (2007/08): 158–90; On the efficacy of the doctrine, see Shashank Joshi, 'India's Military Instrument: A Doctrine Stillborn', *The Journal of Strategic Studies* 36, no. 4 (2013): 512–540.

[64] V.P. Malik, *Kargil—From Surprise to Victory* (New Delhi: Harper Collins, 2010).

[65] Joshi, 'India's Military Instrument'.

[66] Varghese K. George, 'Battlefield Nuke Deployment by Pakistan Raises Risk: U.S', *Hindu*, 30 March 2016.

[67] Jaganath Sankaran, 'The Enduring Power of Bad Ideas: "Cold Start" and Battlefield Nuclear Weapons in South Asia', *Arms Control Wonk*, 4 November

of crisis but as of today many questions regarding forward deployment remain unaddressed inside Pakistan.[68]

Introducing Tactical Nuclear Weapons (TNWs)

From the Pakistani strategic perspective, TNWs are an effective means for dealing with Indian conventional aggression. Pakistan simply has no choice but to escalate the conflict if it has to defend itself. There is no way it can deal with India in the same conventional domain and so it has to reach out to a higher-domain capability to cater to its defence needs. The development of short-range, nuclear-capable ballistic missiles, the 60-km range Hatf IX, or Nasr missile, first tested in 2011, is seen as very much in keeping with this thinking. Indeed, the press release issued at the time of the testing of Nasr by the ISPR was unambiguous: 'The missile has been developed to add deterrence value to Pakistan's Strategic Weapons Development programme at shorter ranges. Nasr, with a range of 60 km, carries nuclear warheads of appropriate yield with high accuracy, shoot and scoot attributes. This quick response system addresses the need to deter evolving threats.'[69]

What impact do TNWs have on strategic stability from Pakistan's perspective? First, Islamabad hopes to dissuade New Delhi by a nuclear deterrent threat so that the latter does not open conventional hostilities with the former. That is, Pakistan's argument is that the ball is in India's court, as the decision to provoke Pakistani nuclear use lies with India. Second, by adopting such a strategy, Pakistan would also think that a tactical nuclear use would not lead to an all-out nuclear war between the two countries. From this perspective, the introduction of TNWs to counter India's conventional offensive does not damage strategic stability; it only enables Pakistan's survival as the Indian conventional offensive has the capability to seriously compromise Pakistan's war-fighting capacity.

2014, available at https://www.armscontrol.org/ACT/201_11/Features/Cold-Start-and-Battlefield-Nuclear-Weapons-in-South-Asia, last accessed on 25 August 2017.

[68] Grateful to Sadia Tasleem for this point.

[69] Inter-Services Public Relations, 'PR-94/2011-ISPR' [press release], 19 April 2011, available at https://www.ispr.gov.pk/front/main.asp?o=t-press_release&id=1721, last accessed on 6 February 2016.

For Pakistan, TNWs are a defensive weapon that will help it to offset India's conventional superiority. It is indeed this offence–defence dilemma that made Khalid Kidwai argue that TNWs are weapons of peace in South Asia.[70]

New Delhi views Pakistan's TNWs as deeply destabilizing. In response to Pakistan's TNWs, New Delhi seems to be contemplating the development of a ballistic missile defence (BMD) shield.[71] Scholars have also argued that New Delhi is rethinking its no-first-use doctrine in response to Pakistan's TNWs.[72] New Delhi began its BMD developments before the beginning of Pakistan's TNW programme. However, the arrival of TNW has infused a sense of urgency into India's BMD programme.

The foregoing discussion sums up the dominant understanding of the India–Pakistan escalation dynamics and ladder, and as is evident, there is absolutely no reference to how CFVs play a role in this escalation ladder—either as an autonomous trigger for escalation or as a force multiplier in an ongoing escalation and the resultant crisis.

Simulated 'Wargames'

South Asian track-two groups and other war games that have in the past been organized to throw light on the Indo-Pak escalation dynamics have also largely ignored the impact of CFVs on escalation. For instance, Brig. (Retd) Gurmeet Kanwal, one of India's foremost thinkers on nuclear

[70] 'Khalid Kidwai: Nuclear Risks in South Asia' [online video], 2015, available at https://pugwash.org/2015/11/02/video-gen-kidwai-on-nuclear-risks-in-south-asia-nagasaki-conference/, last accessed on 8 August 2016. From the keynote address given by Khalid Kidwai at the Pugwash Annual Conference on 2 November 2015.

[71] Happymon Jacob, 'Time to Consider a Trilateral Asian ABM Treat', *Off Ramps Initiative*, Stimson Center South Asia Program, 5 November 2017, available at https://www.stimson.org/sites/default/files/file-attachments/Happymon%20Jacob_Off%20Ramps%20Essay-FINAL.pdf, last accessed on 1 December 2017.

[72] Vipin Narang, 'Plenary: Beyond the Nuclear Threshold: Causes and Consequences of First Use', Carnegie International Nuclear Policy Conference, Washington, DC, 20 March 2017, Report prepared by Stimson Center, available at https://fbfy83yid9j1dqsev3zq0w8n-wpengine.netdna-ssl.com/wp-content/uploads/2013/08/Vipin-Narang-Remarks-Carnegie-Nukefest-2017.pdf, last accessed on 20 March 2017.

strategy, explains the trigger for an India–Pakistan escalation in the following words:

> The Trigger: Dussehra-Diwali holidays, 2015. Tensions between India and Pakistan have escalated. At 1900 hours a day before Diwali (Day 1), serial bomb blasts on multiple targets in crowded markets in New Delhi result in approximately 300 casualties, including 12 foreign tourists. A captured terrorist is found to be a former Major of the Pakistan army. Cutting across party lines, political leaders demand immediate military retaliation against Pakistan. TV anchors join in; passions are inflamed, the voices are shrill. The Response: Day 2. The Indian Director General of Military Operations (DGMO) calls his Pakistani counterpart on the hotline and asks him to hand over the perpetrators of the terrorist strikes within 48 hours or face military action. The Pakistan DGMO expresses sympathy, but denies that the Pakistan army or the ISI [Inter-Services Intelligence] played any role in the attacks. Strategic partners share evidence with India.[73]

This escalation ladder, in Kanwal's view, ends in a nuclear exchange between India and Pakistan with Indian nuclear strikes leading to war termination:

> Day 15. At 0700 hours, India launches four nuclear strikes of appropriate yield on the reserve forces of the Pakistan Army. Two strikes are launched on 4 Corps reserves south-east of Kasur in the Lahore sector and two on 2 Corps (Army Reserve South) near Bahawalpur. Pakistani casualties: 660 civilians killed or wounded, 345 troops killed or wounded, 56 tanks, infantry combat vehicles and missile launchers destroyed or damaged.[74]

Interestingly, several track-two forums and war games have reached similar conclusions, or at least begun with similar triggers for ensuing escalation.[75] Notably, most of the war games have not taken into account

---

[73] Gurmeet Kanwal, 'Worst-case Scenarios: What would Happen if Indo-Pak War Breaks Out?', *Hindustan Times*, 8 October 2015, available at http://www.hindustantimes.com/analysis/indo-pak-tensions-a-fictional-nuclear-war-scenario/story-gundIhC1iC0amJjMFYo3AN.html, last accessed on 29 July 2017.

[74] Kanwal, 'Worst-case Scenarios'.

[75] See, for instance, Feroz H. Khan, 'South Asian Stability Workshop, A Crisis Simulation Exercise', *Calhoun: The NPS Institutional Archive*

the role of CFVs in an India–Pakistan escalation leading up to the nuclear level.

Assessment of the Dominant Narratives on Escalation

In short, we can make the following assessment regarding the literature on India–Pakistan escalation dynamics: (*i*) There is a great deal of focus on rational decision-making, centralized leadership, and controlled and planned escalation, and an unstated belief in the ability to control escalation. Even when bolt-from-the-blue terror strikes trigger escalation, the control exercised by the political class is complete and it's a central decision to escalate or not; (*ii*) Terror strikes are the primary cause behind escalation to higher levels of the escalatory ladder. These strikes are either carried out by autonomous terror groups at the behest of the state (Indian argument) or carried out autonomously (Pakistani argument). Either way, the argument rests on the assumption of terrorist strikes as the trigger for escalation; (*iii*) The debate between nuclear optimists and pessimists that assesses the impact of nuclear weapons on regional stability, however, does not consider lower levels of conflicts such as CFVs; (*iv*) There is some work on local factors and military culture leading to escalation (by Lavoy et al.) but that forms a miniscule minority in the otherwise vast literature on escalation in South Asia. This line of research needs to be further developed; and (*v*) There is a great deal of focus on unresolved conflicts triggering tensions between the two sides but again the assumption in such literature is that escalation is a product of decision-making by rational and centralized actors in order to resolve the 'key' disputes between the two sides such as Kashmir.

There is, however, some work on terror attacks leading to 'inadvertent escalation' between the two sides, but again the focus is on inadvertent escalation following terror attacks.[76] This literature that focuses essentially

DSpace Repository, 2013, available at https://calhoun.nps.edu/bitstream/handle/10945/37069/2013%20008%20South%20Asian%20Stability%20Workshop.pdf;sequence=4, last accessed on 29 July 2017.

[76] Stephen A. Smith, 'Assessing the Risk of Inadvertent Nuclear War between India and Pakistan,' *Calhoun: The NPS Institutional Archive DSpace Repository*, 2002, available at https://calhoun.nps.edu/bitstream/handle/10945/3272/02Dec_Smith_Stephen.pdf?sequence=1&isAllowed=y,

on the accidental use of nuclear weapons in an India–Pakistan conflict is driven by the same assumption of a terror strike initiating crisis, not CFVs.

Interestingly, however, while the academic literature and policymakers in general have not recognized the role played by CFVs in escalation, some among the military leadership on both sides have recognized the importance of CFVs in contributing to escalation. Earlier in 2017, in a statement by the monthly corps commanders' conference presided over by the army chief of Pakistan, the Pakistan Army 'warned that renewed ceasefire violations along the Line of Control (LoC) and the Working Boundary (WB) pose a threat to regional stability'.[77] In June of the same year, *India Today* reported that 'As tension with Pakistan remains at an all-time high over frequent ceasefire violations and funding of terror in Jammu and Kashmir from across the border, Indian Army Chief Gen. Bipin Rawat today said all options are open against the belligerent neighbour'.[78]

The above-mentioned statements from top Indian and Pakistani military officers indicate that the two militaries seem to recognize the gravity of the problem posed by CFVs, at least to some extent.

The Missing Link

In short, then, CFVs, for some curious reason, have been absent from the discussions and debates about South Asian escalation dynamics. It

last accessed on 29 July 2017; Sam Seitz, 'On a Knife's Edge: Conventional and Nuclear Deterrence in South Asia,' *Politics in Theory and Practice*, 30 September 2016, available at https://politicstheorypractice.wordpress.com/2016/09/30/on-a-knifes-edge-conventional-and-nuclear-deterrence-in-south-asia/, last accessed on 29 July 2017; Mahesh Shanker and T.V. Paul, 'Nuclear Doctrines and Stable Strategic Relationships: The Case of South Asia', *International Affairs* 92, no. 1 (2016), available at https://www.chathamhouse.org/sites/files/chathamhouse/publications/ia/INTA92_1_01_ShankarPaul.pdf last accessed on 5 November 2017.

[77] Baqir Sajjad Syed, 'Ceasefire Violations by India Threaten Stability, Warns Army', *Dawn*, 9 February 2017, available at https://www.dawn.com/news/1313677, last accessed on 20 March 2017.

[78] Bijin Jose, 'All Options against Pakistan Open, Says Army chief General Bipin Rawat', *Indiatoday.in*, 6 June 2017, available at http://indiatoday.intoday.in/story/general-bipin-rawat-pakistan-ceasefire-violations-terror/1/971780.html, last accessed on 5 August 2017.

is in itself puzzling how the regular use of high-calibre weapons such as 105 mm mortars, 130 and 155 mm artillery guns, and anti-tank guided missiles by two nuclear-capable countries, which has led to civilian and military casualties, has escaped scholarly scrutiny and policy attention.

There could be several reasons for this lack of focus on CFVs as a trigger for escalation. For one, there is an acute lack of official data describing accurately when, where, and why CFVs take place, and, more importantly, what they lead to. The aggregate annual data released by the respective governments are devoid of any locational or causative details in the absence of which it would be hard to make sense of the data. Second, there is a great deal of operational secrecy with regard to what happens on the front lines of the J&K border making it, again, difficult for the researchers to get access to information that would help them understand the causes and implications of CFVs. Third, a cursory analysis of the literature shows that there is hardly any material on the operational aspects of the contemporary Indian and Pakistani military engagements. The tendency within the literature, by and large, then is to focus on the big picture questions using traditional, mainstream, and Western theoretical formulations.

The reason why, to repeat the obvious, it is problematic to discard discussions on CFVs in the context of escalation is that a great deal of ground gets subsumed under the ambit of CFVs: from low-level firing to major land grabbing to surgical strikes. The very fact that land grabs and surgical strikes have taken place in the past leading to major standoffs between the two countries, even though they were not publicized, goes to show that it is both analytically and policy-wise imprudent to leave out CFVs from the escalation ladder. The argument here is not that CFVs by themselves could trigger a nuclear crisis between India and Pakistan—to argue that would be preposterous—but rather that a standoff or crisis prompted by CFVs could soon be overtaken by higher military and political factors and lead up to a major crisis between the two sides. CFVs, in that sense, could potentially trigger major crises between the two sides, as they have done in the past.

In summary then, CFVs have often led to escalation in the past, and serious India–Pakistan crisis escalation has taken place even in the absence of terrorist attacks, which have been traditionally considered to be the trigger for escalation. Moreover, when CFVs and terrorist violence occur simultaneously or sequentially, the potential for escalation increases manifold.

One could make several counter-arguments. For instance, Rajesh Rajagopalan makes two such arguments.[79] One, he argues that 'though CFVs have been around for decades, not one war or even serious crisis was the result of such escalation. This suggests that central political and military leaders do ensure some control to ensure that CFVs do not lead to escalation beyond a point'; and two, 'Leaders are risk averse and they would prefer to take the political hit of stepping back to the uncertainties of war. So even if things escalate to a crisis, the idea that political leaders will lose control is simply not backed by anything in crisis history'.

It is correct to say that although CFVs have been around for a long time, they have not led to a war between India and Pakistan. But using the same yardstick, it is also correct to say that even though terror attacks against India have taken place several times in the past, no wars have broken out due to terror attacks. Surely, some terror attacks have taken the two rivals on an escalation ladder, some more than the other. So have CFVs: serious CFVs have also escalated the tensions between the two countries. It is not my argument that CFVs have led to Indo-Pak wars, but that CFVs have escalated and have led the two sides to crises situations just as terror attacks have. And yet, the entire focus of the literature examining escalation between India and Pakistan has been on terror attacks and not on CFVs.

Rajagopalan's second argument is that leaders are risk-averse, and hence, they will prevent the breakout of a war that escalates from the lower levels of conflict. That is a fair point and it is applicable to both escalation prompted by terror attacks and CFVs. That said, it is important to note that today, unlike previously, media and public pressure plays a major role in crisis escalation. Escalation is not something that the elite can fashion and calibrate removed from the public and media scrutiny and pressure, especially when the political elites have themselves used rhetoric to fuel passions against the adversary. Moreover, CFVs and the violence produced by CFVs have increasingly become a major point of debate in India, and to some extent, in Pakistan. While it might be true that terror attacks continue to capture the popular imagination more powerfully, CFV-related violence is quickly catching up.

[79] Rajesh Rajagopalan, email correspondence with the author, 12 December 2017.

Conceptualizing Autonomous Military Factors

This book uses the concept of AMFs to explain CFVs. I define AMFs as military factors on the tactical operational field that are not tightly controlled or determined by central political or bureaucratic authorities even though they could be controlled by the central authority if, and when, they wish to. Moreover, while these factors have an autonomous effect on the dynamics of CFVs on the border, their autonomy and robustness depend entirely on the permissibility in a given political context. In other words, strict and unambiguous political directions and political oversight constrain the ability of the AMFs to have an impact on CFVs.

It would also be useful to make a distinction between strategic AMFs and tactical AMFs. The former pertains to the behaviour of the military/army in opposition to the objectives of the political establishment. The latter category of AMFs pertains to the behaviour of the forces at local levels due to various cultural and operational reasons.

AMFs, because of their dependence on central political/bureaucratic oversight, are especially constrained during periods of constructive dialogues between adversaries, in this case India and Pakistan. As we saw in the previous chapter, from 2004 to 2008, the CFVs came down drastically from several thousands to single digits. If the presence of AMFs explains CFVs, how does one explain their absence during the 2004–8 period? I argue that AMFs can also provide a plausible explanation for the reduction of CFVs during that period. The argument from AMFs expects that when the central control on military actions and initiatives is significantly high, their ability to function autonomously would be drastically reduced. This was evident in the India–Pakistan context in the period under discussion.

In the case of the Indian Army and the BSF, such constraints are a direct result of the existing political environment, which either permits, disallows, or is ambiguous about tactical military initiatives. Even though there may not be any specific directives from political and bureaucratic superiors who do not want the bilateral dialogue and CFA to be damaged by the local military initiatives, given the nature of the civil-military relations in India, senior military leadership in the country has never been adventurous and, hence, never thwarts political initiatives. Put differently, Indian armed forces would abide by the political leadership's desire vis-à-vis relations with Pakistan and on managing the conflict on the borders in J&K.

Pakistan, on the other hand, has a different civil-military dynamic, where the military's autonomy often trumps the efforts of the political leadership in Islamabad to forge peace with India or to manage the conflict on the border with India in J&K. Hence, there is no difficulty in explaining the presence of AMFs in the Pakistani context, both at the strategic and tactical levels. There are AMFs present at the strategic level due to the civil-military dissonance in Pakistan. At the tactical level, AMFs exist due to operational and local factors just as they do on the Indian side.

What, however, needs to be explained is the absence of such AMFs that could have ruptured peace with India during the 2004–8 period: that is, had the Pakistani military been hawkish in its behaviour towards India during that period, there would have been a domino effect and the Indian political leadership would not have been in a position, due to domestic political reasons, to stop like response by the Indian military. What then explains the lack of 'autonomous' behaviour of the 'autonomous' Pakistan Army in that period?

What constrained the Pakistani army during that period was the fact that the Pakistan Army was fully on board the peace process during the period in question, essentially because the peace process was led by Pervez Musharraf, the then president of Pakistan, who was also the chief of staff of the Pakistan Army (till November 2007). As a result, then, there was no way the Pakistan Army could have acted on its own, which would have meant going against the wishes of its commander-in-chief. What if a civilian leader was in charge in place of Gen. Musharraf in this period? The ability of the AMFs to act autonomously would then have depended on whether the Pakistan Army was on board the peace process or not.

On the other hand, however, during times of tension or no bilateral talks between the two adversaries, tactical AMFs gain prominence in India for two reasons. One, political leadership in the country remains unfocused and ambiguous about tactical military behaviour along the borders, thus providing a great deal of flexibility to the local military commanders to make autonomous tactical decisions. During such periods, the local commanders do not feel there is a need to seek permission from the central leadership before taking tactical decisions. Former DGMO Vinod Bhatia points out, for instance, that a lot of authority is delegated to local-level commanders:

> Every time I can't be running back to New Delhi to seek permission.
> Everyone has got a certain authority to take certain actions that they

do not consider to have strategic implications. He does take actions within the limits. If he wants a commander's permission, he will ring up the commander. If it is beyond the commander's authority, it will be referred to the general officer commanding (GOC) or Division. So, the authority is delegated. But more often than not, there is ample authority given to the unit commanders on the ground.[80]

This holds true for the Pakistani side as well.

Gen. Panag, in a chilling account of his face-offs with the Pakistani side, writes about how in 2000 the Indian Army under his command had 'pushed the Pakistanis out of the Batalik sector' near Kargil where India and Pakistan fought a limited war in 1999. The Batalik operation, according to Gen. Panag, was to establish moral ascendency. In an article that he wrote long after the operation and in retirement, the general, who went on to command two key commands of the Indian Army (North and Central), dispels widely held notions about centralized control. He writes: 'There is a misinformed perception that our rules of engagement are strict and rigidly-controlled by higher headquarters, with troops having no freedom of action to fire on the LoC as opposed to the adversary. Nothing could be further away from the truth.'[81]

Second, constraining the military during periods of military standoff with the adversary on the borders could be damaging domestically for the political leadership. This has been a key factor behind the relative autonomy enjoyed by the Indian Army on the J&K borders.

In the Pakistani case, however, its army holds a great deal of strategic autonomy in determining the course of action and tactical innovation along the borders in J&K. AMFs, in the Pakistani case, are a constant factor that have both strategic and tactical dimensions. As a result, we should expect both the Indian and Pakistani armies to enjoy great amounts of autonomy when the political/military establishments in New Delhi and Islamabad/Rawalpindi do not issue explicit instructions to hold fire.

[80] Interview with Lt Gen. (Retd) Vinod Bhatia, 19 September 2016, New Delhi.
[81] Lt Gen. H.S. Panag, 'How We Pushed Pak out of the Batalik Sector', *News Laundry*, 6 September 2016, available at https://www.newslaundry.com/2016/09/06/how-we-pushed-pak-out-of-the-batalik-sector, last accessed on 16 September 2016.

Military Culture and Escalation

Jeffrey Legro uses the argument from military culture to explain inadvertent escalation in World War II.[82] In explaining what causes inadvertent escalation, Legro argues that military cultures, beliefs, and norms about the optimal means to fight wars inform and shape the behaviour of militaries. He enhances the argument made by traditional organizational theory, which highlights the significance of formal structure in causing uniform military behaviour, and argues that there is a need to analyse the specific cultural contents that inform the military in order to understand how they influence the military behaviour. Legro proposes that 'a cultural approach contends that differences in belief can lead to dissimilar actions'.

The argument about AMFs is broadly in line with Legro's analysis insofar as beliefs and cultural practices form the central plank of AMFs. However, what Legro's big-picture analysis (for him, there exists a larger belief system or the culture of the force as a whole that determines their behaviour) about 'military cultures, beliefs and norms about the optimal means to fight wars' is not able to adequately explain is the 'tactical innovation and manoeuvres' done by forces on the ground without express political directions or bureaucratic oversight. More significantly, such elements of tactical innovation are not part of the larger belief system or the culture of the force but are developed over the years as SOPs to be adopted in specific contexts to guide operational effectiveness. For analytical purposes, they may be considered as military 'subcultures'.

In other words, to understand how militaries behave in terms of the use of force or exercising restraint, besides focusing on the specific organizational cultures, it is also important to examine the local-level AMFs that are in play.

Political Permissibility, AMFs, and CFVs

Political permissibility plays a determining role in the ability of AMFs to trigger CFVs. In general, we can hypothesize three kinds of scenarios

---

[82] Legro, 'Military Culture and Inadvertent Escalation in World War II', 110.

with regard to the extent of political permissibility available. The first would be what could be termed as permissive political environment. This is when the political environment is permissive for aggressive engagement on the LoC. During times of tension and no talks, the permissibility increases and there would be an increased likelihood of increased action on the LoC/IB. During such a situation, there are likely to be explicit statements from political leadership about the 'autonomy' given to the forces on the ground for firing at the opponent. The CFVs from April 2016 through 2017 have taken place in a politically permissive environment. CFVs tend to rise dramatically during permissive political environments but the influence of AMFs would be reduced given that CFVs are more of a result of political direction or environment rather than due to local factors.

The exact opposite of this is the non-permissive political environment wherein there are explicit directions from the political/ military high commands not to fire at the other side, leading to a drastic reduction in CFVs. The years immediately after the 2003 CFA witnessed a great deal of calm on the borders with CFVs dropping to a minimum even though infiltration into J&K and sporadic, minor terror attacks against India continued to take place. There were no major terror attacks, and Kashmir was calm, and it lasted roughly till 2008. Another phase when this environment was evident was following Prime Minister Narendra Modi's visit to Lahore. Thanks to the rapprochement achieved by his visit, the period from December 2015 to February 2016 hardly witnessed any CFVs, despite the Pathankot Air Force base attack in early January 2016. During such periods of non-permissive environment, CFVs drastically reduced. The AMFs had very little influence on CFVs.

The third kind of situation relating to political permissibility is the indeterminate political environment wherein there is no clear political direction from the leadership on whether or not to fire. This is a 'no war no peace' sort of a situation when the two sides are engaged in occasional talks as well as trade fire. The period from 2010 to 2014 seems to fall in this category. CFVs tend to be moderate during this period but the ability of AMFs to influence CFVs is very high. Presence or absence of permissibility is open to interpretation by local commanders, leading to a great deal of tactical military flexibility.

Interplay among Political Permissibility, Autonomy of Local Military Factors, and CFVs[83]

In order to better understand the interplay of political permissibility, autonomy of local military factors, and CFVs, I propose the three hypotheses, as displayed in Tables 2.1 and 2.2.

Hypothesis 1: Presence of political permissibility allows for local military initiatives but the autonomy available to local commanders is limited. This moderately reduces the ability of AMFs to influence CFVs. However, CFVs would be high due to prevailing political permissibility.

Hypothesis 2: Absence of political permissibility constrains the autonomy of local military factors. This has a constraining effect on CFVs. This also has a debilitating impact on the ability of AMFs to influence CFVs.

Table 2.1 Relationship between political permissibility and CFVs

		Violations		
		Low CFVs	Moderate CFVs	High CFVs
Political permissibility	Low	X^*		
	High			$X^{\#}$
	Indeterminate		$X^{\dagger}$	

Source: Author.
X^* = authority not devolved
$X^{\#}$ = authority may or may not be devolved
$X^{\dagger}$ = authority devolved

Table 2.2 Relationship between political permissibility and the influence of AMFs on CFVs

		Influence of AMFs on CFVs
Political permissibility	Low	X^*
	High	$X^{\#}$
	Indeterminate	$X^{\dagger}$

Source: Author.

[83] I am grateful to Fahd Humayun for sharing his insights with me on this issue.

Hypothesis 3: Indeterminate political permissibility enhances the autonomy of local military factors. This has a moderate effect on CFVs. However, this radically enhances the ability of AMFs to influence CFVs.

***

The burden of this chapter was to conceptualize the India–Pakistan escalation dynamics. The chapter first examined the Cold War literature to see how mainstream literature views escalation. It was noted that even though there are differing traditions in the Cold War literature on escalation, the predominant strand views escalation as a conscious step taken by rational, unitary, and central decision-makers. The chapter thereafter examined the key debates in the literature on escalation dynamics in South Asia and found that the literature borrows from the predominant tradition of the Cold War literature to understand and explain escalation dynamics between India and Pakistan.

More significantly, the chapter also showed that the literature on India–Pakistan escalation dynamics almost entirely focuses on terror attacks as the trigger for escalation. CFVs in the India–Pakistan border in J&K are not viewed as a trigger, something this book strongly challenges. One could retort that since governments are aware that local dynamics can be the source of CFVs, they will be able to manage it from escalating beyond a point. Such an argument would mean that escalation is always a conscious decision, not the unpredictable outcome of CFVs.

The problems with such an argument are that: (*i*) it assumes that the top levels of the governments are fully aware of the dynamic nature of conflict on the front lines and tactical theatres, which the evidence brought about in this book contests; and (*ii*) escalation can be controlled at will by senior decision-makers. This assumption is again problematic. Even if one were to argue that escalation can be controlled by top decision-makers, their ability to do so becomes less convincing in an era of media sensationalism and hyper-nationalism. Unlike during the yesteryears, what happens on the borders, especially when they involve military casualties, does not stay on the border. More so, as pointed out in this chapter, when CFVs and terrorist violence occur simultaneously or sequentially, the potential for escalation dramatically increases.

In sum, this chapter has argued that escalation can and does begin from local factors rather than due to central directives, something the existing literature on South Asian escalation does not account for. The later chapters in the book bring out evidence to show that CFVs indeed can lead to escalation.

3   (Mis)managing the Border

A History of Practices and Mechanisms

STANDING HARDLY 1,000 METRES from each other, the two Indian border outposts (BOPs) near border pillar (BP) no. 1 in the Indian Punjab are visibly dissimilar in appearance. On the right side is a well-fortified post with BSF soldiers wearing bulletproof gear, with their machine guns loaded, pointed at the Pakistani post. This is in contrast to the post on the left of the pillar where the soldiers look more relaxed without any bulletproof gear: they still have their guns pointed at the Pakistani post though. Further, both face Pakistani posts across the border. BP no. 1 is the first pillar at the border between Jammu and Punjab where the IB between India and Pakistan begins, according to Pakistan. The Indian interpretation differs. The Indian post next to BP no. 1 in the Punjab sector on the left is Dhinda forward and the Pakistani post on the other side is called Chak Qazian.

Having been on a tour of the LoC in J&K for the past several days, I was taken aback by this visible contrast. When asked about the reason for this, the BSF officer who accompanied me to BP no. 1 responded:

> The post on your right (Paharpur forward) falls in Jammu in J&K. Since the status of the border between India and Pakistan in J&K is disputed by Pakistan, there is a possibility of firing between the posts when ceasefire is violated by either side. However, the post on your left (Dhinda forward) falls in Punjab where the boundary between India

and Pakistan is not disputed by Pakistan and so there is no danger of fire breaking out between the two sides.[1]

The distance between the two posts is around 1,000 metres but the difference here is often between life and death.

There is palpable tension and insecurity all around, mixed with bravado and heightened doses of nationalism. There is a sense of suspense, fear, and thrill among the young 20-something soldiers posted there, contributed to by an air of uncertainty about what might happen next. A quick burst of machine-gun fire might ring out anytime, and they must take cover and fire back.

I was on a field visit to the LoC and IB (as India refers to it) or WB (as Pakistan refers to it) in J&K where Indian and Pakistani soldiers have been standing eyeball to eyeball for the past many decades, firing at each other not so infrequently. The motivation behind the visit was to understand the reasons behind the CFVs that seemed to occur every now and then despite the CFA of 2003.

About the Chapter

This chapter will examine the management of the India–Pakistan border. Following a brief discussion on the various terminologies used in the context of the India–Pakistan border, the first section will discuss the early role played by the UN monitoring group in helping the management of the India–Pakistan borders in J&K as well as the occasional, though minor, reworking of the border that took place in the 1950s and 1960s. The next section will discuss the various border management practices and mechanisms used by India and Pakistan in managing the IB and LoC. This chapter will help us understand the occurrence of CFVs that happen on the LoC and IB in J&K, which we will examine in the next chapter.

Terminological Clarifications

From the Arabian Sea to the high Himalayas, the India–Pakistan border is about 3323 km in length. Of this, 1,125 km run through J&K, the status of which is disputed between the two countries. On the Indian

---

[1] Interview with BSF Officer 6, 4 June 2016, Jammu.

side, the J&K border is made up of the LoC, which is controlled by the Indian Army, and the IB, which is guarded by the BSF. The IB is 201 km, of which 191.5 km is guarded by the BSF and 10 km is controlled by the army beyond the river Chenab, which flows through the Jammu region into Pakistani Punjab. On the Pakistani side, the WB is manned by the Pakistan Rangers and the Pakistan Army manages the LoC. Borders outside J&K are managed by the BSF and Pakistan Rangers.

As discussed in the previous chapter, the LoC as well as the IB/WB in J&K have their origins in the first India–Pakistan war of 1947–8. At the end of this war over the status of J&K, the warring parties signed the UN-mediated Karachi Agreement in 1949 and defined the CFL, deemed as running from 'Manawar in the south, north to Keran and from Keran east to the glacier area'. The CFL, though considered to be a temporary measure at the time, divided the princely state of J&K into two parts. In 1972, after the Bangladesh war, India and Pakistan delineated the J&K border in accordance with the Simla Agreement and renamed it the LoC. However, this delineation was done only on the map and not on the ground. The India–Pakistan border in other states, that is, Rajasthan, Punjab, and Gujarat, on the other hand, is well demarcated on the ground by the Survey of Pakistan and Survey of India.

Unlike the years prior to the 1971 war when UNMOGIP oversaw the observance of the CFL, there was no mechanism after the Simla Agreement to control and limit the hostilities between the two countries, and as a result, the firing between the two sides and minor incursions into each other's territory were commonplace in the 1980s and 1990s. In 2003, in order to bring peace and stability to the tense border between the two sides, Pakistan offered a unilateral ceasefire, which India accepted. The 2003 CFA was a huge success, although it lasted only for a few years. There were hardly any CFVs on the LoC or the IB/WB in J&K till 2008 or so. CFVs resumed in 2009 and continue to this day.

There is a geographical reason why Pakistan refers to its border with India in Jammu as WB while India calls its border with Pakistan in the Jammu-Sialkot sector as IB. From the Pakistani point of view, what lies beyond its boundary with India in the Jammu-Sialkot sector is the erstwhile princely state of J&K, which according to Pakistan continues to be disputed. Hence, the term 'working boundary' or WB. However, for India, beyond its border with Pakistan in the Jammu-Sialkot sector lies Pakistani Punjab, which India does not claim since it is not part of the erstwhile princely state of J&K. Hence, for New Delhi, this boundary constitutes the IB. Thus, the boundary from the Chenab River in Jammu down to Gujarat is IB for India.

For both India and Pakistan, however, the boundary in Kashmir is unsettled and has resulted from the actual position of troops at the end of the 1971 war. Hence, they both refer to it, as per the Simla Agreement, as the LoC.

For Pakistan, the IB starts from BP no. 1 at the border between Jammu and Punjab. It may also be noted that unlike in the rest of the IB sectors, the IB/WB in Jammu has not been jointly surveyed by Pakistan and India. There are BPs along the Jammu IB/WB that India considers as the border and Pakistan does not. Given this disagreement on the BPs in Jammu, there has been no attempt to jointly maintain those pillars by the two sides unlike the case in the rest of the IB from Punjab to Gujarat.

In short, there are three distinct lines in J&K even from an Indian point of view. The line that separates India's territory from that of Pakistan in J&K in the Jammu sector is the IB, and from Sangam in Jammu to NJ 9842 in the Siachen area is the LoC. The line beyond NJ 9842 separating the territories held by India and Pakistan is referred to as Actual Ground Position Line (AGPL). Then there is the LAC, which forms the effective border between India and China east of AGPL, a line the status of which is being negotiated between the two countries.

The Making of the Line of Control

The Simla Agreement had given birth to the LoC, which replaced the CFL. Let us briefly examine how the LoC was created before we move on to examine the various border management practices between India and Pakistan. The Simla Agreement was followed by several rounds of discussions between the Indian and Pakistani diplomats as well as military officers to work out the modus vivendi of implementing the agreement. While the diplomats discussed the political aspects of implementing the Simla Agreement, as we saw previously, military officers were engaged in determining the LoC in J&K as of 17 December 1971 and ensuring withdrawals to the pre-war IB outside J&K where India or Pakistan had captured each other's territory.

Far from what we might assume, this was hardly a smooth business: there were often major disagreements in determining the LoC and ensuring that it remained uncontested. For instance, there were places where military advances were made even after the ceasefire of 17 December 1972. Two posts near Tithwal in J&K were examples of adverse occupation of posts after the ceasefire. Other such cases included two posts in the Lipa Valley, which India claimed were captured by Pakistan after the ceasefire. In certain sectors, for instance, the senior commanders of the armed forces found it challenging to determine where the LoC lay at the time of the ceasefire. Moreover, they also had to conduct on-the-spot joint inspections and surveys all along the proposed LoC, which involved difficult terrains.[2]

Besides the post-ceasefire occupation issues, the negotiating teams were also confronted with some other disagreements. New Delhi was keen to link the withdrawal of forces along the IB with the delineation of the LoC in Jammu and Kashmir. Pakistan disagreed with this position, initially arguing that the Simla Agreement had separate clauses governing these two issues. Pakistan eventually conceded to this demand. The talks almost reached a breakdown on the Thako Chak issue. Thako Chak, a village located in the Jammu sector, was captured by Pakistan during the war. The village was divided between the IB and the CFL, which according to the Simla Agreement should have been divided between India and Pakistan. India raised objections to such division, and Pakistan disagreed with the Indian position.[3]

The issue was finally settled by India making territorial adjustments in favour of Pakistan in the villages of Dhum and Ghikot areas. Swaran Singh stated in the Indian Parliament on 12 December 1972:

> [The] controversy over the small pocket of Thako Chak about 1.5 sq miles in area in the occupation of Pakistan, had been resolved. Once Pakistan agreed to withdraw its troops from Thako Chak, we agreed, as a gesture of goodwill, to rationalize the line by minor adjustment of mutual claims. In the process, we withdrew our earlier claim in respect

[2] See Pakistan Horizon, 'Statement made at a press conference by the secretary-general of the Ministry of Foreign Affairs, Government of Pakistan, Aziz Ahmed, regarding the delineation of the line of control', in 'Documents', *Pakistan Horizon* 26, no. 1 (First Quarter, 1973): 107.

[3] P.R. Chari, 'Kargil, LoC and the Simla Agreement', Institute of Peace and Conflict Studies, available at http://www.ipcs.org/article/indo-pak/kargil-loc-and-the-simla-agreement-210.html, last accessed on 2 June 2017.

of the villages of Dhum and Ghikot, situated along the line of control, amounting to about 0.45 sq miles in area.[4]

Delineating the Line of Control

The delineation of the LoC in J&K, in accordance with the Simla Agreement of 2 July 1972, was undertaken by the military representatives of India and Pakistan, who held a series of nine meetings alternately at Suchetgarh on the Indian side and Wagah check post on the Pakistani side between 10 August 1972 and 11 December 1972. The LoC was delineated on the map, not on the ground, as was the case in the 1949 Karachi Agreement. The methodology adopted for the delineation was as follows:

> The Line of Control was reproduced on two sets of maps prepared by each side, each set consisting of 27 map sheets formed into 19 mosaics. Each individual mosaic of all four sets of maps with the Line of Control marked on them has been signed by the representatives of the Chiefs of Army Staff of India and Pakistan and each side has exchanged one set of signed mosaics as required under the joint statement by the representative of Government of India and Pakistan signed at Delhi on 29 August 1972.[5]

The delineated LoC, the maps, and documents were jointly prepared and signed by two senior military commanders, Lt Gen. P.S. Bhagat and Lt Gen. Hameed Khan, and exchanged on 11 December 1972 at Suchetgarh, Jammu. It was also decided on 11 December that adjustments on ground positions will be carried out to conform to the new LoC within five days. On 17 December 1972, a mutually agreed upon statement was released in New Delhi and Islamabad at the same time. And finally, on 20 December 1972, an India–Pakistan joint statement was issued regarding the withdrawal of troops to the IB and the delineation of the LoC in J&K.[6]

---

[4] Public Diplomacy Division, Ministry of External Affairs, 'Statement by the External Affairs Minister Swaran Singh in the Lok Sabha on the Finalization of the Line of Control in Jammu and Kashmir, New Delhi, December 12, 1972' in Avtar Singh Bhasin, *India Pakistan Relations 1947–2011: A Documentary Study*, (New Delhi: Geetika Publications, 2012), 1868.

[5] 'Clarifications on the LOC', Ministry of External Affairs, Government of India, available at http://mea.gov.in/in-focus-article.htm?19004/Clarifications+on+LoC, last accessed on 5 January 2017.

[6] 'Clarifications on the LOC'.

Recent MEA Clarifications on the LoC

In a set of clarifications on the LoC issued by the MEA in July 2012, it sought to dispel the notion that the LoC is not properly delineated. The confusions had arisen in the context of certain Pakistani statements on the LoC. In an intercepted conversation between Lt Gen. Mohammad Aziz, chief of general staff, and Gen. Pervez Musharraf, COAS, Pakistan, Gen. Aziz is heard saying that 'the LoC has many areas where the interpretation of either side is not what the other side believes'.[7]

The note of clarification issued by the MEA stated:

> it is a bit surprising to read in newspapers that some people in Pakistan have expressed a doubt that the Line of Control in Kashmir is vague. These statements indicate complete innocence about the meticulous care and thoroughness with which this Line was discussed, surveyed where necessary, identified on ground and delineated on maps giving detailed grid references and description of land marks.[8]

The MEA further clarified that 19 mosaics were made by putting together the 27 maps that were prepared in the nine meetings mentioned previously. More importantly, these maps and mosaics clearly delineated 'the entire stretch of Line of Control running through 740 km starting from Sangam and ending at Pt NJ-9842. Besides the maps, there were 19 Annexures consisting of 40 pages, giving the details of every feature, landmark and coordinates of the Line of Control'.[9]

The MEA note concluded by saying that 'in view of the facts explained above, there should be absolutely no reason for any reservation in anyone's mind in India or Pakistan that there is anything vague or uncertain about the Line of Control in Jammu and Kashmir'.[10]

How should we understand the MEA note in the context of the clarity of the LoC? While it is accurate to say that the LoC was clearly delineated on the map, as best as it can be delineated on a map, the fact remains that the LoC was only *delineated on the map* by coordinating on the ground: it was *not demarcated*, which means the process of marking a boundary on the ground. Second, over the past decades, the LoC, which

---

[7] Jaswant Singh, *In Service of Emergent India: A Call to Honor* (Bloomington, IN: Indiana University Press, 2007), 185.

[8] 'Clarifications on the LOC'.

[9] 'Clarifications on the LOC'.

[10] 'Clarifications on the LOC'.

is only delineated on the map, has been less accurate on the ground in many places for a variety of reasons. In short, then, the MEA is correct in saying that there is no lack of clarity regarding the LoC of 1972 but it would also be inaccurate to say that there exists absolute clarity on the ground just because there is clarity on the map. We will discuss this issue further in Chapter 4 as a potential cause for CFVs.

India–Pakistan Border Management: A Short History

The Role of the UNMOGIP

The UNMOGIP was set up on the recommendation of the United Nations Commission for India and Pakistan (UNCIP), which was mandated by Security Council Resolution 39 (1948) to investigate and mediate the dispute between India and Pakistan over J&K. Although the UNCIP was terminated in March 1951, a United Nations Security Council (UNSC) Resolution 91 (1951) decided that UNMOGIP should continue to supervise the ceasefire in J&K.

Current Status of UNMOGIP

Following the Simla Agreement of 1972, India has maintained 'that the mandate of UNMOGIP had lapsed, since it's mandate related specifically to the ceasefire line under the Karachi Agreement. Pakistan, however, did not accept this position.'[11] Moreover, it is important to note that 'Pakistan has continued to lodge complaints with UNMOGIP about ceasefire violations', whereas 'the military authorities of India have lodged no complaints since January 1972 and have restricted the activities of the UN observers on the Indian side of the Line of Control'.[12]

The primary function of the UNMOGIP is investigation and observation, to 'observe and report, investigate complaints of ceasefire violations and submit its finding to each party and to the Secretary-

---

[11] United Nations Military Observer Group in India and Pakistan, available at http://www.un.org/en/peacekeeping/missions/unmogip/background.shtml, last accessed on 23 February 2017.

[12] United Nations Military Observer Group in India and Pakistan, available at http://www.un.org/en/peacekeeping/missions/unmogip/background.shtml, last accessed on 23 February 2017.

General'.[13] Prior to 1971, if a CFV occurred and a complaint was registered, an UNMOGIP team would go to the location to investigate the violation. The request for investigation however had to come from either the Indian or the Pakistani side. After 1971, while Pakistan continued to request for investigation into violations, India stopped doing so. The UNMOGIP investigation reports are kept confidential and are only given to the UN headquarters.

India has been discouraging the UNMOGIP's work in the country. The new government in the country under Narendra Modi, for instance, had asked the UNMOGIP in 2014 to vacate the government building used as its office in New Delhi[14] since India considers that the utility of the group is long over. Moreover, two Indian Army personnel are usually present at the UNMOGIP office in New Delhi who would seek to know from visitors the nature and reason of their visit to the UNMOGIP office, unusual for a UN office. An unnamed UNMOGIP official pointed out that there is a lot of restriction on the UNMOGIP's movement in India. Any meeting that the UNMOGIP seeks to organize, professional or personal, requires tedious clearances from the military and civilian bureaucracy in India. This, the official pointed out, is in complete contrast to the great amount of freedom of movement enjoyed by the UNMOGIP in Islamabad to meet political and military leaders there. A brigadier-level officer from the Pakistan Army acts as the liaison officer for the UNMOGIP to help contact the political and military leadership in Pakistan.[15]

In discussing the work of the UNMOGIP, the official stated that the liaison office in Delhi only provides administrative support to the HQ in Srinagar. The office in Delhi sets up the political meetings for the UNMOGIP and liaisons with other missions based in New Delhi and elsewhere in India. In J&K, the UNMOGIP has three field stations, for relay and communication purposes. The field stations undertake area

[13] United Nations Military Observer Group in India and Pakistan, available at http://www.un.org/en/peacekeeping/missions/unmogip/background.shtml, last accessed on 23 February 2017.

[14] Shubhajit Roy, '"No Relevance", Centre asks UN Mission to Vacate Delhi Office', *Indian Express*, 8 July 2014, available at http://indianexpress.com/article/india/india-others/no-relevance-centre-asks-un-mission-to-vacate-delhi-office/, last accessed on 7 July 2017.

[15] Discussions with UNMOGIP official 1, 25 July 2016, New Delhi.

reconnaissance, observe unit and troop movement, and undertake field trips. The observations are reported to the HQ.

Over the years, New Delhi has tried to de-emphasize the role of the UNMOGIP and has hampered its functioning in J&K. The UNMOGIP is not allowed to visit any of the operational areas on the Indian side of the LoC and IB on their own. They are supposed to inform the Indian Army about their travel and visit schedule in advance and they have an Indian Army driver to take them around, which further increases the Indian government's control over the functioning of the group. The UNMOGIP vehicles pass from India into Pakistan only through the Octroi border post, located in Jammu around 11 km away from Pakistan's Sialkot.[16] However, there was a time when the UNMOGIP was not only welcome in the region but, more importantly, played a crucial role in resolving many disputes between India and Pakistan in J&K.

Revisiting UNMOGIP's Record on Border Management in J&K

While the Karachi Agreement itself was by far the most detailed India–Pakistan border management agreement pertaining to J&K, even this agreement was further improved upon and interpreted for operational purposes by the UNMOGIP commanders in consultation with the two parties. These interpretations were eventually incorporated into a field regulations manual issued under the authority of Maj Gen. Robert H. Nimmo, chief military observer of the group, and was made available to the two militaries.[17] The manual also had procedures for defining and clarifying the CFL, informing the UNMOGIP regarding military exercises, and organizing meetings between the two militaries along the border.[18] The manual lost its importance by the late 1960s, and by 1972, India had altogether stopped recognizing the UN group.[19]

Until then, however, the two militaries had welcomed the role played by the group, which was stationed in the local army brigade HQs along

---

[16] Interview with BSF Officer 2, 2 June 2016, Jammu.

[17] Pauline Dawson, *The United Nations Military Observer Group in India and Pakistan (UNMOGIP) 1948–1965* (Bombay: Popular Prakashan, 1995), 65.

[18] Dawson, *The United Nations Military Observer Group in India and Pakistan*, 70.

[19] Dawson, *The United Nations Military Observer Group in India and Pakistan*, 64.

the CFL. Dawson writes that the Indian military in the late 1940s used to give advance information regarding the movement of its guns, arms, and so on in order to avoid allegations of CFVs by the Pakistani side.[20] Minor violations were mediated and settled on the spot by the group without turning them into formal complaints.[21]

After the 1965 war, the group played a key role in reinstating status quo antebellum. In a meeting between the two army representatives on 14 September 1966, it was decided that 'any exercises at brigade level or above to be carried out by either side in the State of Jammu and Kashmir would be intimated to the other side through UNMOGIP', and that 'piquets held by either country on the wrong side of the Cease Fire Line will be vacated on a verdict given by the UNMOGIP'.[22] They also agreed to accept the decision of the group in case there was a difference about the specificities concerning the withdrawal of troops.[23]

The CFV decisions of the group, which would investigate the alleged CFVs and then award (or not) a CFV, were usually accepted by the two sides. Sometimes these cross-border firings were not a handiwork of the two armies but done by armed civilians.[24]

During both the 1965 and 1971 wars, the Karachi Agreement was suspended for all practical purposes and the movements of the UNMOGIP were curtailed due to the ongoing war.[25] In any case, after the 1971 war, the observer group's position started getting weaker.

The UNSC Resolution 307 passed at the end of the 1971 war on 21 December 1971 demanded that 'a durable cease-fire and cessation of all

[20] Dawson, *The United Nations Military Observer Group in India and Pakistan*, 66.

[21] Dawson, *The United Nations Military Observer Group in India and Pakistan*, 67.

[22] 'Record of Discussions Held Between C-in-C Designate Pakistan Army and Chief of the Army Staff, India on 13/14 September 1966 at New Delhi', in Bhasin, *India Pakistan Relations 1947–2011*, 1198.

[23] 'Agreement Between the Government of India and the Government of Pakistan on Withdrawal of Troops. New Delhi, 22 January 1966', in Bhasin, *India Pakistan Relations 1947–2011*, 5265.

[24] Dawson, *The United Nations Military Observer Group in India and Pakistan*, 95.

[25] Dawson, *The United Nations Military Observer Group in India and Pakistan*, 266.

hostilities in all areas of conflict be strictly observed and remain in effect until withdrawals take place, as soon as practicable, of all armed forces to their respective territories and to positions which fully respect the cease-fire line in Jammu and Kashmir supervised by the United Nations Military Observer Group in India and Pakistan'.[26]

The problem however was that the line had changed, and India, the victor in the war, was in no mood to go back to the CFL (although, territorially, most of the CFL remained unchanged) nor was it keen to continue the supervision of the UN monitoring group, as the resolution demanded. Pakistan, on the other hand, wanted the group to continue as before, and the group itself was bound by the resolution that required it to continue. India insisted that the resolution did not refer specifically to the CFL. In any case, it was now becoming clear that the group was to report to the UN on the ceasefire as per UNSC Resolution 307, not the Karachi Agreement.

In January 1972, Pakistan asked UNMOGIP to continue its normal functions as before as per the Karachi Agreement even as India continued its restriction on the movement of the group.[27] Then in March that year, India's permanent representative to the UN stated that UNMOGIP had no role to play in Kashmir and stated that CFVs would be dealt with bilaterally.[28] In July 1972, in a briefing for heads of foreign missions on the Simla Agreement, the Indian foreign secretary stated that the UNMOGIP had no supervisory role.[29]

Furthermore, in a statement on 17 May 1972 in the Lok Sabha, Foreign Minister Swaran Singh stated that the CFL no longer existed as it was replaced by a new line on 17 December 1971. The UNMOGIP's functions applied only to the CFL line and so it had no role to perform. Any issues on the line now would be resolved bilaterally through flag

---

[26] 'United Nations Security Council Resolution 307 (1971)', United Nations, 21 December 1971, available at http://www.un.org/en/ga/search/view_doc.asp?symbol=S/RES/307(1971), last accessed on 21 March 2017.

[27] Dawson, *The United Nations Military Observer Group in India and Pakistan*, 270.

[28] Dawson, *The United Nations Military Observer Group in India and Pakistan*, 271.

[29] 'Briefing by Foreign Secretary for Heads of Foreign Mission on the Simla Agreement, New Delhi, July 4, 1972', in Bhasin, *India Pakistan Relations 1947–2011*, 1762.

meetings. UNMOGIP was not present during troop withdrawals based on the LoC, which was completed in December 1972.

In the meantime, Pakistan continued to ask the UN to 'strengthen and enhance the mandate of UNMOGIP'. From 1972, India disallowed the movement of the UNMOGIP to forward areas and Indian authorities refused to accept any communication from the UNMOGIP's field teams.

The UN position was that if India desired the withdrawal of the group from Kashmir it had to officially write to the UNSC who would have to discuss and take a call on the matter. A.G. Noorani quotes C.V. Narasimhan, the then under-secretary general of the UN, who said in New Delhi on 13 October 1972 that 'there has been no written request from New Delhi to withdraw U.N. Observers from the Indian side of the old ceasefire line in Jammu and Kashmir'.[30]

In January 2013, the UN secretary general's spokesperson stated that 'the Secretary-General's position has always been that UNMOGIP can only be terminated by a decision of the Security Council', responding to a debate between Indian and Pakistani envoys during a UNSC open debate on peacekeeping.[31]

In short then, India has, since 1972, ignored the existence of the UNMOGIP for all practical reasons and yet has not written formally to UNSC to withdraw it from J&K. Doing so, it realises, would open a Pandora's box on the Kashmir question, which it knows best to avoid. Hypothetically speaking, an official Indian request to the UNSC to withdraw the UNMOGIP will begin a series of discussions and debates in the Security Council (SC) on Kashmir including potentially on the issue of plebiscite.

Clashes, Negotiations, and Interpretations of the Indo-Pak Border

From the end of the first war in Kashmir until the 1965 war, the India–Pakistan border in J&K, Punjab, and even in other states, had witnessed

---

[30] A.G. Noorani, 'Can't "Disappear" This Body', *Hindu*, 9 February 2013, available at http://www.thehindu.com/opinion/lead/cant-disappear-this-body/article4394238.ece, last accessed on 12 March 2017.

[31] 'UN Mission in Kashmir Can Be Terminated Only By UNSC', *Hindu*, 23 January 2013, available at http://www.thehindu.com/news/national/un-mission-in-kashmir-can-be-terminated-only-by-unsc/article4335377.ece, last accessed on 14 March 2017.

constant interpretations of the Radcliffe Boundary Award to bring about more clarity on the ground, to end occasional clashes between the two sides and armed raids by civilians on either side, and to have negotiations to bring about an end to such issues. In other words, the India–Pakistan boundary making was a process that went on for close to 15 years.

Although the Radcliffe Boundary Award was published in 1947, India and Pakistan continued to firm up the boundary through the 1950s. In May 1949, for instance, the two countries decided to let the other side manage minor parts of their territory so as to stabilize the boundary between East and West Punjab:

> Where the boundary runs near a river, the area of the Indian Dominion, which may be for the time being on the Pakistan side of the river, should be made over for management to the Pakistan Government. Similarly, the area of the Pakistan Dominion, which may be for the time being on the Indian side of a river, should be made over the management to the Indian Government.[32]

While the Radcliffe Award had kept in mind only the existing administrative divisions in deciding the boundary award, in practice however, Ravi and Sutlej Rivers eventually become the de facto boundary between the two sides.[33]

More significantly, through the 1950s, the two sides negotiated four specific contested areas along the Punjab border and, finally in January 1960, arrived at mutually agreed interpretations of the Radcliffe Award with regard to them.

1. Area of the Hussainiwala Headworks:
   a. It was agreed that the Indo-Pakistan boundary in this area should be the pre-partition boundary between Ferozepur and Lahore districts.
2. Area of the Suleimanke Headworks:
   a. It was agreed that an adjustment should be made in the pre-partition boundary of Ferozepur and Montgomery districts, in

---

[32] 'Minutes of the Meeting Held at Circuit House, Amritsar, on the 30th May, 1949, at 11 a.m. to Consider Measures to Stabilize the Boundary between East and West Punjab', in Bhasin, *India Pakistan Relations 1947–2011*, 6943.

[33] Lucy Chester, *Borders and Conflict in South Asia: The Radcliffe Boundary Commission and the Partition of Punjab* (Manchester: Manchester University Press, 2009), 155.

consideration of the fact that the Headworks had been awarded by Sir Cyril Radcliffe to Pakistan. Measures for mutual cooperation in the maintenance of the Left Marginal Bund were also agreed to.
3. Chak Ladheke
   a. The Government of Pakistan dropped their claim to this area.
4. The villages of Theh Sarja Marja, Rakh Hardit Singh, and Pathanke:
   a. The Government of India dropped their claim to these villages.[34]

Before the Border Ground Rules (BGRs) had come into effect in 1960, India and Pakistan had put in place a slew of bilateral mechanisms to reduce friction and resolve them as and when they occurred. In the Inter-Dominion Conference of December 1948, the two sides had agreed that the inspectors general of police of the two Punjabs should meet regularly to review the situation arising out of the border incidents. Later on, the scope of this agreement was extended to other borders between them.[35] Another bilateral meeting later that month decided that if military personnel are found to be involved in border raids, they would be strictly dealt with and if 'the residents of a village are proved to have been involved in such raids, apart from other action, the question of levying collective fine on the village shall be immediately considered by the Provincial Government concerned'.[36] In an important meeting in May 1955 between Indian home minister G.B. Pant and Pakistani interior minister Maj Gen. Iskander Mirza, it was decided 'that all possible steps should be taken to prevent border incidents', and to set up a joint India–Pakistan committee to 'evolve a plan indicating the measures to be adopted for preventing recurrence of such incidents'.[37]

[34] 'Statement by Prime Minister Jawaharlal Nehru in Lok Sabha on Indo-West Pakistan Border Conference. New Delhi, February 9, 1960', in Bhasin, *India Pakistan Relations 1947–2011*, 8864.

[35] 'Aide Memoire Handed over by the Indian High Commissioner in Pakistan to the Pakistan Ministry of Foreign Affairs. Karachi, December 19, 1953', in Bhasin, *India Pakistan Relations 1947–2011*, 335.

[36] 'Agreement on Boundary Disputes and Incidents Reached at the Indo-Pakistan Conference held at New Delhi from 6th to 14th December, 1948', in Bhasin, *India Pakistan Relations 1947–2011*, 6938.

[37] 'Agreed Minutes of the Meeting on Border Incidents and Shrines', Ministry of External Affairs, available at http://mea.gov.in/bilateral-documents. htm?dtl/7714/Agreed+Minutes+of+the+Meeting+on+Border+Incidents+ and+Shrines, last accessed on 8 July 2017.

This committee, in its preliminary report on the following day, stated 'that the greatest single factor for incidents on the Punjab border was the absence of a properly-demarcated boundary'.[38] They also made a temporary arrangement regarding boundary along rivers in Punjab, something that has been a major issue:

> As far as the border in the vicinity of the rivers was concerned the existing river boundaries would be considered as the de facto boundaries without prejudice to the territorial rights of either country. This agreement would not however, entail any evacuation of any of the existing positions or possessions. If, in future, the rivers changed their course, the Inspectors-General of Police of the two Punjabs would meet and make recommendations to the two Central Governments regarding the cultivation of the land which might be thrown on the wrong side of the river as a result of the shifting of the river's course. Until an agreement is reached on this issue, no attempt should be made by nationals of either side, including their armed forces, to exercise or establish control or possession of the areas in question.[39]

In 1957, the two countries also had reached an agreement about the exchange of armed personnel who cross the CFL and the IB between J&K and Pakistani Punjab inadvertently.

An aide-memoire dated 4 February 1955 pointed fingers at Pakistan for inaction with respect to border raids.[40] But it is clear that such incidents were not a one-way traffic. The aide-memoire itself discusses border raids by Indians. The same was extended in 1958 and further provisioned that the determination of 'inadvertent crossing' had to be done by the UN observers and 'the verdict of the U.N. authorities will be accepted as correct and final. If according to the verdict of the U.N. authorities,

---

[38] 'Minutes of the Meeting held between the Home Minister of India Govind Ballabh Pant and Interior Minister of Pakistan Major General Iskander Mirza. New Delhi, May 15, 1955', in Bhasin, *India Pakistan Relations 1947–2011*, 7044.

[39] 'Minutes of the Meeting held between the Home Minister of India Govind Ballabh Pant and Interior Minister of Pakistan Major General Iskander Mirza', in Bhasin, *India Pakistan Relations 1947–2011*, 7044.

[40] 'Aide Memoire Delivered by the Ministry of External Affairs to Pakistan High Commissioner in India M. R. Arshad on 4th February 1955', in Bhasin, *India Pakistan Relations 1947–2011*, 6996.

such individuals were maltreated they should be given compensation to be determined by the U.N. officers.'[41]

Despite the existence of such agreements and goodwill, especially in the 1950s, border incidents continued to take place given the fact that the borders were still getting clarified and firmed up. The many ambiguities that existed on the border along with the lack of cooperation and mechanisms for effective border control led to a number of undesirable incidents. People living on either side of the border were often kidnapped and sometimes killed in border raids. An aide-memoire sent by the MEA to Pakistan high commissioner in India, M.R. Arshad, on 4 February 1955 pointed out this problem: 'No effort is also being made to apprehend and punish the criminals who sometimes happen to be police officials themselves or are sided and abetted by police officials.'[42]

Lucy Chester writes that 'border raids and livestock theft went both ways.... At least some, if not most, of these attacks were motivated by opportunism, rather than religious hatred.... Occasionally, uncertainties over the actual location of the boundary aggravated an already tense situation.'[43]

The UNMOGIP was often involved in defusing such situations in J&K. The Pakistan Army, for instance, complained to the UNMOGIP in April 1963 that India was mistreating the Muslim villagers of the Chaknot village along the LoC in Kashmir, to which the Indian side responded that Pakistan was inciting the villagers against India. India also stated in a letter to the UNSC later that Pakistan was not only blocking the channel that provided water to the village but also fired upon the Indians who were building an alternative channel (which Pakistan claimed was taking place within the prohibited 500 yards).[44] The UN group, while stating

[41] 'Letter from the Pakistan Ministry of Foreign Affairs and Commonwealth Relations to the Ministry of External Affairs Regarding Exchange of Armed Personnel Inadvertently Crossing the Ceasefire Line, No. I(I).9/51/54, March, 11, 1958', in Bhasin, *India Pakistan Relations 1947–2011*, 537

[42] 'Aide Memoire Delivered by the Ministry of External Affairs to Pakistan High Commissioner in India M. R. Arshad on 4th February 1955', in Bhasin, *India Pakistan Relations 1947–2011*, 6996.

[43] Chester, *Borders and Conflict in South Asia*, 154.

[44] 'Shri U. N. Chakravarty's Letter to Security Council on Kashmir', *Foreign Affairs Record* X, no. 1 (January 1964), Ministry of External Affairs, Government of India, available at http://mealib.nic.in/?pdf2552?000, last accessed on 12 September 2016.

that this matter was outside their area of competence, pointed out that since the village was on the Indian side of the LoC, Pakistan should not press for control of the village.[45]

What is important to be noted here is that unlike in the IB, the J&K CFL was not a peaceful place, and the two sides often made claims and counter-claims and fought over the line. They also did not have many agreements and SOPs to manage the border in J&K. The borders outside J&K was far less contentious than the one in J&K, and the presence of the UNMOGIP was the only hope for sanity there, however limited. We will deal more with the skirmishes and violations in J&K in the next chapter.

The Nekowal Incident

Nekowal is a village located on the Indian side of the border in Jammu, bordering Pakistan's Sialkot, in Punjab. On 7 May 1955, an Indian Army major, along with his guards and civilians, was demarcating a line around 500 yards away from the zero line when they were fired upon by the Pakistani side. A total of 12 Indians lost their lives. After the attack, the Pakistanis took away their bodies as well as the tractor in which the Indians were travelling.[46] The UN observers intervened and the bodies were recovered. The UNMOGIP enquiry on 8–9 May found the Pakistani border police to be guilty of the firing and killing the Indians. Based on this enquiry finding, India demanded a monetary compensation of Rs 12,00,000 from the Pakistan government.

After over a year of negotiations, the Pakistan prime minister Mohamad Ali wrote to Indian prime minister Jawaharlal Nehru on 22 August 1956 that: 'I am instructing our High Commissioner in Delhi to hand over to you immediately a cheque for Rs.1,00,000/- representing our ex-gratia contribution towards the rehabilitation of the relatives of those who have lost their lives on the Jammu side of the border as a result of the incident. How this amount is to be disbursed among the persons

---

[45] Dawson, *The United Nations Military Observer Group in India and Pakistan*, 180.

[46] 'Minutes of the Talks held between Prime Minister Jawaharlal Nehru and Pakistan Prime Minister Mohammad Ali and Interior Minister Iskander Mirza, New Delhi, May 14, 1955', in Bhasin, *India Pakistan Relations 1947–2011*, 413.

affected is a matter I propose to leave to your discretion.'[47] Even though the compensation amount was one twelfth of what was demanded and came after a year's negotiations, the gesture was significant: it highlighted the ability of the two prime ministers to admit to misdeeds by their people, provide compensation, and move on.

The correspondence between the two prime ministers on the Nekowal incident shows that demands for monetary compensation were raised even before, but it is unclear whether they were paid or not. Nehru, in his letter of 30 September 1955, wrote to Prime Minister Mohammad Ali that 'I would also remind you that, on previous occasions, the Government of Pakistan itself have asked for compensation and the Government of India have formally informed the Government of Pakistan that they on their part would be prepared to pay compensation in respect of established incidents on the border involving any death.'[48]

The Nekowal incident highlights the fact that the UNMOGIP played a very constructive role in helping India and Pakistan manage the border as well as the willingness of the two governments to negotiate to settle issues such as border firing and incursions, and even pay damages.

Border Ground Rules

The intermittent incidents along the border both in J&K and the IB outside J&K, in particular the Nekowal incident in the Jammu-Sialkot sector discussed earlier, prompted the two counties to negotiate and finalize a set of written down BGRs to manage the borders. Though 13 years was a long wait, one of the key reasons why the ground rules were not negotiated and finalized till 1960 was because the Punjab border was still being formalized through clarifications, interpretations, and negotiations under the Radcliffe award.

Two and a half months after signing the East Pakistan-India ground rules in October 1959, the two sides finalized another set of rules for

---

[47] 'Letter from Pakistan Prime Minister Mohamad Ali to Prime Minister Jawaharlal Nehru. Karachi, August 22, 1956', in Bhasin, *India Pakistan Relations 1947–2011*, 7039.

[48] 'Letter from Prime Minister Jawaharlal Nehru to Pakistan Prime Minister Mohammad Ali, New Delhi, September 30, 1955', in Bhasin, *India Pakistan Relations 1947–2011*, 7018.

the West Pakistan-India border. The ground rules were formulated on 9 January 1960 by Lt Gen. Bakhtiar Rana, corps commander, West Pakistan, and Lt Gen. P.N. Thapar, GOC-in-C, Western Command, India. Two days later, they were signed into agreement by J.G. Kharas and M.J. Desai in New Delhi.

A close reading of the Ground Rules Agreement (GRsA) suggests that this was a very detailed and expansive agreement worked out by the two armies keeping in mind the various causes that might lead to a firing incident. The GRsA was therefore an important instrument to ensure the existence of a peaceful border.

The 1960 GRsA was later updated in August 1961 specifically for the Punjab sector. This revision in the rules for the Punjab sector was important in the light of the territorial exchange that took place on the West Pakistan-Punjab border in January 1961. In other words, the final interpretation of the Radcliffe Award took place only in January 1961, which necessitated a change in the ground rules. Accordingly, an India–Pakistan conference was held in New Delhi from 22 August to 26 August 1961. Pakistan's foreign secretary S.K. Dehlavi and India's commonwealth secretary Y.D. Gundevia signed the agreement after which the ground rules became immediately operative on the West Pakistan-Punjab (India) border.

Some of the salient features of the August 1961 GRsA for Punjab (India) and West Pakistan were the following. It outlined the maintenance of BPs to be carried out by the two sides. It clarified that within the 150 yards belt on either side of the boundary, all towers, pickets, forward posts, and observation posts in existence shall be demolished and no new construction of the aforesaid description erected (except the ones that were retained under rule 7 (c) of the 1960 agreement), but without increase in their height. The rules also had provisions for return of troops crossing accidently, return of straying cattle, return of stolen cattle, specifications for casual flag meetings, or signals with light at night, and specifications for reinstating dislocated pillars. Interestingly, the rules also recommended that the press on both sides should be pursued to exercise restraint and not to publish exaggerated reports or material that is likely to influence the feeling of the population on both sides. Should incorrect reports be published, contradiction at government level should be issued at the earliest opportunity.

These rules, of course, did not include the CFL in J&K since it was still being governed by the Karachi Agreement of 1949. However, the IB/

WB sector in Jammu continues to follow the ground rules as applied to the rest of the IB to this day.

The ground rules survived the 1965 war as the Tashkent Declaration implicitly revived all existing India–Pakistan arrangements and, hence, both sides continued their adherence to the ground rules. The post-1965 war troop withdrawals to establish status quo antebellum was done on the basis of the ground rules and other supplementary rules formulated in January 1966.[49]

Over the next few years, the two sides developed further measures to enhance stability on the IB and CFL. On 25 October 1967, the two army chiefs agreed to the following[50]:

1. (That the) Exchange of information regarding exercises should reach the other side three clear days before the moves for the main exercise take place.
2. The information so exchanged, in addition to the time and place, should also include the level of the exercise.
3. Information on 'Black-Out' exercises would only be exchanged in respect of towns lying within 25 miles of the border/CFL. Such information should also reach the other side three clear days before the actual date of the exercise.

However, as noted in the previous chapter, things changed dramatically after the 1971 war. Not only did India refuse to adhere to the Karachi Agreement, which was applied to the CFL in Kashmir and de-recognized the UNMOGIP, but also more importantly, it refused to adhere to the GRsA along the IB.

Indian Objections

The basic Indian objection to the ground rules, especially in Punjab, was that its military component prevented it from erecting defence structures

---

[49] 'Agreement between the Government of India and the Government of Pakistan on Withdrawal of Troops. New Delhi, 22 January 1966', in Bhasin, *India Pakistan Relations 1947–2011*, 5264.

[50] 'Record of Discussions Held Between the Indian Chief of the Army Staff and Commander in Chief of Pakistan Army Amplifying Decisions Contained in Paras 2 and 3 of the Record of the Meeting Held at New Delhi on September 13–14, 1966, Rawalpindi, October 25, 1967', in Bhasin, *India Pakistan Relations 1947–2011*, 1245.

and deploying troops close to the border. India believed, and continues to do so, that 'while they (Ground Rules) also prevented Pakistan from doing likewise, the application of these provisions worked against us, as the Pakistan defence system in the Punjab sector is based on canals network while ours is not'.[51] However, the official Indian line on the ground rules has been that given that it is a political-military agreement, it automatically stood abrogated with the outbreak of the 1971 war. In November 1972, the Indian Army chief Sam Manekshaw, the general who oversaw the defeat of Pakistan the previous year, conveyed it to his counterpart in Lahore.

Notably, the final Indian draft of the Simla Agreement had a provision which stated that 'a joint body composed of an equal number of representatives, nominated by each government, shall be appointed to establish ground rules and to supervise the effective observance of the Line of Peace and the rest of the border between the two countries'.[52] This was however rejected by the Pakistani side. Had Islamabad accepted this clause, it was perhaps possible to finalize a new set of ground rules without much delay. That said, it was the Indian side that was not keen on the continuation of the 1961 ground rules: For New Delhi, the absence of ground rules was perhaps necessary for fortifying its positions all along the western border.

Through the 1970s, Pakistan continued to protest the Indian unwillingness to abide by the ground rules. An aide-memoire was presented by the Pakistan Ministry of Foreign Affairs (MFA) to the Indian MEA on 15 November 1977, in which Pakistan accuses India of violating the ground rules in Punjab's Khem Karan area. Pakistan further states that Indian construction on the IB was in violation of the ground rules. The BSF officer retorted, according to the memoire, when told that about the violation, 'It may not be out of place to mention that we have the right to do what we like on our side of the border keeping in view that our actions do not transgress the International Border.'[53]

---

[51] Interview with Senior BSF official, 15 June 2016, New Delhi.

[52] 'Final Indian Draft of the "Agreement on Bilateral Relations between the Government of India and the Government of Pakistan, 2 July 1972', in Bhasin, *India Pakistan Relations 1947–2011*, 1750.

[53] 'Aide Memoire Presented by the Pakistan Ministry of Foreign Affairs to Ministry of External Affairs. Islamabad, November 15, 1977', in Bhasin, *India Pakistan Relations 1947–2011*, 8866.

In response to the continuous Pakistani protests, India, in an aide-memoire dated 4 June 1978, informed Pakistan that it considered the GRsA outdated and that it was willing to negotiate a new set of ground rules for the purposes of governing the conduct of the respective security forces on the IB between India and Pakistan. Pakistan reluctantly agreed to it. In its response, Pakistan foreign office responded via its aide-memoire in January 1980 that 'although the Government of Pakistan maintains that the current Border Ground Rules have been working satisfactorily, it had expressed its willingness to consider specific amendments in the existing rules which the Indian Government may suggest. The Government of Pakistan has since been awaiting communication of proposals from the government of India so that the proposed meeting between the representatives of the two countries could take place.'[54]

Pakistan was keen to either stick to the earlier ground rules or make amendments, rather than create an entirely new set of ground rules. It further stated in the same aide-memoire that 'the Government of Pakistan would be grateful to receive the proposal, of the Government of India for revision of the Border Ground Rules 1961 and would, in the meantime, appreciate it if the Border Security Forces of India are instructed to observe the Border Ground Rules 1961 in the interest of peace and tranquillity on the border'.

Finally, in June 1981, the Indian MEA drew up a new draft 'border control guidelines' (notice the new name) and sent them to Pakistan for its consideration. The new draft focused on unauthorized movement of people across the border, straying of cattle, and border crimes particularly smuggling, kidnapping, armed dacoits, and so on. Significantly, though not surprisingly, it made no reference to the military components of the 1960–1 GRsA, in keeping with New Delhi's lack of desire to put controls on military build-up along the border. Pakistan sent its counter-proposal in April next year, which expectedly included the military aspects of the 1960–1 ground rules, making it clear that they were keen on updating the earlier agreement and that military component could not be left out.

Though Pakistan continued to raise the issue with India, there was no momentum on the subject till 1986. During the then Indian foreign

---

[54] 'Aide Memoire from the Pakistan Ministry of Foreign Affairs to the High Commission of India in Pakistan, Islamabad, January 2, 1980', in Bhasin, *India Pakistan Relations 1947–2011*, 8867.

secretary M.K. Rasgotra's visit to Islamabad in August 1982, the Pakistani side reminded him of the need to keep the 1960–1 ground rules in force till the new rules could be negotiated. Rasgotra responded that the 1960–1 ground rules were invalid and had ceased to exist in 1971.[55]

In December 1986, during the visit of Home Secretary C.G. Somiah to Pakistan, the two secretaries agreed that the Ground Rules evolved in 1960–1 need to be reformulated.[56] To do so, they agreed to set up a committee consisting of representatives of MEA and MFA, Home Affairs and Interior, the Director Generals of BSF and Pakistan Rangers. This Committee was to 'study the two draft proposals in this behalf which had been exchanged in 1981–82 by the two sides, take into account the developments and evolution between then and now and expeditiously draft new ground rules for the consideration of the two Governments.'[57] By late 1980s, Pakistan was coming around to the Indian demand for a new set of guidelines instead of reviving the old agreement: in early February 1987, President Zia Ul Haq assured Rajiv Gandhi during his visit to India that he would do all that is possible to ensure Pakistani cooperation on the issue of border ground rules.[58] Coming in the wake of the Brass Tacks crisis, which lasted from November 1986 to early 1987, the new developments were also an attempt by the two sides to reach a rapprochement after the crisis.

Based on the discussion between the Indian home secretary and the Pakistani interior secretary, New Delhi, in consultation with BSF, MHA, MoD, MEA, and the Department of Revenue Intelligence, prepared a fresh draft of 'Border Control Guidelines for the Border Security

---

[55] 'Letter from the Indian Ambassador K. D. Sharma to Secretary (Pak-iraf) in the Ministry of External Affairs Natwar Singh Regarding the Visit of Foreign Secretary to Pakistan. Islamabad, August 15, 1982', in Bhasin, *India Pakistan Relations 1947–2011*, 2714.

[56] 'Joint Press Release Issued on the Visit of Home Secretary C. G. Somiah to Pakistan. Lahore, December 21, 1986', in Bhasin, *India Pakistan Relations 1947–2011*.

[57] 'Joint Press Release Issued on the Visit of Home Secretary C. G. Somiah to Pakistan. Lahore, December 21, 1986', in Bhasin, *India Pakistan Relations 1947–2011*, 2964.

[58] 'Record of Discussions Between Pakistan President Zia-ul-Haq and Prime Minister Rajiv Gandhi. New Delhi, February 21, 1987', in Bhasin, *India Pakistan Relations 1947–2011*, 3027.

forces of India and Pakistan—1987'. This draft also did not include the military provisions of the 1960–1 GRsA. The Indian Army made it clear that there should be nothing in the agreement that would hinder the movement of Indian troops right up to the border and construction of military structures. New issues such as infiltration also found a place in the Indian draft.

The committee for the reformulation of the ground rules met in Lahore on 8–10 September 1987 and agreed on most aspects of the potential agreement except on three issues: (*i*) Pakistan wanted to include in the text of the agreement references to the 1960–1 agreement, which India objected to, arguing that the 1960–1 agreement had ceased to exist; (*ii*) Pakistan insisted on including defence-related provisions, which India did not want. India argued that defence matters pertained outside the purview of the ground rules. For Pakistan, its acceptance of the agreement hinged on this particular aspect; and (*iii*) India wanted to include a reference to the problems of terrorism and the trafficking of arms and ammunition, which Pakistan objected to.

The next meeting of the two secretaries on 14–16 May 1988 decided to ask the India–Pakistan committee to meet within the next three months to finalize the BGRs taking into account new realities. In the meantime, some interim measures were agreed to by the two sides for the management of the borders outside J&K.[59]

They also decided to strengthen cooperation between the border security forces to check the movement of terrorists and smuggling/transfer of arms and ammunition across the border by organizing joint border patrolling in selected sensitive areas of the Punjab Sector of the India–Pakistan border, among other measures such as joint border patrolling.[60] Many of the provisions of these interim guidelines are still being followed. Later in this chapter, we will discuss more on joint patrolling.

In the June 1988 meeting of Indian and Pakistani officials, they went back to the September 1987 discussions on the ground rules and

[59] 'Joint Statement Issued at the End of Second India–Pakistan Home Secretary Level Talks. New Delhi, May 17, 1988', in Bhasin, *India Pakistan Relations 1947–2011*, 3123.

[60] 'Joint statement Issued at the End of Second India–Pakistan Home Secretary Level Talks. New Delhi, May 17, 1988', in Bhasin, *India Pakistan Relations 1947–2011*, 3123.

revisited the three sticking points. Pakistan was willing to make a few more concessions. The Pakistani negotiating team admitted that the issue of the nomenclature of the proposed agreement was a minor one and could be easily sorted out. They also agreed to include paragraphs with references to terrorism, a major victory for the Indian side given how the Punjab insurgency was becoming a major headache for New Delhi, and the Kashmir insurgency had just begun. However, they insisted on the defence-related clauses in the proposed agreement. The Indian side contended that the 'border ground rules provided a framework for cooperation between the border security forces of India and Pakistan. Defence-related provisions which Pakistan wanted to include in the border ground rules were, in fact, within the jurisdiction of Army and not the BSF. Moreover, our MoD was not ready to accept these provisions.'[61]

Even in internal discussions between various ministries in New Delhi, the feeling was that no restrictions on the defence-related clauses in the GRsA were to be allowed. In a letter dated 22 December 1988 to Foreign Secretary K.P.S. Menon, Defence Secretary T.N. Seshan argued, for instance, that 'the Ground Rules are essentially between the BSF and the Pakistan Rangers and relate to the International Border only. There is no compromise on our consistent stand that both the Armed Forces and building of defences on the border should be outsides the purview of these Rules.'[62]

One strategy that New Delhi followed in its negotiations on the issue of BGRs was to highlight how different institutions in India were tasked with different responsibilities with regard to managing the border and hence how it was not possible to have a catch-all agreement on the border issue. This position had become starkly clear by the end of the 1980s. For instance, during the meeting between Indian home secretary J.A. Kalyanakrishnan and Pakistan interior minister Aitzaz Ahsan in Islamabad on 21 May 1989, the former pointed out that 'it would be more practicable if the military and defence elements of border ground rules

[61] 'Record of the Discussions of the Officials Meeting Separately as Mandated by the Foreign Secretaries of India and Pakistan. New Delhi, June 1, 1988', in Bhasin, *India Pakistan Relations 1947–2011*, 3137.
[62] 'Letter from Defence Secretary T.N. Seshan to Foreign Secretary K.P.S. Menon on Siachen, December 22, 1988', in Bhasin, *India Pakistan Relations 1947–2011*, 5327.

are left to the Defence and Foreign Secretaries of the two countries to finalize, while the Home Secretaries finalize arrangements for mutual cooperation in the civil and policing aspects; aspects which fall within their jurisdiction.'[63] The Pakistani side seemed to have bought this line of argument, at least for the time being. Ahsan responded that if Pakistan's interior secretary could find a via media by remitting the defence aspects of the rules to be dealt with by the defence authorities or the foreign secretaries, he (interior minister) would not object to it.[64]

Aziz Khan, then director general, South Asia, at the Pakistan MFA recalled in a recent interview with me, 'When I was director general, Satish Chandra had come to Lahore with the DG BSF and the BSF-Rangers for talks. And there I kept insisting to Satish that these BGRs need to be extended because they had expired.'[65] Khan states that the Indian objection indeed was the defence structures not being allowed in the Pakistani proposals: 'The philosophy behind the agreement was that you should not be able to peep into each other's backyards. Visibility should stop at the line and not beyond. You (Indian side) wanted a higher perspective and you felt … *kya* activity *ho rahi hai woh* monitor *kar lo* [we should monitor the activity that is happening] … and you were particularly perturbed because of the Khalistan issue.'[66]

Recalling the same talks in Lahore, Satish Chandra, then joint secretary in the Afghanistan-Pakistan Division in the MEAs, said, 'There were issues like the height of the tower, distance from the zero-line, and the placement of troops,'[67] on which the Indian and Pakistani positions were quite firm. Chandra says that although both sides wanted a settlement, there was no meeting point of positions on these issues.

[63] 'Summary Record of Discussions between Home Secretary J.A. Kalyanakrishnan and Pakistan Interior Minister Aitzaz Ahsan. Islamabad, May 21, 1989', in Bhasin, *India Pakistan Relations 1947–2011*, 3218.

[64] 'Summary Record of Discussions between Home Secretary J.A. Kalyanakrishnan and Pakistan Interior Minister Aitzaz Ahsan. Islamabad, May 21, 1989', in Bhasin, *India Pakistan Relations 1947–2011*, 3218.

[65] Interview with Aziz Ahmed Khan, former high commissioner to India, honorary vice president at Jinnah University, 15 December 2016, Islamabad.

[66] Interview with Aziz Ahmed Khan, former high commissioner to India, honorary vice president at Jinnah University, 15 December 2016, Islamabad.

[67] Interview with Satish Chandra, former high commissioner to Pakistan, 14 September 2016.

No Progress Since

The first meeting of the India–Pakistan Border Ground Rules Committee was held in Lahore on 8–10 September 1987—there has not been another meeting of the committee since, to finalize the ground rules. The discussions in this regard seemed to have taken place, if not progressed any further than the 1987 discussions, in the India–Pakistan Expert Level Dialogue in Conventional Confidence Building Measures (CBMs). Through the 1990s, clearly, the two sides were preoccupied with one crisis after another, from the Kashmir insurgency to terrorism, nuclear tests, Kargil, Parliament attack, and several minor crises. As a result, there was no serious discussion on the finalization of the ground rules. In 2006, at the 3rd Round of the Pakistan-India Expert Level Dialogue on Conventional CBMs, the two sides agreed to finalize the 'Border Ground Rules for implementation along the international border'.[68] That is what we know as of now.

T.C.A. Raghavan, India's high commissioner to Pakistan from 6 June 2013 till 31 December 2015, pointed out, 'The view that started coming up increasingly after the Simla Agreement was that it places too many constraints on us. And in the 1980s after, you know this whole issue of cross-border infiltration began, then those older views that this is placing too many constraints on us acquired a cutting edge.' 'Moreover', he described the Indian rationale that 'by the 1980s, the cross-border infiltration became the issue that was not anticipated in the 1961 border ground rules. So, the view that emerged was that we will observe the rules but we are not bound by the rules.'[69] He also recalled the Pakistani side bringing up the issue of ground rules when he was the deputy high commissioner in Islamabad (2003–7).

One of the key reasons behind the Indian Army's desire to ensure that its ability to access the border areas is not curtailed by any agreement—an argument that has practically held up the finalization of the BGRs—is due to the experience of the 1965 war, which it did not see coming, and

[68] 'Joint Statement, 3rd Round of Pakistan-India Expert Level Dialogue on Conventional CBMs, April 27 2006', Ministry of External Affairs, Government of India, available at http://www.mea.gov.in/Speeches-Statements.htm?dtl/2176/joint+statement+3rd+round+of+pakistanindia+expert+level+dialogue+on+conventional+cbms, last accessed on 21 April 2016.

[69] Interview with T.C.A. Raghavan, 8 September 2016, New Delhi.

the Punjab insurgency thereafter in the 1980s. Defence of the border, it seems to think, requires a well-fortified border without any constraints.

That said, the ball is in India's court on the question of finalizing the ground rules and it is for New Delhi to decide and intimate the dates for the second round of the ground rules committee meeting. This may now not happen at all since circumstances and events have overtaken the context and contents of the September 1987 meeting of the India–Pakistan Border Ground Rules Committee. The bilateral Expert Level Dialogue on Conventional CBMs, which deals with a host of issues, is too broad a forum to negotiate and finalize the specificities of the ground rules. In any case, it is clear that there seems to be no appetite within the MEA, MoD, or even the MHA to take up the task of finalizing the ground rules. This is notwithstanding the fact that the BSF officials have a different opinion. Senior BSF officials in New Delhi say that they have been reminding the Home ministry to finalize the border ground rules, which they consider are important to manage the border effectively.[70]

Border Management Practices

India has a 3,323 km border with Pakistan, of which 1,125 km runs through J&K, the former princely state, the status of which is disputed between the two countries. On the Indian side, the border is made up of the LoC, which is manned by the Indian Army, and the 201 km-long IB, which is primarily manned by the BSF, save for a 10 km stretch manned by the army beyond the Chenab river. On the Pakistani side, the WB is manned by the Pakistan Rangers, and the Pakistan Army manages the LoC.

While the India–Pakistan borders outside J&K are referred to as the IB, the borders in J&K have different nomenclatures: a major part of the India–Pakistan border in J&K is called LoC (which is broadly located in the Kashmir sector), AGPL (in the Siachen area), and IB/WB in the Jammu sector (see Table 3.1). Unlike the rest of the mutually agreed to and hence undisputed IB, the IB/WB in Jammu/Sialkot sector has not been jointly surveyed by Pakistan and India. The remainder of the India–Pakistan border, on the other hand, is well demarcated on the ground by the Survey of Pakistan and Survey of India.

[70] Interview with BSF IG, BSF DIG, and other senior BSF officials, 25 April 2016, New Delhi.

India and Pakistan jointly or unilaterally employ a number of measures to manage the borders.

Border Management Practices in Jammu and Kashmir

Table 3.1 India–Pakistan corresponding areas on the LoC and IB/WB

Pakistan side	India side
Neelum Valley	Tangdhar
Tithwal	Baramulla
Chakothi	Uri
New Mirpur	Uri
Rawalakot	Poonch
TattaPani	Mendhar
Kotli	Rajouri
Bhimber	Naushera
Sialkot	Jammu, Samba, Kathua
Bajwat	Akhnoor
Chaprar	RS Pura
Charwah	Arnia
Shakargarh	Kathua

Source: Author.

Border Pillars in Jammu and Kashmir

There are BPs along the Jammu-Sialkot IB/WB that India considers as the border though Pakistan does not. The reason behind this lack of agreement on the Jammu border is straightforward: From the Indian side of the Jammu border, what lies on the other side of the border is Pakistani Punjab, which India has no disputes over; from the Pakistani side of the Jammu border, that is, Sialkot, what lies on the India side is Jammu, a province of J&K, which is a disputed territory between the two counties. One of the major problems in managing the borders in Jammu is the complicated pillar system on the Jammu IB. Unlike in Punjab or Rajasthan, where BPs are properly numbered, mutually recognized, and jointly maintained, the pillar system in Jammu is a stark contrast.

The entire LoC has no BPs since the LoC runs roughly through the middle of the erstwhile princely state. On the IB/WB, however, although there are pillars, they are not sequentially numbered since different revenue authorities numbered them at different points of time in history.[71] A senior BSF officer in Jammu pointed out that in the pre-Independence period, the IB used to be a revenue boundary between Punjab and the princely state of J&K, called the Curzon boundary.[72]

More so, Pakistan does not recognize the BPs in IB/WB since it does not consider it to be a settled border. Put simply, while both India and Pakistan do not consider LoC to be final, India considers Jammu border as final but Pakistan does not.

Even though Pakistan does not formally recognize these pillars, they indeed constitute a 'working boundary' for Pakistan, and hence, the two sides see these pillars as constituting the zero line between the two countries, even if only for 'practical purposes'. Given Pakistan's non-recognition of the pillars, if an IB pillar is damaged in the Jammu frontier, it cannot be replaced because Pakistan objects to it. Over the years, some pillars have been damaged due to natural causes, or in some places, there have been no pillars at all. BSF officials in Jammu say that such places are major flashpoints between the two forces.[73] They also accuse the Pakistan Rangers of sometimes removing BPs in J&K, technically referred to by them as the 'nibbling' of pillars.

Patrolling & Deployment on the Indian Side of the LoC

As pointed out earlier, the Indian Army predominantly staffs the Indian side of the LoC with some BSF battalions inducted under the operational command of the army. There are about five to six battalions of the BSF on the LOC. However, the Government of India is currently considering the possibility of 'thinning out' the presence of BSF personnel on the LoC in Kashmir and redeploying them along the IB in Punjab and Jammu.[74] Indian Army, Rashtriya Rifles (RR), and the BSF (under the operational command of the army) operate on the LoC. RR is a CI force drawn from

[71] Interview with BSF Officer 1, 2 June 2016, Jammu.

[72] Interview with BSF Officer 1, 2 June 2016, Jammu.

[73] Interview with BSF Officer 7, 4 June 2016, Jammu.

[74] 'BSF May Be Withdrawn from LoC, Deployed to Secure Indo-Pak International Border', *Economic Times*, 15 March 2016, available at http://economictimes.indiatimes.com/news/defence/bsf-may-be-withdrawn-from-loc-deployed-to-secure-indo-pak-international-border/articleshow/51416201.cms, last accessed on 25 June 2017.

the army and they come under four CI force HQs in J&K. Victor Force oversees CI Anantnag and Pulwana districts in the South Kashmir Valley, and Kilo Force operates in Kupwara and Baramulla districts in the North Kashmir Valley. Both these forces come under the operational control of the 15 Corps based in Kashmir. The Delta Force is deployed in Doda district and the Romeo Force in Poonch and Rajouri districts. These two forces come under the operational control of the 16 Corps headquartered in Nagrota, Jammu. Over all, some reports estimate India to have deployed around 2,00,000 to 2,25,000 troops on the LoC. Pakistan, on the other hand, has about half that number on the LoC.[75]

India has constructed a fence on most of its border with Pakistan. The distance between the fence and the LoC in J&K is normally between 500 metres to 3–4 km. However, there are places where the fence is closer than 500 metres to the zero line. Small patrol parties of the army move around to dominate the area every night. Sometimes these teams lay ambush after patrolling. A patrol party usually consists of about eight people, equipped with mine detectors, sniffer dogs, pocket jammers (for mines), man-pack jammers, and improvised explosive device (IED) detectors, among others. Each party patrols for about four hours with routes varying every day. Ambush is laid in identified infiltration routes or where infiltration is suspected.[76] In places like Kashmir, patrolling in the winter or during rains becomes a hard task when visibility is drastically reduced.

Jammu International Boundary

The IB in J&K is guarded by the BSF. Prior to 1965, J&K Armoured Police used to manage the IB. The army, with the few battalions that it has posted in the IB sector, provides an outer layer of defence to the BSF forward formations since it has no peacetime duty on the IB. It performs counter-insurgency (CI) operations and lets the BSF guard the border. Moreover, the army posts some men with the BSF companies in the forward posts for observation purposes. However, prior to 2003, the army had the operational command in the IB sector and the BSF operated under the army with the command being with the army above the

[75] Praveen Swami, 'The Abyss Ahead of the Line of Control', *Indian Express*, 24 November 2016, available at http://indianexpress.com/article/explained/india-pakistan-relation-army-jammu-kashmir-terrorism-4392082/, last accessed on 10 June 2017.

battalion level. Indeed, in the LoC sector, as pointed out earlier, the BSF battalions function under the operational control of the army. The BSF is given specific areas of responsibility in the LoC sector. BSF also carries out unmanned aerial vehicle (UAV) surveillance as and when required.

While, in Punjab, a battalion is generally responsible for 35 km of area, in J&K, a BSF battalion's area of responsibility reduces to 20 to 22 km given the security perception there. Vehicle patrolling along the fence, foot patrolling on both sides of the fence, zero line patrolling, and so on are performed regularly. The IB fence has 18 gates, and if locals have to go across for farming purposes, they have to get their IDs verified by the BSF officials. There are lady guards, 'kisan' (farmer) guards, and the like who oversee the farmers while they are in the field ahead of the Indian fence.

The relationship between the BSF and the Indian Army is often not so smooth even when the BSF is deployed under the army in the LoC sector, unlike in the Pakistani case where the relationship between the Rangers and the army is seamless. Gen. J.P. Nehra puts it pithily:

> Operational control is on paper. Suddenly, the CO [commanding officer] will vanish because his reporting is different. This is actually a serious problem because although the BSF is well under the operational control of the army, the control is loose. The person who does the administrative control calls the shots and supersedes the operational control. The army does not write their annual confidential report (ACR). Real control lies in the side that writes the ACR and sanctions leaves. When multiple agencies are involved, the command and control need to be sorted out. Even in the hinterland, in terms of intelligence, there is the BSF's G section, Police and CID[Criminal Investigation Department], army intelligence, and the IB. They are all reporting to their own bosses. Many efforts at synthesizing—like MAC [multi agency centre] in HQ Delhi, under MHA, and I think, controlled by the IB—have not really been successful, although they claim it is.[77]

Ajai Shukla agrees with this assessment:

> Only one thing really determines who controls a unit—and that is who writes the CO's ACR? When there is op control, the BSF will obey you up to a point. But when the difficult decisions are to be made, the person will say that he will ask his commander. So, the levels of

---

[76] Interview with Indian Army Officer 1, 18 May 2016, Rajouri.
[77] Interview with Lt Gen. J.P. Nehra (Retd), 3 December 2016, Dwarka.

coordination and inter-force cohesiveness will happen when you place the BSF unit commanders under the army commanders for writing their annual reports.[78]

The BSF has its own complaints too. First of all, it argues that the army does not involve it in any of its exercises although the BSF knows the border like the back of its hand. Second, while the army is keen on getting information and intelligence from the BSF, the favour is almost never returned. Rakesh Sharma also talks about ego issues between the two forces: 'We have regular coordination meetings and I had very good relations at higher levels of the army, but at the operative level on the ground some egoistic commanders would cause problems for us.'

Deployment on the Pakistani Side

The 23 Division of the Pakistan Army is deployed along the LoC. Punjab Rangers are posted along the WB and the Punjab province. FCNA, a division-size formation of the Pakistan Army, is posted along the Siachen as well as sectors up north. The brigade HQ of certain battalions posted along the Pakistani side of Kashmir is at Muzaffarabad. The divisional HQ is situated at Murree, and Corps HQ is in Rawalpindi.[79]

Punjab Rangers are deployed along the WB sectors and operate under the command of the Pakistan Army. Although technically the Punjab Rangers come under the Federal Ministry of Interior, the force, de facto, is filled by Pakistani army officers on deputation. Its head is a serving two-star officer of the Pakistan Army. Moreover, regular soldiers of the Pakistan Army are also deployed along with the Punjab Rangers in the WB sectors.[80] All the commanding officers and wing commanders of the Rangers are army officers. Some Rangers, most of whom start out as constables, rise in the chain up to a point. Some Ranger officers, known as deputy superintendent Rangers, equal to a captain in the army, are directly recruited at the officer level.[81] During the 2003 military standoff, the Pakistan Army was deployed in the Jammu IB along with the Rangers, though this was not done during the Kargil War of 1999.[82] Given such a close relationship between the Pakistan Army and the Rangers (although they technically report to two different ministries), the communication links are smoother than those between BSF and the Indian Army.

Regular infantry units of the Pakistan Army patrol the Pakistani side of the LoC, with its soldiers taking turns to patrol the area as well as guard the post.[83] All units are linked with communication systems at two levels, that is, 'strategic' and 'tactical'. At the strategic level, 'Pakistan Army Strategic Communications' (PASCOM) connects all units to the GHQ. At the tactical level, all units are connected with all tiers of chain of command through 'Pakistan Army Tactical Communication' (PATCOM) systems.[84]

In the Sialkot/Jammu sector, the Pakistan Rangers are deployed at the section level whereas the Indian deployment is at the platoon level, which makes the force ratio at 1:3 in India's favour (one platoon has three sections). This is compensated by Pakistan with its superior number of bunkers on the Jammu IB.[85] While BSF has about 100 BOPs on the Jammu IB, Pakistan Rangers have about 128 of them.

The LoC and IB (Jammu) Fence

The LoC fence came up during the 2001–3 period though construction on the IB fence started before the LoC fence. The fence should ideally have been 150 yards away from the zero line in Jammu (as per the GRsA of 1961) and 500 yards away in Kashmir (as per the Karachi Agreement of 1949), but in some places it is even at 50 yards distance from the zero line on the IB.[86] The fence itself is 8–12 feet wide. Ahead of the fence, there is a 14-feet road, wherever possible. Since the fence was built where it could be best built, the norm of no construction within 150-yard limit was often violated, attracting Pakistani firing. Riverine gaps interrupt the IB fence in several places and measures are taken to plug the gaps, using technological solutions such as laser lights, alarms, and cameras as well as sharp metal obstructions placed on the ground to prevent trespassing.

[83] Interview with Pakistan Army Officer 1, 7 June 2016, Islamabad.

[84] Interview with Pakistan Army Officer 2, 9 June 2016, Islamabad. (Pakistan Army Officer 3, interviewed by M. Faisal, also agreed with this info).

[85] Interview with BSF Officer 4, 3 June 2016, Jammu.

[86] Interview with BSF Officer 1, 2 June 2016, Jammu.

The fence on the LoC is far less effective than the one on the IB due to reasons pertaining to the terrain. The LoC fence, for instance, is often buried in snow during the winter and requires annual repairs after the snow melts. The posts in places like Tangdhar in Kashmir are at a height of 14,000 feet, which gets fully covered by snow during winter months. Sometimes, an Indian officer explained, infiltrators use wooden planks to cross the fence.[87]

In order to further strengthen the surveillance, UAVs are used along the LoC every 10–15 days or so to capture images. The feeds are magnified to see whether new constructions have come up on the Pakistani side. However, if a UAV crosses the LoC, it would amount to a CFV.[88] And when they cross, they risk getting shot down.

Officers who have served on the LoC before the fence came up argue that the fence has fundamentally changed the dynamics along the LoC. "The fence on the Indian side came up in 2002–3. Before that the norm was "grabbers as keepers", especially between 1988 and 2003."[89]

The fence in Kashmir and Rajasthan are the most difficult to maintain: in Kashmir, the winter snow destroys the fence, and in Rajasthan, the shifting sand dunes often buries the fence. Moreover, during rains, the fence gets damages throughout the border, except in Rajasthan where the rainfall is minimal. There are also a number of riverine gaps on the border fence, especially in J&K and Punjab where it is difficult to construct a fence due to running rivers.

The distance between the fence and the LoC in J&K is normally between 500 metres to 3–4 km. However, there are places where the fence is closer than 500 metres to the zero line. Although the fence should ideally be 150 yards away from the zero line in Jammu and 500 yards away in Kashmir, in some places it is even at 50 yards distance from the zero line on the IB.[90] The government's own logic for constructing the fence within the 'prohibited' 150 yards is that it is done in 'keeping in view the geographical terrain and other related constraints on the site'.[91] The entire

---

[87] Interview with Indian Army Officer 7, 16 May 2016, Tangdhar (J&K).

[88] Interview with Indian Army Officer 3, 14 May 2016, Poonch (J&K).

[89] Interview with Indian Army Officer 3, 14 May 2016, Poonch (J&K).

[90] Interview with BSF Officer 1, 2 June 2016, Jammu.

[91] Press Information Bureau, 'Fencing of International Border', Ministry of Defence, Government of India, 5 December 2014, available at http://pib.nic.in/newsite/PrintRelease.aspx?relid=112676, last accessed on 23 July 2017.

IB fence (including in Punjab) is electrified with live 'Cobra' wires running through them even though the same is not the case in the LoC fence.

The IB fence in Punjab came up in 1989 after insurgency in the state, as pointed out earlier. After 1989, when the construction of wire fencing began in the state, Pakistan did not raise too many objections, even though in some places, the fence is closer than 500 yards to the zero line. Pakistan objected, however, to any extension in the Jammu sector and along the LoC given the fact that it does not accept the IB to be final.

In fact, the Pakistani side had explicitly said that fencing on the LoC is not allowed. Maj Gen. Shaukat Sultan, Pakistan's military spokesman, had said in 2003 when India was building the fence: 'Any measure to alter the status of these and any attempt to erect [a] new impediment is a direct violation of international commitments, and Pakistan opposes it. Border fencing is not allowed.'[92] It was then that the BSF started building the fence themselves, in 2001–2, even before the LoC fencing was started. Construction and earth-moving equipment with bulletproof sheets were widely used. Bulletproof sheets were put on vehicles and other equipment, and before construction on the fence began, a bund (embankment) was formed beyond the area where the fence would be. Heavy firing along the IB and LoC during 2001–3 (prior to CFA) can be partly explained by the fence building that was happening at that point of time.[93]

Journalist Praveen Swami reported in September 2001: 'Protective earth walls along with bullet-proof metal shields were put up as defences against fire. Work began under cover of darkness and fog in January this year, and remained undetected for the next four months.'[94] Pakistan also tried to demolish parts of the fence using explosives, whenever possible.[95] See Table 3.2 that shows how the firing increased when India began the construction of the fence in early 2001.

[92] Rama Lakshmi, 'India's Border Fence Extended to Kashmir', *The Washington Post*, 30 July 2003, available at https://www.washingtonpost.com/archive/politics/2003/07/30/indias-border-fence-extended-to-kashmir/39e3e816-9704-4a3b-8d6c-fd46123ce005/?utm_term=.390d52c3e317, last accessed on 10 June 2016.

[93] Interview with BSF Officer 1, 2 June 2016, Jammu.

[94] Praveen Swami, 'Border Barrier', *Frontline* 18, no. 9 (15–28 September 2001), available at http://www.frontline.in/static/html/fl1819/18191290.htm, last accessed on 25 June 2017.

[95] Swami, 'Border Barrier'.

Table 3.2   Firing along the India–Pakistan border in J&K

Month	Pakistan	India
December 2000	682	77
January 2001	181	23
February 2001	7,132	173
March 2001	7,637	1,218
April 2001	29,012	13,426
May 2001	1,29,929	90,417
June 2001	2,59,335	1,61,745
July 2001	1,82,716	1,11,847
August 2001	3,04,425	1,63,820

Source: This table has been adopted from Praveen Swami, 'Border Barrier', *Frontline* 18, no. 19 (15–28 September 2001), available at http://www.frontline.in/static/html/fl1819/18191290.htm.

Landmines

Both India and Pakistan use anti-personnel landmines on the LoC and sometimes even on the IB/WB, like in the Samba sector in Jammu, where infiltration attempts have gone up in the recent years. Mines were placed in the India–Pakistan border area during the wars of 1947, 1965, 1971, and again in 2001 during Operation Parakram. Some of those old mines continue to remain in place. Mined sites are marked and safeguarded with fences and meshes as per Protocol II of the Geneva Convention of 1980.[96] Gen. Waheed confirms that marking of mines is done on the Pakistani side as well: 'Mine fields are always fenced and marked. There are red markers.' Indeed, during the 2001 Operation Parakram, more mines were placed in some areas in the LoC and IB.[97]

Sometimes these mines drift away from the meshed areas due to environmental factors and there have been several mine-related accidents. Sometimes rains take away both mines along with the mesh making the management of mines difficult.[98]

Sometimes the Indian side places mines along the infiltration routes on the border. There is also a related danger, Indian officials recount, of Pakistan

[96] Interview with Indian Army Officer 3, 14 May 2016, Bhimber Gali.
[97] Interview with BSF Officer 6, 4 June 2016, Jammu.
[98] Interview with Lt Gen. (Retd) Tariq Ghazi, 7 November 2016, Bangkok.

Rangers or terrorists placing mines or IEDs along the fence to damage the fence or to frustrate the Indian activities such as patrolling.[99] Former BSF Jammu inspector general (IG) Rakesh Sharma recalls an incident where a deputy inspector general (DIG), along with two others, was blown off by mines in the Ballad post of Samba sector in 2009. Sharma argues that 'it was probably an anti-tank mine planted by Pakistan on our side'.[100]

Certain areas and selected sectors on the Pakistan side also are mined along the LoC. In some sectors, mining is extensive and, in others, limited.[101] However, according to Gen. Waheed, the whole LoC is mined on both sides. Sometimes, every two or three feet, one would get a mine. Gen. Waheed argues 'At times, mines get washed away by waterfalls, heavy rains … they are anti-personnel mines so they are not very deep. A landslide may take the mines away. A number of mine-related accidents have taken place on both sides of the border.[102] A lot of casualties take place on our own side too'.[103] As a result of mine drifting, according to Gen. Yasin, areas which were not supposed to be mined end up having mines.[104]

After the 1971 war, it was during Operation Parakram (after the terrorist attack on the Indian Parliament in 2001) that India and Pakistan undertook a massive mine-laying operation along the border in all states.[105] A landmine monitor report estimates that around two million mines were laid from December 2001 to mid-2002.[106]

[99] Interview with BSF Officer 7, 4 June 2016, Jammu. Also see: 'Army Jawan Injured in Mine Blast along LoC in Jammu and Kashmir', *IndiaTV*, 14 December 2014, available at http://www.indiatvnews.com/news/india/army-jawan-injured-in-mine-blast-along-loc-in-jammu-and-kashmir-45221.html, last accessed on 10 June 2016.

[100] Interview with Rakesh Sharma, 15 September 2016, New Delhi.

[101] Interview with Pakistan Army Officer 1, 7 June 2016, Islamabad.

[102] Shujaat Bukhari, 'Deathtraps along the Border', *Friday Times*, 10 April 2015, available at http://www.thefridaytimes.com/tft/deathtraps-along-the-border/, last accessed on 10 June 2016.

[103] Interview with Gen. Waheed, 15 April 2016, Bangkok.

[104] Interview with Gen. Yasin, 15 April 2016, Bangkok.

[105] Interview with Lt Gen. (Retd) J.P. Nehra, 3 December 2016, New Delhi.

[106] For more, see: 'Landmine and Cluster Monitor Report 2004: India', *Landmine and Cluster Munition Monitor*, Archives 1999–2014, http://archives.the-monitor.org/index.php/publications/display?url=lm/2002/india.html, last accessed on 2 April 2017.

Around 16,000 acres of land in the Jammu region and 1,73,000 acres in Kashmir were also reportedly mined during this period.[107] While the Indian government claims that almost all of this area has been demined, officials on the ground say that a lot of those continue to remain in place and have killed hundreds of civilians and soldiers. A report published by the Landmine & Cluster Munition Monitor showed that 1,074 people were killed and 2,068 were injured by the end of 2012 in J&K in mine-related incidents.[108] The Government of India stated in the Parliament in 2004 that during the period from 1 January 2002 to 30 November 2002, 48 civilians were killed and 236 were injured in landmine blasts in the three states bordering Pakistan, namely Rajasthan, Punjab, and J&K.[109] From 1 January 2000 to 30 April 2002, the government stated in the Parliament that 138 army personnel were also killed in mine- or IED-related accidental blasts.[110] While most of the mines were eventually removed, officials posted in these areas say that these areas are not fully demined.[111] Gen. Bhatia points out that the Indian Army loses 12–15 soldiers every year in divisions deployed in heavily mined areas.[112]

During a visit to the border in Kashmir's Uri, not far from the civilian habitats, I was strictly asked to stay behind soldiers carrying mine detectors so that I do not accidently step on a stray mine and injure myself. The possibility of drifted, and therefore unsecured, mines in the outskirts of the villages was not ruled out by the officers I spoke to. There is a lot of undergrowth in the areas close to the LoC and the IB in Jammu, and it

[107] Bukhari, 'Deathtraps along the Border'.

[108] Peerzada Ashiq, 'More IED Blasts in India than in Afghanistan, Syria: Report', *Hindustan Times*, 7 May 2015, available at http://www.hindustantimes.com/india/more-ied-blasts-in-india-than-in-afghanistan-syria-report/story-a6OHsxDdjrmvvgL1R0YJvN.html, last accessed on 10 June 2016.

[109] Press Information Bureau, 'Persons Killed by Landmine Blast', Ministry of Defence, Government of India, http://pib.nic.in/newsite/erelcontent.aspx?relid=6008, last accessed on 14 May 2017.

[110] Paty Ripple Kyndiah, 'Landmine Casualty', Lok Sabha, Unstarred Question 7533, Ministry of Defence, Government of India, 16 May 2002.

[111] Interview with BSF Officer 6, 4 June 2016, Jammu.

[112] Interview with Lt Gen. (Retd) Vinod Bhatia, 19 September 2016, New Delhi.

is possible that such areas would have drifted mines. This is because it is not an easy task to demine once an area is mined due to practical reasons and prohibitive costs.

Regarding the placement of mines on the Pakistani side, Gen. Waheed says: 'There are mines in front of your positions, in the gaps, in the depths. Everywhere ... as per your tactical plans.'[113]

India and Pakistan have conspicuously not signed the 1997 Ottawa Convention on the Prohibition of the Use, Stockpiling, Production and Transfer of Anti-Personnel Mines and on Their Destruction. India argues that 'it (the Convention) does not adequately address its security concerns. India is, however, party to the Inhumane Weapons Convention and is fully committed to its Amended Protocol II which deals with Anti-Personnel Landmines.'[114]

Cross-LOC Trade and Travel

In the aftermath of the earthquake in October 2005, India and Pakistan agreed to open several trade and travel crossing points on the LoC. Five cross-LoC trade and travel points were opened at:[115]

1. Rawalakot—Poonch (at Chakan Da Bagh)
2. Chakoti—Uri (at Kaman Post)
3. Nauseri—(Tangdhar) Tithwal
4. Tattapani—(Balnoie) Mendhar.
5. Hajipir—Uri (at Silikot)

Cross-LoC trade facilitation points have been set up at Salamabad and Chakan Da Bagh. Over the years, however, trading ties between the two sides have drastically come down due to the deteriorating bilateral relations and the increasing firing on the LoC and Jammu/Sialkot IB.

---

[113] Interview with Lt Gen. (Retd) Waheed Arshad, 15 April 2016, Bangkok.

[114] Simranjit Singh Mann, 'Ban on Landmines', Lok Sabha, Unstarred Question 2599, Ministry of External Affairs, Government of India, 20 March 2002, http://mea.gov.in/lok-sabha.htm?dtl/13427/Q+2599Ban+on+Landmines, last accessed on 4 June 2017.

[115] 'Joint Statement, India–Pakistan Discussions on Opening of Crossing Points across the LoC, October 29, 2005', Ministry of External Affairs, Government of India, http://bit.ly/2aVmVYN, last accessed on 4 June 2017.

The Flag System and Flag Meetings

The flag system given in Table 3.3, is of great importance in the day-to-day management of the border as it forms the most basic tool of communication between the two sides. And yet, it is clear from this table that there is no uniform system of flag use on the border.

Table 3.3 The flag system

Sr no	Flag colour	Used by	Purpose	Remarks
1.	White	Indian and Pakistan armies	Indicate Truce/ Peace—LoC and IB To signal that firing is being stopped To indicate to rebuild a fallen wall or to undertake repair works	
2.	Red	India/Pakistan	Raised when an issue is not sorted out, and firing continues. To undertake operational work during peacetime. To object to construction being carried out by the other side.	According to Gen. Waheed, when you raise a red flag, it means there is an issue or a concern.
3.	Green	India/Pakistan on LoC	To signal to the post on the other side to check the issue after firing has started on a different post other than the one to which flag is being shown.	The green flag protocol/ provision was agreed at the brigadier-level flag meeting held on 21 September 2015 at Chakan

Sr no	Flag colour	Used by	Purpose	Remarks
				Da Bagh— (*Source*: Indian Army Officer 3).
4.	Black and White chequered	India/Pakistan on the LoC	To warn about crossers.	The black and white chequered flag protocol/ provision was agreed at the brigadier-level flag meeting held on 21 September 2015 at Chakan Da Bagh.[116]
5.	Orange	India—BSF on the IB	Casual contact/ call for flag meeting.	
6.	Blue	Pakistan— Rangers on the WB	Casual contact/ call for flag meeting.	
7.	Whistle	India/Pakistan	Casual contact/ Call for a flag meeting.	When the flag cannot be seen.
8.	Red light	India	To raise objection.	Used at night when flag can not be seen.

Source: Author.

Flag Meetings

The most basic level of communication between the Indian and Pakistani sides on the LoC and IB/WB is the flag meeting between local commanders. In the Jammu IB sector, as is the case with the IB outside J&K, casual meetings take place anywhere on the border between local

---

[116] 'India, Pak Armies Decide to Defuse Tensions on LoC at Flag Meeting', *Tribune*, 21 September 2015, available at http://www.tribuneindia.com/news/jammu-kashmir/india-pak-armies-decide-to-defuse-tensions-on-loc-at-flag-meeting/135932.html, last accessed on 10 June 2016.

company commanders. In order to initiate a casual contact, the company commander on either side would walk up to the zero line, wave an orange flag in the Indian case, and a blue flag by the Pakistani side, which will be responded to by the counterpart company commander. However, if due to low visibility, the flag would not be visible, a whistle is used to alert the other side.

Rakesh Sharma explains how the local-level meeting is organized in the IB sector in Jammu:

> A flag is shown which prompts the other party to ask what we want. We ask them for casual contact with their company commander. The two company commanders get together where one tells the other that his company is getting close to the IB and some people appear to be engaging in suspicious movement and so that needs to be taken care of. The other also says that the road being built on the other side is coming within 150 metres of the IB and that needs to be taken care of. Both parties agree to the terms and sort it out.[117]

The aim of such meetings is local conflict resolution. As Gen. Hasnain points out: 'They are not part of the political dialogue but are just border conferences to temporarily dilute a military standoff in a situation where political parleys are not possible.'[118] While for local purposes, flag meetings can be very helpful, 'participants are not empowered to dilute the established positions'.[119] Sometimes the atmosphere of tension is so high that such meetings would have no effect on the ground. Hasnain points out that 'there have been times when firing has recommenced in the vicinity of a flag meeting, even as the local commanders returned to their respective sides after the meeting'.[120] Post-CFA, the decision to hold regular flag meetings between local commanders was taken in 2005 during the meeting of the second round of the 'Expert Level Talks between India and Pakistan and Conventional Confidence Building Measures'.

---

[117] Interview with Rakesh Sharma, 15 September 2016, New Delhi.

[118] Syed Ata Hasnain, 'Meeting Point', *Indian Express*, 9 January 2014, available at http://indianexpress.com/article/opinion/columns/meeting-point-4/, last accessed on 10 June 2016.

[119] Hasnain, 'Meeting Point'.

[120] Hasnain, 'Meeting Point'.

Then there are more structured flag meetings. While casual flag meetings can take place anywhere between local company commanders on the zero line, formal meetings are held with more preparation. 'Tent meetings', as they are called on the IB in Jammu, take place at the DIG level—whichever side calls the meeting pitches the tent on their side and invites the other side (who come with men and weapons) for the meeting with proper agenda and advance notice. There are however no joint SOPs on weapons that can be carried to such meetings by either side and how many men could be present in such meetings.[121]

While the LoC has a number of places where such meetings can take place, meetings in the Jammu IB/WB are held only at the Octroi post, a post on the India–Pakistan border in Jammu-Sialkot region. The Octroi post serves as the only formal communication point on the IB/WB in Jammu-Sialkot, which means that protest or other communication notes are handed over to either side only from here. Moreover, in the entire Jammu-Sialkot sector, this is the only place with a phone link between the two sides (also note there is no phone link between the Indian state of J&K and Pakistan). At their biannual meeting held in New Delhi from 12 to 15 September 2015, the BSF and Pakistan Rangers had decided to exchange phone numbers at multiple levels for better communication.[122] This decision has not yet been implemented.

Including the local-level casual contact that happens regularly, though informally, on the Jammu IB/WB, most meetings are not properly institutionalized. For instance, the talks at the director general (DG) level are supposed to be held biannually, and they should ideally happen every six months; however, they actually meet only once a year. The commandant/wing commander meetings are also supposed to take place once in six months; the company-commander-level meetings are supposed to take place once a month. However, none of these are really institutionalized.[123] With regard to the minutes of the

[121] Interview with BSF Officer 5, 3 June 2016, Jammu.

[122] Aman Sharma, 'BSF Dominates Talks with Pakistan Rangers, Has Its Way on Major Points', *Economic Times*, 14 September 2015, available at http://economictimes.indiatimes.com/news/defence/bsf-dominates-talks-with-pakistan-rangers-has-its-way-on-major-points/articleshow/48949576.cms, last accessed on 10 June 2016.

[123] Interview with BSF Officer 5, 3 June 2016, Jammu.

meetings, only at the DG-level meeting are the minutes signed by both sides: without written and signed minutes of the decisions taken at the lower levels, it is unlikely that verbal commitment would have any force on the ground.

There is no Simultaneous Coordinated Patrolling (SCP) in between the two sides in J&K unlike in Punjab and other places. In the 2015 September meeting of the Pakistan Rangers and BSF, 'both sides discussed ways to strengthen measures to coordinate border patrolling on the respective sides of the border and address each other's concerns in a time bound manner'.[124] However, there has not yet been any decision to introduce SCP in the Jammu sector.

Flag meetings also take place in the LoC sector in Kashmir. There are occasional casual contacts to resolve local issues. Then there are higher-level meetings between senior officials. The agenda of the higher-level flag meetings are pre-decided and the meetings are video-recorded.[125] On 21 September 2015, during a brigade-level flag meeting in the Rajouri sector, the two sides agreed on the use of green and chequered flags.[126] Sometimes, a whistle is used to indicate request for a flag meeting if visibility is low and the flag cannot be seen. In the LoC sector, a white flag is used to indicate peace or truce, red to raise an objection, green to signal to the post on the other side to check the issue after firing has started on a different post other than the one to which flag is being shown, and black and white chequered to warn the other side about crossers.[127]

The company commander is the lowest ranking officer who can attend a flag meeting.[128] 'Flag meetings are held with a great deal of cordiality and mutual respect. Both sides know each other so well and sometimes it becomes an exercise in hospitality, to see who is a better host', an army officer described the manner in which such meetings are held on

---

[124] 'BSF, Pak Rangers Reach Consensus during Meeting in Lahore: MEA', *Hindustan Times*, 28 July 2016, available at http://www.hindustantimes.com/india-news/bsf-pak-rangers-reach-consensus-during-meeting-in-lahore-mea/story-jceTV9lb66rIZlVSkDDvVN.html, last accessed on 10 June 2017.

[125] Interview with Indian Army Officer 3, 14 May 2016, Poonch (J&K).

[126] Interview with Indian Army Officer 3, 14 May 2016, Poonch (J&K).

[127] Interview with Army Officer 1, 13 May 2016, Rajouri.

[128] Interview with Army Officer 3, 14 May 2016, Kashmir.

the LoC.[129] While casual meetings are an effective way of dealing with minor issues, such meetings do not take place during tense periods.[130]

Flag meetings at the local levels have been a constant feature on the LoC, except, of course, when the border is highly tense. Gen. Ghazi recalls that pre-notifying the Indian side of any activity on his side was always done as a practice: 'We would just have a flag meeting or even raise our voice and tell the other side if there would be any civilian activity. So, for instance, we would shout across that there are these four civilians who are coming with their pitchers to get water and we are coming along with them and the other side would respond and tell us to get them in one by one.'[131]

Army officers on the Pakistani side say that if any side wishes to rebuild a fallen wall or to undertake repair works, it has to raise a white flag to notify the other side.[132] Two types of flags, that is, white flag and red flag, are raised to discuss issues when firing has already started. To signal that firing is being stopped, a white flag is raised. A red flag is raised when an issue is not sorted out and firing continues.[133] There are occasions when one side raises a white flag for a flag meeting but does not turn up for the meeting.[134] When tensions run high, requests for flag meetings are not responded to for an entire week.[135] There have been occasional reports of misbehaviour in the context of flag meetings (besides not turning up for such meetings occasionally). In January 2015, Pakistan's *Dawn* newspaper reported, quoting a spokesman for Punjab Rangers, that 'a commander of the Indian Border Security Force in Shakargarh sector sought a flag meeting at 11 am this morning, but when our men reached there, BSF

[129] Interview with Indian Army Officer 5, 14 May 2016, Kashmir.

[130] Interview with Ajay Shukla, 6 September 2016, New Delhi; and Interview with Lt Gen. (Retd) Amjad Shuaib, 18 December 2016, Rawalpindi.

[131] Interview with Gen. Ghazi, 7 November 2017, Bangkok.

[132] Bhukari, 'Deathtraps along the Border'.

[133] M. Faisal's conversations with Pakistan Army Officers 1 and 2, 7 and 9 June 2016 respectively, Islamabad.

[134] Rediff, 'Pak Shows White Flags But Doesn't Turn Up for Flag Meet', *Rediff*, 28 October 2013, available at http://www.rediff.com/news/report/pak-shows-white-flags-but-doesnt-turn-up-for-flag-meet/20131028.htm, last accessed on 10 June 2016.

[135] Interview with Indian Army Officer 2, 13 May 2016, Udhampur.

soldiers started shooting at them'.[136] Such developments indicate a disturbing breakdown in the existing communication links between the two sides.

There is clearly a need to have a lot more flag meetings and to respect the sanctity of such meetings. To give a comparative example, the number of flag meetings held on a highly contentious and live border such as the India–Pakistan one (see Table 3.4) is significantly lower than those held on the rather peaceful India–China border, where not a single shot has been fired since 1962 (see Table 3.5).

Table 3.4 Flag meetings held on the India–Pakistan LoC in J&K from 2010 to 2013

Year	Number of flag meetings
2010	17
2011	09
2012	07
2013	08

Source: Author.

Table 3.5 Flag meetings held on the India–China LAC from 2010 to 2013

Year	Number of flag meetings
2010	32
2011	43
2012	24
2013	34

Source: Press Information Bureau, 'Commanders Flag Meetings', Ministry of Defence, Government of India, 17 December 2013, available at http://pib.nic.in/newsite/PrintRelease.aspx?relid=101910, last accessed on 22 June 2017.

Protest Notes

'Protest notes' are a major form of communication between the two sides. Though protests can be lodged informally during the zero line in a casual

---

[136] 'India Kills 2 Troops Invited to Meeting', *Dawn*, 1 January 2015, available at https://www.dawn.com/news/1154352, last accessed on 10 June 2016.

meeting, formal protest notes are exchanged through the Octroi post in the Jammu sector. Sometimes, advance notifications are given by either side to reduce misunderstandings.[137] A protest note is given to object to an activity undertaken by the other side. It is usually addressed to the BSF commandant (equivalent to a wing commander or Lt Col on the Pakistani side). While the local company commander may write the protest note but it goes from the commandant of the battalion. The Indian protest note will carry the name of the Pakistani post and the BP number. The name of the Indian post is not mentioned. On an average, 10 to 15 protest notes are sent each month from one side to the other.[138]

The Hotline System

Hotline messages (HLMs) (see Figure 3.1) are widely used on the LoC to communicate with the other side. These messages may contain routine information, prior notifications of activities undertaken by either side, requests for clarifications on what is happening on the other side, responses to queries from the other side, and so on. For instance, HLMs are used to give advance notification regarding civilian activities such as blasts for earth-moving purposes so as to avoid misunderstandings.

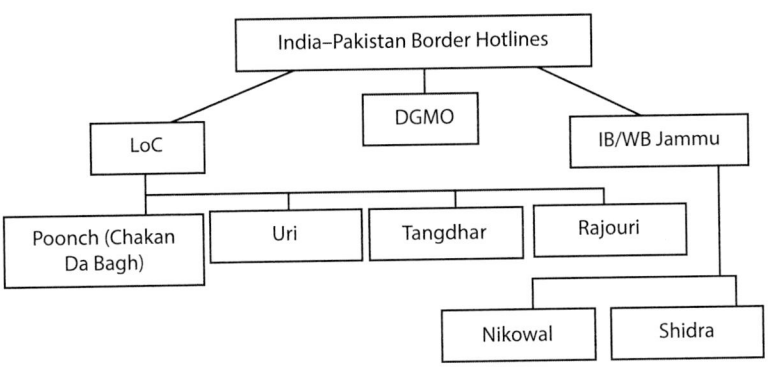

Figure 3.1   India–Pakistan hotline links in J&K
Source: Author.

[137] Interview with BSF Officer 1, 2 June 2016, Jammu.
[138] Interview with BSF Officer 4, 3 June 2016, Jammu.

These messages are also used for non-military communication such as to coordinate bus travel or trade-related issues.[139]

On an average, 50–60 HLMs are sent/received per month from each hotline point. HLM response from the other side comes within a day or two.[140] Every hotline sent across to the other side is vetted by the army hierarchy. As a result, every hotline message goes up to a division level.[141]

An officer on the Indian side in Kashmir pointed out that sometimes the Indian side receives two to three hotline messages every day. The Indian side responds to these messages at the corresponding level of hierarchy. There are four hotlines operating on the LoC: Tithwal (Tangdhar), Uri, Rajouri, and Poonch (Chakan Da Bagh).[142]

Pakistani officers noted that sometimes there is hardly any contact with the Indian side for days together, and on other occasions, there is hectic activity.[143] They also pointed out that response time varies drastically.[144] Indian officials complain that sometimes Pakistan does not accept protest notes at all.[145] Again, as is the case with flag meetings, it is important to preserve the sanctity of the most basic form of communication on the LoC/IB—exchange of protest notes.

The DGMO Hotline

The highest level military contact between India and Pakistan is the DGMO hotline. The DGMOs talk to each other on a dedicated phone line every

[139] Interview with Lt Gen. (Retd) Vinod Bhatia, 19 September 2016, New Delhi.

[140] Interview with Indian Army Officer 7, 16 May 2016, Tangdhar.

[141] Interview with Lt Gen. (Retd) Vinod Bhatia, 19 September 2016, New Delhi.

[142] Interview with Indian Army Officer 6, 15 May 2016, Kupwara.

[143] Interview with Pakistan Army Officers 2, 9 June 2016, Islamabad; Interview with Pakistan Army Officer 3, 12 June 2016, Islamabad.

[144] Interview with Pakistan Army Officers 2, 9 June 2016, Islamabad; Interview with Pakistan Army Officer 3, 12 June 2016, Islamabad.

[145] 'Pakistan Rangers Not Accepting Protest Notes over Ceasefire: BSF', *Indian Express*, 6 January 2015, available at http://indianexpress.com/article/india/india-others/pakistan-rangers-not-accepting-protest-notes-over-ceasefire-bsf/, last accessed on 10 September 2016.

Tuesday morning. Sometimes they may shift it to another day if one of the DGMOs is busy. At times, the additional DGMOs speak if the DGMOs are not available. After the phone conversation, the information is selectively disseminated to the military intelligence/ military operations (MI/MO) directorates on the Indian side, which then issues a daily directive/bulletin that is sent to the principal staff officers to keep them in the loop about what is happening on the border. This bulletin carries a small report with bullet points highlighting what information was exchanged and what was spoken.[146]

Gen. Arshad points out that what is spoken over the phone is based on a previously agreed upon agenda, and that the DGMO hotline is always recorded. Gen. Majid recalls: 'Normally, the contact is established by the respective staff officers and then the DGMOs take over to discuss substantive aspects. Although their conversation is mostly focused on military matters, especially the issues raised by either side, the exchange of pleasantries and light chat is also not uncommon.'[147]

Although the DGMO hotline conversation is scheduled for Tuesdays, they can initiate a conversation anytime through a procedure called 'special hotline conversation' if serious issues come up on other days.[148] Gen. Bhatia, who was the Indian DGMO from October 2012 to February 2014, confirms, underlining the importance that the two sides attach to the DMGO hotline, that even on other days DGMOs can place what is called a 'special hotline' if there is an urgent matter to be dealt with. Gen. Majid says that such special hotlines are often used in times of emergencies: 'For instance, once an Indian guy fell into the river and got washed away to the Pakistani side. A message came from the Indian side that the DGMO would like to speak—in a very short time the two sides were engaged—it was not a Tuesday.'

DGMO talks are normally very useful in resolving issues even if held during times of tension. Gen. Majid points out, 'Even in times of tensions, initial pleasantries are exchanged to start with. Then you get straight on to the issue—this is what we are seeing and how do you explain it, there is no justification. There needs to be a check on this—we think it is deliberate and should not lead to escalation. Or, sometimes, help is sought from each

---

[146] Interview with Lt Gen. (Retd) Ata Hasnain, 5 June 2016, New Delhi.
[147] Interview with Gen. Majid, 14 April 2016, Bangkok.
[148] Interview with Lt Gen. (Retd) Waheed Arshad, 15 April 2016, Bangkok.

other because someone has crossed over or fallen from a post on to the other side. Once we used the helicopter to help. For instance, help was also sought during earthquakes.'

Gen. Bhatia recalls one of his non-Tuesday conversations with his counterpart Gen. Riaz to underline how the two sides treat the communication link with a great deal of importance: 'This was on 29 November 2013, and something happened and I wanted to speak to the DGMO. So, I told the staff, "Please tell the DGMO that I want to speak to him." So, after about an hour, he came on the line and said, "I hope all okay," and I said, "Not really, that's why I called you." He said, "Sir, sorry, I took time because the handing over charge of the chief was going on." Kayani was handing over to Raheel Sharif. So he left that and came. So that is the importance of it. This happened at 6 o'clock in the evening.'[149]

The Tuesday DGMO conversation, the timing of which is decided by the Military Operations staff on both sides in advance, continues to be the most useful and important contact between the two militaries.

While the DGMOs discuss LoC-related issues, the IB-related issues are discussed by BSF and Rangers through the phone link in Jammu. However, when DGMOs talk on Tuesdays, sometimes issues from the IB/WB also come up for discussion. The BSF informs the discussion points to its IG Operations who forwards it to the DGMO's office.[150]

Only the sector HQ Jammu contacts Pakistan Rangers by phone. The reason for just one phone link on the Indian side of the IB is that the Pakistani side has only one sector for IB (Sialkot). Jammu DIG HQ has a phone connection that is used two or three times a month on an average but the communications are not recorded. And as pointed out earlier, only the meetings between the DGs BSF and Rangers are recorded.[151]

The DGMO Meeting of December 2013

While there is a bilateral provision for the two DGMOs to meet, they rarely do. Gen. Bhatia, who was the Indian DGMO from October

[149] Interview with Lt Gen. (Retd) Vinod Bhatia, 19 September 2016, New Delhi.

[150] Interview with Rakesh Sharma, 15 September 2016, New Delhi.

[151] Interview with Rakesh Sharma, 15 September 2016, New Delhi.

2012 to February 2014, had represented the Indian side for a DGMO-level meeting with his Pakistani counterpart Maj Gen. Aamer Riaz that took place after a gap of 14 years during the height of the CFVs in December 2013. This was the first meeting of the two DGMOs that took place after the Kargil War. Significantly, there has not been another meeting between the two DGMOs after the meeting in December 2013.

In a conversation between the general and the author as given below, Gen. Bhatia describes how the meeting took place after a gap of more than a dozen years:

Gen. Vinod Bhatia (VB): I think it was 28 September, when the two prime ministers met on the sidelines of the UN General Assembly, they decided then that DGMOs should meet to talk about the CFVs because CFVs were occuring unabated. The CFVs are not good for either side, more so for the Pakistani side. So, this we heard from the media that the DGMOs were going to meet. Nothing happened. And one fine day in December, Gen. Riaz called up and said, 'Sir, I would like to invite you to Pakistan for the DGMO talks on the CFVs.'

Happymon Jacob (HJ): This was to Wagah?

VB: Yes. I said fine. Give me a date and I will be there.

HJ: So, didn't you check with the government first?

VB: No, I did not. But you can't tell their DGMO that I will check back and come. It's a question of moral ascendency, you see! In any case, this was in the pipeline. I said, let me know the date and time. So, he asked, 'Would the 24th, Tuesday be okay, would that be fine?' I said, 'Fine.' And so I went there. I took some of my staff along and we also took some staff from the 15 Corps along. He walked me through the gate at Wagah. It was very cordial. Initially, we just talked.

HJ: So, you first had a one-on-one with Gen. Riaz?

VB: Yes, we talked between ourselves till the staff settled down and all that.... Then we walked off and let the staff do the detail work. Then we sat down with tea and had a very interesting conversation. He said his parents had gone to Pakistan from a village near Kapurthala. Then I said, 'My parents are from Multan.' So, he said, 'Arre sir *pehle batana tha na* (you should have told me), I would have got some Multani Sohanhalwa for you.' So, I said, 'My mother would have liked that very much.' So, I just told him that. That finished there.

HJ: So, what was the result of the meeting?

VB: The charter was to sustain the ceasefire and we both agreed to do that.

Cross-LoC Dynamics

The following figures (Figures 3.2, 3.3, and 3.4) explain the cross-LoC dynamics in detail by way of illustrating the various India–Pakistan Hotlines as operational in J&K, the locations of flag meetings between the two forces, and the LOC crossing and trading points.

Villages Ahead of the Fence

In many places along the LoC and IB, several Indian villages are located ahead of the border fence. Pakistan does not have a border fence and so technically there are no villages ahead of the fence, even though there are villages close to the zero line. Some of them are traditional settlements

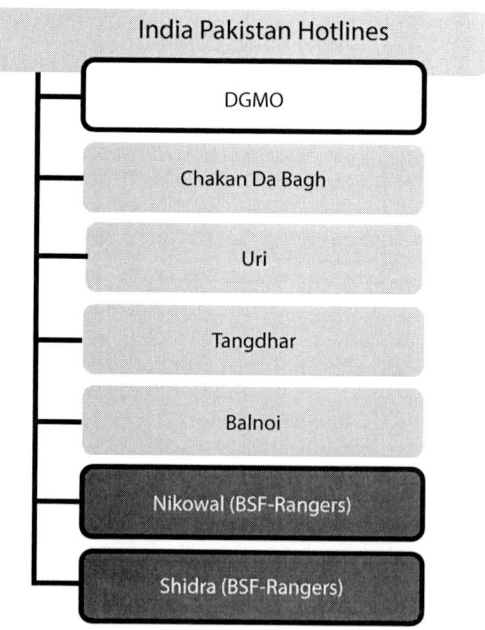

Figure 3.2   India–Pakistan hotlines in J&K

Source: Author.

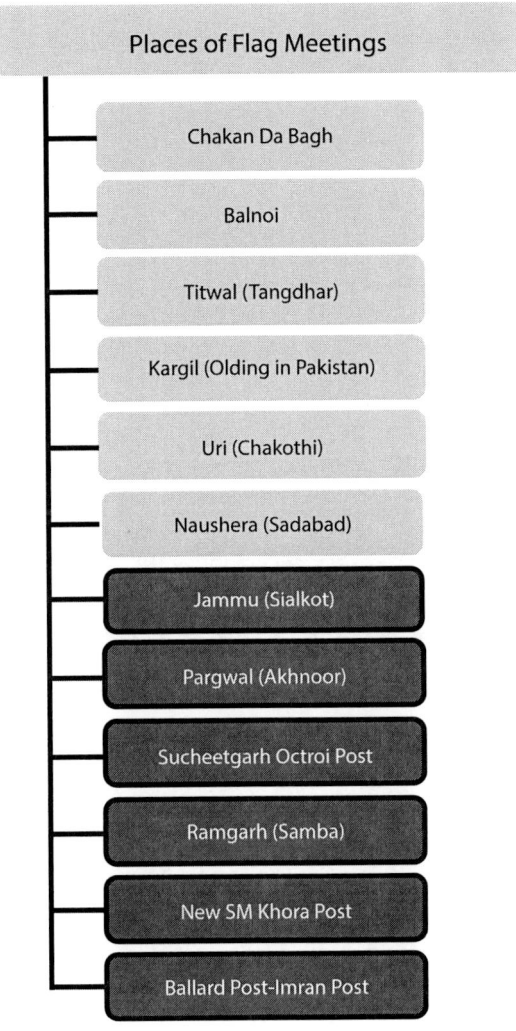

Figure 3.3 Places of flag meetings
Source: Author.

where villagers continue to live in their ancestral homes, and in some cases, farmers from nearby villages cultivate the land that lies ahead of the fence close to the zero line. In the Jammu division alone (including Kathua, Samba, Jammu, Rajouri, and Poonch), there are around 590

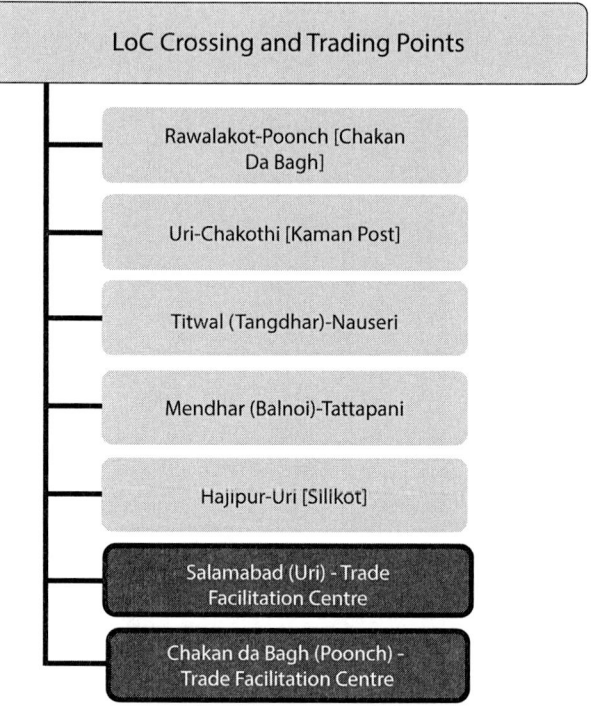

Figure 3.4 LOC crossing and trading points
Source: Author.

villages between 0 and 5 km from the IB/LoC, of which 448 villages are vulnerable due to CFVs, according to the Indian MHA.[152]

Major violations result in the mass displacement of people from their habitats. In 2014 alone, 73,368 persons from Jammu, Kathua, and Samba were displaced, due to CFVs.[153] While it is common for villagers to live

[152] Press Information Bureau, 'Ceasefire Violations', Ministry of Home Affairs, Government of India, 11 December 2015, available at http://pib.nic.in/newsite/PrintRelease.aspx?relid=133036, last accessed on 22 July 2016.

[153] Press Information Bureau, 'Exodus of People from J&K after Ceasefire Violation by Pakistan', Ministry of Home Affairs, Government of India, 3 December 2014, available at http://pib.nic.in/newsite/PrintRelease.aspx?relid=112489, last accessed on 22 July 2016.

in their homes ahead of the fence along the LoC in the Kashmir sector, this is not the case in Jammu. In the Jammu sector, people live in homes behind the fence and go across to their farms located ahead of the fence only for farming activities.

Those travelling beyond the fence to engage in farming activities are regulated by a proper identification system. People living on the Indian side but ahead of the fence and close to the LoC are provided with biometric IDs, which are verified by the army personnel stationed at the gates of the fence.[154]

In the Tithwal area of Kashmir alone, there are 13 villages with an approximate population of 5,000 located ahead of the fence. Although Indian officials insist that they do not allow the Indian and Pakistani villagers to interact with each other, villagers living close to the line, especially those who have kinship ties, often interact undetected by the two forces. The Pakistani village, for instance, is as close as 500 metres from the Indian village located ahead of the fence in Rajouri, with divided families living on both sides. Such interactions were far more frequent before the 1980s, but they have certainly not disappeared. Some estimate that in the Bimbergali area, 40 per cent of those living ahead of the fence close to the zero line have relatives living on the other side. It is only reasonable then to assume that those families try and meet each other without being caught by the forces on either side.

This can lead to CFVs. As Brig. Salik puts it: 'On the Pakistani side, the civilian population is right on the zero line and sometimes even ahead of the forward post. Sometimes people cross inadvertently—they might go after cattle that runs across. People would go across to attend marriages and come back. People familiar with the territory can easily bypass despite the difficult terrain.'[155] In one such major incident in 2012, a Kashmiri grandmother who ran away to the Pakistani side from India's Charonda village triggered an action-reaction sequence of CFVs by the Pakistani and Indian soldiers.[156]

[154] Interview with Indian Army Officer 7, 16 May 2016, Tangdhar.

[155] Interview with Brig. Naeem Ahmad Salik, Pakistan Army, 13 April 2016, Bangkok.

[156] Praveen Swami, 'Runaway Grandmother Sparked Savage Skirmish on LoC', *Hindu*, 10 January 2013, available at http://www.thehindu.com/news/national/runaway-grandmother-sparked-savage-skirmish-on-loc/article4291426.ece, last accessed on 10 June 2016.

Over the years, the presence of the Indian and Pakistani troops has increased on the LoC. Prior to such massive troop presence as pointed out earlier, villagers also used to engage in raiding across the LoC. UNMOGIP routinely stepped in to deal with many such instances of robbery, smuggling, cattle thieving, and encroachments to cut grass in the 1950s and 1960s. Both India and Pakistan actively sought UNMOGIP help in resolving such cases during those years.[157]

Return of Crossers

Standard operating procedure on the Indian side in case of those who cross either the LoC or the IB inadvertently is to send the crosser to J&K police custody for interrogation and then return them if they are found innocent by the police and other agencies.[158] Gen. Majid says, 'Normally, you inform the other side as you get to know. And there is no institutionalized arrangement. Inevitably, it takes time. The agreement on inadvertent crossings has been on the table; we are stuck because the political climate changed.'[159]

However, there are times when the forces on the ground take a more compassionate position. An army officer in Kashmir narrated, 'Once an 11-year-old Pakistani child was sent back in 3 days from the Tithwal crossing point/bridge. The Pakistani side however takes a long time to return Indians who stray across to the other side. In case of adult crossings, the intelligence agencies and police get involved.'[160]

When someone crosses into the Indian territory, the person will go through certain procedures before the authorities determine how he/she needs to be dealt with. Officials say:

> Through body language and other mannerisms, we come to know whether the person is up to some mischief or not. We blow whistle as a warning. If the person is not carrying any weapon or does not have any ulterior motive, he surrenders. We then take him to the joint interrogation centre where officials of other intelligence agencies also join us. We cannot take him to our border outpost, since there

---

[157] Dawson, *The United Nations Military Observer Group in India and Pakistan*, 96.

[158] Interview with Indian Army Officer 3, 14 May 2016, Bhimber Gali.

[159] Interview with Gen. Majid, 14 April 2016, Bangkok.

[160] Interview with Indian Army Officer 7, 16 May 2016, Tangdhar.

is a chance that he could have been sent by the enemy to spy on our infrastructure. After all the agencies are convinced that the person is innocent, we inform our counterparts and return him or her within 24 hours. If any one of the sister agencies raises a doubt, the person is handed over to the local police.[161]

Sometimes even soldiers who inadvertently cross into the other side are returned. Indian Army soldier Chandu Babulal Chavan, who had inadvertently crossed into Pakistan in September 2016, was returned to India by Pakistan in January 2017.

The issue of speedy return of inadvertent crossers has been periodically taken up at bilateral meetings between the two countries. Such an agreement was reached during the Second and Third Rounds of the Expert-Level Dialogue on Conventional CBMs in 2005 and 2006 respectively. During the DGMOs meeting at Wagah on 24 December 2013, it was 'decided to inform each other if any innocent civilian inadvertently crosses Line of Control, in order to ensure his/her early return'.[162] However, a formal set of SOPs is yet to be put in place to deal with crossers.

***

This chapter, along with the previous chapter, was intended to set the stage for the forthcoming discussion on why CFVs occur on the India–Pakistan border in J&K. To put the CFVs in perspective, a historical understanding was deemed necessary.

In concluding this chapter, let me recapture the key points made here. First, even though the UNMOGIP is an 'institution non grata' for New Delhi today, there was a time especially in the 1950s and 1960s when both India and Pakistan actively sought the mediation, assistance, and good offices of the UN group to settle their differences on the LoC and IB in J&K, to manage the border, as well as to further clarify and

[161] Vijaita Singh, 'Sunday Anchor: Home Is Where the Border is', *Hindu*, 6 September 2015, available at http://www.thehindu.com/sunday-anchor/home-is-where-the-border-is/article7620260.ece, last accessed on 5 April 2017.

[162] Inter-Services Public Relations, Press Release 'No PR-211/2013-ISPR', 24 December 2013, available at https://www.ispr.gov.pk/front/t-press_release.asp?date=2013/12/24&print=1, last accessed on 10 March 2017.

settle the borders in the state. The early role played by the group and the contribution it made in terms of establishing important SOPs did play a role in the management of the border in the later years. Even though the group is unable to carry out its duties today, many of the practices established by the group and the clarifications made by the group are still in force in the border management systems on the LoC, surely for want of new practices and SOPs.

Second, what comes out clearly from the preceding discussion is the acute absence of clear, unambiguous, and mutually agreed upon agreements or SOPs to manage the border. There have been a few such rules/mechanisms put in place at various points of time. But for the most part, those managing the border are is groping in the dark, which makes the management of a disputed border even more dangerous. Even though the IB outside J&K is undisputed, there are still no ground rules that the two sides have agreed to for it's management. The lack of SOPs is something the next chapter will discuss further as a cause of CFVs.

Third, this chapter has also highlighted that the boundary-making process outside of J&K was not a one-time affair: it took close to one and a half decades for the entire boundary to be interpreted, mutually agreed upon, and finally fixed, based on the broad directives given by the Radcliffe commission.

Four, it is important to recall today that while the boundary was still being fixed, both sides showed a great amount of willingness to be flexible, to negotiate, and sometimes even to give up land that they were holding based on the original Radcliffe Award. It is instructive that despite the initial communal carnage that resulted from the Partition, especially in Punjab, and the bitterness of the first India–Pakistan war over J&K, the political and military leaderships of the two counties were willing to go through this process of negotiations and talks and make concessions.

The inability of the two sides to finalize the ground rules needs to be underscored. While it is clearly the unwillingness of the Indian side to include the military-related issues (read: fortifications close to the zero line, within 150 yards) in the agreement that has prevented the agreement from getting finalized, the Indian concern about the IB comes from the experience of the 1965 war wherein it was caught off guard. While India and Pakistan continued to abide by the GRsA after the 1965 war, which had no winners, the Indian victory in 1971 and its experience of fighting the 1971 war itself convinced India that it would be better for it to avoid having anything in writing that would potentially hinder its defence preparedness on the border with Pakistan. Pakistan's active sponsorship of the Punjab militancy and then the Kashmir insurgency further cemented this Indian belief.

4 Lull before the Storm

The 2003 Ceasefire Agreement and After

One day I was in the bunker and the sahayak came to me and said, 'Subedar sahib bol rahen hain ki Lieutenant sahib ko bolo ki apna radio uncha karenge.' I said, 'Humare subedar sahib toh yahan hai hi nahi'. And he says, 'Humare subedar sahib nahi, Pakistan ke subedar saheb'. He was saying that 'Lieutenant sahib ko bol do ke radio uncha karen, humein All India Radio ka Urdu programme sunana hai. Hamara apna radio kharab hai.'

(One day I was in the bunker and the sahayak came to me and said, 'Sir, the subedar is asking me to tell the lieutenant to turn up the volume of the radio.' I said, 'But our subedar is not here.' And he says, 'Not our subedar, but Pakistan's subedar'. He was saying that 'Tell the Lieutenant sahib to turn up the volume of the radio so that we can listen to the Urdu programme of the All India Radio. Our radio is not working'.)

—Lt Gen. (Retd) T.K. Sapru[1]

THIS CHAPTER WILL OFFER a historical and statistical analysis of CFVs in J&K to put them in proper perspective before attempting to, in the next chapter, explain why they occur. The chapter is divided into two broad sections. The first section will focus on the occurrence of CFVs prior to 2003 when the current CFA was signed and explain the immediate background to the CFA of 2003. The second section will analyse the various data sets on CFVs, including the one this book has put together, and draw conclusions regarding the locations, causes, and various other factors relating to CFVs. This section will also discuss how

---

[1] Interview with Lt Gen. (Retd) T.K. Sapru, 10 October 2016, Chandigarh.

CFVs are counted, how they spread horizontally and vertically, and the existing explanations for the occurrence of CFVs.

This chapter serves as a precursor to the following chapter, which problematizes and challenges the existing explanations for CFVs and offers several alternative explanations.

Cross-Border Firing Prior to 2003

The CFA of 2003 was the fourth ceasefire that India and Pakistan agreed to since 1947: the first was at the end of the 1947 Kashmir war; the second one ended the 1965 war; the third one in December 1971; and, finally, the 2003 CFA. The first three were war termination ceasefires, but the 2003 CFA was to end a particularly tense period in India–Pakistan relations that witnessed several thousands of CFVs on an annual basis on the LoC and IB/WB in the Jammu/Sialkot sector of J&K. The 2003 CFA is the only one that was agreed to without any direct external pressure or mediation. While the first three CFAs had detailed war termination agreements that accompanied them, the 2003 CFA was simply a telephone conversation between the two DGMOs in November that year.

All four CFAs, including the 2003 one, witnessed a relatively calm period of no violations for a few years after they were signed, before they started breaking up, leading to cross-border firing. In a sense, this is to be expected given the fact that except the Karachi Agreement of 1949, none of the other CFAs were properly written down to explain what the CFA entails. But before we come to the latest CFA of 2003, let us briefly examine the cross-border firing that used to take place prior to the 2003 agreement, since 1947.

Phase One: 1949–65

The first phase from 1949 (Karachi Agreement) to the end of the 1965 war was relatively calm between the two forces, thanks primarily to the presence of the UNMOGIP in Kashmir, located in the brigade HQs on both sides, and the high degree of willingness to communicate with each other and resolve issues. Their presence acted as a major deterrent on both sides as neither of the newly independent countries wanted to be seen as initiating a military standoff on the LoC in clear violation of the UN strictures, which during those years was a very powerful international body. There were, however, several major and minor incidents that took place on the border, many of which were a result of the activities of the civilians living in those areas, some of whose villages, families, and livelihoods were cut off due to the de facto division of the princely state. Moreover, it is important to remember that during those years there was neither a fence on the border as there is now, nor were there tens of thousands of troops guarding the CFL—(as it was called before the Simla Agreement) in J&K as is the case today. The line dividing the two sides of the princely state was not very clear to the troops guarding the border and even lesser to the local population. Sometimes, even when the local population was aware of the boundary, they chose to ignore it.

As a result, there were several instances of civilians and troops crossing the line both advertently and inadvertently. Pakistan, in fact, encouraged the crossing of civilians, implicitly making the argument that the CFL was 'merely for the two armies, but that civilians, as Kashmiris, could go anywhere in Kashmir'.[2] The Pakistani side also, as they continue to do even today, encouraged Pakistani civilians to cultivate their land up to the zero line. Whereas the Indian forces not only prohibited cultivation near the zero line but also took stern action against those crossing the line to the Pakistani side. In fact, the UNMOGIP often brought it to the attention of the Pakistani authorities to exercise strict control over the civilians on their side, stating that it provokes the Indian troops.[3] Such incidents were not limited to J&K alone—the Punjab border reported quite a few of them. Indeed, Punjab reported several firing incidents involving civilians as well as troops.

Not only were the civilians crossing the line in J&K, even soldiers of the two armies used to cross the line inadvertently. So much so that the two countries even had an agreement to exchange those armed personnel who crossed the CFL, and the adjoining border between Jammu and West Pakistan inadvertently. Ironically, even today, there are such incidents being reported from the LoC in J&K.[4]

[2] Pauline Dawson, *The United Nations Military Observer Group in India and Pakistan (UNMOGIP) 1948–1965* (Bombay: Popular Prakashan, 1995), 98.

[3] Dawson, *The United Nations Military Observer Group in India and Pakistan*, 98.

[4] Rahul Singh, 'Soldier Inadvertently Crossed LoC, Pak Has Been Informed: Indian Army Source', *Hindustan Times*, 30 September 2016, available at http://www.hindustantimes.com/india-news/soldier-inadvertently-crosses-loc-pak-has-been-informed-indian-army-source/story-XlTFmHzcPSRbTa1UytmNtN.html, last accessed on 1 December 2016.

The two sides often accused each other of crossing the line and firing at each other, but the presence and intervention of the UNMOGIP was a major stabilizing factor, especially in controlling the behaviour of the troops on both sides. There were worries among the troops and the army leadership on both sides about the UNMOGIP investigating alleged violations and then awarding it against their side, which made them careful about not being the guilty party. There were also many trumped-up allegations of CFVs, which when investigated by the UNMOGIP turned out to be attempts to hassle the opponent.

At the same time, many allegations turned out to be accurate as well. In May 1960, for instance, Pakistan accused India of violating the CFL in Sudpura in the Tangdhar–Domel sector of Kashmir, which was eventually awarded against India by UNMOGIP which determined that Indian personnel had indeed fired across the line.[5] On 21 August 1964, in his letter to the president of the Security Council on Kashmir, India's permanent representative to the United Nations B.N. Chakravarty gave an exhaustive list of Pakistani violations of the CFL and the many instances where UNMOGIP determined that Pakistani complaints against India were not to be awarded. Clearly, he did not mention any of those instances where the UNMOGIP awarded violations against India.[6]

By and large, the period from 1949 to 1960 was calm, compared to the years that followed. As Tremblay and Schofield point out, CFVs started spiking after Ayub Khan came to power in Pakistan through a military coup as he was 'determined to stop and reverse Indian attempts to incorporate Kashmir into India.'[7]

This deterioration of bilateral relations was reflected in the reports of the UNMOGIP. In a clear departure from the previous years, Dawson writes, 'There was a surge in the number of incidents which neither party seemed disposed to take any specific action to prevent, in spite of a promise

---

[5] Dawson, *The United Nations Military Observer Group in India and Pakistan*, 169.

[6] 'Shri B. N. Chakravarty's Letter to the President of Security Council on Kashmir', Ministry of External Affairs, Government of India, available at http://mealib.nic.in/?pdf2552?000, last accessed on 22 June 2017.

[7] Reeta Tremblay and Julian Schofield, 'Renewing UNMOGIP: The Passing Problem of Kashmir', *Peacekeeping & International Relations* 27, no. 6 (Nov/Dec 1998): 14.

of cooperation with UNMOGIP, and suggestions by Gen. Nimmo such as the replacement of the units concerned.'[8]

Chakravarty's letter gives an exhaustive account of Pakistan's violations in 1964 that were awarded against Pakistan by the UN Group. He writes:[9]

> The following awards given in March and June, 1964 only by the Chief Military Observer against Pakistan speak for themselves
>
> - Jammu case 312, 17 March, 1964 'Border Violations by Pakistan. An organized armed party crossed the border and fired on Indian police and troops.'
> - Galuthi Case 745, 7 June, 1964 'Violation by Pakistan. These posts were constructed by Pakistan troops who later filled them in and camouflaged them in order to deceive UN Observers. They have since been re-opened and used by Pakistan troops.'
> - Punch Case 271, 21 June, 1964 'Violation by Pakistan for armed forces crossing the cease fire line and raiding an Indian post, killing two Indians and taking away one of the bodies.'
> - Galuthi Case 746, 21 June, 1964 'A well planned attack by organized armed party resulting in 2 policemen being seriously wounded, Violation by Pakistan.'
> - Naushera Case 160, 21 June, 1964 'An armed group of Pakistan troops crossed CFL and fired on Indian positions. Violation by Pakistan.'
> - URI Case 82, 21 June, 1964 'Investigation of this case and physical evidence found at the scene of the incident clearly indicated an organized raid by armed personnel from the Pakistan side of the CFL. Violations by Pakistan.'
> - Tangdhar Case 107, 27 June, 1964 'Planning and execution indicate regular troops responsible. Killing range 60 yards of 7 policemen at waterhole, 3 killed and 3 seriously wounded. Scene of ambush 1,000 yards on Indian side of CFL and on reverse side of high ridge. Action unprovoked as no previous incident in this vicinity. Violations by Pakistan.

[8] Dawson, *The United Nations Military Observer Group in India and Pakistan*, 178.

[9] 'Shri B. N. Chakravarty's Letter to the President of Security Council on Kashmir', Ministry of External Affairs, Government of India, available at http://mealib.nic.in/?pdf2552?000, last accessed on 22 June 2017.

The above-mentioned cases are brought up here not to argue that only Pakistan violated the CFL but to give a flavour of the kind of violations that were taking place in the 1960s, especially closer to the 1965 war. India's defence minister Y.B. Chavan pointed out this marked increase in violation in a statement in the Parliament on 16 August 1965: 'In the seven months period from January to July (1965), the number of incidents on the ceasefire line was over 1,800 compared to 1522 in the whole year 1964 and 448 in the year 1963.'[10]

The 1965 war, which did not throw up a clear victor, ended with the Tashkent Agreement mediated by the Soviet Union. The CFA of 22 September, and the Tashkent Declaration of 10 January 1966, which envisaged 'all armed personnel of the two countries shall be withdrawn not later than 25 February 1966 to the positions they held prior to 5 August 1965, and both sides shall observe the ceasefire terms on the Ceasefire Line', however, could not ensure that the CFL remained calm thereafter even though the CFVs came down significantly till the two sides fought the next war in another six years, in 1971.

1965–71: Inter-war Years

Between the two wars, there still were complaints of transgressions and violence on the border. In October 1966, Maharaja Krishna Rasgotra, officer on special duty (Kashmir) in the MEA, wrote to the heads of mission in New Delhi complaining that 'in recent months Pakistan has been sending small parties of infiltrators into Kashmir in breach of the ceasefire agreement and Tashkent Declaration'.[11]

Despite the occasional complaints, there seemed to be a genuine effort to ensure that such infractions of the CFA do not happen. In a meeting held in New Delhi on 13–14 September 1966, the two army chiefs agreed to exchange advance information on military exercises to be held along the CFL. They also agreed that 'in order to prevent avoidable incidents along

[10] 'Defence Minister, Shri Y.B. Chavan's Statement in Parliament on August 16, 1965', Ministry of External Affairs, Government of India, available at http://mealib.nic.in/?pdf2553?000, last accessed on 25 June 2017.

[11] 'Letter from the Officer on Special Duty (Kashmir) in the Ministry of External Affairs M. Rasgotra to the Heads of Mission. New Delhi, October 6, 1966', in Bhasin, *India Pakistan Relations 1947-2011: A Documentary Study* (New Delhi: Geetika Publications, 2012), 1191.

the Cease-Fire Line/the working boundary as agreed to by the military commanders, local commanders should resort to the agreed methods of solving disputes/disagreements by holding joint meeting at various levels through the good offices of the UN Observers'.[12]

Lt Gen. T.K. Sapru, the former GOC of India's Western Command, recalled in an interview recently: 'I can tell you of 1969, 1970 ... 1971, there was never any cross-LOC firing'. Even in 1971, well before the start of the war at the end of the year, things were cordial between the two sides. Lt Gen. Sapru recalls an interesting incident to drive home his point:

> One day I was in the bunker and the sahayak came to me and said, *'Subedar sahib bol rahen hain ki Lieutenant sahib ko bolo ki apna radio uncha karenge'.* I said, *'Humare subedar sahib toh yahan hai hi nahi'.* And he says, *'Humare subedar sahib nahi, Pakistan ke subedar sahib'.* He was saying, *'Lieutenant sahib ko bol do ke radio uncha karen, humein All India Radio ka Urdu programme sunana hai. Hamara apna radio kharab hai'.* So those were also the times ... although we were going to fight a war with them in the next six/seven months from then—this I am talking of April/ May of 1971. Sometimes, it could happen that people saw each other, waved at each other also; rarely, in those days, we exchanged fire.[13]

The Shock and After: Post-1971

The 1971 war, though fought primarily on the eastern front, also saw action on the western front, including in J&K and as we discussed in Chapter 2, the territories that were captured by either side during the war were not returned. As a result, the CFL ceased to exist and the new nomenclature given to the dividing line in J&K in place of CFL was LoC. The 1971 defeat was a huge blow to Pakistan—militarily, psychologically, and with long-lasting implications for domestic politics. Within Pakistan, it set off a series of events culminating in the hanging of Zulfikar Ali Bhutto in 1979 by Pakistan's military regime. The confidence that Pakistan derived

---

[12] 'Record of Discussions Held Between the Indian Chief of the Army Staff and Commander in Chief of Pakistan Army Amplifying Decisions Contained in Paras 2 and 3 of the Record of the Meeting Held at New Delhi on September 13–14, 1966. Rawalpindi, October 25, 1967', in Bhasin, *India Pakistan Relations 1947–2011*, 1245.

[13] Interview with Lt Gen. (Retd) T.K. Sapru, 10 October 2016, Chandigarh.

from its alliance with the Unites States and China in the 1960s did not seem to have paid off in 1971. It took another decade for Pakistan to re-emerge as the lynchpin of regional geopolitics—when the Soviet Union invaded Afghanistan and its Cold War rival, the United States, decided to fight the red army in Afghanistan by using Pakistan as a willing partner and proxy. As a result, the Kashmir borders were relatively quiet during the 1970s, if not entirely.

Lt Gen. Sapru argues that even though there was occasional firing across the line, they were never intended to kill anyone unless there was an intentional crossing of the LoC: 'In 1971, I was at a post called Sarla ... we used to play basketball in the evening and the Pakistani post opposite would wave and watch us, even used to start clapping sometimes ... they didn't have a basketball court. They would be there on the line but we never fired at each other.'[14]

Lt Gen. J.P. Nehra, former deputy army chief of India, used to be posted on the LoC in the mid-1970s, which he recalls as being peaceful with hardly any trespassing by either side except cattle straying across since Pakistani civilians used to cultivate till the zero line. When cattle strayed across or were intentionally brought to the Indian side to graze, he says, Indian soldiers would fire in the vicinity just to scare them away and to act as deterrent. This fire was sometimes returned by Pakistani soldiers posted on the other side of the line, again not intended to hit anyone.[15]

It is however not the argument here that there were no violations at all in the early 1970s; there were several of them, but they were fewer in number than in the late 1970s. On 12 May 1972, for instance, the Indian minister of defence, Jagjivan Ram informed the Parliament that in May of that year alone Pakistan had committed 49 CFVs.[16]

However, this began to change in the late 1970s given the new-found confidence Pakistan started deriving from the Afghan war and its close relationship with the Western block and the incoming money and weapons. Lt Gen. Harcharanjit Singh Panag, the former GOC of the

---

[14] Interview with Lt Gen. (Retd) T.K. Sapru, 10 October 2016, Chandigarh.
[15] Interview with Lt Gen. (Retd) J.P. Nehra, 3 December 2016, New Delhi.
[16] 'Statement in the Lok Sabha on 12 May 1972 by the Minister of Defence, Shri Jagjivan Ram', Ministry of External Affairs, Government of India, available at http://mealib.nic.in/?pdf2560?000, last accessed on 25 June 2017.

Northern and Central Commands of the Indian Army, attributes this to
Pakistan regaining its confidence from the shock of 1971:

> Pakistan initially was reeling under the impact of having lost half its
> country. They were totally taken aback … the insult and shock. But as
> the shock wore off by the late 1970s, as they recovered and recouped,
> the LoC started warming up; there were more firings and deliberate
> attempts were made to engage the enemy posts by both sides and
> even small bunkers became bones of contention—you made it so we
> must remove it … harping back to the 1949 agreement. Then both
> sides moved their heavier direct firing weapons onto the LoC to cause
> more damage to each other. I think it was more because Pakistan, after
> recovering from the 1971 debacle, was now flexing its muscle. This
> situation lasted nearly about a decade plus up to 1990.[17]

As a result of this new aggression, Lt Gen. Panag points out, both
sides started making new fortifications along the line to defend against
aggression and to close the many gaps between posts of which there
used to be many: 'LoC warfare intensified with Pakistan becoming more
belligerent and the danger of posts and areas getting occupied increased
… also there was a requirement of occupying more and more area; so the
density of troops also increased … by both sides.'[18]

The Indian non-recognition of the UNMOGIP also contributed to
the occurrence of CFVs as there was no neutral party to either award
violations, which in the past acted as a deterrent, and to ensure that the
two sides had a neutral arbiter to turn to in case of severe disagreements.
With the UNMOGIP now reduced to a mere spectator, several AMFs on
the ground started influencing the situation on the borders in J&K.

Pakistan continued to lodge complains with the UNMOGIP, as
they still do, and which India has refrained from doing since 1972. In
1981 itself, Pakistan lodged 152 CFV complaints with the group, which
included complaints about firing, defence construction, and overhead
flights. The Indian view seemed to be that there was no agreement now
to prevent them from making defence construction since the Karachi
Agreement did not hold after the Simla Agreement came into being, the

---

[17] Interview with Lt Gen. (Retd) H.S. Panag, 19 September 2016,
Chandigarh.
[18] Interview with Lt Gen. (Retd) H.S. Panag, 19 September 2016,
Chandigarh.

latter being silent on such construction.[19] After 1979, UNMOGIP, given the Indian intransigence about the body, decided that it would henceforth record violations but would not condemn them.[20]

The Lull before the Storm—1980s

The 1980s were relatively calm till the onset of militancy in Kashmir, actively backed by the Pakistani security agencies. Gen. Tariq Ghazi of the Pakistan Army, who had served in Kashmir during the 1980s, says that there was no fear among the troops on either side about getting shot at except during periods of tension. There was a general understanding among both the military leaderships that it was important 'to calm down and talk about it, and the situation would cool down'.[21]

The calm of the early 1980s was disturbed by the Indian military operation, Operation Meghdoot, that captured the Siachen Glacier in April 1984, pre-empting Pakistani plans to do so. Not only did it lead to a great deal of firing in the Siachen area, but this rekindled tension in the rest of the LoC as well.

Then came the Kashmir insurgency in the late 1980s, and it had a striking effect on the situation on the J&K borders, but more so on the LoC than the IB. Pavan Nair, a retired Indian Army officer, writes evocatively about this dramatic shift:

> Till the late eighties, the LoC was mostly quiet. Militancy in the Valley with covert support from Pakistan changed the situation overnight. Shelling and exchange of fire became the order of the day. Infiltration by militants was covered by artillery, mortar and small arms fire from the Pakistani side. A few odd casualties of soldiers as well as civilians were a daily occurrence on both sides of the line. The number of civilian casualties both in terms of dead and wounded was far more since troops were mostly sheltered in bunkers and trenches. It is difficult to estimate the total casualties over a period of nearly 14 years till a ceasefire came

---

[19] Dawson, *The United Nations Military Observer Group in India and Pakistan*, 183.

[20] Dawson, *The United Nations Military Observer Group in India and Pakistan*, 283.

[21] Interview with Lt Gen. (Retd) Tariq Ghazi, 7 November 2016, Bangkok.

into effect in November 2003, but it would be in the thousands killed and maimed on each side.[22]

A senior serving Indian Army brigadier in Kashmir, who was a young officer serving in the valley at the start of the insurgency, recalls vividly that with the onset of the insurgency, 'all hell broke loose' and 'grabbers as keepers' became the norm (referring to minor land grabs that would be carried out by either side). He refers to the situation then as 'Diwali everyday'![23]

Lt Gen. Panag agrees with this assessment:

> Pakistan decided to apply the Afghanistan model in Jammu and Kashmir so they started facilitating the infiltration of militants into J&K. They would divert our attention by firing on us and there would be retaliatory fire. Then if we knew that certain posts are being used for facilitating infiltration, we would punish them even more. Their operations required them to fire at us and divert our attention ... our response was to punish them and block the infiltration routes.[24]

Infiltration and the consequent increase in the 'free-for-all' firing across the LoC and, to a lesser extent, on the Jammu IB, also meant that the Indian side decided to further strengthen the LoC. For example, 'the entire valley was looked after by the 19 Division of the Indian Army during 1965, 1971, and even after the 1971 war. But somewhere around 1991–2, one additional division—the 28 Division—was brought in to occupy the LoC, and some more additions—one or two brigades—were made. So, on the whole, on the LoC, the number of troops went up by 40 per cent approximately'.[25] More troops meant more posts and more firing and more return fire, something several Indian and Pakistani army officials refer to as 'free-for-all' firing. With UNMOGIP ceasing to be a consideration, there was no looking over one's shoulder—troops fired at will.

---

[22] Pavan Nair, 'Skirmishing on the Line of Control', *Economic and Political Weekly* 48, no. 2 (26 January 2013), available at http://www.epw.in/journal/2013/04/web-exclusives/skirmishing-line-control.html#sthash.hwjngvvY.dpuf, last accessed on 20 June 2017.

[23] Interview with Army Officer 3, 14 May 2016, Poonch (J&K).

[24] Interview with Lt Gen. (Retd) H.S. Panag, 19 September 2016, Chandigarh.

[25] Interview with Lt Gen. (Retd) H.S. Panag, 19 September 2016, Chandigarh.

Lt Gen. Sapru attests to the sudden spike in the firing that was taking place in the early 1990s. Heavy weapons such as mortars and artillery were available to the forces to be used in times of need. Recalling the intensity of firing in the early 1990s, Lt Gen. Sapru says, 'At times, it was so bad, let us say in the 25 Division sector when I was the colonel GS (General Staff) there, there would be times when there would be almost 100 thousand rounds fired in one night, in the whole Division sector.'[26] Such 'free-for-all' firing, he admits today, was 'purposeless and meaningless'.

Use of heavy weapons like the artillery was normal in the 1990s, recollects Lt Gen. Nandal, former GOC of the Jammu-based 16 Corps: 'The artillery is not being used after the ceasefire has come in to place in 2003. It used to be very regular earlier (in the 1990s). If not the artillery, heavy mortar would be fired. It was bad in the 1990s.'[27]

In the middle of such a tense period, the two sides had tried to take a few modest steps in order to maintain some amount of tranquillity on the border. They attempted to negotiate an 'Agreement on The Maintenance of Peace and Tranquillity Along the Line of Control'. India sent a non-paper (a non-binding paper) to Pakistan on 24 January 1994 proposing several measures to stabilize the LoC such as: 'Neither side will undertake specified levels of military exercises in mutually identified zones'; 'In case of contingencies or other problems arising in the areas along the Line of Control, the two sides shall deal with them through meetings and friendly consultations between border personnel of the two countries', among others.[28]

Pakistan responded to the Indian proposal (on 19 February 1994) with a counter-proposal. But its counter-proposal did not focus on practical measures to contain the violence on the LoC but instead focused on 'UN Resolutions on J&K', 'de-induction of Indian troops from Jammu and Kashmir', 'strengthen the size and presence of the UNMOGIP', and 'adherence to the Karachi Agreement'.[29] Clearly, that was the end of that proposal.

[26] Interview with Lt Gen. (Retd) T.K. Sapru, 10 October 2016, Chandigarh.

[27] Interview with Lt Gen. (Retd) A.S. Nandal, 23 September 2016, Gurgaon.

[28] 'Suggestions and Confidence-Building Measures sent by the Government of India to the Government of Pakistan on 24 January 1994', in Bhasin, *India Pakistan Relations 1947–2011*, 3452.

[29] 'Comments by the Government of Pakistan on the Non-paper No.1 given by India on January 24, 1994 for the Improvement in India–Pakistan Relations

The CFVs continued unabated through the 1990s. By the late 1990s, militancy in J&K was crushed by the Indian state, though primarily through the use of force. In May 1998, India and Pakistan conducted nuclear tests and declared themselves as nuclear weapons states. However, soon after the tests, Prime Minister Vajpayee made a historic trip to Lahore in February 1999 and signed several treaties and agreements during his meeting with his Pakistani counterpart.

However, at around the same time, the Pakistan Army, under Gen. Pervez Musharraf, had already intruded into the Kargil sector of J&K. Upon detecting the intrusion, India used military force to expel the intruders and relations between the two sides slid further into uncertainty.

The end of the Kargil War did not stop the firing on the LoC. Firing across the border by the two armies was routine and worse than it is today. However, Vajpayee attempted to make peace with Pakistan once again and invited Gen. Musharraf to the northern Indian city of Agra, better known as the location of the Taj Mahal, for a summit meeting, which again failed to achieve anything.[30] In December 2001, Pakistan-based terrorists carried out an attack against the Indian Parliament, killing seven security personnel.[31] This led to a mass mobilization of Indian troops along the border. Though Operation Parakram, as the Indian military build-up was called, did not lead to a hot war between the two sides, firing between the two sides reached a new height. 'We', Lt Gen. Nehra recalls, 'used to call them fire assaults—destroying Pakistani posts with direct weapons and heavy weapons. Civilians from the vicinity had to be evacuated.'[32]

---

and its Counter Proposals, Islamabad, February 19, 1994', in Bhasin, *India Pakistan Relations 1947–2011*, 3470.

[30] G. Parthasarathy, 'Missed Opportunities from Simla to Agra', *Tribune*, 7 March 2004, available at http://www.tribuneindia.com/2004/20040307/ spectrum/book4.htm, last accessed on 23 April 2017.

[31] B. Muralidhar Reddy, 'Jaish behind Parliament Attack: Ex-ISI Chief', *Hindu*, 7 March 2004, available at http://www.thehindu.com/2004/03/07/ stories/2004030703320900.htm, last accessed on 4 January 2017.

[32] Interview with Lt Gen. (Retd) J.P. Nehra, 3 December 2016, New Delhi.

Run-up to the CFA

Bilateral tension persisted through 2002 thanks to yet another terror strike against an Indian military facility in J&K.[33] India's fence-building activity on the J&K border with Pakistan from 2001 or so was another reason why firing incidents had reached a new high during the period between 2001 and 2003.[34]

Forces on both sides were doing everything they could in order to achieve their own dominance on the LoC. Ajai Shukla recalls, 'We mounted raids on the Pakistan posts. Sometimes troops actually crossed the border to establish psychological dominance.' Comparing to the spike in the CFVs in 2013–15 period, Shukla says, 'It's much better today and so when people say "My God! The ceasefire is collapsing", I say, "What are you talking about? The LoC is a picnic today." Back then, there was not a day when two to three soldiers were not killed, seven to eight injured.'[35] Lt Gen. Panag agrees to it, saying that 'post-Kargil, there was a lot of intensity of firing up to 2003, phenomenal amounts. We used to have large scale artillery duels, cross border raids were launched, many casualties, capturing posts....'[36]

In July 2003, four months before the CFA was agreed to by the two armies, there was yet another audacious terrorist attack on the Indian Army's top brass in Jammu. A terrorist attack by al-Shuhda Brigade injured Northern Army Commander Lt Gen. Hari Prasad. Also under attack that day were senior officers Lt Gen. T.P.S. Brar, GOC 16 Corps, Maj Gen. T.K. Sapru, GOC 10 Division, Maj Gen. D. Khanna, and Brig. Baldev Singh. Brig. V.K. Govil, of the 16 Corps, was killed in the attack, along with seven soldiers.[37] This further vitiated the relations between the two sides.

[33] Luv Puri, '30 Killed in Jammu Suicide Attack', *Hindu*, 15 May 2002, available at http://www.thehindu.com/2002/05/15/stories/2002051503030100.htm, last accessed on 1 February 2017.

[34] Interview with BSF Officer 7, 4 June 2016, Jammu.

[35] Interview with Col Ajai Shukla, 6 September 2016, New Delhi.

[36] Interview with Lt Gen. (Retd) H.S. Panag, 19 September 2016, Chandigarh.

[37] Praveen Swami, 'A Message Loud and Clear', *Frontline* 20, no. 16 (2–15 August 2003), available at http://www.frontline.in/static/html/fl2016/stories/20030815003503600.htm, last accessed on 1 February 2017.

Then in November 2003, after registering over 2,800 CFVs that year, guns across the lines in Jammu as well as Kashmir fell silent. India and Pakistan started talking about all outstanding disputes, including, most importantly, Kashmir, and there was a reduction in the infiltration into J&K from the Pakistani side. In January 2004, on the sidelines of the SAARC summit meeting in Islamabad, Pakistan president Pervez Musharraf had a quiet discussion with Tariq Aziz and Brajesh Mishra and things started picking up, and the 'Composite Dialogue' began.[38]

Guns fell silent in the state because there was clear and unambiguous political direction to do so, and even if the Pakistan Army wanted to go against the wishes of the government in Islamabad, they could not do so because its own chief was the country's political boss. Gen. Ghazi describes the change on the ground on the LoC: 'After 2003, things became very quiet. The troops could sit out at the bunkers and sun themselves and wave at each other. If there was any support to Mujahidin, that too was pulled back. The Indian side cut down on its rhetoric on cross-border movement and went about building its fencing on the LOC unhindered.'[39]

The CFA of 2003

As discussed previously, the run-up to the CFA of 2003 was a tense period.

There were 4,134 CFVs in 2001 and it went up to 5,767 in 2002, as per official Indian records.

The ceasefire offer from Pakistan came in the wake of this rather tense period of bilateral relations. On the night of 23 November 2003, Pakistan prime minister Mir Zafarullah Khan Jamali announced that Islamabad would implement a unilateral ceasefire with India beginning from the Eid-ul-Fitr holidays. According to Aziz Ahmed Khan, who was Pakistan's high commissioner in New Delhi during those days, the declaration was unilateral and Prime Minister Jamali had not consulted his Indian counterpart, Vajpayee, before making the announcement. Gen. Waheed, though, claims that the Indian government was informed before the Pakistani DGMO made the phone call.

Other accounts have suggested that a lot of spadework was done before the agreement was reached. In the preceding months of the

---

[38] Interview with Aziz Ahmed Khan, 15 December 2016, Islamabad.
[39] Interview with Lt Gen. (Retd) Tariq Ghazi, 7 November 2016, Bangkok.

ceasefire, the then RAW chief C.D. Sahay and his ISI counterpart Gen. Ehsan-ul-Haq met in undisclosed locations to chalk out a CFA. This was accepted by the two political leaderships who asked the respective armies to implement it.

After Prime Minister Jamali made the statement, the ceasefire offer was communicated via a telephone call between the DGMOs of the two armies.[40] The following day, New Delhi welcomed Jamali's statement, and it led to the first ever successful India–Pakistan CFA.[41] The CFA covered the area from the AGPL in Siachen to the LoC and the IB/WB. The IB along the Punjab, Rajasthan, Gujarat, and Sindh did not fall under the ambit of this agreement since there was no firing taking place along these borders.

Lt Gen. (Retd) Waheed Arshad, who was Pakistan's deputy director military operations[42] at the Military Operations Directorate in Rawalpindi when the two countries finalized the ceasefire, says that the two sides had agreed to the following things when the telephone call was made by Pakistan's director military operations Gen. A.P. Kayani to the officiating Indian DGMO, Gen. A.S. Bhaiya:

> One was that both sides will make all efforts not to undertake any activity that would lead to a dent in the ceasefire. We decided that we should not have any new construction. Even if the improvement of defence (construction) has to take place, it should be with prior information. Moreover, that we should activate and institute measures to have communication arrangements … already there were four/five places where we had decided to have such arrangements but they were

[40] Amit Baruah and Sandeep Dikshit, 'India, Pak. Ceasefire Comes into Being', *Hindu*, 26 November 2003, available at http://www.thehindu. com/2003/11/26/stories/2003112604940100.htm, last accessed on 1 February 2017.

[41] Baruah and Dikshit, 'India, Pak. Ceasefire comes into being'. Earlier, in 2000, Indian leader Atal Behari Vajpayee had announced a Ramadan ceasefire, which did not last very long. See 'Responses to India's Offer of Cease-fire', *South Asia Terrorism Portal*, http://www.satp.or'g/satporgtp/countries/india/states/ jandk/documents/papers/Response_Ceasefire.htm, last accessed on 21 March 2017.

[42] While Pakistan's DGMO is the counterpart officer of India's DGMO, Pakistan's DGMO is a two-star officer, and the Indian DGMO holds a three-star rank.

not functional because the LoC used to be hot and those things were not functioning.[43]

However, it may be noted that this was a telephone conversation and no bilateral agreement was signed agreeing to the specifics Lt Gen. Arshad points out. Nor has the Indian side ever confirmed the contents of the CFA as described by Arshad.

Answering why Pakistan decided to offer a unilateral ceasefire, Lt Gen. Arshad argues:

When General Musharraf took over, there were very concerted efforts to improve our relations with the Indian Army. It was the post-Kargil era. Since there were a lot of reforms and forward movement within Pakistan's internal dynamics, there was a lot of positivity about the country taking a new direction and reducing the issues of conflict with neighbours, stabilizing the country, improving the economy, and things like that. So, there was a very considered opinion from the Musharraf government that we should make all efforts to reduce the conflict.[44]

The CFA was only communicated verbally between the DGMOs, not written down, although both sides recorded the exchange as is the case with all DGMO-level phone conversations. Lt Gen. (Retd) Asif Yasin Malik of the Pakistan Army says the reason why this was not written down was because it was informal in nature: 'In any case, (even) at the political level also, there was no agreement that was signed by either government. So if its (CFA's) origin was informal, then how could people in the implementation stage write it down?'[45]

Khan says that during his years as the high commissioner (he stayed on till the end of 2006, witnessing one of the finest phases of recent India–Pakistan bilateral history), not only was there no discussion between the two sides about formalizing the CFA, no one even felt a need to do so since the borders were peaceful. In more recent years, however, the Pakistani side, for obvious reasons, has been asking India to formalize the CFA. In 2015, for instance, Pakistan's high commissioner in New Delhi called for a formalization of the agreement.[46] Lt Gen. Arshad echoed

---

[43] Interview with Lt Gen. (Retd) Waheed Arshad, 15 April 2016, Bangkok.

[44] Interview with Lt Gen. (Retd) Waheed Arshad, 15 April 2016, Bangkok.

[45] Interview with Lt Gen. (Retd) Asif Yasin Malik, 15 April 2016, Bangkok.

[46] 'Formalise 2003 India–Pakistan Ceasefire Agreement: Abdul Basit', NDTV, 30 October 2015, available at http://www.ndtv.com/

this sentiment: 'We had proposed to sit and talk about the arrangement that we already have along the LoC, discuss that, and put it as a formal agreement. Obviously, when you start discussing, there are 10 things that might get added to it to make sure that it is a proper agreement.'[47]

Indian officials also support the codification of the CFA, especially those serving currently on the front lines. So does Col Shukla, who argues: 'Every single piece of written documentation is a help, no doubt about that. But merely writing a CFA is not as helpful as writing down the modalities and the procedures at the local level, the procedures for calling flag meetings, the procedures for de-escalation of the situation that may have blown out of control. The modalities are more important.'[48]

New Delhi has not yet responded to formalizing the 2003 CFA even though the 'notional CFA' that seems to exist started falling apart since 2012 or so. Conversations with officials in India suggest that the reluctance comes from concerns that India would not be able to respond to Pakistan militarily if terrorist infiltration and attacks persisted despite a formal agreement. Moreover, G.K. Pillai, former Indian home secretary, believes that there is no point in having agreements if there is no goodwill (meaning, if Pakistan is unwilling to stop terrorism): 'One can codify anything one wants but there must be goodwill on both sides for it to work.'[49]

Notice the difference between the responses of the military officers and bureaucrats on the need to formalize the CFA.

The Kashmir Talks and the Reduction in CFVs

A solution to the Kashmir dispute was being seriously negotiated by the two governments from 2004 to 2007. Though not officially acknowledged by either India or Pakistan, details of the proposed solution to the Kashmir standoff have since surfaced. Several of those involved in those negotiations, including the former foreign minister of Pakistan Khursheed Mehmood Kasuri, have spoken/written about them. In April 2010, Kasuri

india-news/formalise-2003-india-pakistan-ceasefire-agreement-abdul-basit-1238292, last accessed on 2 March 2017.

[47] Interview with Aziz Ahmed Khan, 15 December 2016, Bangkok.
[48] Interview with Col Ajai Shukla, 6 September 2016, New Delhi.
[49] Interview with G.K. Pillai, 21 September 2016, New Delhi.

stated that 'the previous Musharraf government had completed almost 90 per cent of the spadework on the half-a-century old Kashmir dispute by 2007 as the whole exercise just needed the formal signature of all the three parties to the issue—Pakistan, India, and representatives of Kashmir'.[50] He also argued that the 'near-deal' on Kashmir was the result of three years of quiet diplomacy that proposed a formula for peace characterized by 'loose autonomy that stopped short of the azadi (freedom) and self-governance aspirations ... to be introduced on both sides of the disputed frontier', which was understood to be 'between complete independence and autonomy'.[51]

Kasuri has written that the Kashmir deal was to be signed in March 2007 when the Indian prime minister was to have been invited to visit Pakistan to do so. However, by early 2007, Musharraf started losing domestic legitimacy in Pakistan and Prime Minister Singh realized he did not have the political support from his own party in India, the risk-averse Congress party, to see the deal through.[52] Developments in 2008 further deteriorated the bilateral relationship, with a series of terrorist attacks of Pakistani origin being carried out against India. Following the July 2008 car bomb attack on the Indian embassy in Kabul that killed 57 people, including senior Indian officials, India's foreign secretary Shivshankar Menon stated that the peace process was 'under stress'.[53] Then, after terrorist attacks in Bangalore (Karnataka) and Ahmedabad (Gujarat) during the same month, Menon declared that 'India–Pakistan relations were at a four-year low'.[54]

---

[50] B. Dogar and R. Roy, 'Kashmir Solution just a Signature Away: Kasuri', Aman Ki Asha, available at www.amankiasha.com, last accessed on 2 April 2017.

[51] Ranjan Roy, 'Kashmir Pact Was Just a Signature Away', Times of India, 24 April 2010, available at http://timesofindia.indiatimes.com/article show/5850851.cms?utm_source=contentofinterest&utm_medium=text&utm_ campaign=cppst, last accessed on 20 September 2018. For more on this, see Khurshid Mahmud Kasuri, Neither a Hawk nor a Dove: An Insider's Account of Pakistan's Foreign Policy (Oxford: Oxford University Press, 2015).

[52] A.S. Dulat and A. Sinha, Kashmir: The Vajpayee Years (New Delhi: Harper Collins, 2015), 22, 280–1.

[53] 'India Says Dialogue under Stress', BBC, 21 July 2008, available at http:// news.bbc.co.uk, last accessed on 3 March 2017.

[54] Ministry of External Affairs, Government of India, 'Briefing by Foreign Secretary after India–Pakistan Foreign Secretary-Level Talks', media briefing, 21

Breakdown of the Ceasefire

The CFA of 2003 held till 2009 when CFVs started spiking, though nowhere close to the pre-2003 numbers. The LoC and IB started heating up in 2009 primarily because of the many developments in the previous year.

What really damaged the bilateral relations was the Mumbai terror attack carried out by LeT—a Pakistan-based terrorist organization—in November 2008. Between November 2008 and February 2009, there existed a serious possibility of a military confrontation between the two nuclear rivals. In January 2009, New Delhi cancelled the previously scheduled talks on the Sir Creek maritime dispute, and the composite dialogue remained officially suspended for over two years thereafter.

In close to a year, the Indo-Pak relationship deteriorated so much that from signing a peace deal on Kashmir, India and Pakistan almost went to war. CFVs reached a new high in 2013. The relationship went into a tailspin once again. However, while the two sides were trading bullets, they were also willing to engage in a dialogue process with each other. The 'no war, no peace' situation continued till May 2014, when the hard-line Indian leader Narendra Modi came to power in New Delhi.

2014, Enter the Modi Regime

However, when the BJP government came to power in New Delhi under the leadership of Narendra Modi in May 2014, many hoped that relations with Pakistan would improve based on the assumption that it would take a strong leader to make a lasting deal with Pakistan.

This initial belief about Modi's changed attitude towards Pakistan was further strengthened when he invited the Pakistani prime minister, Nawaz Sharif, to New Delhi for his swearing-in ceremony in May 2014, which the latter accepted. However, this friendliness did not last very long as terror strikes against India continued apace, as did the CFVs. But, Modi's impromptu visit to Pakistan in December 2015, to the surprise of Indians and Pakistanis alike, to meet Nawaz Sharif was widely seen as a breakthrough.

July 2008, available at http://www.mea.gov.in/media-briefings.htm?dtl/3202/Briefing+by+Foreign+Secretary+after+IndiaPakistan+Foreign+Secretary+level+talks, last accessed on 2 April 2017.

By the end of 2015, it seemed that New Delhi had found a consistent Pakistan policy: the meeting of the Indian and Pakistani national security advisers in Bangkok in early December 2015, which they followed up with occasional phone conversations, the visit of the external affairs minister to Islamabad soon thereafter, and finally the impromptu visit of Modi to Lahore. The two prime ministers had briefly met in Paris during the COP 21 conference, besides an officially unconfirmed closed-door meeting in Kathmandu, Nepal, during the SAARC meeting in 2015.[55] There was a great deal of diplomatic activity during this phase.

Pathankot Attack and After

This bilateral optimism soon hit a 'not-so-unexpected' roadblock: a terror strike against India. This time, the target was an airbase in Pathankot, in the Indian Punjab. The attack on the strategic airbase, close to the Pakistan border, led to the killing of seven people and was, at that point, reported to be the handiwork of Pakistan-based terror outfits. Despite the opposition's criticism of Modi's policy towards Pakistan, the two sides managed the political fallout of the Pathankot terror attack admirably well. They also decided to jointly investigate the attack. India allowed the first ever visit of a Pakistani joint investigation team (JIT) to the site of the terror attack in Pathankot, which at the time was indicative of a new-found rhythm in the India–Pakistan relationship.

Pakistan also reciprocated Modi's efforts. It reportedly provided intelligence warning about a possible terror strike in Gujarat by LeT and Jaish-e-Mohammed (JeM) cadres in early March 2016; earlier, in mid-February, the Pakistan government had lodged a first information report against 'unknown persons' in the Pathankot terror attack case; and JeM (a terror organization based in Pakistan) chief Masood Azhar was placed under custody after the Pathankot airbase attack. Moreover, Sharif also started making political overtures to India. In February 2016, he stated at a rally in Muzaffarabad: 'Vajpayee told me that he was stabbed in the back because of Pakistan's misadventure in Kargil, especially during the process of [the] Lahore Declaration. Vajpayee was

[55] Happymon Jacob, 'A Christmas Course Correction', *Hindu*, 24 March 2016, available at http://www.thehindu.com/todays-paper/tp-opinion/a-christmas-course-correction/article8038253.ece, last accessed on 1 July 2017.

right. I would have said the same thing—he was certainly backstabbed [in Kargil].'56

In the spirit of the joint investigation on the Pathankot attack, Islamabad was supposed to host an Indian National Investigative Agency (NIA) team in Islamabad, which never took place. This eventually sowed seeds of bitterness between the two countries.57

More importantly, the borders in Kashmir, which witnessed rising instances of firings (CFVs), had become silent since the engagement began in December 2015. While the rapprochement was welcome in the larger scheme of India–Pakistan relations, it did not have much political support within India. With Pakistan not finalizing its plans to invite the Indian investigative team to Islamabad, the dialogue process was already losing steam when an Indian Army base was attacked in Kashmir's Uri in September 2016. The two sides had managed to begin a useful engagement but failed to follow up primarily due to the lack of reciprocity from Islamabad's side.

Uri Attack and the 'Surgical Strikes'

The attack on the Indian Army camp in Uri in J&K carried out by Pakistan-based terror group LeT took the lives of 19 Indian soldiers, leading to a huge outcry in the country.

New Delhi, then, decided to respond militarily to the militant attack on Uri and carried out what it called 'surgical strikes' against Pakistan on 29 September 2016. From a military point of view, the cross-LoC operation was limited and carefully calibrated: there was no targeting of Pakistani military installations as the operation was claimed to be against terror camps and not against the Pakistan Army, and the DGMO telephoned his Pakistani counterpart after the operations ended and conveyed the counter-terrorist intent behind the strike. The DGMO further clarified

---

56 'Kargil "Misadventure", Was "Stab" in Atal Vajpayee's Back: Nawaz Sharif, *Economic Times*, 18 February 2016, available at http://economictimes. indiatimes.com/news/defence/kargil-misadventure-was-stab-in-atal-vajpayees-back-nawaz-sharif/articleshow/51035959.cms, last accessed on 15 January 2017.

57 Happymon Jacob, 'The Pathankot Paradigm', *Hindu*, 2 April 2016, available at http://www.thehindu.com/opinion/lead/The-Pathankot-paradigm/article14213873.ece, last accessed on 1 July 2017.

that the 'Indian Army conducted surgical strikes at several of these launch pads "along" Line of Control'. Pakistan refused to acknowledge the attack and hence did not counter or respond to the surgical strikes.

Does this mean that Pakistan displayed a certain amount of tolerance for the Indian military action given that it was carried out after 19 Indian soldiers were killed, and national anger was mounting in India? It is true that Pakistan decided not to respond conventionally but it did respond in various ways thereafter to the Indian strikes. Responding to the surgical strikes with matching force would not have been a smart strategy for Pakistan, given that it would have been hard for the Pakistan Army to pull it off. This, in my reckoning, perhaps explains the Pakistani inaction and the refusal to acknowledge the Indian attack. Pakistan, however, could be seen as having used a low-cost strategy to respond to the Indian strikes in the most practical and feasible manner from Rawalpindi's point of view, and 'at a time and place of its choosing'—by firing on the border in J&K and organizing (or helping to organize) coordinated attacks on Indian Army bases/convoys through its proxies such as the JeM and LeT.

Consider this: In late November 2016, terrorists attacked an Indian Army camp at Nagrota in J&K, killing seven soldiers. In the following month, an Indian Army convoy was attacked by terrorists in Pampore in Kashmir, killing three soldiers. These cheap strategies seemed to make up Pakistan's response to New Delhi's surgical strikes.[58]

The result of the strikes has, therefore, created more challenges, both on the LoC and IB/WB as well as inside Kashmir. Terror attacks in Kashmir have been spiking, for instance. Lt Gen. Devraj Anbu, the Northern Army commander of the Indian Army, under whose charge comes Kashmir, stated in a press conference at his headquarters in Udhampur: 'Large number of terrorist camps and launch pads exist across south & north of Pir Panjal, they have not decreased ... Launch pads and terrorist camps have increased since last year.'[59] Let us also

[58] Happymon Jacob, 'A Year of Living Dangerously', *Hindu*, 22 December 2016, available at http://www.thehindu.com/opinion/lead/A-year-of-living-dangerously/article16919538.ece/ucbrowser/?hbt=uc, last accessed on 1 December 2017.

[59] 'One Year of Surgical Strikes: Indian Army Says it will Cross LoC Again if Required', *Financial Express*, 7 September 2017, available at http://

look at some figures from J&K. Credible media reports show that 110 militants and 38 army personnel were killed between January and September 2016 (that is, prior to the surgical strikes). However, between the surgical strikes (October 2016) and mid-2018, 178 militants and 69 army personnel have been killed. Forty-four army personnel were killed between January and September 2018, compared to 38 last year between January and September (including those killed in the Uri army base attack).

The net result of the Uri attack and its aftermath led to another spike in the CFVs in J&K, a throwback to the situation in 2013.

New Delhi's Strategies to Deal with CFVs

Ever since the CFA of 2003, New Delhi seems to have followed three broad strategies to deal with the violence on the J&K border: 'talks over bullets', 'talks and bullets', and 'disproportionate bombardment'.[60]

The years immediately after the 2003 CFA witnessed a great deal of calm on the borders with violations dropping to a minimum despite infiltration into J&K and sporadic, minor terror attacks against India taking place. There were no major terror attacks, and Kashmir was calm. Bilateral talks drastically reduced violence during that phase which lasted roughly till 2008.

The period following Prime Minister Narendra Modi's visit to Lahore is another example of this phase. Thanks to the rapprochement achieved by his visit, the period from December 2015 to February 2016 hardly witnessed any CFVs, despite the Pathankot Air Force base attack in early January 2016.

The second strategy has been to engage in talks while proportionately responding to Pakistani provocations. The period from 2010 to 2012 seems to fall in this category. India and Pakistan engaged in talks during this time and CFVs reduced significantly—India reported 70 violations

---

www.financialexpress.com/india-news/big-blow-for-pakistan-indian-army-threatens-more-surgical-strikes-says-will-cross-loc-if-required/844925/, last accessed on 23 October 2017.

[60] Happymon Jacob, 'The Strategy of Conflict', *Hindu*, 16 March 2018, available at http://www.thehindu.com/opinion/lead/the-strategy-of-conflict/article23264085.ece?homepage=true, last accessed on 20 March 2018.

in 2010, 62 in 2011, and 114 in 2012. In 2010, the two foreign secretaries met in New Delhi, followed by the two foreign ministers meeting in Islamabad. In 2011, the two foreign secretaries met in Thimphu, and in 2012, the Indian and Pakistani foreign ministers issued a joint statement in Islamabad. Both talks and firing persisted, though at moderate levels.

The third Indian strategy could be termed as disproportionate bombardment of the Pakistani side using high-calibre weapons and not showing any desire to engage in negotiations or concessions and shunning Pakistani suggestions thereof. India's reported rejection, in January 2018, of a Pakistani proposal for a meeting between the Indian and Pakistani DGMOs, saying it first wanted to see a drop in infiltration levels, is a result of this strategy.

Violations since April 2016 are largely informed by this strategy. Despite the rising terrorist attacks inside J&K and the increasing CFVs, there has been hardly any dialogue. Pakistan accused India of violating the ceasefire 389 times from April to December 2016, and in 2017 over 2,000 times. India accused Pakistan of 449 violations in 2016, and 860 in 2017.

Understanding CFVs

This section will compare the various data sets on CFVs and what the data shows, how CFVs are defined by the Indian and Pakistani forces and study the existing explanations for CFVs.

Methods Used to Create the Data Set on CFVs

There is no systematic official data on CFVs available in the public domain in India or in Pakistan specifying the causes for CFVs and the places where CFVs take place. CFVs are reported in India and in Pakistan by the security forces through set channels to the concerned government departments, the MoD, and the MHA in the case of India. Aggregate numbers of yearly CFVs are often, not always, released by the two governments without indicating the specific places or when and how they occurred. While the UNMOGIP reports the CFVs to the UN headquarters, this information is not shared publicly. In any case, the Indian side has not been reporting the CFVs to UNMOGIP since 1972, after the Simla Agreement. Therefore, the UNMOGIP data would only include 'alleged' CFVs reported by Pakistan.

To overcome this lack of meaningful data, two new data sets (separately, for India and for Pakistan) were created for this project by listing all the CFVs reported in open sources in India and Pakistan, from 2002 to early 2018. Open sources primarily include print media reports and digital media reports (newspapers, mostly English-language national dailies and, in some cases, even non-Indian and non-Pakistani press reports). Media reports usually include the date, location, and in some cases the cause of the CFVs and casualties as indicated by the security officials. However, it should be noted that not all CFVs get reported in the press, and since the reporting of the CFVs is bound to be lower than the actual occurrences of violations, the number of CFVs listed in the book's data sets is significantly lower than the number of CFVs accounted for in the official records. However, the data set created for this book is able to provide a chronological record of the CFVs through the years from 2002 to 2017, and is very helpful in understanding the patterns, locations, and the major causes of CFVs between India and Pakistan.

Interestingly, in recent years, social media has also been an important open source for information on CFVs. All major governmental agencies in India and Pakistan—the Indian MoD, MHA, BSF, Army HQs, and Pakistani ISPR have regularly updated twitter handles, which can be resourceful for obtaining information on CFVs. Individual listings and reports on the government websites like the Press Information Bureau (PIB) website are mostly sporadic (site search engines are unable to generate relevant data in an organized manner), unavailable (links are outdated giving the HTTP 404 Not Found errors), or missing (press release is not done for each violation).

As part of the research for this book, CFV data was collected with the following details: date of the CFV/date of the CFV as reported, area where CFV took place, location of the CFV—LOC/IB, reason given for CFV/ trigger event, additional information (including casualties occurred), and source of information. CFVs were first tabulated chronologically year-wise from 2002 to 2017. Based on the listings for all the years, subsidiary data sets tabulating the CFVs reason-wise, location-wise, and area-wise were created (see Table 4.1). The Indian and the Pakistani data sets were consolidated into an additional data sheet to compare the locations, areas, and reasons for CFVs reported by each side. The individual and comparative data sets were then graphically represented in the form of bar

Table 4.1 Consolidated data on CFVs and related casualties in J&K

Year	Indian official data *		Pak official data #		CFVs listed according to the data set created for the book **	
	CFVs***	Casualties (Personnel)	CFVs	Casualties (Personnel)	India	Pakistan
2001	4134	NA	NA	Nil	NA	NA
2002	5767	NA	NA	Nil	0	96
2003	2841	NA	11	Nil	1	30
2004	4	Nil	6	Nil	0	0
2005	6	Nil	9	Nil	1	1
2006	3	Nil	9	1	0	2
2007	21	3 (A)****	18	Nil	1	3
2008	86	6	30	Nil	8	2
2009	35	6	46	Nil	7	5
2010	70	5	113	Nil	13	16
2011	62	3	104	2	14	6
2012	114	4	252	2	20	5
2013	347	5	464	5	25	46
2014	583	3	315	3	30	51
2015	405	10	248	16	40	55
2016	449	13	382	38	57	54
2017	971	19	1,970	NA	117	62
2018	633 (till Feb. 2018)	10 (till Feb. 2018)	690 (till 22 Mar. 2018)	NA	NA	NA

Sources:
*Figures for India from official data sources such as MoD, MHA, Parliament briefings, and PIB releases.
Figures for Pakistan from official data sources such as Pakistan National Assembly records.
** Data set for the project consists of individual CFV listings for India and for Pakistan sourced from print media (newspaper), online media (newspapers), and official data sources such as PIB Press releases for India and ISPR for Pakistan.

(Cont'd)

Table 4.1 *(Cont'd)*

*** All the CFVs reported by India for the years 2002, 2003, 2005, 2006, and 2007 were on the LoC. In 2008, of the 86 violations, 77 were on the LoC and 9 on the IB in Jammu; in 2009, out of 35 CFVs, 28 were on the LoC and 9 on the IB in Jammu; in 2010, out of 70 CFVs, 44 were on the LoC and 26 on the IB in Jammu; in 2011, out of the 62 CFVs reported, 51 were on the LoC and 11 on the IB in Jammu; in 2012, 93 violations took place on the LoC and 22 on the Jammu IB, totalling 114; in 2016, out of 449 CFVs, 228 were on the LoC and 221 on the IB in Jammu; in 2017, 860 violations have been reported on the LoC and 111 violations on the IB in J&K. Official India data up to February 2018 states that of the 633 violations by Pakistan, 432 were along the LoC and 201 were along the IB in J&K. CFV data for 2018 is in the process of collection for the month of March 2018 and onward.
**** (A)—Army, NA—Not Available, Nil—Zero.

charts and pie charts. The areas of CFVs on the Indian and the Pakistani sides were plotted on maps (see Figure 4.1).

What the Data Shows

Based on the data collected for this book, the most affected areas by CFVs on the Indian side are Poonch and Jammu, followed by Samba and Rajouri. Indeed, all four places started witnessing higher incidence of CFVs from 2012. On the Pakistan side, the areas with high incidence of CFVs are Sialkot, Rawalakot, Kotli, and Shakargarh. These areas witnessed high incidence of CFVs in 2013, 2014, and 2015. These eight highly CFV-prone locations are in corresponding locations on either side of the LoC and IB/WB. For instance, Sialkot in Pakistan is physically opposite to Jammu and Samba in India; Kotli in Pakistan is opposite to Rajouri in India; Rawalakot in Pakistan is opposite to Poonch in India; and Shakargarh in Pakistan is opposite to Kathua in India, not too far from Jammu and Samba.

On why CFVs take place, data collected from the official Indian sources do not provide any real insights. Even the newspaper reports do not provide any real insights into why CFVs occur. In 2015, for instance, the major causes listed in unofficial reports were: 'unprovoked firing', 'not stated', 'cross fire', 'inadvertent crossing', and 'cover fire'. In 2014, the causes mentioned were: 'unprovoked firing', 'not stated', 'others', 'infiltration', 'cross fire', 'inadvertent crossing', and construction. In fact, 2014 is the only year when construction is mentioned as a cause for CFVs. Infiltration (of militants into J&K) as a trigger for CFVs is mentioned since 2008.

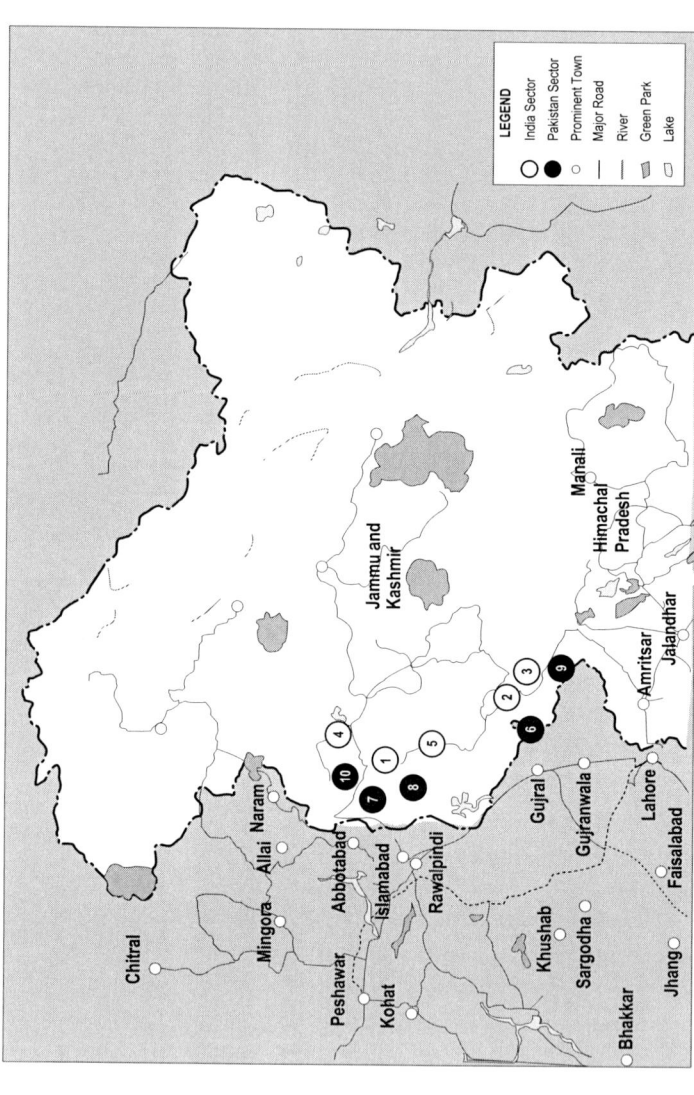

Figure 4.1 Areas with high intensity of CFVs: 1—Poonch, 2—Jammu, 3—Samba, 4—Baramulla, 5—Rajouri, 6—Sialkot, 7—Rawalakot, 8—Kotli, 9—Shakargarh, 10—Chakothi

Source: Author.

Disclaimer: This map does not claim to represent the authentic domestic or international boundaries of India. This map is not to scale and is provided for illustrative purposes only.

Data collected from official and non-official sources on the Pakistani side is even more restrictive as far as its explanatory power is concerned. In 2015, Pakistani data merely mention three causes: 'unprovoked', 'not stated', and 'crossfire'. In 2014 and 2013, there is an addition of 'inadvertent crossing' contributing in a minor way to CFVs.

Both Indian and Pakistani officials, serving and retired, cited defence construction along the IB/WB and LoC, by both sides, as a major reason for CFVs. However, the reports in the media or official documents hardly ever mention this as a major cause for CFVs. Given such acute lack of explanations for causation of CFVs, this book has relied extensively on oral evidence to fix causation. Next chapter, using such oral evidence, explains why CFVs occur on the India–Pakistan borders in J&K.

Graphical Representation of Indian Data

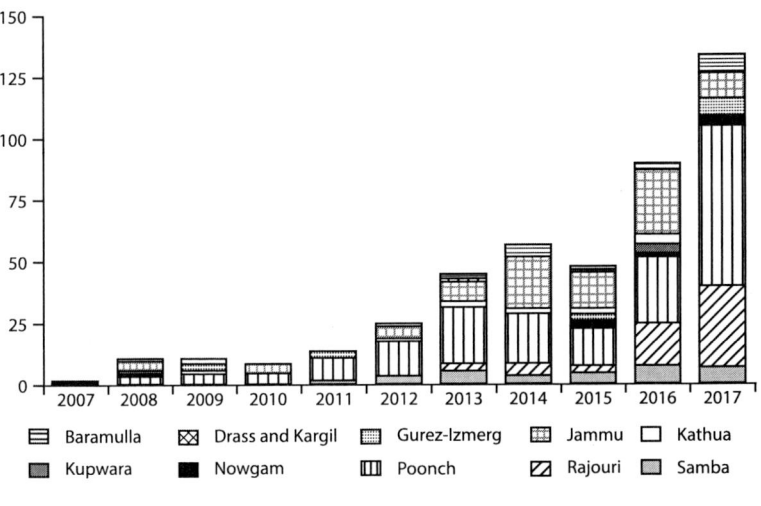

(*Cont'd*)

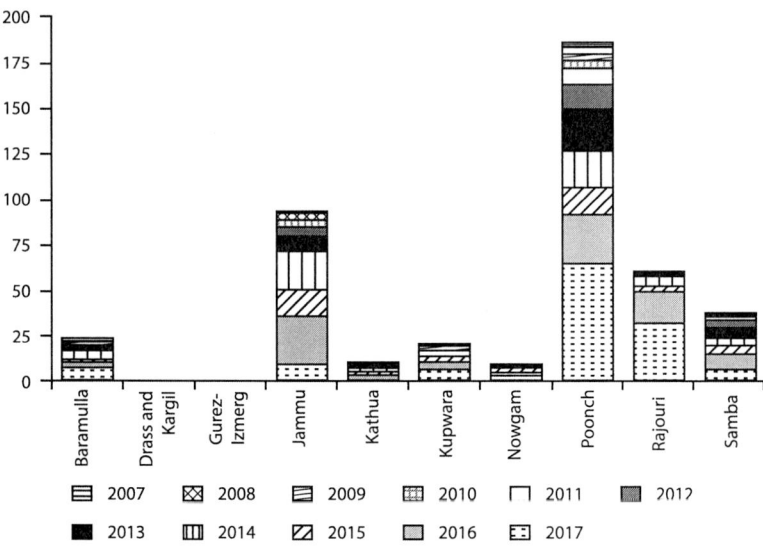

Figure 4.2 The number of CFVs at sector/district for each year (India)
Source: Author.

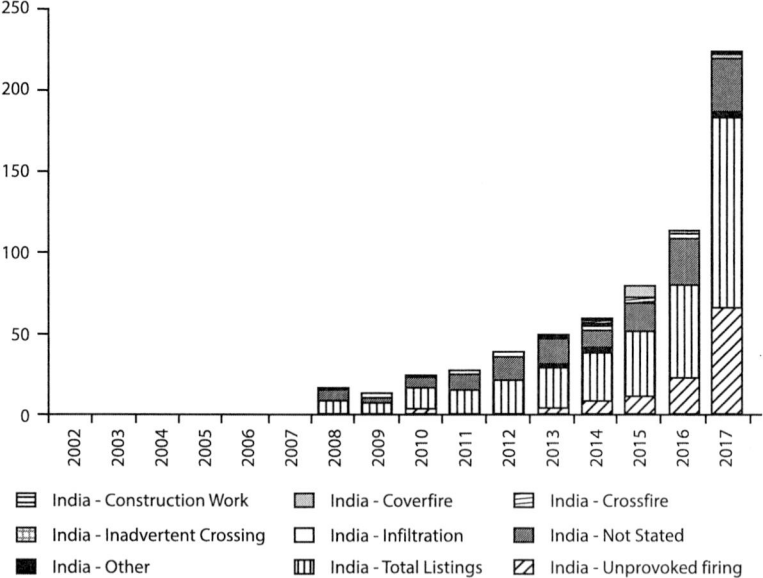

Figure 4.3 Causes of CFVs each year—numbers (India)
Source: Author.

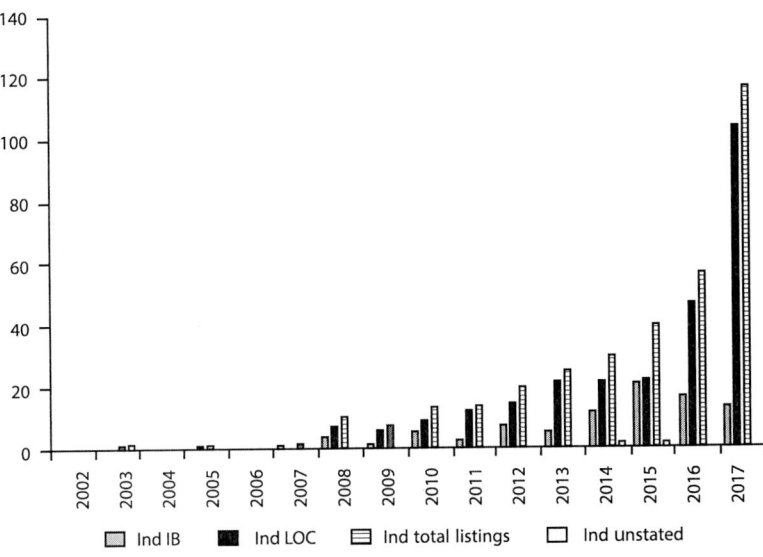

Figure 4.4 Comparative data on the CFVs on the LoC/IB (India)

Source: Author.

Pakistan side	India side
14: Neelum Valley	1 - Tangdhar
15: Tithwal	2 - Baramulla
16: Chakothi	3 - Uri
17: New Mirpur	
18: Rawalakot	4 - Poonch
19: TattaPani	5 - Mendhar
20 - Kotli	6 - Rajouri
21 - Bhimber	7 - Naushera
22 - Sialkot	8 - Jammu, 9 - Samba, 10 - Kathua
23 - Bajwat	11 - Akhnoor
24 - Chaprar	12 - RS Pura
25 - Charwah	13 - Arnia
26 - Shakargarh	

(Cont'd)

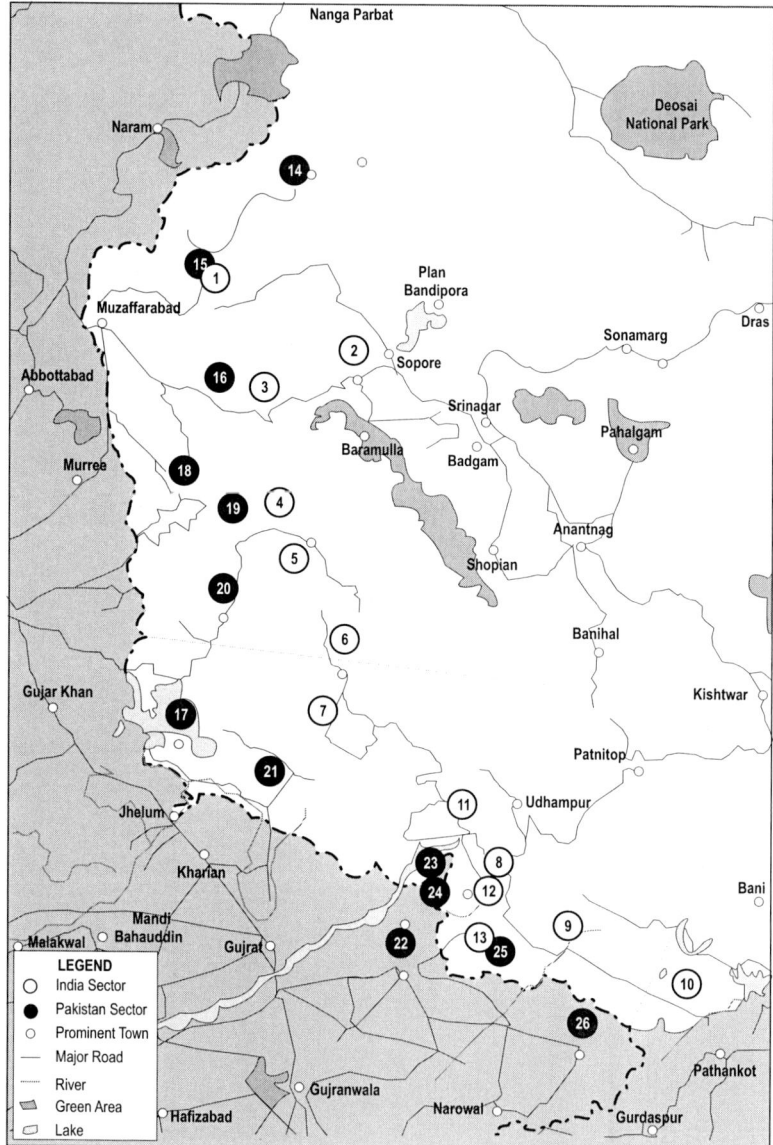

Figure 4.5 Locations reporting CFVs on the Indian and Pakistani sides

Source: Author.

Disclaimer: This map does not claim to represent the authentic domestic or international boundaries of India. This map is not to scale and is provided for illustrative purposes only.

Graphical Representation of Pakistani Data

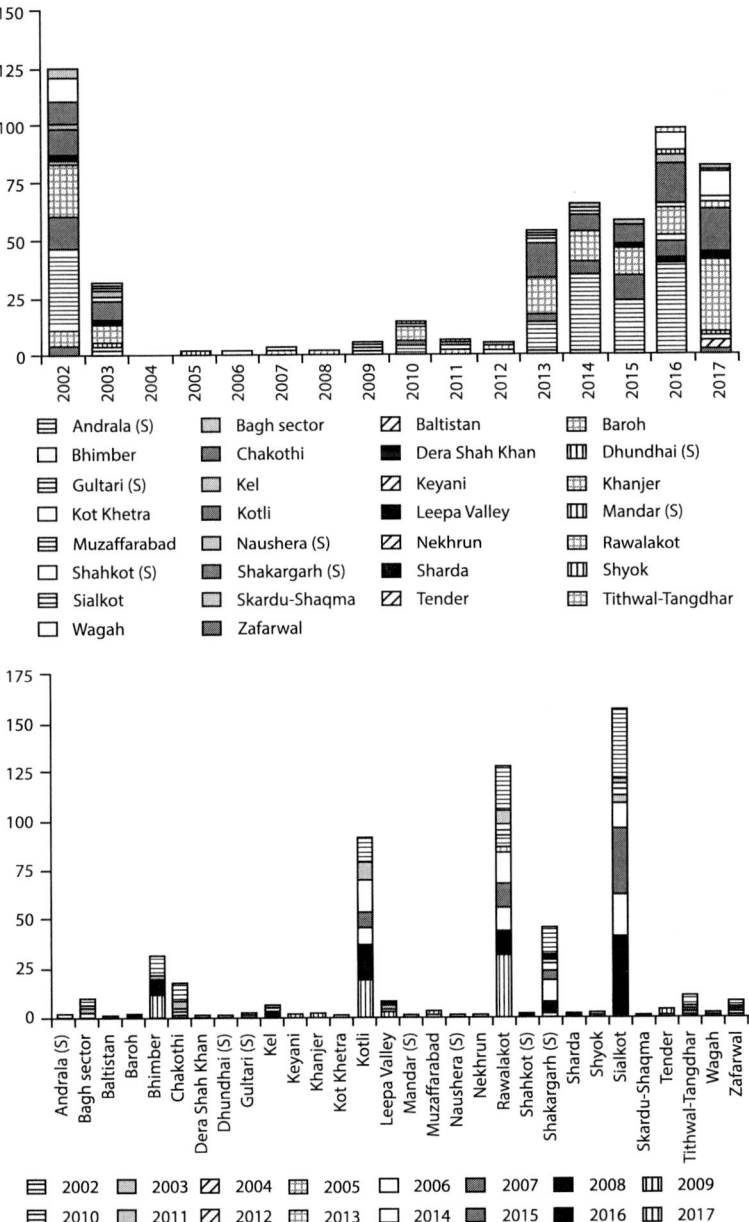

Figure 4.6   The number of CFVs at sector/district for each year (Pakistan)
Source: Author.

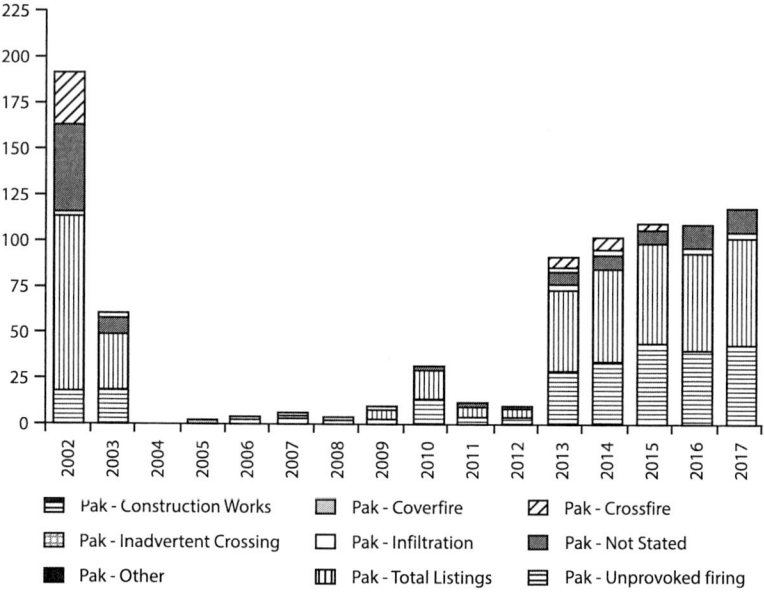

Figure 4.7 Causes of CFVs each year—numbers (Pakistan)
Source: Author.

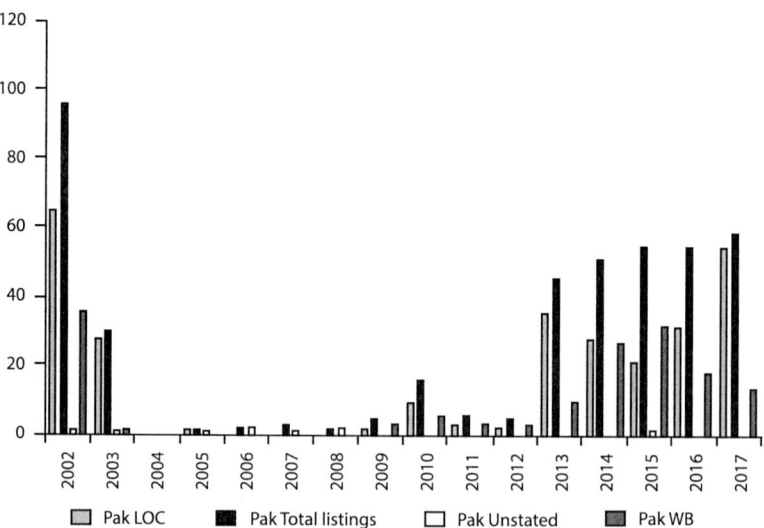

Figure 4.8 Comparative data on the CFVs on the LoC/IB (Pakistan)
Source: Author.

Comparative Graphs—India and Pakistan

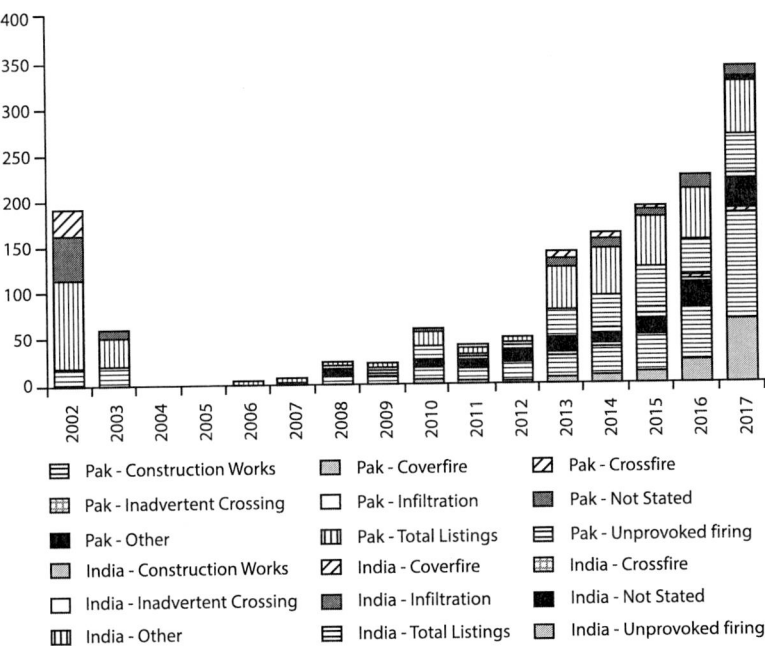

Figure 4.9 Reason-wise CFVs

Source: Author.

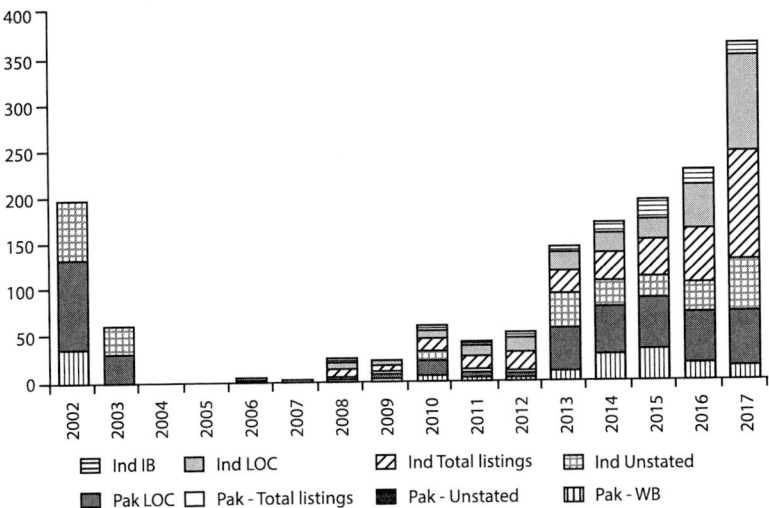

Figure 4.10 Comparative data on LoC and IB/WB

Source: Author.

How Are CFVs Counted?

Understanding what a CFV entails and how CFVs are counted is correspondingly important. On the ground, there is no universal rule for counting CFVs. A violation generally does not consist of one shot; a CFV might be thousands of shots fired by a range of weapons from personal firearms to artillery. The violation might include multiple exchanges of fire across multiple areas within a period of 24 hours in reaction to an initial violation. The armies of India and Pakistan, as well as the BSF and Pakistan Rangers, generally use this method to count the CFVs. Moreover, not all CFVs are reported to the higher political authorities on either side or, sometimes, even on the chain of command of the force guarding the border. As Lt Gen. Nandal, former chief of the Jammu-based 16 Corps says, although the situation report is sent to the HQ every day, not all CFVs are reported.[61] Reporting depends on a variety of situational factors, including whether it might be advantageous to the forces to play up or play down violations in a particular area.[62] In short, a great deal of subjectivity goes into counting CFVs, with local-level officials often making a subjective determination on what should be counted as a CFV.

The local commanders of the Indian Army report the CFVs to the DGMO and the army HQs. The violations on the IB in Jammu are reported by the BSF to the sector HQs and then to the BSF HQ in Delhi. Reports are consolidated at the HQs and sent to respective ministries— MHA in case of the BSF and MoD in case of the Army.

The BSF counts CFVs using the following method. A period of 24 hours from the first shot fired is taken to count one CFV in an area. For instance, in Samba, if the firing starts at 6 a.m., then all the firings till 6 a.m. next day are counted as one CFV. Sometimes there could be tens of thousands of shots fired by the other side in 24 hours. If the firing takes place at 6 a.m. in Samba, and the next one at 8 a.m. in Samba, then it is counted as one CFV. If the firing starts at 6 a.m. and next one is at 5 p.m., it is still counted as one CFV. If firing starts at 10 p.m. at night in Jammu, then the firing till 10 p.m. next day is counted as one CFV. Therefore, the 24 hours starts at a place depending on when the firing breaks out in that area. Sometimes, when the firing is continuous, the 24 hours might extend to 26 hours too.

[61] Interview with Lt Gen. (Retd) A.S. Nandal, 23 September 2016, Gurgaon.
[62] Interview with officials (unnamed) in J&K, 11 June 2016.

Gen. Vinod Bhatia, a former Indian DGMO, says that the counting adopted by the Indian Army is slightly different. While the BSF has taken time (24-hour period) as a unit of measurement, the army counts a CFV in terms of continuity in a given area. Normally, a CFV is counted as 'one' when Pakistan fires at the Indian posts in any given area, either a single round or sporadic fire on any one day. In other words, instead of 24 hours, the Indian Army would count continuity and location on a given day for counting CFVs. He explains further to throw light on how areas are taken into consideration while counting CFVs: 'Let say, there is CFV say in Akhnoor sector, one in Bimbergali sector, one in Poonch sector, one in Rampur sector, one in Uri sector, so there will be 6 CFVs.'[63] But firing happening in one sector (which would have several hundred units), or in the area of responsibility (AOR) of one battalion would be counted as one CFV. The Pakistan Army has a similar method of counting CFVs.

Counting of CFVs gets more complicated when we take into consideration the issue of multiple areas involved in CFVs. Gen. Yasin says that a single CFV in one location could potentially have reactions in five or six places. Even then, it is counted as only one violation.[64] Pakistani army officers say that they make a distinction between minor violations and major violations. Only when more than 200 rounds of mortar are fired, it is called a major violation. Anything below that is a minor CFV.[65]

There is yet another complication when it comes to counting the violations given how each side calls the other side as the violator. Lt Gen. Panag explains: 'We will report his firing and that we responded; he will report our firing and that he responded. So, the violation will get counted actually generally by both sides, as one violation. But both sides say that the other has violated.'[66] This then explains why the media in India and Pakistan habitually reports, quoting military sources, that it is 'the other side' that initiated the firing.

[63] Interview with Lt Gen. (Retd) Vinod Bhatia, 19 September 2016, New Delhi.

[64] Interview with Lt Gen. (Retd) Asif Yasin Malik, 15 April 2016, Bangkok.

[65] Interview with GOC, 12 Division, Pakistan Army, 13 December 2017, Murree, Pakistan.

[66] Interview with Lt Gen. (Retd) H.S. Panag, 19 September 2016, Chandigarh.

The GOC of 12 Division of the Pakistan Army based in Murree told this author that only when more than 200 rounds of motor are fired, it is called major violation; anything below is minor. While this is an important piece of information, the data put out by official sources does not reflect this distinction.

It is also important to understand what is not a CFV. Speculative firing that soldiers undertake for a variety of tactical reasons is not counted. Firing on one's own side is not counted as CFV: Only firing for effect is considered as violation—stray firing without effect often does not get counted.

How Do CFVs Proliferate?

CFVs occurring in one location often spread to other areas within a sector or sometimes even to other sectors depending on the severity of the damage. Such horizontal proliferation of CFVs is more of a rule than exception. One of the reasons why CFVs tend to spread horizontally is because firing by one's opponent is not necessarily responded to in the same location. The response is carried out where the responding side has dominance. As Gen. Bhatia succinctly points out: 'If you fire at me, it is not that I will retaliate immediately. I may retaliate immediately; I may retaliate a little while later. Once a CFV is there, I may retaliate immediately to keep you quiet. Or I may retaliate little later to make sure that you get hit.'[67]

The point is to send a message to the opponent: 'You hit me where I am weak, I will hit you where you are weak'—and both sides are aware of each other's weak points. Col Shukla describes the thinking that leads to such horizontal proliferation: 'When a CFV takes place, it is not that you are firing on me and I am firing back on you. There are certain posts that are dominated comprehensively from the Pakistani side by fire and observation, and when the time comes, they will hammer the Indian post. But I will not hammer back from here. Another post that dominates the Pakistani post somewhere else will do it. So, when the CFV takes place, there is a well-established procedure that unleashes itself'.[68]

Then there is vertical proliferation of CFVs, which happens when firing that starts with personal weapons escalate into firing with heavy

---

[67] Interview with Lt Gen. (Retd) Vinod Bhatia, 19 Septemeber 2016, New Delhi.
[68] Interview with Col Ajai Shukla, 6 September 2016, New Delhi.

weapons like mortars or artillery. As a senior Pakistani general pointed out,[69] normal firing from automatic weapons will be responded to immediately without waiting for permission from above. However, in the case of using high-calibre weapons, commanding officers will be the authority to initiate their use. As far as weapons like mortars and artillery are concerned, permission must come from higher HQs. This gives a form of inbuilt check mechanism on the level of escalation.

CFVs that start with automatic weapons can often escalate vertically and go up to the level of higher-calibre guns like the medium and heavy machine guns, then to artillery, howitzers, field guns, rocket launchers, and so on. The use of such weapons is often used in what officers describe as 'fire assaults'. Lt Gen. Sapru defines them as 'very heavy, concentrated dose of fire using mortars and sometimes artillery, specifically targeted on one or two posts to try and destroy it to the extent possible'.[70] For the purposes of fire assaults, these weapons systems were taken up to posts on mules-back, to site them in deflated positions, and then fire. He confirmed that such weapons have been used extensively on the LoC. Officials on the IB confirm that during the 2014 standoff, heavy weapons were moved from Punjab to carry out coordinated firing in Jammu.[71] In November 2016, the Indian Army used artillery guns 'to raze four positions of Pakistan army' in the Keran sector of the LoC.[72]

Such escalation happens with the knowledge of the higher-ups in the hierarchy because the heavy weapons are not provided to the units or even battalions. Heavy weapons, usually with the brigades or divisions, can only be used with the permission of the officers commanding those formations.

Existing Explanations for CFVs

What are the causes behind CFVs? A cursory glance at the existing literature, government documents, academic writings, or analysis in

---

[69] Interview with Pakistan Official 4, 17 January 2017, Rawalpindi.

[70] Interview with Lt Gen. (Retd) T.K. Sapru, 10 October 2016, Chandigarh.

[71] Interview with Senior retired BSF officer, on condition of anonymity.

[72] 'Army Used Artillery Guns to "Destroy" Pakistani Posts across LoC', *Times of India*, 4 November 2016, available at http://timesofindia.indiatimes.com/india/Army-used-artillery-guns-to-destroy-Pakistani-posts-across-LoC/articleshow/55250508.cms, last accessed on 2 December 2017.

the media throws up a regular set of explanations for CFVs, widely disseminated and consumed. The next chapter is an attempt to de-mythify those explanations. But before we get to that, let us examine what the existing explanations are.

The most common cause attributed in the media for a CFV is 'unprovoked firing'. Until 2012, Indian sources commonly reported the cause of CFVs to be closely associated with infiltration bids. From 2013 onwards, the reports do not seem to link CFVs with infiltration bids. In the years 2013, 2014, and 2015, 'construction work', 'intentional firing to obstruct work', 'ambush by security forces', and 'intrusion' have also been noted as causes of CFVs. In 2015 and 2014, there was one media report each, linking CFVs with construction activity along the LoC/IB. For instance, the CFV reported on 23 October 2015 in the Samba sector on the IB stated that the violation was intended at 'targeting BSF Naka mound and civilian labourers who were carrying out construction work on the culvert inside the Indian Territory in the Samba sector'.[73] In similar vein, on 30 November 2014, a CFV that was reported also in the Samba sector stated that 'Pakistan rangers on Sunday opened fire on Indian border posts after objecting to construction by Border Security Force on the Indian side in Samba sector in Jammu and Kashmir'.[74]

The data collected from open sources have sometimes, though not very frequently, mentioned 'inadvertent crossing' by itself as a cause for CFV on the LoC or IB. The *Hindu* reported on 20 October 2014 that there was an intentional CFV by the Pakistani troops in Jammu sector to prevent farmers from harvesting their crops.

---

[73] 'Pakistan Provokes India Again, Kills Labourer on International Border', *DNA*, 24 October 2015, available at http://www.dnaindia.com/india/report-pakistan-provokes-india-again-kills-labourer-on-international-border-2137893, last accessed on 3 April 2016.

[74] 'We are constructing a boundary wall in the area inside our territory. This is part of the construction project to provide better living condition to our forces, to which Pakistani side has regularly raised objection', a senior BSF official said. He said that a party of the Pakistani Rangers asked the Indian side to stop the construction work, which the BSF refused. See: 'Pakistan violates Ceasefire, Objects to Construction on Indian Side', *Hindu*, 30 November 2014, available at http://www.thehindu.com/news/national/pakistan-violates-ceasefire-objects-to-construction-on-indian-side/article6648688.ece, last accessed on 23 March 2017.

What do government reports say about the causes behind CFVs? Here's a flavour. The 2014–15 annual report of the Indian MoD says that 'the terrorist infrastructure across the border remains intact and Pakistan's frustration manifested itself in CFVs and high-visibility, audacious attacks by foreign terrorists'.[75] The following year, the annual report said that CFVs were politically motivated: 'Pakistan continues to calibrate violence to keep the LC alive and to showcase issue of unresolved/unsettled borders in J&K'.[76] The 2016–17 report says that Pakistan-based 'outfits continued to be encouraged to infiltrate into India under the cover of massive cross-LoC and cross-border firing in Jammu and Kashmir and other areas throughout the year'.[77]

The 2015–16 annual report of the MEA has this to say about the causes of CFVs: 'Continued terrorism emanating from Pakistan remained a core concern. The months of July and August saw an increase in the number of Cease Fire Violations (CFVs) and unprovoked firing, along the International Border (IB) and Line of Control (LoC), leading to death of defence personnel and civilians'.[78] In October 2015, Abhishek Singh from the Permanent Mission of India to the United Nations stated at the UN: 'The world knows that the primary reason for firing is to provide cover to terrorists crossing the border. It needs no imagination to figure out which side initiates this exchange'.[79] The director general of BSF stated in

[75] Ministry of Defence, *Annual Report 2014–15* (New Delhi: Ministry of Defence, Government of India), available at http://ddpmod.gov.in/sites/default/files/Annual%20report%202014-2015.pdf, last accessed on 27 June 2017.

[76] Ministry of Defence, *Annual Report 2015–16* (New Delhi: Ministry of Defence, Government of India), available at http://ddpmod.gov.in/sites/default/files/Annual%20Report%20MOD_2016.pdf, last accessed on 27 June 2017.

[77] Ministry of Defence, *Annual Report 2016–17* (New Delhi: Ministry of Defence, Government of India), available at http://www.mod.nic.in/writereaddata/AnnualReport1617.pdf, last accessed on 27 June 2017.

[78] Ministry of External Affairs, *Annual Report 2015–16* (New Delhi: Ministry of External Affairs, Government of India), available at https://www.mea.gov.in/Uploads/PublicationDocs/26525_26525_External_Affairs_English_AR_2015-16_Final_compressed.pdf, last accessed on 27 June 2017.

[79] 'India Responds to Nawaz Sharif's U.N. speech', *Hindu*, 1 October 2015, http://www.thehindu.com/news/national/india-responds-to-nawaz-sharifs-speech-at-un/article7710260.ece, last accessed on 3 March 2017.

November 2015 that the 'Pakistan Army engages in wilful violation of the ceasefire agreement along the Line of Control so as to provide fire cover to infiltrators'.[80]

Reasons identified by analysts have been more diverse and non-uniform in terms of what causes CFVs. There is a wide range of arguments in the public domain. Betwa Sharma argued that 'Pakistan's ceasefire violations have often been aimed at helping militants cross the border/ LoC'.[81] Pushpta Das of the Institute of Defence Studies and Analyses (IDSA), a Delhi-based think tank of the Indian MoD, identifies two causes—to provide cover fire to terrorists and traffickers attempting to infiltrate into India, and to contest the status of the border in Jammu.[82] Anil Khamboj attributes the reason to the Pakistan Army's attempt at derailing the IndiaPakistan peace process: 'Whenever there had been any initiative for peace process or bilateral talks between India and Pakistan, ceasefire violation occurred.'[83] Kashmir-based journalist Shujaat Bukhari attributes CFVs to defence construction in the border areas.[84] Academic Sreeram Chaulia argues that 'much of the bad blood at the LoC is linked to infiltration of jihadists into India from Pakistani terrain under the cover of official army shelling'.[85] Zahoor Ahmad Rather and Deepika

---

[80] 'Escalating the Proxy War', Pioneer, 30 November 2015, available at http://www.dailypioneer.com/columnists/edit/escalating-the-proxy-war.html, last accessed on 1 December 2016.

[81] Betwa Sharma, 'Why India Needs To Read Nawaz Sharif's UNGA Speech More Closely', Huffington Post, 1 October 2015, available at http://www.huffingtonpost.in/2015/10/01/nawaz-sharif_n_8225782.html?m=false, last accessed on 3 April 2017.

[82] Pushpita Das, 'Issues in the Management of the India–Pakistan International Border', Strategic Analysis 38, no. 3 (2014): 307–24.

[83] Debobrat Ghose, 'Why is Pakistan Violating Ceasefire along LoC? Because It Needs to Prop Up India as External Enemy, Say Experts', Firstpost, 18 August 2015, available at http://www.firstpost.com/india/why-is-pakistan-violating-ceasefire-along-loc-because-it-needs-to-prop-up-india-as-external-enemy-say-experts-2396422.html, last accessed on 22 December 2016.

[84] 'Ceasefire Violations', Frontline, http://www.frontline.in/the-nation/ceasefire-violations/article5037702.ece, last accessed on 12 January 2017.

[85] Sreeram Chaulia, 'Ceasefire Violation: How India is Misreading the "Suicidal Logic" of Pakistani Army', Economic Times, 12 October 2014, available

Gupta argued that CFVs are used by the Pakistan Army to support the terror organizations in J&K.[86]

Praveen Swamy, one of the most informed and connected national security journalists in the country, argued in 2014 that 'to push enhanced numbers of jihadists into Kashmir, Pakistan needed to engage Indian defences on the LoC—creating gaps infiltrators could exploit'.[87] In his other reports, he has also identified construction activity as well as the unauthorized crossing of civilians as causes for CFVs.[88]

Retired Indian Army official Vivek Chadha, currently associated with IDSA, argues that it is part of Pakistan's larger strategy to keep the LoC destabilized.[89] Gen. (Retd) Dhruv Katoch links CFVs with Pakistan's domestic compulsions.[90] Gen. (Retd) Ata Hasnain identifies several causes for CFVs—from Pakistan's need to keep the Kashmir issue alive[91] to aiding infiltration into J&K, and as 'an instrument of diplomacy to send

---

at https://economictimes.indiatimes.com/news/politics-and-nation/ceasefire-violation-how-india-is-misreading-the-suicidal-logic-of-pakistani-army/articleshow/44784759.cms, last accessed on 22 December 2017.

[86] Zahoor Ahmad Rather and Deepika Gupta, 'Ceasefire Violation—Pakistan's Transgression on the line of Control, A Situation growing more Serious', *International Research Journal of Social Sciences* 3, no. 1 (January 2014), http://www.isca.in/IJSS/Archive/v3/i1/9.ISCA-IRJSS-2013-211.pdf, last accessed on 20 July 2017.

[87] Praveen Swami, 'Shooting Ourselves in the Foot', *Indian Express*, 21 October 2014, available at http://indianexpress.com/article/opinion/columns/shooting-ourselves-in-the-foot/99/, last accessed on 22 December 2016.

[88] Praveen Swami, 'Runaway Grandmother Sparked Savage Skirmish on LoC', *Hindu*, 10 January 2013, available at http://www.thehindu.com/news/national/runaway-grandmother-sparked-savage-skirmish-on-loc/article4291426.ece, last accessed on 22 December 2016.

[89] Ask an Expert, 'Abhinav Upadhyay Asked: In the Backdrop of Recent Skirmishes Along the LoC, How Can India Create Strong Disincentives for Such Hostile Actions by Pakistan?', Institute of Defence Studies and Analyses, available at http://www.idsa.in/askanexpert/recentskirmishesalongtheLoC, last accessed on 22 December 2016.

[90] Ghose, 'Why Is Pakistan Violating Ceasefire along LoC?'.

[91] Syed Ata Hasnain, 'Looking beyond a Tattered Truce', *Hindu*, 1 October 2014, available at http://www.thehindu.com/opinion/op-ed/looking-beyond-a-tattered-truce/article6367256.ece, last accessed on 21 March 2017.

veiled messages.[92] By far the best, though extremely brief, account of why CFVs take place is provided by Gen. (Retd) Ashok Mehta: to keep 'the LoC hot and alive in order to internationalize the Kashmir issue'; feuding local commanders; testing the mettle of opposing new battalions on the LoC; tit-for-tat tactical responses; aiding infiltration and maintaining moral ascendency across the Line; Border Action Teams (BAT) laying ambushes; and planting IEDs and raiding posts.[93]

As is to be expected, the Pakistani arguments have been exactly the opposite. Former Pakistan high commissioner to India Abdul Basit stated in August 2015 that unprovoked firing by the Indian side leads to CFVs.[94] Director general South Asia division at Pakistan's Foreign Office in Islamabad, Mohammad Faisal, claimed in 2015 that 'Indian troops are deliberately targeting the civilian population.'[95] Pakistan's army chief Gen. Qamar Javed Bajwa argued in February 2017 that India engages in unprovoked CFVs along the LoC: 'On one side it is an effort to divert world's attention from her [Indian] atrocities against the innocent Kashmiris, and on the other, it is an attempt to dilute our response against terrorism and militancy.'[96] In October 2016, Foreign Office spokesperson Nafees Zakaria stated that 'during the 2014 provincial assembly elections (in J&K), India violated ceasefire agreement more than 200 times' and that Pakistan 'never violated the ceasefire agreement.'[97] In November

[92] Ghose, 'Why Is Pakistan Violating Ceasefire along LoC?'.

[93] Ashok K. Mehta, 'A Line without Ceasefires', Hindu, 18 October 2014, available at http://www.thehindu.com/opinion/lead/a-line-without-ceasefires/article6512297.ece, last accessed on 22 December 2016.

[94] 'Ceasefire Violations: Pak Envoy Abdul Basit Blames India Even as Firing Continues', DNA, 16 August 2015, available at http://www.dnaindia.com/india/report-ceasefire-violations-pak-envoy-abdul-basit-blames-india-even-as-firing-continues-2115049, last accessed on 22 December 2017.

[95] Ali Hussain, 'India Wants to Discuss Only Terrorism, NA Body Told', Business Recorder, 2017, available at http://epaper.brecorder.com/m/2015/10/28/11-page/538022-news.html, last accessed on 22 December 2017.

[96] Tariq Naqash, 'Pakistan Aware of Designs behind Ceasefire Violations: COAS', Dawn, 22 February 2017, available at https://www.dawn.com/news/1316231, last accessed on 22 March 2017.

[97] Syed Sammer Abbas, '"India Violated Ceasefire Agreement More than 90 Times This Year", FO Claims', Dawn, 17 October 2016, available at https://www.dawn.com/news/1290533, last accessed on 1 March 2017.

2016, a Pakistan National assembly resolution condemned 'unprovoked firing by the Indian forces' on the border.[98]

This cursory analysis, which represents a cross-section of opinions in India and Pakistan on why CFVs occur, shows that a vast majority of the analysis falls severely short in throwing adequate light on why CFVs take place. Even the rare analysis that gives a little glimpse about the multi-causality behind CFVs does not seem to provide any detailed, explanatory analysis.

***

The discussion in this chapter has clearly shown that CFVs are not a new phenomenon that began after the 2003 CFA agreed to by the two militaries. There is a history to it. Ever since the 1948 ceasefire came into force and the signing of the Karachi Agreement the following year, there have been CFVs. However, their frequency, intensity, purpose, and impact have changed depending on a variety of factors, including the thinking within Pakistan on the Kashmir issue, domestic politics in J&K, the impact of a war (like 1965, 1971) on the two parties, and the manner in which the two sides have engaged in a dialogue with each other on the Kashmir question. The difference between post-2003 and after the previous CFAs is that CFVs have a tendency to trigger escalation today unlike in the previous decade. One reasons could be the fact that the CFVs do not remain unknown to the larger public today.

It is important to keep in mind this broad-stroke historical narrative that this chapter has offered while we attempt to understand the causes and impact of contemporary CFVs in J&K.

It is also pertinent to note that the two governments do not have any viable mechanisms on the ground to control the outbreak of CFVs; even the mechanisms they have had (such as the Karachi Agreement of 1948 and the ground rules agreement of 1961) have been rendered unenforceable over the years. As a result, the two countries are left with hardly any legal or treaty mechanisms to deal with CFVs.

---

[98] Ijaz Kakakhel, 'Lower House Blasts India over Ceasefire Violations at LoC', *Daily Times*, 19 November 2016, available at http://dailytimes.com.pk/pakistan/19-Nov-16/lower-house-blasts-india-over-ceasefire-violations-at-loc, last accessed on 22 March 2017.

What is also clear from the previous discussion is that CFAs (be it the one following the Karachi Agreement, or the CFA that ended the 1965 war or the 1971 war or the 2003 agreement) tend to hold: (*i*) for a few years after the agreement has been arrived at by the two sides and (*ii*) when the two countries have a dialogue process, especially on the J&K question. These two factors have been constant since 1947.

The data presented in this chapter also underlines that the data made available from official sources have very little explanatory power to tell us where CFVs happen, let alone tell us why they happen. The data set created by this book using open sources (newspapers from India and Pakistan), though not numerically robust, has been more successful in throwing light on the locations of CFVs on the LoC and IB in J&K. The information of the locations of CFVs thus collected show that CFVs, in general, tend to occur in six locations. The most affected areas by CFVs on the Indian side are Poonch and Jammu followed by Samba and Rajouri. All four places started witnessing higher incidence of CFVs from 2012. On the Pakistan side, the areas with high incidence of CFVs are Sialkot, Rawalakot, Kotli, and Shakargarh. These areas also witnessed high incidence of CFVs in 2013, 2014, and 2015. These eight highly CFV-prone locations are in corresponding locations on either side of the LoC and IB/WB. Two each of these locales are guarded by the Indian and Pakistani armies and two each by the BSF and Rangers. The next chapter will throw more light on why CFVs are concentrated in these areas.

While the data set offered in this book tells us more about CFVs in terms of where they occur, it still does not tell us why they occur. The staple of reasons cited in the official and non-official literature is uninspiring. This then means that there is a need to go beyond the official as well as the open source data in order to understand why CFVs occur. This book does precisely that, in the next chapter, by collecting oral evidence from both India and Pakistan to examine the causes of CFVs.

5   Military Gamesmanship and Moral Ascendency

Explaining Ceasefire Violations

At times, we do not even take the government into confidence. You just say that it happened. Let us say I want to do an operation as an army commander. Something happens and I am asked what is happening, there are some reports, and so on. I will say that the enemy had attacked us and we responded and captured a post—in any case, it was always ours ... they had illegally claimed it.

—Lt Gen. (Retd) H.S. Panag[1]

WHY DO CFVs HAPPEN? We have already examined the standard existing explanations in the official and even non-official discourses on why CFVs take place, and why they are sorely inadequate. This chapter probes deeper and offers several fresh explanations for CFVs.

The previous chapter discussed the various ceasefires between India and Pakistan in the past and showed that there is a history of violence along the India–Pakistan border in J&K preceding the CFA of 2003. It also analysed the data on CFVs to determine their locations and timelines. It concluded with a brief assessment of the conventional discourses regarding what causes CFVs. This chapter unearths several hitherto unexamined causes behind the CFVs in J&K. Although the focus of this chapter is to explain the triggers for the CFVs from 2003 onwards, several of these causative explanations pre-date 2003, especially the 1990s when the firing between the two forces were at a high, or as many officers describe it as 'a free-for-all era'.

---

[1] Interview with Lt Gen. (Retd) H.S. Panag, 19 September 2016, Chandigarh.

This chapter discusses the causes of CFVs using a template of five specific types of causes: operational reasons, politico-strategic reasons, retributive reasons, cultural factors, and inadvertent firing. The order in which these causes have been identified here is based on their ability to cause CFVs.

This chapter also explains CFVs using the concept of AMFs, which was discussed in Chapter 2. A large chunk of the causes of CFVs as identified below falls under the category of AMFs.

Table 5.1 categorizes the causes of CFVs based on their type, key features, relationship with AMFs, impact on CFVs, the kind of CBMs are required to address them, and their relative ranking based on this ability to cause CFVs.

Table 5.1 A detailed typology of CFVs[2]

	Types of CFVs				
	Politico-strategic	Retributive	Operational	Inadvertent	Cultural factors
Key features	Kashmir; leaders visiting; important days; summit meetings; domestic political angles; aggressive governments; UNMOGIP visits	Land grab attempts; sniping leading to CFVs; revenge firing and 'honour killings'; 'surgical strikes'; sabotage; 'releasing pressure elsewhere'	Defence construction on the LoC and IB in J&K, and fence repair; lack of clarity of the line leading to land grab; personality traits of commanders; emotional state and CFVs; command and control (C&C) issues;	Lack of clarity of the line leading to inadvertent crossing; accidental firing and CFVs; unauthorized crossing of civilians	Honour and prestige; 'moral ascendancy'; testing the 'new boys'

[2] The author is grateful to Toby Dalton for suggesting the importance of a typology.

	Types of CFVs				
	Politico-strategic	Retributive	Operational	Inadvertent	Cultural factors
			institutional mechanisms		
Impact on CFVs	Moderate to high	Low to moderate	High	Low to moderate	Moderate to high
Relationship with AMFs	Low	Moderate to high	High	High	High
What kind of CBMs needed	Political CBMs and rapprochement	Military CBMs, more flag meetings, DGMO meetings	CBMs relating to management of LoC and more meetings between the two militaries	Military CBMs, more flag meetings, DGMO meetings	Military CBMs, more flag meetings, DGMO meetings
Ranking	2	3	1	5	4

Source: Author.

Terrorist Infiltration and CFVs: A Revisionist Account

On the Pakistani side, till 1993–94, the firing used to be to divert the Army or BSF attention from a particular area, so that we could push people through or receive people from the other side. People would come from Indian Kashmir to train.

—Retired Pakistani Lt General[3]

It is a very wrong thing to say that to cover infiltration, they are firing. To cover infiltration, you want the people to be relaxing rather than being alert. It is a known and acknowledged fact that if the enemy is asleep, relaxing, and not alert, the infiltration is easier.

—Lt Gen. (Retd) T.K. Sapru[4]

[3] Interview with Retired Pakistani Lt General on condition of anonymity, 2016.
[4] Interview with Lt Gen. (Retd) T.K. Sapru, 10 October 2016, Chandigarh.

They want to help the infiltration by firing on the posts so that the attention gets diverted to the cross L[o]C firing. If he is firing at you, you also fire back, so you will be engaging him. This is giving an opportunity to the infiltrator to intrude in one hour or two to three hours.

—Lt Gen. (Retd) Om Prakash[5]

Let me begin this chapter by de-mythifying the prominent causal linkage that is often made between CFVs and terrorist infiltration into J&K from Pakistan. New Delhi and several analysts, as highlighted in the previous chapter, have consistently made the argument that one of the major reasons for CFVs is the infiltration attempt by Pakistan-based terrorists into J&K, that Pakistani forces initiate covering fire for militants seeking to cross the border. However, as the above-mentioned statements indicate that such an argument is not without inherent complications.

Those supporting the 'infiltration-leads-to-CFVs' logic argue that this is an undeniable fact. The Pakistani side, they say, would 'fire to support, assist, confuse, divert you'[6] and to keep 'our heads down'.[7] Brig. Kanwal makes the argument more nuanced by saying, 'If they want surprise, they will not fire. If there is interception and the Pak guy on the post can see that the firing has broken out at the Indian side, then they will fire back— advance support to infiltrators by firing does not make sense but this is often used as an excuse to fire back'.[8] In other words, the infiltration-CFV link is a complicated one.

There are also other ways in which terrorists can trigger CFVs between the two armies. A senior retired Indian general recounted a case in which a few militants fired on the Indian soldiers and ran, provoking Indian retaliation against a Pakistani post, which in turn provoked Pakistani counter-fire.[9] Col Shukla argues that around 50 per cent of all CFVs are infiltration-related, and says that 'the day infiltration stops, you can have ceasefire on the LoC that actually works'.[10] Indian officers also accuse Pakistani forces of planting mines or IEDs on the Indian

[5] Interview with Lt Gen. (Retd) Om Prakash, 27 September 2016, Gurgaon.
[6] Interview with Lt Gen. (Retd) J.P. Nehra, 3 December 2016, New Delhi; Interview with BSF Officer 1, 2 June 2016, Jammu.
[7] Interview with Lt Gen. (Retd) A.S. Nandal, 23 September 2016, Gurgaon.
[8] Interview with Brig. (Retd) Gurmeet Kanwal, 4 May 2016, Bangkok.
[9] Interview with Senior Retired Indian Army Official, 22 January 2016, New Delhi.
[10] Interview with Col Ajai Shukla, 6 September 2016, New Delhi.

side in order to curtail Indian reconnaissance activities and to facilitate infiltration.[11] Infiltrators could also get caught in them, but if indeed the Pakistani forces have planted them, they would be able to guide the former on how to navigate them.

Some Pakistanis agree that there was a time when infiltration-linked CFVs used to happen, during the thick of the Kashmir insurgency. A senior retired Pakistani general, for instance, said, requesting anonymity, that 'on the Pakistani side, till 1993–4, the firing used to be to divert the army's or BSF's attention from a particular area, so that we could push people through or receive people from the other side. People would come from Indian Kashmir to train.'[12] Another Pakistani general uses a different logic to explain the occurrence of CFVs: 'When an Indian unit, which is going back from the LoC for administrative or other reasons, gets ambushed on the way back, and its soldiers are wounded or killed, then in anger, Indian posts open fire on locals on the Pakistan side and even target Pakistani posts. This, then, becomes a CFV and it can escalate further.'[13] Aziz Ahmed Khan, former Pakistani high commissioner to India, says that the Pakistan Army giving aid to militants ended in 2004: 'I am personally convinced also that the official, as India claims, patronage of cross-LoC infiltration was given up by us in 2004 and we have stuck by that. The Pakistani side says that they are no longer interested in infiltration. That part is over.'[14]

While terrorist infiltration is often made out to be a key reason behind CFVs, officers based on the ground say that this might sometimes take place but not very frequently, especially since the fence has come up.

In any case, data does not seem to support the infiltration-leads-to-CFVs theory. If we juxtapose the data on infiltration and CFVs, there appears no correlation between militant infiltration and CFVs in J&K.

Table 5.2 and Figure 5.1, based on official Indian data on CFVs and terrorist infiltration into J&K, show that even when CFVs were at their lowest in the 2004–7 period, instances of attempted infiltration were no less than 500. Moreover, when CFVs went up after 2011, infiltration was actually reported to have declined. This shows that the

[11] Interview with Indian Army Officer 4, 15 May 2016, Bhimber Gali.

[12] Interview with Retired Pakistani General (name withheld on request), April 2016, Bangkok.

[13] Interview with Pakistani Official 4, 17 January 2017, Rawalpindi.

[14] Interview with Aziz Ahmed Khan, 15 December 2016, Islamabad.

Table 5.2 Comparative data on CFVs and infiltration

Year	CFVs as per Indian official sources	Number of terrorists attempting to infiltrate—commonly referred to as 'infiltration attempts or infiltration bids'	Number of terrorists successfully infiltrating
2001	4,134 incidents of cross-LoC fire		
2002	5,767 incidents of cross-LoC fire	1,504	
2003	2,841 incidents of cross-LoC fire	1,314–73	
2004	4 (LoC-1)	507–37	
2005	6 (LoC)	597	231
2006	3 (LoC)	572–3	317
2007	21 (LoC)	535	311
2008	86 (77 LoC + 9 IB)	342	57
2009	35 (28 LoC + 9 IB)	485	113
2010	70 (44 LoC + 26 IB)	489	95
2011	62 (51 LoC + 11 IB)	247	52
2012	114 (93 LoC + 22 IB)	264	121
2013	347	277	97
2014	583	221–2	65
2015	405	121	36
2016	437	364	105

Source: Based on response by the MHA in the Parliament of India to Unstarred Questions 1336, 1112, 398, 917, 2146 and 2848, and Starred Question 90.

data does not support the argument about a direct link between CFVs and infiltration.

While one could potentially make the argument that the reduction in infiltration and increase in the CFVs are linked (that is, CFVs went up while foiling infiltration attempts), a consistent analysis of the data on CFVs and infiltration from 2004 to 2016 does not lend much credibility to such an argument. If the argument about the causative relationship

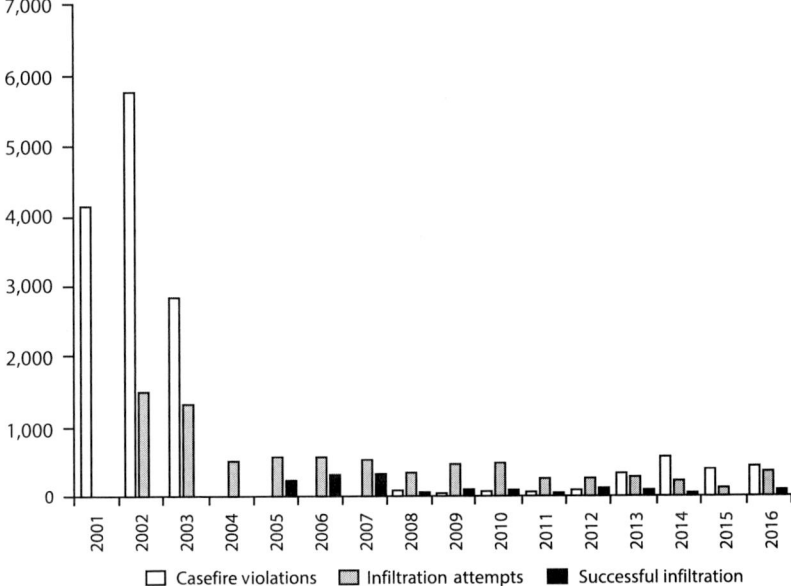

Figure 5.1 Comparing CFVs and terrorist infiltration attempts in J&K.
Source: Author (based on Table 5.2).

between CFVs and infiltration should hold, then there has to be a consistent relationship between the two data sets.

While interactions with military officers on both sides make it obvious that infiltration is indeed one of the triggers for CFVs, the data indicates that it is not one of the primary causes as is often claimed.

In other words, the argument here is not that CFVs and terrorist infiltration in J&K are not linked at all, but that the data does not support the claim that this is the 'most important cause', let alone the only cause behind CFVs, as claimed in the official Indian sources and by analysts.

More importantly, it is also not the argument that infiltration does not take place across the LoC or the IB in Jammu; they do as per official and unofficial accounts. Pakistan uses terror organizations in the larger context of conventional imbalance and strategic revisionism. However, the link between CFVs and infiltration is more tenuous than is usually understood.

If terrorist infiltration is not the primary reason behind CFVs, what are the causes of CFVs? The remainder of this chapter is an attempt to understand the several little-known factors that lead to CFVs between the two sides.

Operational Reasons

The most prominent reason for CFVs can be broadly categorized as 'operational reasons'. This broad category includes several causes such as defence construction and fence repair on the LoC and IB, lack of clarity of the LoC leading to land grab, personality traits of local commanders, emotional state and CFVs, C&C issues, and lack of institutional mechanisms.

Defence Construction on the LoC and IB

> *There's only one legality on the LoC—that is the sniper rifle. If you can do it without getting shot at, you will be able to do it. If I am a commander and someone cites the Karachi Agreement to me, I will say f*** the Karachi Agreement.*
>
> —Col Ajai Shukla, Indian Army[15]

Both Indian and Pakistani officials, serving as well as retired, cited defence construction along the two borders in J&K as a major contributing factor to CFVs. Surprisingly, however, neither the media nor official documents hardly ever mention it as one. The evidence gathered from interviews and field visits strongly supports the argument that construction-related activities form the most important trigger of CFVs.

The Karachi Agreement of 1949 stipulated that no new defence construction should be undertaken and no troops placed within 500 yards of the LoC. The restriction was reduced to 150 yards on the IB under the Border Ground Rules Agreement of 1960. At the Second Expert-Level Talks in August 2005, Pakistan proposed no defence works and no new posts, which India accepted. In January 2006, during the India–Pakistan foreign secretary talks in New Delhi, the Indian side gave the Pakistani side a non-paper[16]—an unsigned document that, because it cites no

---

[15] Interview with Col Ajai Shukla, 6 September 2016, New Delhi.

[16] 'On India–Pakistan Foreign Secretary Level Talks in New Delhi', Ministry of External Affairs, Government of India, available at http://www.mea.gov.in/media-briefings.htm?dtl/2730/On+IndiaPakistan+Foreign+Secretary+level+talks+in+New+Delhi, last accessed on 2 September 2016.

names and bears no signatures, can serve as a detailed yet deniable basis for a deal. In April that year, though they had held no related discussions since January, the two sides agreed at the third round of expert-level talks to not develop any 'new posts and defence works along the LoC'.

Despite these restrictions, new construction on both the LoC and the IB in Jammu is a regular occurrence, typically leading to a spate of CFVs. Field research in the area confirmed the presence of new defence construction within the restricted area. Officer interviewees, both serving and retired, also reported the existence of such construction, remarking that they often lead to CFVs. For instance, at the BOP Pittal in the Jammu sector, which is less than 150 yards from the border, officers posted there pointed out that they have built such constructions in the past 'but by the time the Rangers objected, it was late'.[17] Such construction activities happen on both sides of the LoC and IB/WB, as was observed during the field visits.

Open-source data compiled for this book show two instances of major CFVs being linked to construction activities. Two instances may not seem a lot, but it is important to note that causes of CFVs are almost never declared by either side except in vague terms. Therefore, even occasional references to a specific trigger are significant.

The issue of legality regarding new construction within 500/ 150 yards is complicated. Officials from the Indian MEA, as noted in the previous chapters, have consistently maintained that both the Karachi Agreement and the Ground Rules Agreement are not valid as opposed to the uniform Pakistani view that they are both valid on the ground. Army and BSF officials on the Indian side, both serving and retired, argue that given the fact that there is no other agreement that can be used to manage the borders, they abide by the ban on construction. And yet, as we shall see later, they regularly engage in construction activity within the 'prohibited' area provoking CFVs.

In any case, legality is for lip service. As Col Shukla forthrightly puts it: 'There's only one legality on the LoC—that is the sniper rifle. If you can do it without getting shot at, you will be able to do it. If I am a commander and someone cites the Karachi Agreement to me, I will say f*** the Karachi Agreement.'[18]

---

[17] Interview with BSF Officer 2, 2 June 2016, Jammu.
[18] Interview with Col Ajai Shukla, 6 September 2016, New Delhi.

The problem then is that there is no real agreement on defence construction along the LoC and IB/WB. As Gen. Tariq Majid points out, all we have is a 'tacit understanding'.

Gen. Hasnain admits that construction activity on the LoC is one of the main reasons for the infringement of the ceasefire. These activities, which typically take place at night by both India as well as Pakistan, lead to firing. He justifies the construction as the Simla Accord is silent on the issue, which effectively overrides the Karachi Agreement of 1949 that had prevented construction activity within 500 yards from the CFL (now LoC).[19]

Retired Pakistani general Sikander Afzal agrees that both sides engage in construction activities leading to CFVs. He describes how the dynamics progresses on the ground:

> When one side starts making bunkers, the other side will raise a flag (white flag for a meeting/red flag for a violation). Objection is indicated. If there is no response from the other side and work continues, then first a round of rifle shots are fired, then a few bursts of machine guns, then more machine guns—all at the target. The local commander will inform the top leadership about what has happened and what he is doing. If there is no negative reply, then the firing continues. This leads to counter-fire.[20]

It is easier to make bunkers in the LoC sector than in the IB sector given the fact that the latter is mostly flatland and defence construction on the flatland without drawing the adversary's attention is tough. Hence, Gen. Afzal says:

> The bunker construction is done in early summer—when the grasses grow up to a height of 3 feet so the other side cannot detect construction. That is why, in order to deny the other side the advantage, both sides set fire to the scrub and grass. The wind or breeze takes the fire on to the other side and burns the grass there and allows better visibility of what is happening on that side.[21]

Serving Pakistani officials also pointed out that disagreements between local commanders over a certain construction, fortification, and so on, can lead to CFVs.[22]

[19] Interview with Lt Gen. (Retd) Syed Ata Hasnain, 5 June 2015, New Delhi.
[20] Interview with Lt Gen. (Retd) Sikander Afzal, 16 April 2016, Bangkok.
[21] Interview with Lt Gen. (Retd) Sikander Afzal, 16 April 2016, Bangkok.
[22] Interview with Pakistani Official 1, 7 June 2016, Islamabad; Interview with Pakistani Official 2, 9 June 2016, Islamabad; Interview with Pakistani Official 3, 12 June 2016, Islamabad. All shared a similar assessment.

Both sides try to take all available precautions to ensure that their construction activity is undetected. They work at night, use camouflage, and make the most of thick foliage for additional cover. During a field visit to the IB in Punjab, where new construction within 150 yards is rare, construction activity on both sides was clearly under way at night. However, construction at night is resisted by the adversary by bringing in night vision equipment.[23]

Construction can be the result of a local need and decision or something that is approved from the higher-ups. Gen. Arshad explains the link between construction and CFVs:

> Sometimes construction is going on and you raise a flag or shout out but the other side does not stop. So, you fire a couple of shots on one side to send a message. The other side then turns around and fires back. This leads to a localized breakdown of ceasefire. At times, it does not expand, and at times, it does. But when it is a political decision to upgrade, then it is a widespread activity. This can lead to a lot of casualties as happened in 2013.[24]

Bhatia agrees to this link between CFVs and defence construction: 'I will raise the red flag and if he does not, I have the right to fire.'[25] A senior BSF officer in Jammu confirms that this is roughly the SOP followed in the IB as well with regard to objecting to fresh construction, but is quick to mention that construction remains a key cause behind CFVs.[26]

Engaging in constant construction on one's side and denying the other side an opportunity to construct is a never-ending game of wits being played by the two forces. Geographical advantage, concentration of forces, and availability of camouflage help either side to get the better of the other side. As Lt Gen. Nandal says matter-of-factly: 'If they are building up their defences, we have to fire. And similarly, they will fire if we construct. Neither wants the other to do up their defences.'[27]

---

[23] Interview with Lt Gen. (Retd) H.S. Panag, 19 September 2016, Chandigarh.

[24] Interview with Lt Gen. (Retd) Waheed Arshad, 15 April 2016, Bangkok.

[25] Interview with Lt Gen. (Retd) Vinod Bhatia, 19 September 2016, New Delhi.

[26] Interview with BSF Officer 1, 2 June 2016, Jammu; and interview with BSF Officer 4, 3 June 2016, Jammu.

[27] Interview with Lt Gen. (Retd) A.S. Nandal, 23 September 2016, Gurgaon.

In any case, engaging in defence construction is not a new pheno-menon. They have taken place prior to 2003 leading to firing. Brig. Kanwal recalls how during 2001–2 when he was posted in the Gurez sector in Kashmir, they had to engage in new construction. Gen. Majid concurs on the existence of new construction within the restricted area going way back to early 2000s.

Construction activity reached a new height during the peaceful period in the mid-2000s. As Col Shukla recalls, 'After the ceasefire, the construction became much more feasible and both sides took advantage of the ceasefire to improve defence works that had been falling into disrepair as a result of the constant firing.'[28] During this period, however, construction-related activities did not lead to CFVs.

Prior to 1971, it was difficult to make defence constructions at will given the presence of UNMOGIP. Post-1971, such considerations did not matter. As Gen. Panag recalls: 'Both sides have violated the (defence construction) norm with impunity over the years. Whatever area you have, constructions have been done. In the 1950s and 1960s, the UN observers would come and check. After that, it has never been respected.'[29] Elaborating the action–reaction firing resulting from defence construction, Gen. Panag says that if the other side objects to the construction, the constructing side would simply fire back. While UNMOGIP is present on the Pakistani side, Pakistani forces do not seem to bother about UNMOGIP while carrying out construction work, given that the UN body has virtually stopped telling either side how to manage the border. They merely send classified reports to the UN—hardly a deterrent.

Gen. Sapru contrasts the role the UN group played before 1971 and after 1971 with regard to inspecting new constructions by saying that prior to 1971, UNMOGIP would come very frequently and would go to the extent of checking the size of the loophole in the bunker. If the peephole was 10 by 10 inches and it had increased to 12 by 12 inches, the group would raise questions. Gen. Sapru recalls, the UNMOGIP 'had a record of all our field fortifications on all our posts, as to how many bunkers, trenches, firing ranges, and loopholes there are. We did entertain them before 1971 and we did adhere to whatever they said. After 1971, we have not accepted them at all, now we do not allow them to be anywhere close.'[30]

[28] Interview with Col Ajai Shukla, 6 September 2016, New Delhi.
[29] Interview with Lt Gen. (Retd) H.S. Panag, 3 March 2017, Bangkok.
[30] Interview with Lt Gen. (Retd) T.K. Sapru, 10 October 2016, Chandigarh.

Several serving Pakistani army officials who are deployed on the LoC indicated that new construction would lead to CFVs. Brig. Akhtar Khan agreed that the Pakistani side would fire when the Indian side reconstructs the fence that gets damaged after the winter snow melts (if the fence falls within 500 yards of the zero line).[31] Brig. Noor also pointed out that repair works of existing construction often invites firing. [32]

Most of the time, undertaking construction does not require the consent of the higher-ups. These activities are/were mostly local initiatives catering to local/tactical requirements.

WHY ARE DEFENCE CONSTRUCTIONS UNDERTAKEN?

Why would the two sides construct defence works if it could almost certainly lead to CFVs, and potential loss of life? There are several operational reasons for doing so. Here are a host of them.

Gen. Hasnain explains why it is sometimes important to make new constructions, from an Indian point of view:

> There are a few villages across the LoC fence that are not easily monitored. In the instant case, the local commander complained of not having enough observation facilities. He was allowed to construct a few bunkers in the area close to the LoC. This is how it started; the Pakistani side objected to the bunkers, fired on them and at the village, in which three civilians died; our side retaliated in which a JCO [junior commissioned officer] of the Pakistani army was killed. This led to escalation over a period of time and increase in tension, which, as usually happens, moved across the Inter-Corps boundary into the Mendhar-Poonch sector, culminating in the Pakistani action of ambush against an Indian Army patrol and beheading of two Indian soldiers.[33]

There are other reasons as well. Officers argue that because the terrain of LoC/IB is not even, not all posts are 500/150 yards from the zero line, so sometimes you need to rebuild/repair within 150 yards in order to observe movements near the zero line. Although repairs are not usually objected to, they could be if they are within 150 yards. The LoC, after all, is not the outcome of a well-thought-out exercise keeping in mind the

31 Interview with Brig. Akhtar Khan, 13 December 2017, Muzaffarabad.
32 Interview with Brig. Noor, 14 December 2017, Rawalakot.
33 Interview with Lt Gen. (Retd) Syed Ata Hasnain, 5 June 2015, New Delhi.

distance requirements of the Karachi Agreement; it is the line that came up when hostilities ceased in 1948.

During interactions with officers on the ground, what becomes clear is that they would need to engage in construction one way or another in order to be able to manage the border. As Gen. Bhatia says, 'Sometimes we have to and sometimes he has to (engage in construction).'[34] Gen. H.S. Panag, former Northern Army commander of the Indian Army, says, 'As an army commander, it did not even bother me … I authorized construction as per the operational situation.'[35] Gen. Ghazi says that when a new commander is appointed in a new area, he has his own plan as to how he wants to fight the battle, which could mean more construction.[36]

New construction is also linked to counter-infiltration strategies. The Indian side believes that they need to have posts at places because it gives them better observation and security, and better control over the area where infiltration is taking place,[37] or because new positions stem from the fact that, as Brig. Sahgal points out, 'soil erosions take place, the mountains are young, there is snowfall, now you're bringing in ground censors that must be deployed in such a way that they get a wide arc.'[38] Col Shukla explains how construction on the Pakistani side can aid an infiltrator: 'If you have allowed construction, then the infiltrator will just move from construction to construction and you will not be able to observe him.'[39]

One's ability to operate during tense periods becomes much better if there are adequate constructions like tunnels, passageways, ditches, and the like. Sometimes, construction is required to man one's own areas better.[40]

Yet another logic for bunker construction is that it is often a 'cyclical activity'. One side builds a bunker, and as a result, the other side has to adjust its own bunker in order to observe the other side. This, Gen. Yasin says, becomes a 'cycle of unending activity'.[41]

[34] Interview with Lt Gen. (Retd) Vinod Bhatia, 19 September 2016, New Delhi.
[35] Interview with Lt Gen. (Retd) H.S. Panag, 19 September 2016, Chandigarh.
[36] Interview with Lt Gen. (Retd) Tariq Ghazi, 7 November 2016, Bangkok.
[37] Interview with Lt Gen. (Retd) Waheed Arshad, 15 April 2016, Bangkok.
[38] Interview with Brig. (Retd) Arun Sahgal, 4 November 2016, Bangkok.
[39] Interview with Col Ajai Shukla, 6 September 2016, New Delhi.
[40] Interview with Lt Gen. (Retd) Tariq Ghazi, 7 November 2016, Bangkok.
[41] Interview with Lt Gen. (Retd) Yasin, 15 April 2016, Bangkok.

Why Is New Construction Objected To?

There are several reasons why new construction is objected to. One, it provides enhanced observation capability to the sides building it.[42] Two, during a stand-off, tactically built defence construction would help in holding ground.[43] As Indian general Nandal unambiguously put it, 'Someday we will have to launch an assault in war',[44] and the constructions of the adversary would become impediments. Gen. Sikander Afzal pointed out that 'construction strengthens the other side's capability to fire back'.[45] Moreover, as Pakistan's Waheed Arshad observed, 'It also gives more military advantage to the side which has better positions, more positions, and flexibility at the tactical and sub-tactical level. A ceasefire can break down ... then what? There is a military connotation to it.'[46]

In short then, the rampant defence construction is driven by the need for enhanced observation capability as well as to prepare for higher military contingencies, which often in turn lead to a cyclical process of reaction to the other side's construction.

What Kind of Construction Is Allowed?

There is a clear lack of clarity about what kind of construction is allowed and what is not, which complicates matters even more. Some officers argue that although new construction is explicitly not permitted, repair work on existing construction is allowed, which could include increasing the height of existing construction or expanding construction within the same premise. There is, however, no consensus on this.

On the distinction between new construction and maintenance works, Gen. Tariq Majid explained:

> An upkeep of the existing defence structures and restoration of their damaged parts forms part of the maintenance / repair work but any addition or modification to an existing structure that helps improve defence posture or combat capability is viewed in excess of the maintenance work and, therefore, is disallowed by the opponent side.[47]

[42] Interview with Lt Gen. (Retd) Om Prakash, 27 September 2016, Gurgaon.
[43] Interview with Lt Gen. (Retd) Sikandar Afzal, 16 April 2016, Bangkok.
[44] Interview with Lt Gen. (Retd) A.S. Nandal, 23 September 2016, Gurgaon.
[45] Interview with Lt Gen. (Retd) Sikander Afzal, 16 April 2016, Bangkok.
[46] Interview with Lt Gen. (Retd) Waheed Arshad, 15 April 2016, Bangkok.
[47] Interview with Lt Gen. (Retd) Tariq Majid, 14 April 2016, Bangkok.

By giving an example, he further clarified:

> A defended post normally comprises an assortment of fighting, observation, living, and storage bunkers as well as communication trenches. If any of these get damaged due to weather hazards like excessive snow or rains, the repair of the damaged parts would be taken as maintenance work and is normally not objected to. However, if in the process, any additional bunker is constructed or alterations are made to reconfigure the bunkers/post, it will be contested.[48]

Brig. Ali echoes Gen. Majid's argument that already existing constructions can be improved with prior notification to the other side about the work that will be undertaken. Gen. Afzal also claims that repair works are allowed: 'The other side is not stopped from repairs. The unwritten rule is to inform the other side that repair work is being done. Extension of existing bunker is considered as new construction. Living bunkers are invariably on the reverse slope and not visible to the enemy side. So they will not matter.'[49]

There is also a difference between extension and improvement. While an improvement of the existing construction is fine, extension is not. In explaining this concept, Arshad says, 'A post is a set of living and fighting bunkers—three or five or 10 bunkers. Extension may mean from four to six bunkers, so extension is not accepted. Anything which is subject to interpretation is a conflict issue. Living bunkers nobody bothers mostly because they are normally in the rear.'[50] This is confusing given that some officers I talked to confirmed that extension is not new construction. I also witnessed such extension works happening on both sides.

Some other officers take a completely different view. Bhatia, for instance, says that even modifications to the existing construction are not allowed. Lt Gen. (Retd) Tariq Ghazi, former Pakistan defence secretary, brings up a new complication about the issue of new construction. According to him, when old constructions made with wood and mud are replaced with new ones made from concrete, there could be CFVs. Moreover, he argues that either side is unlikely to let the adversary improve or add upon what existed on the front line. Between improvement

---

[48] Interview with Lt Gen. (Retd) Tariq Majid, 14 April 2016, Bangkok.
[49] Interview with Brig. (Retd) Ghazanfar Ali, 11 April 2016, Lahore.
[50] Interview with Lt Gen. (Retd) Waheed Arshad, 15 April 2016, Bangkok.

and addition, he says, the latter is unacceptable.[51] However, a lot of surreptitious improvement takes place.

Another interpretation about new construction that this author heard from officers posted on the LoC on the Indian side is that what gives the adversary a military advantage is what is objected to usually. In other words, given the rampant construction that happens on the LoC and IB, what the other side looks at is whether something gives the side that is constructing a military advantage or not. As a senior army officer in Tangdhar argues, 'A post consists of multiple bunkers. If a new bunker is constructed within a post, it is not objected to. However, if within 25 metres from a bunker, another construction is carried out, then there can be objection.'[52] Pakistani officials point out that the SOP is that if any side wishes to re-build a fallen wall or to undertake repair works, it has to raise a white flag to notify the other side.[53]

The other issue to be considered is the repair works on the Indian border fence after the winter snow and rainfall. Since the fence is often within the 150/500-yard limit, the repair works carried out on it often leads to firing. Pakistani officials confirm this: 'The fencing done by India along the LoC gets damaged during the snowfall. In certain sectors, Indian forces attempt to repair it, which is a blatant violation, as Kashmir being a disputed territory, no side can fence it. Pakistan continues to contest such fencing efforts.'[54]

Moreover, the determination of whether a particular construction is within 150/500 yards or not is often made with the naked eye.[55] Col Shukla stresses that even though the estimation is made with the naked eye, thanks to the lack of any other verification mechanism, such estimates are pretty accurate:

In every OP [observation post], you have an observation chart in front of you giving the precise distance. Other than that, there is whole system of visual estimation. For instance, how large a figure appears at a

51 Interview with Lt Gen. (Retd) Tariq Ghazi, 7 November 2016, Bangkok.
52 Interview with Indian Army Officer 7, 16 May 2016, Tangdhar (J&K).
53 Interview with Pakistani Official 1, 7 June 2016, Islamabad; Interview with Pakistani Official 2, 9 June 2016, Islamabad; Interview with Pakistani Official 3, 12 June 2016, Islamabad.
54 Interview with Pakistan Army Officer 3, 12 June 2016, Islamabad.
55 Interview with BSF Officer 1, 2 June 2016, Jammu.

certain distance. As a trained soldier, you will know how the figure will appear at 200, at 300, and at 600. At 600, you know it becomes difficult to estimate the movement of the limbs. At 500, it fits on your foresight. These are all things that we know as soldiers.[56]

And yet, disputes on the determination of the distance can also lead to stand-offs. The absence of a mutually accepted system to verify the distance leads to a situation where both sides raise objections to any construction they can see, whether or not it is within the prescribed area which, as a result, becomes a tit-for-tat situation.[57]

What seems to be clear then is that there exists an ad hoc arrangement on the LoC and IB/WB regarding defence construction within 500/150 yards: whether or not it will be objected to depends on a number of subjective factors such as how the adversary views a certain construction, the measure of the distance made with naked eye by the adversary, and the tactical advantage that a certain construction provides, among others.

Even though both sides make fresh constructions, they are not unanimous about legally allowing new construction. On why Pakistan may not accept an agreement on allowing new construction within the 150/500 yards, Tariq Majid says, 'The idea was to reduce deployments as much, so that the possibility of escalation reduces. The LoC, although not demarcated, is generally well known to both sides. The focus is to be thinning or maintaining the existing levels of existing constructions on the LOC since it is not the permanent line.'[58]

Lack of Clarity of the Line

> *There is no clarity with respect to the Line of Control. The clarity is with respect to perceptions.*
>
> —Brig. (Retd) Arun Sahgal[59]

Sometimes, though infrequently, lack of clarity of the line can lead to stand-offs and CFVs. As pointed out earlier, unlike the IB in Punjab, Rajasthan, Sindh, and Gujarat, the Kashmir LoC is not surveyed and demarcated by the two countries' official surveyors. Moreover, unlike in

---

[56] Interview with Col Ajai Shukla, 6 September 2016, New Delhi.
[57] Interview with Rakesh Sharma, 15 September 2016, New Delhi; and interview with Lt Gen. (Retd) Om Prakash, 27 September 2016, Gurgaon.
[58] Interview with Lt Gen. (Retd) Tariq Majid, 14 April 2016, Bangkok.
[59] Interview with Brig. (Retd) Arun Sahgal, 4 November 2016, Bangkok.

Jammu, there are not even pillars (even though Jammu has pillars, they are not recognized by Pakistan) on the LoC. As a result, sometimes there could be a genuine confusion on the ground, especially after the winter snow, heavy rains, or similar natural developments. Rivers sometimes change course and the previously understood LoC could become confusing. Or sometimes such developments could be used as a cover for deliberate incursions. Gen. Bhatia points out that sometimes the Pakistani soldiers get confused about the zero line since Pakistan does not have a fence along the LoC. They could sometimes get lost or disoriented and lose the way.

Brig. (Retd) Naeem Salik agrees that there are occasional issues relating to clarity on the ground: 'It is not a straight line—it zigzags and goes back and forth. If you are going from one post to another, and in between there is an intervening area which belongs to the other side, it can be mistaken.'[60] He says, for instance, that in the Sialkot/Jammu sector, people do get lost particularly near the river Ravi since there is a lot of undergrowth in those areas.

In any case, as pointed out earlier, the LoC has only been delineated on a map and not demarcated on the ground. Translating what is on the map to how it should be on the ground could pose a major problem. Gen. Panag explains: 'You mark it on a large-scale map with a thick pen and translate it onto a small-scale map—there is bound to be dispute here and dispute there.'[61] He has written elsewhere explaining this issue further: 'When the Line of Control was demarcated after the Simla Agreement, it was done with a 'thick pen' on a small scale map—1/4 inch to a mile or one centimetre to 2.5 km scale. Once interpreted on a large-scale map—one inch to a mile or one centimetre to 500 metres—the differences become glaring, with claims and counter claims by both sides on the ground.'[62]

So when we read together the lack of absolute clarity on the ground and the occasional jostling for small chunks of land, what emerges is high potential for CFVs, as has happened in the past, deliberately or otherwise.

[60] Interview with Brig (Retd) Naeem Ahmad Salik, 13 April 2016, Bangkok.

[61] Interview with Lt Gen. (Retd) H.S. Panag, 3 March 2017, Bangkok.

[62] Lt Gen. H.S. Panag, 'The "Lost" Operation against Pakistan in Chorbat-la', New Laundry, 14 September 2014, available at https://www.newslaundry. com/2016/09/14/the-lost-operation-against-pakistan-in-chorbat-la,   last accessed on 2 September 2016.

In September 2016, it was reported that an Indian soldier, Chandu Chavan, 'inadvertently crossed over' from his post on the Mendhar sector of the LoC.[63] In February 2013, Pakistan reported a similar incident of a Pakistani soldier crossing over to the Indian side in the Khoi Ratta sector.[64] If indeed these were inadvertent crossings, the argument that the lack of clarity or confusion about the zero line could contribute to the inadvertent crossings has some merit, which further strengthens the argument that there could be genuine confusion about the zero line.

Brig. Kanwal supports this theory, arguing that while in strongly held areas like Tangdhar, the LoC is well understood, in lightly held areas such as Gurez and Machil, it is more of a perception: 'So when I construct a bunker where I think my territory lies, the Pakistani guy fires because he says it is on their side.'[65] Weather can cause lack of clarity on the LoC. A serving Indian brigadier in Kashmir agrees and says that 'on the ground, the LoC is an assumed line.'[66]

However, most officials say that clarity is only a problem in rare circumstances. When asked whether non-demarcation of the LoC causes ambiguity amongst troops on either side and the resulting wrong perception of transgression could lead to escalation, Gen. Tariq Majid replied, 'The LOC, though not demarcated on the ground, is generally well known to troops on both sides. Given the difficult nature of terrain along the LoC, however, the possibility of misunderstanding sometimes cannot be ruled out.'

Sometimes, when new units arrive, the adversary tries to take advantage by edging past the traditionally held area, thinking that the new unit may not know the existing positions that well. Gen. Panag describes a scenario wherein it is possible for such mind games to translate into

---

[63] 'Soldier Chandu Chavan, Who Inadvertently Strayed Across LoC in 2016, Handed Over to India,' *Indian Express*, updated 21 January 2017, available at http://indianexpress.com/article/india/pakistan-army-announces-return-of-indian-soldier-who-crossed-over-loc-accidentally-4485043/, last accessed on 5 March 2017.

[64] 'India Kills Pakistani Soldier for Inadvertently Crossing LoC', *News*, 16 February 2013, available at https://www.thenews.com.pk/archive/print/628648-india-kills-pakistani-soldier-for-inadvertently-crossing-loc, last accessed on 3 January 2017.

[65] Interview with Brig. (Retd) Gurmeet Kanwal, 4 May 2016, Bangkok.

[66] Interview with Indian Army Officer 7, 16 May 2016, Tangdhar (J&K).

reality on the ground. For instance, Gen. Panag says, 'There is a certain *nallah* (small stream), near the LoC. The previous unit has left and the enemy has moved there. If the new unit says that the areas is doubtful whether it is ours or theirs and lets it be, then it will become a routine.'[67]

It is not always possible to physically guard every inch of the held territory, especially because the forces are not posted on the zero line but way behind it. Moreover, the LoC is not a clearly identified straight line. And since in the mountainous areas it is not possible to patrol the difficult terrain, the adversary could potentially occupy an area. This may or may not be due to lack of clarity but would lead to CFVs either way.

Brig. Sahgal put it with remarkable lucidity: 'There is no clarity with respect to the line. The clarity is with respect to perceptions.' The question then is whether there can be differences of opinion on the question of perceptions. And if so, what would that lead to? He also says, 'Nobody knows for sure where exactly the zero line is, since there are no markings.'[68]

Sometimes, a serving general in Kashmir said, rivers or small streams can change course, which could cause confusion on the ground.[69] Gen. Ghazi gave a concrete example to show how lack of clarity can lead to CFVs:

In the area where the Tawi flows into the Chenab, it creates a huge floodplain. When the floods come, the troops end up withdrawing from there. After the floods recede, CFVs invariably take place because the topographic changes give rise to fresh or conflicting claims and so on. In areas where both sides are vulnerable, there are usually no CFVs. Where one side is vulnerable, there is greater danger of CFVs.[70]

There are, however, others who disagree that there is any scope for confusion or there is any lack of clarity. Gen. Amjad Shuaib retorts:

It is very rare to change positions due to environmental factors, because with passage of time, both sides have developed permanent defences/posts in such a way that these can meet all-weather requirements. Hence, there have been no CFVs on account of any change in positions due to environmental factors.[71]

[67] Interview with Lt Gen. (Retd) H.S. Panag, 3 March 2017, Bangkok.
[68] Interview with Brig. (Retd) Arun Sahgal, 4 November 2016, Bangkok.
[69] Interview with Indian Army Officer 6, 15 May 2016, Kupwara.
[70] Interview with Lt Gen. (Retd) Tariq Ghazi, 7 November 2016, Bangkok.
[71] Interview with Lt Gen. (Retd) Amjad Shuaib, 18 December 2016, Rawalpindi.

Indian general Om Prakash agrees to this assessment and argues that 'crossing and grabbing of territory happens by design'.[72] Col Shukla adds weight to this argument by saying that the LoC is 'written in stone'.[73]

In sum, while there is a clear difference of opinion on whether or not there is a certain amount of lack of clarity with regard to the zero line in the LoC sector, and whether such lack of clarity can lead to CFVs, what is clear is that the line is a 'notional one' and that it is possible to have occasional confusion and lack of clarity about it, leading potentially to CFVs. During fieldtrips to the LoC, the impression I got was that while the LoC is not demarcated on the ground, there is an understanding of where the line is, even though there could be an occasional genuine case of misunderstandings for the several reasons cited previously.

Personality Traits of Commanders

There is a mindset or an approach that travels down. If local commanders feel that the top person is strict and cautious, they will not be adventurous.

—Brig. (Retd) Naeem Salik[74]

On 10 January 2013, Indian journalist Saikat Datta reported in the *Daily News and Analysis*, using sources in the MoD and MHA, that a cross-border raid by the *ghatak* (commando) platoon of the 9th Maratha Light Infantry (MLI) based in the Uri sector of Kashmir a few days ago might have led to the killing and beheading of two Indian soldiers. Datta reported that Brig. Gulab Singh Rawat, commander of the 161 Brigade stationed in the Churchunda sub-sector, had asked the CO (a colonel) of 9 MLI to take 'proactive action' against a Pakistani post that was harassing Indian positions, which led to casualties on the Pakistani side. Brig. Rawat's action led to the Pakistani counter-operation and the beheadings. The report also suggested that Brig. Rawat had a track record of being very aggressive.[75] An inquiry was ordered against Brig. Rawat.

---

[72] Interview with Lt Gen. (Retd) Om Prakash, 27 September 2016, Gurgaon.
[73] Interview with Col Ajai Shukla, 6 September 2016, New Delhi.
[74] Interview with Brig. (Retd) Naeem Ahmad Salik, 13 April 2016, Bangkok.
[75] Saikat Dutta, '"DNA" Exclusive: Uri Commander's Forceful Retaliation led to Beheadings?,' *DNA*, 10 January 2013, available at http://www.dnaindia. com/india/report-dna-exclusive-uri-commander-s-forceful-retaliation-led-to-beheadings-1787448, last accessed on 5 December 2017.

This was 2013 when the United Progressive Alliance (UPA) government led by Manmohan Singh was still in charge in New Delhi and Singh was keen on resolving issues with Pakistan. Since 2014, things have drastically changed with the new right-wing government in New Delhi, which has consistently used an aggressive line with regard to the stand-off on the borders in Kashmir. Many political and military leaders have often asked, and publicly so, the Indian Army in Kashmir to be on the offensive.[76]

As discussed earlier, the general environment of permissiveness influences the behaviour of troops and commanders posted on the LoC and IB. Within the larger context of such permissiveness, the autonomy available to the local commanders varies, which has an effect on the behaviour of the local commanders. More significantly, the personality traits of the local commanders matter a great deal in determining how they respond to certain situations on the ground. Some commanders tend to be 'trigger-happy' and their actions often lead to CFVs.[77]

While it is widely accepted that 'a commander on the spot can take all necessary action to safeguard the security of his post and his troops',[78] what that action is would sometimes depend on the commander himself, his views, and how he perceives the limits of permissibility that exists. In a not-so-tightly-controlled environment, an order such as 'I am not sitting on your head. There should be no infiltration from this area and you do not have to call me up to ask how many rounds to fire. You should take action that you deem appropriate and at the right time, give your report',[79] could mean different things to different commanders.

The overarching military culture is based on aggression, domination, and winning. That simply is the nature of the beast. Ajai Shukla makes this big-picture argument succinctly:

---

[76] Fayaz Wani, 'Amid Ceasefire Violations by Pakistan Troops, Army Chief asks Soldiers to be Aggressive in Approach', *New Indian Express*, 15 November 2016, available at http://www.newindianexpress.com/nation/2016/nov/15/amid-ceasefire-violations-by-pakistan-troops--army-chief-asks-soldiers-to-be-aggressive-in-approach-1538903.html, last accessed on 6 December 2017.

[77] Pavan Nair, 'Skirmishing on the Line of Control', *Economic and Political Weekly* 48, no. 4 (26 January 2013), available at http://www.epw.in/journal/2013/04/web-exclusives/skirmishing-line-control.html, last accessed on 1 July 2017.

[78] Interview with Lt Gen. (Retd) H.S. Panag, 19 September 2016, Chandigarh.

[79] Interview with Lt Gen. (Retd) J.P. Nehra, 3 December 2016, New Delhi.

In my opinion, the single biggest reason is the personality of the local commander. All this business of covering fire and civilian targeting, they are there to a certain degree, but essentially, both armies, being fairly aggressive beasts, believe in maintaining psychological domination over the opposition at any given point in time. That leads to confrontations, and escalation of local confrontations can frequently lead to exchange of local fire. When the exchange of local fire is not controlled by local commanders, it leads to exchange of mortar fire, which can escalate to exchange of artillery fire. That is the real reason.[80]

The issue of moral ascendency, which we discussed earlier in great detail, feeds into this culture of aggression and domination. Sometimes political permissiveness is exacerbated by the outlook of the top military leadership. Brig. Salik believes that 'there is a mindset or an approach which travels down. If local commanders feel that the top person is strict and cautious, they will not be adventurous.'[81]

In any case, local/tactical military activities take place on the front line and the beliefs and personality of the man in charge of that locality make a huge difference. Different commanders would have different understanding of how much force calibration should take place at each level.[82] The very fact that 'two commanders can act differently in the same situation' indicates the level of influence the personality of the commander makes in a given situation even though there is a set understanding of 'how much' a commander is able to go.[83]

For instance, when confronted with a tactical situation, certain commanders 'might think that it (firing from the other side) is not worth making a big deal out of, (as) we will only end up creating a situation that will escalate and people will get killed on both sides and then go back to normal.'[84] In such situations, 'non-aggressive COs will try and negotiate with the other side'[85] through flag meetings and the like. As pointed out earlier while discussing the issue of moral ascendency, the characteristics of units and troops also matter along with that of the commander. As Sahgal points out: 'Sometimes the characteristic of the troops plays out.

---

[80] Interview with Col Ajai Shukla, 6 September 2016, New Delhi.
[81] Interview with Brig. (Retd) Naeem Ahmad Salik, 13 April 2016, Bangkok.
[82] Interview with Lt Gen. (Retd) Om Prakash, 27 September 2016, Gurgaon.
[83] Interview with Lt Gen. (Retd) Om Prakash, 27 Septmeber 2016, Gurgaon.
[84] Interview with Col Ajai Shukla, 6 September 2016, New Delhi.
[85] Interview with Brig. (Retd) Arun Sahgal, 4 November 2016, Bangkok.

There are troops that are less aggressive. For instance, the presence of Gorkha or Sikh battalions leads to "peaceful border". Pathan battalions are also very aggressive.'[86]

Gen. Panag agrees with the argument that different commanders deal with things differently—some are aggressive and some are balanced. The more balanced ones are likely to ask themselves whether the aggressive reaction would hamper their CI efforts. He recalls the case of 'an interesting brigade commander in 2001, he was commanding a brigade in Chamb-Jaurian. He was very aggressive and organized many trans-LoC raids. He had several successes but they also struck back. So, these people went across and cut heads and got them back.'[87]

Local initiatives undertaken by local commanders sometimes may not even be known to the senior leadership of the force. Gen. Waheed explains: 'Sometimes, people up the ladder do not even know about the construction activity happening on the Indian or Pakistani side. A lot of things happen on the LoC—construction of walls, for instance, at a post—without information passing up the ladder for a variety of reasons.'[88]

Sometimes, the not-so-aggressive commanders, who would prefer the resolution of the issue rather than aggressive action, may come under pressure from his senior officers who are more aggressive; sometimes, the pressure may be from his subordinates who want retribution:

At times, orders will be given right from the top ... sometimes an army commander will say, 'What are you doing? Are you wearing bangles?' Sometimes it happens at the lower end ... he does not want to tell that we have been shamed. So even if you are trying to tell them to not be hasty, they will not listen and take action. Or sometimes, the aggressive commander may initiate.[89]

Gen. Salik agrees to the argument about aggressive brigade commanders giving down orders to be more aggressive and fire back:

It also depends on the mindset of the brigade commander—some commanders will pull people up for firing; some commanders might say retaliate accordingly if fired upon; some commanders might say

[86] Interview with Brig. (Retd) Arun Sahgal, 4 November 2016, Bangkok.
[87] Interview with Lt Gen. (Retd) H.S. Panag, 19 September 2016, Chandigarh.
[88] Interview with Lt Gen. (Retd) Waheed Arshad, 15 April 2016, Bangkok.
[89] Interview with Lt Gen. (Retd) H.S. Panag, 3 March 2017, Bangkok.

use any weapon to take the post out. Basically, it travels down, right from the top. You have a mindset or an approach that travels down. If commanders feel that the top person is strict and cautious, they will not ... it happens ... depends a lot on the personalities.[90]

Aggression, as a rule, seems to be more preferred than diplomacy since what matters when it comes to writing the officer's ACR is how well he held the line and defeated infiltration attempts from the Pakistani side.[91] Even though it is difficult to determine whether a commander has succeeded or not, pro-active action may often be seen as an indication of holding the line successfully and countering infiltration—thereby leading to more display of aggression. A senior general of the Pakistan Army explains the 'promotion angle' further:

> Local commanders on the posts in those areas are captains and majors and JCOs. And CO is a Lt Col and many a times, the CO is maybe 36 or 37 years old, a relatively young man. Now they have to be promoted to higher ranks, and some want to prove they are very exceptional; thus, they try to look for opportunity and take advantage.[92]

Moreover, with no treaty mechanism or international norms to stop them from being aggressive and the only thing that matters is how well the LoC was defended and infiltrators pushed back, innovative tactical measures, with a potential for triggering CFVs, are not constrained as often as they should.

On being asked whether sometimes soldiers and commanders take things into their own hands, Gen. Majid responded that 'troops are normally disciplined but some people could be stupid'. What make the situation worse, over and above the fact that some commanders are trigger-happy, is the presence of heavy weapons in the vicinity of the LoC and IB in J&K.

Firing with small weapons could be contained sooner and easier than when the stand-off graduates to the use of heavy weapons. In the year 2000, for instance, the Indian Army decided to move forward around six Vijayanta tanks to the forward posts in Lalyani. Having spent a month building access to tanks to Lalyali, one morning, the Indian Army

[90] Interview with Brig. (Retd) Naeem Ahmad Salik, 13 April 2016, Bangkok.
[91] Interview with Lt Gen. (Retd) H.S. Panag, 3 March 2017, Bangkok.
[92] Interview with Pakistani Official 4, 17 January 2017, Rawalpindi.

suddenly had Vijayanta tanks open up fire in the area. Under tank fire and being taken by complete surprise, the Pakistani side was in utter shock.[93]

Increasingly, heavier weapon systems are being used on the LoC and IB in J&K. The calibre of weapons used on the border have also graduated from short-range personal weapons to 105 mm mortars, 130 and 155 mm artillery guns, and anti-tank guided missiles.[94]

Some officers disagree that it is possible for local commanders to act independently. Indian and Pakistani officers who are currently deployed on the field typically argue that such instances of local-level commanders taking things into their own hands may have happened in the past, but does not happen anymore, especially due to improved communication networks, both on one's own side and bilaterally. A Kashmir-based general insists that 'today, there is a huge communication network in the LoC areas. The army uses all kinds of communication methods, such that no post remains isolated. If there is firing, hotlines are used to clarify or find out what is happening.'[95] An Indian brigadier agrees with this assessment that some local commanders may try to behave macho and take action but such attempts these days are deterred by the communication that goes up to the higher levels.[96] Better communication and absence of isolated posts have led to fewer CFVs today—local-level issues tend to get contained. 'Macho behaviour is unlikely, due to double oversight, counter oversight, and communications network'. Gen. Yasin says that there were more such incidents before the CFA.[97]

Emotional State and CFVs

> *Monotony breaking will also include shooting holes into the clothes left for drying by the troops on the other side of the border. There are few avenues for entertainment.*
>
> —Lt Gen. (Retd) Sikandar Afzal[98]

[93] Interview with Col Ajai Shukla, 6 September 2016, New Delhi.

[94] Happymon Jacob, 'The Strategy of Conflict', *Hindu*, 16 March 2018, available at http://www.thehindu.com/opinion/lead/the-strategy-of-conflict/article23264085.ece?homepage=true, last accessed on 20 March 2018.

[95] Interview with Indian Army Officer 6, 15 May 2016, Kupwara.

[96] Interview with Indian Army Officer 7, 16 May 2016, Tangdhar (J&K).

[97] Interview with Lt Gen. (Retd) Asif Yasin Malik, 15 April 2016, Bangkok.

[98] Interview with Lt Gen. (Retd) Sikander Afzal, 16 April 2016, Bangkok.

CFVs can also be triggered by the emotional state of soldiers and commanders resulting from the adverse operational environment that the forces find themselves in. Extreme psychological stress often leads to venting in the form of kinetic action. Pakistani officials agreed to this assessment: 'At times, CFVs are a result of emotional state/frustration of local commanders/soldiers in a certain sector. Being deployed in a state of no hot conflict/no peace affects emotional stability of the men and officers. Conditions are also harsh. Thus, to vent their frustration, soldiers/commanders resort to firing.' They said, though, that such instances are infrequent.[99] They also pointed out that in the 1990s, incidence of emotionally charged exchange of fire was high. But now, situation has changed.[100]

In highly tense operational environments, there are also other related psychological factors at play, adding to the violence on the border. Gen. Yasin points out:

> On both the sides, there are active troops sitting. Whether by intent or accident, if one of my soldiers is hit, then as a battalion commander, I have to respond. I must try and kill at least one guy on the other side. This is an unwritten thing, which is clear in a soldier's mind. This is a reality; it cannot be found in books. I remember we had earmarked places—if there is a contingency, such and such place will be taken out.[101]

Gen. Afzal rules out the possibility of accidental CFVs: 'There is no inadvertent firing. The main causes are bunkers and defence works/constructions; second is to break the monotony; third, pre-planned firing (with political consent—LoC/WB) and fourth, testing fire (when there is change in battalion—related to LoC only).'[102]

Fun and Gamesmanship

Sometimes, sheer misunderstanding or accidents can lead to CFVs. Gen. Afzal of the Pakistan Army says that sometimes when India wins an

---

[99] Interview with Pakistani Official 1, 7 June 2016, Islamabad; Interview with Pakistani Official 2, 9 June 2016, Islamabad.
[100] Interview with Pakistani Official 2, 9 June 2016; Interview with Pakistani Official 3, 12 June 2016, Islamabad.
[101] Interview with Lt Gen. (Retd) Asif Yasin Malik, 15 April 2016, Bangkok.
[102] Interview with Lt Gen. (Retd) Sikander Afzal, 16 April 2016, Bangkok.

India–Pakistan cricket match, the Indian side fires in celebration and vice versa when Pakistan wins. On Eid, the Pakistani side would engage in celebratory fire. Although the firing might not be targeted on the posts and troops on the other side, firing can sometimes inadvertently lead to firing at each other. In any case, he argues, firing is a monotony breaker: 'Monotony breaking will also include shooting holes into the clothes left for drying by the troops on the other side of the border. There are few avenues for entertainment.'[103] Gen. Nehra agrees with this assessment of troops firing for fun.[104] Gens. Nandal and Bhatia also recall how the victorious side would engage in celebratory firing with the adversary not responding to such firing.[105]

Referring to the 1980s, senior Pakistani general Ghazi says how CFVs were often a result of gamesmanship and mirth:

> Then there are silly occasions such as when you have visitors, for instance, senior officials, college students, or even families, causing CFVs. So, you want to show them this live fire and drama being staged and so you initiate a CFV. That was gamesmanship. Both sides engaged in it, and when one side was doing it, the other would just tuck themselves in and wait for it to get over.[106]

The emotional state of soldiers needs to be taken and analysed seriously given how emotional, psychological, and similar issues have increased suicide rates within the armed forces. A news report claimed that 597 Indian military personnel committed suicide in the five years between 2009 and 2013,[107] many of them in J&K, which is considered to

---

[103] Interview with Lt Gen. (Retd) Sikander Afzal, 16 April 2016, Bangkok.

[104] Interview with Lt. Gen (Retd) J.P. Nehra, 3 December 2016, New Delhi.

[105] Interview with Lt Gen. (Retd) A.S. Nandal, 23 September 2016, Gurgaon; Interview with Lt Gen. (Retd) Vinod Bhatia, 19 September 2016, New Delhi.

[106] Interview with Lt Gen. (Retd) Tariq Ghazi, 7 November 2016, Bangkok.

[107] Rajat Pandit, '597 Military Personnel have Committed Suicide in Last 5 Years, Government Says', *Times of India*, 22 July 2014, available at http://timesofindia.indiatimes.com/india/597-military-personnel-have-committed-suicide-in-last-5-years-government-says/articleshow/38873826.cms, last accessed on 11 March 2017.

be a difficult posting. Another report gave figures going back to 2003.[108] Several reports indicate that suicide and fratricide trends in the Indian Army soldiers posted in J&K and its border are disturbingly high. One such report indicated that 'the Indian Army has lost nearly 500 personnel to suicides and fratricides in less than five years, even though cases of fratricide or men killing their own people are rare'.[109]

In a widely reported incident in the Samba district of J&K in August 2012, officers and jawans (soldiers) of the 16th Cavalry regiment of the Indian Army were engaged in a stand-off after a soldier committed suicide.[110] The soldiers had accused certain officers of harassment. While there is no material connection between suicide rates in the army and CFVs, what would be useful to note is the psychological state of the troops deployed on the LoC, where such psychological pressure would be much more, and the potential implications for their behaviour on the LoC and IB.

Revenge Firing and 'Honour Killings'

CFVs are often part of a series of events, one violation leading to the other and another. Politicians[111] and army officials[112] often rationalize CFVs,

---

[108] Nitin Gokhale, 'Blog: Suicides in Army—A Comprehensive Review Needed', NDTV, 11 August 2012, available at http://www.ndtv.com/india-news/blog-suicides-in-army-a-comprehensive-review-needed-496357, last accessed on 11 March 2017.

[109] Abhishek Bhalla, 'Fratricide, Suicide Cases in the Army on the Rise', *DNA*, 19 July 2017, available at http://www.dnaindia.com/india/report-fratricide-suicide-cases-in-the-army-on-the-rise-2506532, last accessed on 11 September 2017.

[110] 'Jawan's Suicide Led to Unrest Among Troops in Samba', *Outlook*, 3 September 2012, available at http://www.outlookindia.com/newswire/story/jawans-suicide-led-to-unrest-among-troops-in-samba/774029, last accessed on 11 March 2017.

[111] 'India Retaliating Appropriately to Pak Ceasefire Violations: Nirmala Sitharaman', *Indian Express*, 5 March 2018, available at http://indianexpress.com/article/india/india-retaliating-appropriately-to-pak-ceasefire-violations-nirmala-sitharaman-5087242/, last accessed on 5 March 2018.

[112] 'Will Continue Giving Befitting Reply: Army Vice Chief on Ceasefire Violation by Pakistan', *Economic Times*, 5 February 2018, available at https://economictimes.indiatimes.com/news/defence/will-continue-giving-befitting-reply-army-vice-chief-on-ceasefire-violation-by-pakistan/articleshow/62787673.cms, last accessed on 6 February 2018.

referring back to an earlier attack by the other side—the other side may have fired in a particular sector in response to an attack elsewhere, constituting a vicious cycle of killings and firings. The timelines of various significant CFVs reveals that the action–reaction–retaliation cycle is a key component of the firing that takes place on the J&K borders. CFVs initiated by one side are usually responded to by the other side using roughly the same calibre, creating a near perfect symmetry of violations between the two militaries.[113]

To the uninitiated, CFVs may look spatially and temporally distinct and unconnected, but they may actually be interlinked due to operational and tactical reasons. Gen. Nandal says that deliberate operations are often carried out to get back at the adversary for causing casualties, with coordinated efforts including the use of artillery.

Firing for revenge is one of the most essential ingredients of local military dynamics. Brig. Sahgal explains this mindset:

> If in firing or through BAT actions or through infiltration, a battalion suffers casualties, there is no question of the battalion pulling out of the sector, without causing similar or greater damage. This is the standard rule up there.... The unwritten law of the jungle, as far as violations are concerned, is that any provocation, any casualty by either side is always responded to.'[114]

Gen. Afzal agrees that if there has been a casualty on either side, then the return firing that follows cannot be seen as 'out of control' firing, but intentional.[115] The local commander might tell the superior commanders that he seeks revenge and firing then may be permitted by higher-ups in some places.

In early May 2017, the *Indian Express* reported that the attack and beheading of the Indian soldiers on the Indian side of the LoC in the Krishna Ghati sector of Kashmir was a revenge for the killing of around 10 soldiers in an Indian artillery assault on 17 April against the Pakistan Army. The *Express* report reads:

> The lethal ambush came days after the largest Indian fire assault since last year, targeting Pakistani posts across a large swathe of the

[113] Happymon Jacob, 'Data Exposes what India & Pakistan Don't Reveal about the Constant "Ceasefire Violations"', *Print*, 3 April 2018, available at https://theprint.in/opinion/india-pakistan-constant-ceasefire-violations/46434/, last accessed on 3 April 2018.

[114] Interview with Brig. (Retd) Arun Sahgal, 4 November 2016, Bangkok.

[115] Interview with Lt Gen (Retd) Sikander Afzal, 16 April 2016, Bangkok.

LoC in Poonch and Rajouri. The Pakistan Army had made no official statement on the 17 April fire assault by India. However, Indian military observers estimate that up to ten Pakistani soldiers may have been killed or injured in fire directed at a position identified on Indian maps by the codename Pimple, facing Kirpan post.[116]

What is important to note for our purposes are two things: one, the interlinked nature of the firing across the LoC or IB/WB, and two, the unending cycle of action-reaction firing.

Command and Control Issues

Though rarely, inter- and intra-organizational dynamics and other related C&C issues trigger, increase, or sustain CFVs. The very fact that there is no one overarching institutional or doctrinal framework when it comes to border management in India means a possibility of organizational politics playing a role in border mismanagement. Let us take the case of the BSF, which comes directly under the Indian Home Ministry. Notwithstanding the fact that the BSF is a fine paramilitary force, it often comes under pressure from local politicians and the home ministry in New Delhi for holding or violating the CFA of 2003. IPS officers, as opposed to career BSF officers, occupy most of the top posts in the organization, which not only impacts the professionalism of the force but also leads to a situation wherein it can be easily influenced by New Delhi's political class, which wants to use CFVs for political ends.

More significantly, there is a great deal of bureaucratic politics within the MHA. The Kargil review committee talked about the need for a department of border management, which led to the creation of the post of secretary border management (SBH). However, the SBH has hardly any real border management power as the home secretary did not want to give any powers away. As a result of this power struggle, the post of SBH is sidelined and it is merely tasked with managing the infrastructure development in the border areas.[117] The home secretary, who manages the vast home ministry bureaucracy dealing with intelligence functions to

---

[116] Praveen Swami, 'Pakistan Army Brass Ordered Attack to Avenge Losses on Line of Control', *Indian Express*, 3 May 2017, available at http://indianexpress.com/article/india/pakistan-army-brass-ordered-attack-to-avenge-losses-on-line-of-control-4638185/, last accessed on 14 September 2017.

[117] Interview with BSF Officer 21, 16 September 2016, New Delhi.

migrations issues, has no time to effectively manage the border, and the SBH does not have the powers to do so. The result being that there is no senior body to plan and synchronize the border guarding itself nor does it have a proper border management doctrine.

G.K. Pillai, former union home secretary, admitted to not having a uniform border management policy: 'We do not have any uniform border policy because our borders are quite diverse. The Gujarat and Rajasthan borders are handled quite differently from the Punjab borders and the Punjab border is handled differently from the J&K border.'[118] The coordination between the BSF, Army, MHA, and MoD on operational matters is mostly ad hoc in nature as there are no formal forums for deliberations and strategy planning.

On the one hand, then, there is no uniform policy on border management in India, which results in ad hoc policymaking, and the BSF tends to come under pressure from the political bosses in New Delhi, on the other. A senior army officer in Kashmir pointed out on condition of anonymity, 'The CFVs in areas manned by the BSF could be politically motivated. The BSF gets its directions from the home ministry and home secretary.'[119] Gen. Om Prakash supports this argument by saying, 'The training matters. Like there is a difference between the army and the BSF, or the army and the CRPF. Their training, their ethos, and their moral values are different … sometimes recklessly, carelessly, they open up. We cannot sit idle then and have to punish them back. We [the army] go by planned methods.'[120]

There is also a third dimension of playing one-upmanship between the army and the BSF. In today's media age, when CFVs on the LoC and IB often become part of the national political and security discourse, there is often a competition between the BSF and the army to increase their respective visibility in such discourses, which invariably has an impact on CFVs. More visibility means more attention, which potentially means more resources.

On the Pakistani side, there appears to be no inter-organizational dissonance between the Rangers and the Pakistan Army since the former

[118] Interview with G.K. Pillai, 21 September 2016, New Delhi.
[119] Interview with Indian Army Officer 2, 13 May 2016, Udhampur.
[120] Interview with Lt Gen. (Retd) Om Prakash, 27 September 2016, Gurgaon.

is officered by the latter.[121] However, as pointed out earlier, given their subservient position vis-à-vis the Pakistan Army, the Pak Rangers have to often initiate CFVs and sniping in the Sialkot-Jammu sector to suit the Pakistan Army's interests and designs, which eventually become difficult for its own operations in the sector.

On the LoC sector, Pakistan's Mujahid Battalions are often reported to be more aggressive than regular army battalions. Mujahid Battalions are semi-regular forces raised in times of emergency and are locally recruited and more often locally deployed with rare deployments far from home. Given that they are not regular troops, they are activated for a brief period every year to keep them up to date and well trained.[122] According to Gen. Bhatia, Mujahid Battalions have a tendency to violate the CFA more often than the disciplined army battalions. The Pakistan Army, according to Gen. Bhatia, would violate the CFA as a planned measure, but the Mujahids will do it for the heck of it.[123] In fact, several CFVs in the past have been linked specifically to the Mujahid Battalions.[124]

[121] Conversations with Pakistani army officials reveal that they do not believe that there is an organizational disconnect given that the Rangers is officered by the Pakistan Army.

[122] Interview with Lt Gen. (Retd) Tariq Ghazi, 7 November 2016, Bangkok.

[123] Interview with Lt Gen. (Retd) Vinod Bhatia, 19 September 2016, New Delhi.

[124] Rajat Pandit, 'Pak Fire goes Beyond LoC, Hits Kargil after 10 years', *Times of India*, 17 August 2013, available at http://epaper.timesofindia. com/Repository/getFiles.asp?style=OliveXLib:LowLevelEntityToPrint_ TOINEW&Type=text/html&Locale=english-skin-custom&Path=TOIM/ 2013/08/17&ID=Ar00106, last accessed on 11 March 2017; Ravi Krishnan Khajuria, 'Pakistan's latest Barbaric Act: Bodies of Two Indian Soldiers Mutilated, Army Vows Appropriate Response', *Hindustan Times*, 28 May 2017, available at http://www.hindustantimes.com/india-news/pakistan-mutilates-bodies-of-two-indian-soldiers-army-vows-revenge/story-MuI5fTZdmRyavJNnAqwlPI. html, last accessed on 12 August 2017; and Rahul Datta, 'Pak Planning Kargil Dobaara?', *Pioneer*, 17 August 2013, available at http://www.dailypioneer.com/ todays-newspaper/pak-planning-kargil-dobaara.html, last accessed on 11 March 2017.

Lack of Legal, Treaty, and Institutional Mechanisms

Well, we have always abided by the strictures of the Karachi Agreement especially when it comes to the issue of defence construction. MEA might differ, but then diplomats do not have to manage a live border, I have to.

—Serving General of the Indian Army[125]

There is hardly a formal treaty or legal basis for border management between India and Pakistan both in J&K and outside of it. Final ratification of the 'ground rules' of 1960–1 is still pending in both Islamabad and New Delhi. Even though the two sides have not yet signed the rules, they tend to abide by it in Punjab, Rajasthan, and Gujarat.

The question of rules is a very complicated issue on the India–Pakistan border in J&K. The two sides do adhere to the ground rules in the Jammu-Sialkot sector, even though India maintains that the observance of the ground rules is an ad hoc arrangement and Pakistan claims that the border itself is ad hoc.[126] Officials in Pakistan said they will continue to follow 1961 rules till new rules are finalized by both sides and a new agreement is signed that overrides it,[127] something the Indian forces also agree with. This again is an ad hoc arrangement with little legal basis.

Senior BSF officials in New Delhi that I spoke to pointed out that they have been demanding that the MHA takes steps to finalize the rules with Pakistan, given that doing so would enable the BSF to better manage the India–Pakistan border. Former Indian home secretary G.K. Pillai agreed that even though the ground rules are not signed, the forces on the ground have to go by them: 'Strictly speaking, if there is construction within 150 yards and objections are raised, the construction will have to be razed down.'[128]

According to the Pakistani foreign ministry officials, India and Pakistan had during bilateral talks in 2006 agreed to formulate and

---

[125] Interview with serving general of the Indian Army on condition of anonymity.

[126] Interview with Pakistani Official 3, 12 June 2016, Islamabad.

[127] Interview with Pakistani Official 3, 12 June 2016, Islamabad; Interview with Pakistani Official 4, 17 January 2017, Rawalpindi.

[128] Interview with G.K. Pillai, 21 September 2016, New Delhi.

finalize new border rules. And, they say, it is on the basis of the 2006 agreement that both sides will proceed on the ground rules, when the talks resume.[129] But there has been no movement so far in this direction.

Even though the borders in Punjab, Rajasthan, and Gujarat have not had any significant issues under the non-finalized ground rules, this remains a serious problem in the Jammu sector. When combined with Pakistan's non-recognition of the finality of the border and the recurrent CFVs that happen in the region, lack of rules to govern the border management is a serious challenge.

The Indian and Pakistani positions on the various agreements in J&K and their adherence to those agreements get still more complicated. India has consistently argued that the Simla Agreement of 1972 (which brought the LoC into existence) made the Karachi Agreement of 1949 irrelevant, something Pakistan disagrees with saying that the Karachi Agreement is still valid. However, when it comes to the day-to-day management of the LoC, both the forces seem to go by the strictures of the Karachi Agreement given that there are no other detailed agreements to go by. It gets even more complicated now: despite the fact that the Indian and Pakistani militaries in Kashmir adhere to the Karachi Agreement, they both violate the provisions of the agreement at will.

In other words, at the bilateral political level between New Delhi and Islamabad, there is no consensus on the Karachi Agreement, but the two militaries abide by the Karachi Agreement due to the lack of any agreement on the ground, and yet, both the armies violate the agreement when they find it necessary for their tactical purposes.

For instance, the Karachi Agreement states that there should be no new defence construction within 500 yards of the LoC, which is 'adhered to' by both the armies, at least theoretically; the Simla Agreement does not address the defence construction issue at all. When pointed out to a senior serving Indian Army officer in Kashmir that India takes cognizance of the Simla Agreement and not the Karachi Agreement and hence the 500 yards stipulation has no validity under the Simla Agreement, the officer said that they have always followed the stipulations of the Karachi Agreement, explicitly disagreeing with the MEA's take on the matter. Gen.

---

[129] Interview with Pakistani Official 2, 9 June 2016, Islamabad; Interview with Pakistani Official 3, 17 January 2017, Rawalpindi.

Panag agrees with the serving officer by saying that 'there are no rules for enforcement. The only rules that exist are the 1949 ones, which are still to be respected.'[130]

Col Shukla argues tersely: 'See, the defence ministry has to deal with the situations on ground and the foreign ministry has to deal with the situation in the debating forums. In the debating forums, the position is clear, the Karachi Agreement was superseded by the Simla Agreement.'[131]

Other Indian Army officers disagree about adhering to the Simla Agreement. Gen. Hasnain, for instance, argues: 'The Pakistan Army continues to follow the Karachi Agreement on the LoC. Under the Karachi Agreement, no fresh bunkers were to be constructed within 500 yards of the LoC. The Karachi Agreement was effectively overruled by the Simla Agreement. The Simla Agreement has no such restriction on defence construction and, in fact, is silent on it.' 'This is why', he contends, 'India does not object to Pakistan constructing new bunkers. In the last couple of years in Uri, 500 yards from the LoC, Pakistan has constructed huge network of communication trenches; India has never objected. However, Pakistan continuously objects to Indian construction and even maintenance activity.'[132] Pakistani officials disagree with the claim that Indian troops do not object to construction on the Pakistani side.

Pakistani officials also argue that the Karachi Agreement is valid. Former Pakistani ambassadors to India Aziz Ahmed Khan and Salman Bashir agree with this position. However, from a purely chronological point of view, the Simla Agreement overrides the Karachi Agreement, but since the Simla Agreement does not prescribe rules for managing the LoC, the two militaries seem to abide by the Karachi Agreement.

In sum, then, a very complicated and confusing picture emerges from the preceding discussion: the IB/WB segment of the J&K border is managed by the Rangers and BSF using the India–Pakistan Ground Rules Agreement of 1961. However, this agreement has not been accepted by New Delhi since the 1970s, even though the forces on the ground adhere to several of its provisions since there is no other treaty mechanism to go by. But as is the case with the Karachi Agreement, the two forces—BSF

---

130 Interview with Lt Gen. (Retd) H.S. Panag, 3 March 2017, Bangkok.
131 Interview with Col Ajai Shukla, 6 September 2016, New Delhi.
132 Interview with Lt Gen. (Retd) Syed Ata Hasnain, 5 June 2015, New Delhi.

and the Rangers—violate the provisions of this treaty at will. This is over and above the fact that there is no clearly written down CFA, an issue that was discussed in the previous chapter.

Moreover, the two sides also do not have sufficient mutually agreed upon SOPs to manage the contentious borders both in the LoC and IB/WB sectors. Both the Indian and Pakistani sides have their own individual SOPs to be followed in managing their respective sides of the LoC and IB/WB. However, there is an inadequate number of joint SOPs between them. The lack of joint SOPs has major implications on the ground.

When a new section/company takes over a post on either side of the LoC or IB/WB, detailed instructions are given to them in writing. The units get to know about their movement about six months in advance. Therefore, the troops know what to do in a situation while on the border.[133] Pakistani officials agree by pointing out that 'these SOPs are given to each new unit'.[134] Hardly anything is left to imagination on unfriendly terrains such as the LoC. As Gen. Majid points out, 'Almost everything, including how the response would be. They are written down clear instructions—it is very comprehensive.'[135]

But there are very few joint SOPs even though it is the absence of such joint SOPs that often lead to CFVs. There are many relevant examples. As one Pakistani official pointed out, India's zero line patrolling, ahead of the fence, when done in an unannounced manner, can be misperceived by the Pakistani troops: 'Such movements lead to misreading of the situation by soldiers, as they can treat it as hostile and CFVs can happen.'[136]

There are no joint SOPs, for instance, on how to respond if there is a movement on the zero line at night. Both sides pointed out that any movement near the fence at night would be fired upon without any questions. This could however pose a problem given that there are villagers living close to the zero line. Then there are villagers on both sides engaging in activities—cutting grass, drawing water, and so on—which could lead to tension or stand-offs between the two sides, for which there are neither working arrangements or SOPs jointly agreed to by both sides.

---

[133] Interview with Indian Army Officer 7, 16 May 2016, Tangdhar (J&K).
[134] Interview with Pakistani Official 2, 9 June 2016, Islamabad.
[135] Interview with Lt Gen. (Retd) Tariq Majid, 14 April 2016, Bangkok.
[136] Interview with Pakistani Official 2, 9 June 2016, Islamabad.

A senior BSF officer in Jammu gave this author a scenario where things could have gone wrong due to lack of proper joint SOPs:

> If you are firing to tackle something on your side at night, you shoot a red light in the air—this is an SOP—to indicate to your side and the other side of your activity. On 17 May 2016, there was one bust of fire from the other side. If it was accidental, they should have shown the red light in the air—but they did not. However, the Indian side understood it was accidental and therefore did not respond.[137]

This could have, as they often do, led to CFVs.

The above-mentioned operational reasons constitute the most significant trigger for CFVs, most of which are either not recognized as triggers or not analysed sufficiently. The second most significant trigger for CFVs are the politico-strategic reasons.

Politico-strategic Reasons for CFVs

Political Factors Causing CFVs

> *Nothing happens, nothing major actually happens without a reason. Even if you look at the Uri attack, it had happened two days before the UN General Assembly. Before that, you had Ufa on 15 July. On 20 July, you had Hiranagar. 24–25 December, you had the prime minister going; 2 January, you had Pathankot. In September, before the prime ministers met, 26 September, you had Samba. I can go on and on. So, there is a linkage between the attacks and the political diplomatic developments.*

> —Gen. Vinod Bhatia[138]

A 2015 Stimson Center report by Julia Thompson offers two important findings on CFV.[139] First, the relationship between CFVs and India–Pakistan diplomatic progress is not statistically significant. CFVs do occasionally occur within the same time frame as high-level bilateral meetings between India and Pakistan, but there is no predictable pattern

[137] Interview with BSF Officer 1, 2 June 2016, Jammu.
[138] Interview with Lt Gen. (Retd) Vinod Bhatia, 19 September 2016, New Delhi.
[139] Julia Thompson, 'The Dynamics of Violence along the Kashmir Divide, 2003–2015', Stimson Center, 11 December 2008, available at https://www.stimson.org/sites/default/files/dynamics-violence-kashmir-divide.pdf, last accessed on 7 February 2016.

to it. Second, there is a lack of any direct, causal relationship—or even a correlation—between high-level bilateral meetings and upticks in violence along the LoC between 2005 and 2015.

While this book agrees in general with Thompson's findings, it, based on the interactions with the officers on the ground, however, argues that 'political factors' are indeed an undeniable cause for CFVs. Officers on the Indian side of the LoC and IB repeatedly spoke of three types of political factors behind CFVs: visit of Indian leaders to J&K; days of national importance such as Independence Day, especially when they coincide with periods of tension; and 'Pakistan's attempts at keeping the Kashmir issue alive'.

There are several political angles to CFVs. CFVs often take place not only because there is a permissive political environment, but also because there are perceived political gains to be made from initiating or sustaining CFVs. Pakistani Gen. Shuaib argues that ever since Modi came into power in New Delhi, India has frequently been using heavy weapons to initiate CFVs.[140] Decisions at the level of the central government and national political mood can often translate into CFVs on the borders. Gen. Afzal says that unless the top leadership wants CFVs to continue, it can be ended early on before it spirals as the DGMO will get to know of the firing within the hour itself. But if the CFVs go on for several days, we can assume that there is an intent behind the firing.[141] Gen. Nandal points out that diplomatic and political stand-offs have a direct bearing on the situation on the ground.[142] This is supported by a Pakistani general who states:

> At times, political environment acts as a catalyst. When political tensions are very high, they have an impact on the military engagement. We are living in an information age. The soldier in the forward-most post is as affected by the media as the man in a city. Psychological mind set becomes agitated, and in such environments, people tend to react and display hostility.[143]

[140] Interview with Lt Gen. (Retd) Amjad Shuaib, 18 December 2016, Rawalpindi.
[141] Interview with Lt Gen (Retd) Sikander Afzal, 16 April 2016, Bangkok.
[142] Interview with Lt Gen. (Retd) A.S. Nandal, 23 September 2016, Gurgaon.
[143] Interview with Pakistani Official 4, 17 January 2017, Rawalpindi.

This insight from the Pakistani officer, which highlights the impact of the media on soldiers on the front lines, is an important one.

But more specifically, Pakistan, given that it considers Kashmir as an unresolved issue, feels that the way to keep the issue on the radar of the international community is to keep the temperature high on the LoC and IB. While sometimes the firing may be to physically enable infiltrators to cross the border, sometimes it is to keep the Kashmir issue alive. Several Indian serving and retired officials testify to it.[144] Some retired Pakistani officials also corroborated it. CFVs are an easy way to attract the international community's attention to J&K, some argue.[145] A senior BSF officer in Jammu argues that 'CFVs take place because Pakistan wants to keep the temperature boiling in J&K. The Pak army commands the Rangers and it is the Pak army policy to fire.'[146]

Gen. Ata Hasnain argues:

> Every time the situation improves in the valley, Pakistan feels the need to bring it back into international limelight. A major violation is able to ensure that people do not forget the Kashmir conflict. Infiltration-related CFVs are also linked to (intention to disrupt or to send message/ to warn against) high-profile events in India/Pakistan or India–Pakistan events like high-profile diplomatic exchange or visit of leaders.[147]

On such occasions, as Gen. Om Prakash (who took over the Indian Army's Srinagar-based 15 Corps from Hasnain in 2012) argued, Pakistan tries to increase the number of casualties to up the ante, because a lower number would not attract the attention of the international media.

Visits of Indian leaders to J&K are often accompanied by CFVs. A senior BSF officer in Jammu pointed out that when Modi visited J&K in April 2016, there were CFVs in Samba.[148] Gen. Nandal testifies to

---

[144] Interview with BSF Officer 1, 2 June 2016, Jammu; Interview with BSF Officer 2, 2 June 2016, Jammu.

[145] Interview with BSF Officers 5, 3 June 2016, Jammu; Interview with BSF Officer 6, 4 June 2016, Jammu,.

[146] Interview with BSF Officer 2, 2 June 2016, Jammu.

[147] Interview with Lt Gen. (Retd) Syed Ata Hasnain, 5 June 2015, New Delhi.

[148] Interview with BSF Officer 1, 2 June 2016, Jammu. See also: 'Hours before Modi's Visit to J&K, Pak Violates Ceasefire, BSF Retaliates', *Deccan Chronicle*, 19 April 2016, available at http://www.deccanchronicle.com/nation/current-affairs/190416/hours-before-modi-s-visit-to-j-k-pak-violates-ceasefire-bsf-retaliates.html, last accessed on 3 January 2017.

212 • Line on Fire

its frequent occurrence and explains its underlying logic: 'It is symbolic. This is a disputed territory and this is an issue that Pakistan would like to highlight. The PM cannot simply go and say everything is alright (if there is a CFV). If there is a major incident, all security forces get deployed. It also undermines your authority.'[149]

To the question 'do political factors lead to CFVs? For instance, prime minister's visit or a UN Assembly meeting?', Gen. Tariq Ghazi of the Pakistan Army responded: 'They do, yes. If you want to highlight terrorism or human rights abuses, you will use that to make your point in these international forums. So, the whole game is played at a certain level between the militaries. Post-2003, these military games have reduced.'[150]

Pakistani officials also sometimes, though not very often, refer to political causes behind CFVs. In recent years, since the arrival of the Modi government in New Delhi, they insist, CFVs have also become politically motivated. The message from the Modi government appears to be that it will deal with Pakistan through force.[151]

Pakistani army officials interviewed in 2017 have invariably indicated that they believe that political factors are behind CFVs in the recent past. During my visit to the Pakistani side of the LoC in December 2017, most Pakistan Army officers underlined this. The GOC of the Pakistan Army's 12 Division in Murree, Gen. Azar Abbas, stressed the importance of understanding the underlying political dynamics that causes CFVs. He specifically referred to what he believed was a policy direction from the new government in New Delhi to fire at the Pakistani posts.[152] This feeling was echoed by Brig. Akthar Khan of 1-AK Brigade based in Muzaffarabad,[153] Brig. Noor of the 2-AK Brigade in Rawalakot,[154] and chief of general staff of the Pakistan Army, Gen. Bilal Akbar, in the army

---

[149] Interview with Lt Gen. (Retd) A.S. Nandal, 23 September 2016, Gurgaon.
[150] Interview with Lt Gen. (Retd) Tariq Ghazi, 7 November 2016, Bangkok.
[151] Pakistan Army officers 1, 2, and 3 were unanimous in their view that the current Modi government is hawkish towards Pakistan. It aims to punish Pakistan through use of force.
[152] Interview with Gen. Azar Abbas, 13 December 2017, Murree, Pakistan.
[153] Interview with Brig. Akhtar Khan, 13 December 2017, Muzaffarabad.
[154] Interview with Brig. Noor, 14 December 2017, Rawalakot.

GHQ in Rawalpindi.[155] Brig. Khan stated that the Indian Army fires at the Pakistani side to deflect attention from the insurgency in Kashmir, an argument strongly agreed to by Brig. Noor.

The field visits of UNMOGIP is sometimes used by the Pakistani side for provoking CFVs. Ajai Shukla explains: 'The Pakistan Army will arrange an UNMOGIP visit to, say, the Langur sector and two hours before the UNMOGIP is scheduled to visit, they will open fire with everything in that sector, provoking the Indian side to retaliate. And they will make sure that UNMOGIP is visiting at the time the Indian retaliation comes in', thereby making the Indian side look as the violator. Several Indian officers, including Gen. Bhatia, agree that this is done by the Pakistan Army to keep the Kashmir issue alive.

Special days of either side often witness CFVs. Forces often watch out, for instances, that can ruin their country's special day. Gen. Nandal argues: 'In J&K, there is a calendar listing all the major holidays like Republic Day, Independence Day, Diwali, or Holi, and they try to ruin that for you.' Brig. Ali makes a counter-argument: 'In 2015, on Bakr-Eid, six women and four children were killed by Indian firing in Shakargarh, Narowal sector.'[156] While on a filed visit to the Bimbergali brigade near the LoC, I heard witness accounts of the death of Karamatullah Khan—the head of the Balakote village on the LoC—who was killed along with six others travelling in a car when it was hit by a Pakistani 120 mm shell.[157] The firing by Pakistan took place on the Indian Independence day in 2015.

Domestic Politics and CFVs

Domestic politics in India and civil–military relations in Pakistan also lead to CFVs. A senior Indian general in Kashmir argued that since the BSF comes under the MHA, the BJP government in New Delhi finds it

[155] Interview with Lt Gen. Bilal Akbar, 15 December 2017, GHQ, Rawalpindi.

[156] Imran Sadiq, 'Two Pakistani Minors Killed in Shakargarh Cross-Border Firing: DCO', *Dawn*, 26 October 2015, available at https://www.dawn.com/news/1215495, last accessed on 3 January 2017.

[157] Anindita Sanyal, 'Pakistan Using Heavy Shells—A First since Ceasefire Agreement: Sources', NDTV, 16 August 2015, available at http://www.ndtv.com/india-news/pakistan-using-heavy-shells-a-first-since-ceasefire-agreement-sources-1207926, last accessed on 3 January 2017.

easier to manipulate it (by issuing informal instructions through the home ministry officials) for posturing in the IB sector in Jammu for domestic political purposes.[158] He also pointed out that there was a great deal of firing on the LoC by the Pakistan Army when Nawaz Sharif was elected as the prime minister of Pakistan in 2013, given the history between him and the Pakistan Army.

T.C.A. Raghavan, India's former high commissioner to Pakistan, argues that 'CFVs are often a way for the Pakistan Army to send a message to its political leaders: do not go too far on India; and the second is their internal transitions within Pakistan.'[159] More specifically, Raghavan believes that CFVs often result from the internal developments within the Pakistan Army such as the appointment of a new chief. Sometimes, he argues, junior officers try and get attention of the new chief by becoming active on the LoC.

Anil Kamboj, a retired BSF IG, agrees with Raghavan's assessment: 'Whenever there had been any initiative for peace process or bilateral talks between India and Pakistan, CFV occurred. Pakistan's ISI and army will never let the political leadership override their decision.'[160] A serving brigadier in Kashmir gives the example of the Ufa bilateral meeting between Prime Ministers Modi and Sharif on 9 July 2015. The eve of the meeting witnessed CFVs and deaths.[161]

Pakistanis disagree with this assessment. Gen. Afzal, for instance, points out that this is no more the case and may have been the case in the past: 'The argument about the Pakistani army wanting to gain an upper hand in political processes may be true 20 to 30 years ago. It has not been true since 2000—that is when I became a brigade commander and was

---

[158] Interview with Indian Army Officer 2, 13 May 2016, Udhampur.

[159] Interview with T.C.A. Raghavan, 8 September 2016, New Delhi.

[160] Debobrat Ghose, 'Why Is Pakistan Violating Ceasefire along LoC? Because It Needs to Prop up India as External Enemy, Say Experts', *Firstpost*, 18 August 2015, available at http://www.firstpost.com/india/why-is-pakistan-violating-ceasefire-along-loc-because-it-needs-to-prop-up-india-as-external-enemy-say-experts-2396422.html, last accessed on 3 January 2017.

[161] Sudhi Ranjan Sen, 'Ceasefire Violation on the Eve of India–Pakistan Talks, BSF Jawan Killed', NDTV, 9 July 2015, available at http://www.ndtv.com/india-news/bsf-jawan-killed-in-firing-by-pak-troops-from-across-the-border-in-jammu-and-kashmir-779863, last accessed on 3 January 2017.

senior enough to be aware of the political thinking in the army vis-á-vis national affairs.'

Many senior officers agree that a lot of the firing happens due to local factors. And yet there are occasions when the instructions come from the top. The use of mortars in CFVs is an indication of higher-level military, if not explicitly political, clearance for firing. Gen. Sikander Afzal, for instance, argued that 'mortar fire cannot be controlled by any level below the battalion level—permission from top is needed for the battalion to move the mortars anywhere—so it has to be a political decision to fire. Any fire beyond rifles and machine guns has to have the concurrence of the highest authority.'[162] While this does not necessarily suggest 'political' approval, it certainly involves permission from the higher echelons of the military.

Gen. Ghazi argues that political directions (or directions from higher-ups) to fire may be issued to Indian or Pakistani troops for a variety of reasons: 'to put pressure, to keep them engaged, cause casualties as a matter of retribution, show aggressive response, create an excuse for putting the blame somewhere, and cover for activities being done under the cover of fire.'

Several serving Pakistani officials also alluded to how the government in New Delhi has tried to use the 'surgical strike' and 'CFV' narratives to garner domestic popularity and win elections.[163] Brig. Noor noted that 'national politics often gets played out on the LoC.'[164] Brig. Khan argued that media pressure and political rhetoric often act as force multipliers when the CFVs begin.[165]

THE 2014 CFVs IN JAMMU

In September–October 2014, months after the BJP-led government of Prime Minister Narendra Modi came to power in a landslide victory in New Delhi, incessant firing and shelling in the Jammu region led to more

---

[162] Interview with Lt Gen. (Retd) Sikandar Afzal, 16 April 2016, Bangkok.
[163] Interview with Brig. Akhtar Khan, 13 December 2017, Muzaffarabad; Interview with Pakistan Army Officer 5, 13 December 2017; Interview with Pakistan Army Officer 6, 14 December 2017; Interview with Pakistan Army Officer 7, 13 December 2017, Islamabad.
[164] Interview with Brig. Noor, 14 December 2017, Rawalakot.
[165] Interview with Brig. Akhtar Khan, 13 December 2017, Muzaffarabad.

than 30,000 local villagers being displaced and led to tens of civilian and military casualties on both sides of the Jammu-Sialkot border. The firing was unprecedented in its intensity, as were the casualties.

September and October of 2014 were also important months for J&K. The election campaign for the local assembly election was in full swing, and the recently elected BJP government in New Delhi was engaged in a feverish campaign in the Jammu region, the only part of the Muslim-majority J&K state that has a Hindu majority, where BJP hoped to win the maximum number of seats. Since the BJP knew that its chances in the Kashmir Valley were slim, despite the so-called 'Modi wave' that brought the BJP to power in New Delhi earlier in the year, they focused all efforts on the Jammu region. To win maximum number of seats in Jammu, the BJP government had to do two things: play up the infiltration and terrorism from Pakistan into J&K[166] and put focus on the cross-border firing by Pakistan, which has been a major nuisance for the people of the Jammu region.

Summer in Jammu from August 2014 onwards was far from normal, or calm. In August that year, the BSF HQ in New Delhi, which reports to the MHA under Home Minister Rajnath Singh, appointed Rakesh Sharma, a local officer from the Jammu region, as the inspector general of the force in Jammu. Soon after Sharma was sent to Jammu, the BSF decided to increase the heat on the Pak Rangers in the Jammu-Sialkot border, which according to some reports caught Pakistan by surprise.[167]

BSF higher-ups decided to graduate the firing from small arms to mortar shelling. As part of a major plan, the BSF moved over 100 high-calibre guns (for shelling) from Punjab and Kashmir sectors to the Jammu

---

[166] 'Modi's J&K Rhetoric Meant for Elections', *Deccan Chronicle*, 14 August 2014, available at http://www.deccanchronicle.com/140814/commentary-op-ed/article/modi%E2%80%99s-jk-rhetoric-meant-elections, last accessed on 3 January 2017.

[167] Abhishek Bhalla and Gautam Dutt, 'Islamabad Shocked as Indian Army Launches "Massive" Retaliation to Border Firing ... and Confident PM Modi Promises "Everything will be All Right Soon"', Mail Online India, 9 October 2014, available at http://www.dailymail.co.uk/indiahome/indianews/article-2785698/Islamabad-shocked-Indian-Army-launches-massive-retaliation-border-firing-confident-PM-Modi-promises-right-soon.html, last accessed on 3 January 2017.

sector. They were used on the 192 km Jammu border with Pakistan in a coordinated manner, pulverizing the Pakistani posts.

In Sharma's own words, 'From 2013 to 2014, there were not many incidents. There were small incidences of couple of days of firing, and in between these incidences, there was small-arm firing mixed with some mortar fire. (However), from July 2014 onwards till October 2015, there was very little small-arm fire; heavy mortar was used in major cross-border firing.'

The J&K elections and the newly elected BJP government's past rhetoric about giving Pakistan a befitting response on the border, and the months-long firing, clearly had an influence on the high incidence of CFVs that took place in the Jammu sector in late 2014.

The Jammu and Kashmir Legislative Assembly election was held in five phases from 25 November to 20 December 2014, and BJP made history by winning 25 of the 37 seats in the Jammu province, emerging as the second largest party in Jammu and Kashmir, which helped it to become a coalition partner in the government in the state for the first time in history.

Retributive Reasons

'Land Grab' and CFVs

> In 2001, when the insurgency was at its peak, we had decided that we will alter the status of the LoC. The Pakistani positions were selected all along, from Batalik to Chamb-Jaurian, roughly per brigade about one-two, total about 25–30 posts ... one fine day, we are going to alter the status, which would hurt Pakistan.
>
> —Lt Gen. (Retd) H.S. Panag[168]

Land grabbing also could lead to CFVs, even though such things happen very rarely. Even though they happen rarely, they have happened throughout the past decades. There are basically two kinds of land grabs that can lead to heightened levels of tension between the two sides: opportunistic land grab, which happens due to an opportunity that presents itself, and aggressive land grab, which is a result of a lot more pre-planning and strategizing. But before we get to various cases of that, let us briefly analyse the historical record of grabbing adversary's land and posts.

---

[168] Interview with Lt Gen. (Retd) H.S. Panag, 3 March 2017, Bangkok.

The difference between the IB and LoC is that the former is a settled boundary whereas the latter is not. Given that fundamental difference, force was used to alter the status of the LoC (when it was CFL) until the Simla Agreement of 1972. The AGPL is still not a settled boundary and, hence, open to potential land grab.[169] Even though the LoC is a semi-settled boundary, since the Simla Agreement prohibits the two sides from altering it by force, the concept of 'holders-keepers' is still valid there, which Gen. Bhatia explains as 'what you have, you keep; what you hold, you keep; and what you occupy also, you keep'. Gen. Hasnain calls it the 'grabbers, keepers' concept and defines it so: 'Any side grabbing a piece of ground for a tactical advantage gets to keep it unless forcibly evicted'.[170]

The practice of capturing vacant land and posts was more common prior to 1971. But even after 1971, there have been several instances of land/post capture. Gen. Ghazi explains the dynamics behind such activities:

> In some areas, troops have gone across the LoC and occupied positions because they found them vacant and have occupied them. There were some areas that were vacant. Post-1971, when the LoC was demarcated, there were gaps that were controlled by patrols, firing, and observation because there were not enough troops. But, after a period, as better means and more personnel became available, incursions into vacant areas became the norm and, in many cases, went unchallenged. Wherever there was opportunity, both sides engaged in it. This went on for some time until it reduced because the existing gaps were closed and the number of troops also increased, so as not to allow it anymore. The number of troops positioned along the LoC has seen a steady rise in terms of number of positions, number of people guarding them, and the kind of weaponry and devices being set up to monitor it. As a result, such activity has drastically reduced over a period of time.[171]

One important rationale for the land grab post-1971 was to retake the lost territories. A senior retired Pakistan Army officer, who refused

[169] Interview with Col Ajai Shukla, 6 September 2016, New Delhi.

[170] Lt Gen. (Retd) Syed Ata Hasnain, 'The LoC/IB and Fire Assaults: What's this all About?', Daily Excelsior, 2 November 2016, available at http://www.dailyexcelsior.com/locib-fire-assaults-whats/, last accessed on 2 September 2017.

[171] Interview with Lt Gen. (Retd) Tariq Ghazi, 7 November 2016, Bangkok.

to be named, said that land grabbing used to take place after 1971 till mid-late 1990s in order to regain the areas lost during the 1971 war, in particular along the LoC. 'When it was realized that regaining was not possible', he says, 'attempts were made to improve tactical positions on ground.' Recall that unlike in other states, territorial status quo antebellum was not established in J&K at the end of the 1971 war.

This argument also clarifies to a great extent why CFVs are so rampant in places like Poonch, Jammu, Samba, and Rajouri on the Indian side, and Sialkot, Rawalakot, Kotli, and Shakargarh on the Pakistan side: these places had witnessed pitched battles during the 1965 and 1971 wars. Since it is not possible to fight and regain territory outside J&K along the IB, land grabbing and CFVs take place here. A history of land grabbing and CFVs in these areas have now become sort of a norm. This is a line of enquiry that requires a great deal more future research focus.

Gen. Om Prakash forthrightly stated that such instances of capturing and establishing one's posts across the line has happened throughout the India–Pakistan stand-off on the LoC, including in the recent years, which are often carried out to gain tactical advantage. A Pakistani general[172] believes that this has not happened after the CFA came into being in 2003. A serving Indian general in the Kashmir Valley says that such activities are not common these days but do happen once in a while.

However, it is important to note that not many such instances come out in the open given the amount of secrecy attached to such missions and that the commander under whose watch land/post was lost would lose face. As Col Shukla points out: 'For a local commander, it is a big deal to have lost it but no local commander wants to make it appear that it was lost on his watch. So, a lot of times, these things are played down and it does not come out.'[173]

The most common form of land grab is the opportunistic kind, that is, making use of a given opportunity to get the better of the adversary and capturing his land or post. During my field visit, I heard Indian officers talk of both sides grabbing small chunks of territory, which have led to CFVs and persistent tension in the area.

To test this theory, I asked Gen. Majid a question: 'Hypothetically speaking, if you know there is a piece of land that belongs to the other side

---

[172] Interview with Pakistani Official 4, 17 January 2017, Rawalpindi.
[173] Interview with Col Ajai Shukla, 6 September 2016, New Delhi.

but is not occupied—would you move in?' He did not say 'no': 'There have been instances—it happened in the Kamar sector. Unless it is allowed by somebody, it does not just happen. The Indians tried to snatch the Javed post on the Pakistani side—a proper operation was planned and there was escalation.'[174] I asked Brig. Kanwal a similar question as to whether he would occupy if an area was not being occupied by the Pakistani side: 'We will occupy it', was his prompt answer.[175]

Post-Kargil, the Indian Army, however, has tried to paint the picture that it was agreed to by the two sides in the Simla Agreement that they would withdraw from their posts in the harsher winter months to return once the winter is over. The routine Kargil War briefing at the Kargil War Memorial in Drass is proof of this innovative argument, which obviously has no treaty basis in the Simla Agreement of 1972.[176]

Gen. Arshad talked of the same sector during my interview with him: 'The Indian Army has violated many areas in the Chakma sector—we call it the Kamar sector—they have made a lot of ingress in the area. Many times, in the winters, you vacate a position and somebody comes and sits there. At many places, both sides are ... there are few areas ... less from our side and more from the Indian side ... there has been ingress.'[177] Sometimes, land grab is carried out in a particular sector in order to balance losses in other sectors.[178]

Gen. Nandal asserts that given the fact that the LoC is not well defined, land grabbing takes place from time to time. Both Nandal and Om Prakash recalled an instance where in Kirni village of the Poonch sector, the Pakistan Army came and occupied well into the Indian territory in the early 1990s. The intruders had also made fortifications in the village. It was later vacated by the Indian Army by force.

There is a constant fear of opportunistic land grab by the other side. Gen. Nandal recalls an incident from the time he was posted on the LoC on how his men had to take pre-emptive steps to offset a potential land grab attempt by the Pakistani troops:

[174] Interview with Lt Gen. (Retd) Tariq Majid, 14 April 2016, Bangkok.
[175] Interview with Brig. (Retd) Gurmeet Kanwal, 4 May 2016, Bangkok.
[176] 'Kargil War Briefing: Live from Kargil War Memorial', YouTube video, available at https://www.youtube.com/watch?v=nfGST9O2vA0, last accessed on 10 October 2017.
[177] Interview with Lt Gen. (Retd) Waheed Arshad, 15 April 2016, Bangkok.
[178] Interview with Brig. (Retd) Naeem Ahmad Salik, 13 April 2016, Bangkok.

Once on our side, there was a house just next to the LoC of a widow named Makhni Begum, just 15 metres from the Pakistani post. One day, the lady migrated to the other side and the house became vacant. We were worried that the Pakistani side may come and position themselves here, make bunkers, and occupy it. So, we had to blow the house up.[179]

The result of opportunistic land grabbing, which has drastically come down over the years, is persistent tension and firing. While this has dissuaded the two sides from engaging in such activities, given the many uncertainties and ambiguities that exist on the LoC and IB, this cannot be ruled out entirely.

Besides the opportunistic land grab operations, there are also more well-planned strategically thought out aggressive land grab operations and counter-operations. The Kargil operation by the Pakistan Army was one such well-known one and does not need to be repeated here. Let us look at a few other instances of such offensive operations.

In 2001–2 during Operation Parakram, the war preparations after the attack on the Indian Parliament in December that year, the Indian Army detected intrusions in the Indian territory called Point 3260 in the Machil-Neelam-Gurez sector of Kashmir. In December 2002, Defence Minister George Fernandes told the Indian Parliament that in the last week of July 2002, there was a Pakistani intrusion approximately 800 metres on the Indian side of the LoC in the area of Point 3260, which is 1,800 metres east of Loonda post.[180] Since the post was not considered strategically important and was hence left unguarded, it was occupied by the Pakistani troops. In a joint operation of the Indian Army and the air force, the post was eventually taken back.[181]

There have been occasions when one side or the other pulled a surprise on the other and captured an unmanned area, especially after

[179] Interview with Lt Gen. (Retd) A.S. Nandal, 23 September 2016, Gurgaon.
[180] Press Information Bureau, 'Vacating Loonda Post in LoC, Kashmir', Ministry of Defence, Government of India, available at http://pib.nic.in/archive/releases98/lyr2002/rdec2002/04122002/r041220024.html, last accessed on 5 July 2016.
[181] Arjun Subramaniam, 'From Kargil to Parakram, A Lesson in Forceful Persuasion', Hindu, 27 July 2012, available at http://www.thehindu.com/opinion/op-ed/from-kargil-to-parakram-a-lesson-in-forceful-persuasion/article3687855.ece, last accessed on 21 September 2017.

wars and conflicts. Gen. Panag describes one such incident that took place in the Batalik–Yaldor–Chorbat-la sector in the year 2000. After the Kargil War was over, some of the territories were left uncaptured by either side 'due to initial errors of judgment and the onset of winter'. In April 2000, the decision was taken to capture a key point in the sector, Point 5310, which had to be done undertaking a torturous journey to the mountain top, during which the attacking party suffered one casualty in a freak accident. Capturing Point 5310 would provide the Indian Army a dominant physical position vis-à-vis the Pakistani side given the advantage of height the point would provide. The point was captured and it was only in May that the Pakistani troops posited far below could detect the Indian capture of Point 5310, but it was too late to do anything by then. Gen. Panag writes:

> On 20th May 2000, Pakistani troops, tried to get observation over us by climbing the slopes of Dolmi Barak, a peak 20,000 feet high on eastern flank of Karubar Bowl, to set up a post. I arranged a Konkurs Missile Launcher with a range of four kilometres from the Mechanised Infantry unit and personally supervised the firing to bring this post down.[182]

Kargil in 1999, perhaps, was the biggest land grab in the history of India–Pakistan relations, a capture that the Pakistan Army could not sustain as it was pushed back from the captured territory eventually. Have there been similar plans made by either country even if not carried out eventually? Here are a few such cases.

THE 2001 'ALTER THE LOC PLAN'

In an interview with me in Bangkok in March 2017, Gen. H.S. Panag discussed the details of such a plan made by the Indian Army in 2001 to alter the LoC with Pakistan, though the meticulously prepared plan was never carried out as various geopolitical developments eventually overwhelmed the decision. Most of the details Panag discussed were later endorsed by Gen. Nanavatty in an interview in New Delhi.

---

[182] Lt Gen. H.S. Panag, 'The "Lost" Operation against Pakistan in Chorbat La', 14 September 2016, *News Laundry*; https://www.newslaundry.com/2016/09/14/the-lost-operation-against-pakistan-in-chorbat-la, last accessed on 3 October 2018.

As per the plan, which was discussed at length in Chapter 1, three posts each were selected from the Batalik sector, where Gen. Panag was posted during those days, right up to Chamb-Jaurian, roughly 1–2 posts per brigade. A total of about 25–30 posts were finally selected for capture. The basic rationale behind the plan was to ease the pressure from the Pakistan-sponsored insurgency. The Northern Command of the Indian Army had made the overall plan with the approval of the army HQ in New Delhi. Gen. Panag then was only a brigade commander and he was in charge of carrying out the operation on three Pakistani posts.

The previous year had witnessed several small-scale and successful operations of this kind. With the tacit understanding and green signal from the army's higher-ups, local units of the army 'adopted a calibrated offensive action across' the LoC 'to sanitise areas of infiltration' on the Pakistani side.[183]

The success of these minor operations and the success of the Kargil War had emboldened the Indian Army.

Lt Gen. Rustom K. Nanavatty, the then commander-in-chief of the Indian Army's Northern Command, was the overall in charge of the operation and had personally overseen the preparations. Gen. Panag recalls Nanavatty flying into the former's brigade HQ to decide the objectives and details of the operation. The general and the brigadier then went up to the LoC on the Indian side and the army commander was shown the three posts that were marked out to be captured. Panag's brigade was holding around 70 km of frontage of the LoC, so the objectives were spread out. Nanavatty approved the plan before returning to his command headquarters in J&K's Udhampur district.

9/11 changed everything, including the geopolitics in South Asia, thanks partly to changing US strategic calculations vis-à-vis Pakistan. The operation was called off. It is worth recalling here that followed by the September 2001 attacks in New York, the Indian Parliament was attacked in December that year, leading to a major military stand-off between India and Pakistan, which lasted several months.

In October that year, the operation was called off.

---

[183] Pravin Sawhney, 'At the Crossroad', Force Newsmagazine, 26 January 2014, available at http://forcenewsmagazine.blogspot.de/2014/01/at-cross-road.html, last accessed on 21 September 2017.

224 • Line on Fire

THE CAPTURE OF MALABELA

Malabela is in the Chicken Neck area of the Jammu sector guarded by the BSF. Chicken Neck is strategically significant for both India and Pakistan. An islet between the river Chenab and one of its subsidiaries, Chandra Bagha, the Chicken Neck provides Pakistan with a quick and short access to the bridge at Akhnoor over the Chenab and enables it to reach Jammu early on in case of a hot war. The beak of the Chicken Neck area is pointed towards the bridge: while India calls it a neck that can be easily strangled, given that it is surrounded on all three sides by the Indian forces, Pakistan calls it a 'dagger', piercing into the Indian territory.

The Malabela area, consisting of around 25 acres with a frontage of around 700 metres, 400 of which is not fenced, has been an area of contention for more than a decade and a half now. The reason for this recurrent violence in the area is that a part of the Malabela area was captured by the Indian forces during the 2001–2 military stand-off, Operation Parakram, between India and Pakistan. Although no war was fought between the two countries, several small-scale operations were carried out, and one such operation was organized here. Despite the fact that the area is well fortified by the BSF, tunnelling underneath the fence has been reported and so has tampering with BPs. In any case, one of the results of the land grab in 2001–2 is incessant CFVs in the area.[184]

Sniping and CFVs

> *In 2011, Pakistani snipers got two of our men through a loophole in the bunker. And then we sorted them out.*
>
> —Lt Gen. (Retd) A.S. Nandal[185]

---

[184] 'Even as India Lodges Protest, Pakistan Targets Border Villages with Mortar Bombs', *DNA*, 16 July 2015, available at http://www.dnaindia.com/india/report-even-as-india-lodges-protest-pakistan-targets-border-villages-with-mortar-bombs-2105047, last accessed on 11 March 2017; 'Woman Killed as Pak Rangers Violate Ceasefire', *Hindu*, 15 July 2015, available at http://www.thehindu.com/news/national/bsf-jawan-injured-in-firing-by-pakistan-rangers/article7424706.ece, last accessed on 21 September 2017.

[185] Interview with Lt Gen. (Retd) A.S. Nandal, 23 September 2016, New Delhi.

Indian officers cite that sniper attacks by Pakistani soldiers or Rangers or even terrorists are also a significant catalyst of CFVs. In fact, there have been several reports of sniping incidents both on the LoC and IB in J&K.[186] But what is the rationale behind sniping and how does it escalate tensions? Syed Ata Hasnain argues that sniping (as it is informally termed) is undertaken to create confusion and help infiltration. Rakesh Sharma of the BSF remarked that sniping takes a serious toll on morale: 'A man standing on duty at the post is always under tremendous fear of being watched by the opposite side through a telescopic rifle and of being shot at any moment.'[187]

'You could get sniped at through the peephole of the bunker if the enemy is determined, and it has happened in the past', an Indian soldier in Kashmir told me when I observed during a field visit to a forward area on the LoC that well-fortified bunkers would be a safe place to be in during times of tension.[188]

A mid-level BSF officer in Jammu pointed out that, unlike firing, sniping is less escalatory because it has deniability and yet it can unsettle the fire-receiving side and lead to counter-fire. The officer also argues that the Pakistan Army, unlike the Rangers, is desirous of escalating tensions with India. He also argued that the Pakistan Army sometimes hires professional snipers to use against Indian troops.[189] Two senior BSF officers in Jammu confirmed this: 'Snipers come from the army or ISI [Inter-Services Intelligence]. The Pakistan Rangers have to participate nonetheless' and that 'Pakistan hires professional snipers and sniping is done to harass the Indian border domination and for psychological damage. Pakistan Rangers are not happy about sniping because they take the blame.'[190]

---

[186] PTI, 'Army Jawan Killed in Pak Sniper Firing in Kashmir', *Deccan Chronicle*, 9 November 2016, available at http://www.deccanchronicle.com/nation/current-affairs/091116/army-jawan-killed-in-pak-sniper-firing-in-kashmir.html, last accessed on 21 September 2017; 'JCO Killed in Sniper Fire from Pakistan at LoC', Indiatoday.in, 25 August 2015, available at http://indiatoday.intoday.in/story/jco-killed-in-sniper-fire-from-pakistan-at-loc/1/460916.html, last accessed on 21 September 2017.

[187] Interview with Rakesh Sharma, 15 September 2016, New Delhi.

[188] Interview with Indian Army Officer 4, 15 May 2016, Bhimber Gali.

[189] Interview with BSF Officer 5, 3 June 2016, Jammu.

[190] Interview with BSF Officer 6, 4 June 2016, Jammu.

Taking anti-sniping measures is not easy. Retaliation using fire assaults is usually the response. As Nandal puts it, 'The only way is to not give the other side a target. Do not become a target. In 2011, Pakistani snipers got two of our men through a loophole in the bunker. And then we sorted them out. We had to give them back four or five casualties.'[191] Rakesh Sharma says that the BSF has of late become aware of the damage it causes and, hence, is taking some measures to avoid getting caught in the sniper's target: 'We have equipped the soldiers sufficiently and modified tour duty points so that anti-sniping measures are in place. For more than two years now, there has not been a single case of sniping. So, we have all the measures, be it physical, technical, or briefing.'[192]

Indian media reports have attributed Pakistani sniping to its commandoes belonging to the Special Service Group.[193] Media reports indicate that considerably more snipers are at work on the Pakistani side than the Indian, prompting an Indian newspaper even to report that 'Army losing sniper edge over Pakistan on LoC'.[194]

Sniping, the officers pointed out, often lead to heavy CFVs precisely because one is compelled to respond to the death of a soldier on one's side. Rakesh Sharma says that sniping invariably escalates the situation on the border and doing so has actually prevented sniping by the Pakistani side:

> After they sniped, I decided that the best way is to be aggressive. So, it was decided that if I am fired upon, my neighbouring posts will retaliate as fast as possible without waiting for orders. He will kill the sniper as early as possible using whatever fire he needs to. The point is to teach them a lesson. We have made it very clear that if they engage in sniping, counter-sniping will be intense till the target has been neutralized. So,

[191] Interview with Lt Gen. (Retd) A.S. Nandal, 23 September 2016, Gurgaon.

[192] Interview with Rakesh Sharma, 15 September 2016, New Delhi.

[193] Pradip R. Sagar, 'Pakistan's SSG Commandoes Targeting Indian Soldiers along LoC', New Indian Express, 31 October 2016, available at http://www.newindianexpress.com/nation/2016/oct/31/pakistans-ssg-commandoes-targetting-indian-soldiers-along-loc-1533561.html, last accessed on 11 March 2017.

[194] Pradip R. Sagar, 'Army Losing Sniper Edge over Pakistan on LoC', The New Indian Express, 12 February 2017, available at http://www.newindianexpress.com/thesundaystandard/2017/feb/12/army-losing-sniper-edge-over-pakistan-on-loc-1569609.html, last accessed on 11 March 2017.

they did that once and paid the penalty. We engulfed their area in heavy firing, and in the bargain, we might have caused some casualties.[195]

Honour and Prestige

If I have commanded a battalion there and have done a lot of fire exchange with the other side as a part of psychological dominance, the officer who replaces me will inherit that confrontation … and that goes on.

—Col Ajai Shukla (Retd)[196]

Personal and regimental honour are the lifeblood of soldiery around the world; Indian and Pakistani militaries are no different. *Izzat* (or honour) is a powerful tool for motivation, which leads men in arms to kill and to get in harm's way without any hesitation or asking any questions, at a mere nod of their COs. This unique feeling of comradery, fraternity, and discipline can also, however, cause more violence.

Responding in kind to the aggression or an attack by the other side is seen as an important element in this hyper-nationalist cosmology. As a senior Pakistani general put it, 'After Indians kill one of our men, it becomes a matter of honour for Pakistanis to respond in kind'.[197] In situations of that kind, which every commander knows will occur from time to time, honour and strategy make a deadly combination.

And the other side knows that there will be no let-up till one retaliatory kill is made.

'Bezzati Ho Gayi' ('We Have Been Humiliated')

Honour goes beyond mere revenge for the fallen men on one's side—it is also about the prestige and history of the regiment, handed down through generations and held sacrosanct. While the blood of the dead should be avenged, the honour of the living needs to be preserved as well. Those who have a reputation of being brave must continue that tradition, others will have to earn it—either way, the result is aggression and blood feuds.

Gen. Panag explains how it works in real life on the front lines using an appropriate example. Every regiment, he says, has an honorary colonel, a patriarch of some kind. One day, suddenly he would read in the

---

[195] Interview with Rakesh Sharma, 15 September 2016, New Delhi.
[196] Interview with Col Ajai Shukla, 6 September 2016, New Delhi.
[197] Interview with Pakistani Official 4, 17 January 2017, Rawalpindi.

newspapers that 13 Rajputana Rifles, for instance, has had an incident and suffered casualties. He, stationed somewhere else, would call up the CO and say, 'Bezzati ho gayi', that the regiment has been shamed and now the CO must do something. This will then become a matter of 'safekeeping' the regimental prestige and honour for the CO who would be psychologically compelled to act, to take revenge. A failure to do so would not only be a personal setback for the CO but also a collective shame for the regiment. And shame is not something a soldier can live with.

Gen. Ghazi of the Pakistan Army gives a similar example from the time he was posted as the CO on the LoC in 1990:

> When I went to take command in the area opposite Poonch sector, the orders were in place to curb unnecessary firing by our troops. Earlier, due to some construction activities undertaken by our side, the Indians had blasted our posts with big-calibre anti-aircraft guns and three guys were killed on our side. The LoC had been very live as a result and the divisional commander (GOC) felt that needless provocations had to stop. My predecessor had issued orders not to fire even a single bullet without his personal permission, even if the other side was firing. The morale of the unit plummeted. The CO was removed and I was posted in his place. When I arrived to take command, I found some troops from the unit standing on the road, blocking my way. They were all Northern Light Infantry (NLI) troops who had a different sense of loyalty and were far more independent-minded than others. When I got out of the jeep, I was told that I wouldn't be allowed to proceed to my HQ until the problem of 'murdaar maut'—a humiliating death— was sorted out. I was taken aback by what some may see as mutinous behaviour but I realized that they were right. The other side was firing and these guys had to duck down and keep quiet on the orders of their officers! They were really riled up. So, I asked them to load the nearest weapon they had, identify the target, and fire to their heart's content. Around five or six men fired for a long time. It uplifted the morale of the battalion immediately and we bonded in a mutual affection that survives to this day. It is another matter that I had hell to pay before my GOC that day for initiating a major CFV on my first day in command![198]

There is also the element of a regiment's history preceding its induction in a particular area. The adversary on the other side of the newly

---

[198] Interview with Lt Gen. (Retd) Tariq Ghazi, 7 November 2016, Bangkok.

inducted sector/area would come to know about the reputation of the incoming unit/battalion and this may trigger a certain behaviour on the other side. As Gen. Panag says, 'each unit has its own reputation, which is known to both sides. Within the army, the individual commanders are chosen for the job depending upon the unit's characteristics, its performance, and its value systems that are assigned to it.'[199] He recalls the reputation of the 4 Sikh regiment when he was part of it and was sent to the LoC in 1968: 'In 1968, when my unit, 4 Sikh, went to a sector that witnessed sporadic firing, our CO sent a message to the other side that *"jo ho gaya, so ho gaya ab 4 Sikh aa gayee hai"* ["what is done is done, now 4 Sikh (Indian Army unit) has arrived"]. So now if you guys do any mischief, you are going to have it.' This had a calming effect in the area. Put differently, aggressive regiments often lend peace to an area.

Sometimes, certain locations have a history of aggressive deployment, patrolling, and violence, which tends to be handed down to the new incoming units, which stick to the behaviour patterns of their predecessors. Col Shukla explains it: 'If I have commanded a battalion there and have done a lot of fire exchange with the other side as part of psychological dominance, the officer who replaces me will inherit that confrontation … and that goes on.'[200] The contours of such military subcultures and their implications should be carefully analysed to understand how and why certain areas report more violence, and sometimes calm.

'Surgical Strikes'

We got back five dead bodies and strewed them outside our posts, saying that the Pakistanis attacked us. That is life on the LoC.

—Retired Indian Army Colonel[201]

On 29 September 2016, the Indian Army's DGMO Lt Gen. Ranbir Singh made a public announcement about a 'surgical strike' that the Indian Army had conducted across the LoC that morning in order to take out terrorist launch pads in the Pakistani territory. He stressed

---

[199] Interview with Lt Gen. (Retd) H.S. Panag, 3 March 2017, Bangkok.
[200] Interview with Col Ajai Shukla, 6 September 2016, New Delhi.
[201] Interview with retired colonel of the Indian Army on condition of anonymity, 3 November 2016, New Delhi.

that the strike was to 'pre-empt infiltration by terrorists'.[202] The strike was in response to a terrorist attack on an Indian Army base at Uri on 18 September that had killed 19 soldiers. Despite calls by the media and the opposition parties, the government refused to put out any video evidence of the operation.

Pakistan, in turn, refused to acknowledge that India had carried out the surgical strike. Since then several reports have claimed that this was not the first ever surgical strike carried out by India on Pakistani soil. *India Today* reported in October 2016 that 'in March 1998, Indian Special Forces had crossed the LoC to carry out a strike, and in January 2000 crossed the Neelam river to the Nadala enclave for another mission'. The same report cited several such instances of 'surgical strikes'.[203] In fact, in a statement before the parliamentary panel on external affairs, India's foreign secretary officially stated that such strikes had been conducted previously as well—'target specific, limited-calibre, counter-terrorist operations have taken place in the past as well'—but this was the first time that the government made it public.[204] Clearly, the public announcement had two aims: domestic political gains and deterrence.

A senior leader of the UPA regime, for instance, clarified, 'Such operations have been carried out before, even during the time of Manmohan Singh ji but he never publicised it and kept beating the drum about it.'[205]

---

[202] 'Surgical Strikes: Full Text of Indian Army DGMO Lt Gen. Ranbir Singh's Press Conference', *Indian Express*, 29 September 2016, available at http://indianexpress.com/article/india/india-news-india/pakistan-infiltration-attempts-indian-army-surgical-strikes-line-of-control-jammu-and-kashmir-uri-poonch-pok-3055874/, last accessed on 11 March 2017.

[203] Javed Ansari, 'Ghatak Surgical Strikes Not First of its Kind, India Carried Several Similar Strikes in Last 10 years', Indiatoday.in, 3 October 2016, available at http://indiatoday.intoday.in/story/surgical-strikes-india-pakistan-loc-pok-indian-army-government/1/779426.html, last accessed on 11 March 2017.

[204] PTI, 'Cross-LoC Strikes Happened in Past Too: FS Contradicts Parrikar', Rediff.com, 19 October 2016, available at https://www.rediff.com/news/report/cross-loc-strikes-happened-in-past-too/20161018.htm, last accessed on 19 November 2018.

[205] 'Surgical Strikes also Carried Out under Manmohan Singh, We Never Publicised It: Congress', *DNA*, 2 October 2016, http://www.dnaindia.com/india/report-surgical-strikes-als-carried-out-under-manmohan-singh-we-never-pubilcised-it-congress-2260658, last accessed on 11 March 2017.

It is widely reported that Pakistan uses what is generally known as BATs to carry out attacks of the kind that was carried out on the Uri army base in September 2016. An Indian news agency, PTI, defined the Pakistan Army's BATs as follows: 'The SSG (special services group) forms the core of BAT. Its primary task is to dominate the LoC by carrying out disruptive actions in the form of surreptitious raids.'[206]

In early May 2017, India accused Pakistan of killing and beheading two of its soldiers on the Indian side of the LoC in the Krishna Ghati sector of Kashmir. The Indian patrol came under fire from automatic weapons and a 'BAT', consisting of jihadi fighters, came over to the Indian side, reports claimed. The terrorists, with the help of the Pakistan Army's covering fire, carried out the attack and returned to their side of the LoC, taking back the heads of the soldiers.[207]

As is evident, then, 'surgical strikes' and BAT actions have not only been a major part of the India–Pakistan military stand-off on the LoC but also have been a key cause behind political and diplomatic escalation between the two sides. Thanks to the sensationalist media coverage of these incidents, political leaderships in the two countries find it difficult to ignore them and it forces them to issue statements and public orders for 'teaching the other side a lesson'. This then necessitates that we take a closer look at this issue.

There are then three sets of questions we must seek answers for: First, was the September 2016 'surgical strike' the first one ever conducted by the Indian military against Pakistan? Or have there been other attacks in the past? Second, perhaps more importantly, has Pakistan ever conducted such operations on the Indian soil in Kashmir?[208] Finally, does India

---

[206] 'Mutilating of Jawans "Pre-planned Operation by Pakistan Army"', *Indian Express*, 1 May 2017, available at http://indianexpress.com/article/india/mutilating-of-jawans-pre-planned-operation-by-pakistan-army/, last accessed on 12 August 2017,

[207] Ajai Shukla, 'Army Weighs Retaliation for Beheading of Two Soldiers', Broadsword [web blog], 3 May 2017, http://ajaishukla.blogspot.de/2017/05/army-weighs-retaliation-for-beheading.html, last accessed on 11 September 2017.

[208] 'No Comments, Says MEA on Foreign Secy's Remark on Surgical Strike', *Deccan Chronicle*, 20 October 2016, available at http://www.deccanchronicle.com/nation/current-affairs/201016/no-comments-says-mea-on-foreign-secys-remark-on-surgical-strike.html?fromNewsdog=1, last accessed on 11 March 2017.

have BAT teams? If indeed the Indian Army has carried out cross-LoC operations in the past, what kind of forces carried it out? If they are special forces and not called BAT, does that difference in the name matter given that the purpose is the same?

But before we answer these questions, let us consider the official statement made by the Indian foreign secretary to the parliamentary panel on external affairs as a working definition for 'surgical strikes': 'target specific, limited-calibre, counter-terrorist operations across the LoC'. In the Pakistani case, however, we may have to delete the phrase 'counter-terrorist' from our definition.

WERE THERE 'SURGICAL STRIKES' PRIOR TO SEPTEMBER 2016?

Several serving and retired military officers interviewed for this book have said so in no ambiguous terms that surgical strikes have been carried out several times in the past and they have created conditions that triggered CFVs. Gen. T.K. Sapru, former Northern Indian Army commander, says:

> It was going on all the time; only thing is that it was not advertised ... it did not get reported in the media, as happens today. The beheadings for example ... there was action thereafter ... I do not want to say when exactly but there were beheadings carried out of the other side. We got the heads back. It happens even without the nation being told ... it shouldn't be advertised. When they do something, they attribute it to the jihadis though they could well be totally controlled, organized, and trained by the ISI and the army but ultimately what comes in is this, at least what is visible. At times, they have sent in their regulars ... quick raids ... but then we have sent in our regulars too. We can't say that jihadis do this for us ... so we use our own army.[209]

Gen. Bhatia recalls an incident from August 2013 when the Pakistani army team had carried out a surgical operation and killed five Indian soldiers in the Poonch sector of the LoC. This was responded to by the Indian Army, according to him, because the 'balance sheet had to be maintained'. Col Shukla recalls a similar operation in 1999 during the Kargil stand-off when 'across the line, we launched physical assaults, captured Pakistani posts—there was one post near where the LoC starts in Munnawar Tawi, near the Beas River—which took the Pakistanis by

---

[209] Interview with Gen. (Retd) T.K. Sapru, 10 October 2016, Chandigarh.

surprise. Indian troops attacked a Pakistani post and killed 19 soldiers and got back a visitors' book in which Musharraf had signed two weeks before the attack took place.'[210]

Another retired Indian officer said on condition of anonymity that his battalion had gone into the Pakistani side on the LoC and 'got back five dead bodies and strewed them outside our posts saying that the Pakistanis attacked us. That is life on the LoC.'[211]

A retired Indian brigadier recalls an incident in 1986 when in the Akhnoor sector, the Pakistan Army had crossed over into the Indian side and killed six Indian soldiers. He says that the then GOC ordered a counter-strike across the LoC. In the well-coordinated counter-operation, 'twenty heads in *boris* (cloth bags) were brought back.'[212]

In January 2013, the news that Lance Naik Sudhakar Singh and Lance Naik Hemraj Singh of 13 Rajputana Rifles were killed, with the latter being beheaded by the Pakistan Army, had made ripples in the Indian media. According to media reports, the trigger was the construction of a bunker in the Churunda village of the Mendhar sector of Kashmir, which the Pakistan Army first objected to and then fired at the Indian bunker with 120 mm mortars. Thereafter, Pakistan claimed that the Indian Army carried out a cross-LoC raid on Sawan Patra post across Churunda, killing one Pakistani soldier and critically injuring another. Several incidents unfolded over the next few days and eventually Sudhakar Singh and Hemraj Singh were ambushed on the Indian side of the LoC (but beyond the fence) by Pakistan's 29 Baloch regiment.[213] This incident showcases how bunker construction, CFVs, surgical operations, and escalation are closely interlinked.

Gen. Sapru recollected another incident in a recent interview: 'During the time of one of my predecessors, the Pakistanis had raided one of our

[210] Interview with Lt Gen. (Retd) Vinod Bhatia, 19 September 2016, New Delhi.

[211] Interview with Indian Army Colonel (name withheld), 3 November 2016, New Delhi.

[212] Interview with Retired Indian Brigadier (name withheld), May 2016, New Delhi.

[213] Shishir Gupta, 'Provoked? A Look at the Indo-Pak Relationship', *Hindustan Times*, 13 January 2013, available at http://www.hindustantimes.com/delhi/provoked-a-look-at-the-indo-pak-relationship/story-uq3orbhbUCF hu9ztmpVsBJ.html, last accessed on 11 March 2017.

forward posts on the LoC and killed about 20 of our soldiers. We had then raided one of theirs and killed about 25 troops, followed by a big fire assault. Their post was literally razed to the ground.'[214]

HAS PAKISTAN EVER CARRIED OUT A SURGICAL STRIKE AGAINST INDIA?

In a tell-all but off-the-record conversation with me in mid-2016, a retired senior Pakistani general narrated a chilling incident of beheading and surgical operations, arguing that 'head-hunting' is an old habit that the two sides have been engaging in:

> In the mid-80s, the so-called Mujahideens went across and brought back two heads with them. From where they had brought these heads, not a single round was fired at that location for about six months by the Indians. The Mujahideen were telling them that if fired upon and stopped from crossing, there will be more heads that will be beheaded. The repercussion was that at village Kaluchak, a small village south of Chamb on the Pakistani side, 15 special force commandos came from the Indian side at night and slaughtered 11 villagers in their sleep. What explains beheading? Nothing. Our side still maintains that there was no beheading—no one went to the other side and no one came back. I know the story because I was stationed in Chamb and went to inspect the village.[215]

A retired commander of the 15 Corps in Kashmir argues that BAT action is far more well thought out than is usually understood. He claims that BATs, which are special teams comprising of Pakistan special forces, high-profile terrorists, and sometimes local guides, 'come in and sit and wait for months and carry out an action once in a year or two years or once in six months. This is a trans-LoC operation. They would not strike at posts but will wait to strike at the logistic parties. Lots of logistics targets—during summer, there is construction of the LoC fence going on.'[216]

Pakistan officially does not acknowledge the presence of BATs though several retired officials are willing to admit to their presence in off-the-record conversations. Gen. Tariq Ghazi insists that Pakistan does

[214] Interview with Lt Gen. (Retd) T.K. Sapru, 10 October 2016, Chandigarh.
[215] Interview with Retd Army General (name withheld), 15 April 2016, Bangkok.
[216] Interview with Senior retired Lt Gen., Indian Army (name withheld), 21 July 2016, New Delhi.

not have BATs and that they 'are the product of an imagination run wild. It is a fabrication that front-line troops in India have concocted, contrary to reality.'

DOES THE INDIAN ARMY HAVE 'BATs'?

What about the Indian Army? Does it have 'BATs'? A serving brigadier, who has organized several cross-border raids in the past, claims that the Indian Army has BATs, which are constituted as and when needed though they are not a permanent fixture. Gen. Nandal, when asked whether the Indian Army has BATs, did not rule it out but merely said, 'This started only lately. BAT did not exist earlier. This was started by Pakistan.'[217]

Gen. Panag also indirectly acknowledged its existence in the army by saying that BATs have mixed composition, but when the Indian Army does it, it is done by regular troops. The Pakistan Army, he says, has a little more advantage because they can do cross-border raids with dispensable militants. And if the militants are caught, for them, it is 'so what?' But when one of our soldiers gets caught on that side, 'it is a big deal for us.'[218] He acknowledged that cross-border raids have taken place several times before, but were not publicized:

In the past, depending on the situation, these raids were organized. Generally, when the raids were organized we never really went for the launch pad targets, but for posts. So we will go in surreptitiously, carry out a few kills or physically capture the post, bring a dead body back. Why do people bring heads back? For evidence ... it is just a brutal part of the whole thing.[219]

He also argues that it is perhaps not a smart thing to publicize these operations. Gen. Nehra agrees with him: 'As a military officer, I feel, when we do a covert operation, we should not publicize it.'[220]

Serving Pakistani army officers, deployed on the LoC, insisted that the Indian Army plants IEDs in many places on the Pakistani side of the LoC, especially in Chakoti and Krishna Ghati sectors. They allege that

[217] Interview with Lt Gen. (Retd) A.S. Nandal, 23 September 2016, New Delhi.

[218] Interview with Lt Gen. (Retd) H.S. Panag, 3 March 2017, Bangkok.

[219] Interview with Lt Gen. (Retd) H.S. Panag, 3 March 2017, Bangkok.

[220] Interview with Lt Gen. (Retd) J.P. Nehra, 3 December 2016, New Delhi.

the Indian side often pays off people living on either side of the LoC to plant IEDs.[221]

In short then, what the foregoing discussion tells is the following: Surgical strikes are nothing new. As a matter of fact, they have been a regular feature of the life on the LoC for several decades now; both the rival armies have staged such operations; and both the forces have special troops that carry out these operations, whether or not they are called BATs. Surgical strikes, it is clear, represent the extreme violent end of the spectrum in the military engagement between the two forces on the J&K borders. However, surgical strikes do not seem to take place in a tactical vacuum: they are often a result of long spells of CFVs, infiltration, and targeted killings or attack on military bases, and in any case, lead to incessant CFVs in their wake.

'Releasing Pressure Elsewhere'

Sometimes, CFVs take place in an area for no apparent reason, often baffling the local officers. How does one account for that? Why would someone fire with an explicit intent to cause damage when everything has been peaceful in that area and the firing side knows fully well that it would not go unresponded to? The answer is linked to military strategy, the positioning of troops, and which side has an advantage in a particular area. To put it simply: the firing side may have chosen that location because it has an advantage, either geographically or in terms of availability of heavy weapons or troops to pulverize the opponent's posts, over the adversary in that sector, in order to respond to firing taking place elsewhere.

Col Shukla explains:

> When a CFV takes place, it is not that you are firing on me and I am firing back on you. There are certain posts that are dominated comprehensively from the Pakistani side by fire and observation, and when the time comes, they will hammer the Indian post. But I will not hammer back from here. Another post that dominates the Pakistani post somewhere else will do it. So, when the CFV takes place, there is a well-established procedure, peculiar to that sector, which unleashes itself.[222]

---

[221] Interview with Gen. Azar Abbas, 13 December 2017, Murree, Pakistan.
[222] Interview with Col Ajai Shukla, 6 September 2016, New Delhi.

Gen. Waheed says that the location of the response can be anywhere within a 200 km radius of the location where the initial firing took place: 'If fired at in one area, it is not necessary that you respond in the same area. If there are no good targets on the other side to respond to, the brigade commander will decide to respond where we have an upper hand, so we can give a better response to the other side.'[223]

Even within an area, troops choose to fire at posts they can. When under intense incoming fire and geographically disadvantaged location, troops would be forced to target posts where they have a clear advantage. This is often coordinated in advance given the fact that troops know that firing from the other side is a possibility and it should be responded to in a different location. As Gen. Yasin explains it: 'When the Indian would fire at my A post, my guy at B post would fire at the Indian side. It is the dynamic of the terrain and the tactical position. If it is a large-scale violation, then you may shift it by 50 km.'[224] In other words, firing by the Pakistan Army in the Poonch sector could potentially be responded to by the Indian Army in the Rajouri sector. This dynamics of releasing of pressure elsewhere could work at the brigade, battalion, or even at a division level.

This also means that troops guarding geographically 'disadvantaged' areas would have to perforce 'behave themselves' not to get shot by the adversary. Geography often determines one's behaviour. Gen. Ghazi recalls an example: 'When I was commanding an area in the Poonch sector, we had an area surrounded on three sides by Indian positions. We had to deliberately keep this area quiet because the slightest disturbance meant those positions would not get their reinforcements and so on and that may also lead to other CFVs.'[225]

Sabotage

Placing of IEDs and mines, Indian officers testify, is another major irritation that triggers CFVs and stand-offs on the LoC and IB/WB. A senior Indian Army commander argues: 'Irritants on the LoC are trans-LoC movement from Pakistan (infiltration), incidents taking place

---

[223] Interview with Lt Gen. (Retd) Waheed Arshad, 15 April 2016, Bangkok.
[224] Interview with Lt Gen. (Retd) Asif Yasin Malik, 15 April 2016, Bangkok.
[225] Interview with Lt Gen. (Retd) Tariq Ghazi, 7 November 2016, Bangkok.

across the LoC like placing of mines, sniping, and IED placement. On the Indian side, Pakistani soldiers place mines/IEDs to frustrate Indian operations.[226] Another army officer in Hamirpur (Rajouri) explains why IEDs and mines are placed close to the fence: 'Planting of IEDs happens often along with shallow infiltration with the intention of damaging our reconnaissance activities.'[227] Government of India reports often cite Pakistani troops planting mines on the Indian side.[228]

In 2009 in the Samba sector of Jammu, a senior BSF DIG, O.P. Tanwar, was blown up and killed on the Indian side of the fencing by an anti-tank mine. Newspaper reports, though, at the time, quoting sources in the BSF, had reported that the mine may have been planted by terrorists from the Pakistani side.[229] However, BSF's Rakesh Sharma, in a recent interview, gave a contrary view. He thinks the accident may have been caused by mines planted by Pakistan Rangers on their side: 'We speculated that it may have been an anti-tank mine planted by Pakistan on their side. The Basantar River has changed its course many times over the last 10 years. The mine must have washed over with it and happened to come under the tire of the jeep, which passed directly above it.'[230]

The foregoing discussion leads to an undeniable conclusion: that retributive factors are a major cause of CFVs on the LoC and IB in J&K. Violations in J&K have a certain amount of cyclicity inherent in it.

Cultural Factors Leading to CFVs

Testing the 'New Boys'

> Roar at night like a bigger tiger and show the Pakistanis that this is even bigger than the earlier one. I asked them (the newly inducted BSF troops) to show the Pakistani Rangers that every time a new battalion moves in, the

---

[226] Interview with Indian Army Officer 2, 13 May 2016, Udhampur.

[227] Interview with Indian Army Officer 4, 15 May 2016, Bhimber Gali.

[228] Press Information Bureau, 'Planting of Landmines by Pakistan', Ministry of Defence, Government of India, 11 March 2013, available at http://pib.nic.in/newsite/PrintRelease.aspx?relid=93392, last accessed on 5 July 2016.

[229] Shujaat Bukhari, 'Senior BSF Officer Killed in Jammu Mine Blast', *Hindu*, 11 November 2009, available at http://www.thehindu.com/news/national/Senior-BSF-officer-killed-in-Jammu-mine-blast/article16892528.ece, last accessed on 11 March 2017.

[230] Interview with Rakesh Sharma, 15 September 2016, New Delhi.

stronger it will be. So their strategy of testing our battalions on arrival would not be able to achieve anything.

—Rakesh Sharma[231]

CFVs also occur due to inherent cultural traits and biases of military organizations guarding the LoC and the IB/WB. However, it would be overstating the case to argue that a certain general military culture gives rise to CFVs. Instead, it would be more plausible to argue that certain military subcultures, contingent on spatio-temporal factors, contribute to CFVs. Let us examine some of them here.

An important local-level factor that leads to CFVs both on the LoC and IB/WB is what is often referred to as 'testing the new boys': one side testing the 'resolve' of the new battalion that gets posted in the counterpart sector. Both serving and retired officers from the two armies, BSF and Rangers, often refer to this as a ceasefire trigger.

Indian general Ata Hasnain remarked, 'CFVs can also result from ego problems—when a new unit comes in on one side, the other side will try to test them.' Gurmeet Kanwal said the same. A serving BSF commander in Jammu argued that 'when a new battalion is inducted, the Pakistani side tests by firing and violating the CFA.'[232] Pakistani general Afzal agreed to it: 'When battalions change on both sides, to test the other side and to show one's ascendency, one side might fire close to the other side.'[233] Senior retired Indian generals Panag, Nandal, and Bhatia also agreed to the existence of this phenomenon.

Gen. Bhatia, the former Indian DGMO, explains the underlying logic why these kinds of CFVs happen. When a new battalion takes over an AOR, there is an extended handing/taking-over period, which could extend from 4–6 weeks. This period is also sometimes the most dangerous time because that location has double the normal number of troops stationed there. This leads to slightly slack responsibility by the outgoing unit who are basically looking at going away, and the new unit is not fully familiar with the area and area-specific SOPs. So this becomes a time of weakness for that particular area. The other side, recognizing this weakness, sometimes takes advantage of this. This is done by both the sides, Gen. Bhatia claims.

231 Interview with Rakesh Sharma, 15 September 2016, New Delhi.
232 Interview with BSF Officer 6, 4 June 2016, Jammu.
233 Interview with Lt Gen. (Retd) Sikander Afzal, 16 April 2016, Bangkok.

Gen. Nandal agrees that maximum casualties within a unit occur when it is being inducted into a new area or being de-inducted from an area. When being inducted, the unit is not familiar with the area, and when being de-inducted, it tends to lower the guard.

Col Shukla not only pointed out that this is standard and routine on the LoC, but also further brought in another dimension to the testing fire thesis—sometimes, the departing battalion makes a parting show of strength. He recalls, 'Whenever a new battalion is coming in a place, if you are a G1 Ops staff officer sitting in the corps HQs like me, I tell the outgoing battalion that we know you are leaving the sector, do not try that "last night" attack on the enemy opposite you, just let it pass. Get into your trucks and go back.'[234]

Serving BSF officers in Jammu's Pittal post attributed the CFVs that started on 16 July 2014, and lasted for over a month, to Pakistan Rangers' attempts at testing the newly posted BSF battalion on the Indian side:

> There were multiple reasons behind the firing on 16 July 2014. First, the 192 Battalion of the BSF had come to Jammu from Ganganagar of Rajasthan—this was a new battalion. The Pak side wanted to test the new battalion, so they fired and sniped. Battalion was only ten days old on the Pittal BOP. Indian forces retaliated. One killed and three injured on the Indian side—one Ranger killed on nearby post. The firing went on for 45 days.[235]

Another BSF officer in Jammu spoke about the time when his 89 Battalion arrived in Jammu from Tripura, how it was treated with firing by the Pakistani side.[236] BSG IG Rakesh Sharma recalls: 'In 2014, there were three battalions that were changed and all three of them came under

---

[234] Interview with Col Ajai Shukla, 6 September 2016, New Delhi.
[235] Interview with BSF Officer 2, 2 June 2016, Jammu; See also: 'One BSF Jawan Dead, Three Injured in Pak Firing', *Times of India*, 16 July 2014, available at http://timesofindia.indiatimes.com/india/One-BSF-jawan-dead-three-injured-in-Pak-firing/articleshow/38478589.cms, last accessed on 11 March 2017; 'Pakistan Targets 15 Border Outposts, Shells Villages in Jammu', *Economic Times*, 20 July 2014, available at http://articles.economictimes.indiatimes.com/2014-07-20/news/51780181_1_pakistan-rangers-ceasefire-violation-s-pura, last accessed on 11 March 2017.
[236] Interview with BSF Officer 4, 3 June 2016, Jammu.

heavy firing in the Jammu region ... Pittal (post) was one, Mukesh was another, Pindi was yet another.'[237]

Gen. Ghazi acknowledges the existence of this practice of showing the incoming unit the opponent's strength, which leads to CFVs, a practice, he says, that goes back to the 1970s. Gen. Ghazi, however, believes that during those days, it was not a very serious issue since both sides knew that it was going to happen. So the incoming side would respond and after that things would quiet down and there would be peace and harmony. Moreover, he says 'Usually, since all your positions are protected, and most of it being small-arm exchanges, it did not lead to casualties.' In any case, 'it was mostly a show of strength and chivalric welcome to the incoming unit'.

Much of this chivalry and show of strength remains limited to the local area, according to Gen. Afzal, and is often carried out to break monotony and in gamesmanship: 'When battalions change on both sides, to test the other side and to show ones' ascendency, one side might fire close to the other side. When you live on the border for a long time, all these things are done to also break the monotony. This testing fire happens occasionally. These things might not even get reported.'[238]

A related factor is when the new unit would want to assert themselves, especially when posted to places that have a history of tension and CFVs. Brig. Salik argues that sometimes a new battalion would want to assert themselves to the other side. They take an aggressive posture and interfere with the patrolling, thereby leading to CFVs. In other words, sometimes the 'new boys' get tested, and sometimes the 'new boys' test the opponent to avoid getting tested. In this cycle of testing, counter-testing, and pre-emptive testing, a lot of fire gets exchanged.

'Moral Ascendency'

> *Moral ascendency is often an invitation to savagery.*
>
> —Lt Gen. (Retd) Sikander Afzal[239]

Then there is what many Indian and Pakistani officers refer to as the complex notion of moral ascendancy. Gen. Hasnain says that 'on the

---

[237] Interview with Rakesh Sharma, 15 September 2016, New Delhi.

[238] Interview with Lt Gen. (Retd) Sikander Afzal, 16 April 2016, Bangkok.

[239] Interview with Lt Gen. (Retd) Sikander Afzal, 16 April 2016, Bangkok.

LOC, there is a concept called moral ascendancy—"I am the better Army" and "I dominate you by my morale, training, and capability". It is a macho game that adversaries in eyeball-to-eyeball contact indulge in,[240] something another Kashmir-based serving army officer agrees to when he says that 'troops sometimes look for moral ascendancy and domination'.[241] Gen. Bhatia, the former DGMO, says it is the self-belief of a combat unit as soldiers and group than the adversary. It is a psyche to be inculcated in the soldiers to dominate the other side—'like a boxer, when he starts punching hard, the other guy starts ducking. When he ducks, the boxer who punches starts punching even more', gaining dominance over the opponent.[242]

So what does moral ascendency mean on the ground? Om Prakash argues that it encourages the troops to become more active and more confident of themselves. Gen. Panag describes how it works on the ground:

> You got the enemy opposite you. Let us say you are at a higher post
> ... if he shows any kind of aggression and you respond aggressively, he
> suffers a casualty and says, let us not repeat. Let us say you get more
> imaginative and sends more patrols out ... in the end, he pulls back and
> does not do anything more. So you have achieved moral ascendency.[243]

Troops also achieve ascendency over the opponent by firing and dominating, by crumbling the opponent's defence works, pinning down his movements, eventually forcing him to move only at night.[244] Brig. Sahgal, who recalls these games being played from the early 1980s, says that 'through your domination and positions in that area, and constantly keeping the other's head down by continuous fire you are assuring your moral ascendency'.[245] Such carefully built psychological sense of superiority is lost, he says, when one's soldiers get beheaded by the other side, referring to the recent spate of beheading in the border. 'So you have to rebuild the morale of the battalion.'

[240] Interview with Lt Gen. (Retd) Syed Ata Hasnain, 5 June 2015, New Delhi.

[241] Interview with Indian Army Officer 5, 14 May 2016, Kashmir.

[242] Interview with Lt Gen. (Retd) Vinod Bhatia, 19 September 2016, New Delhi.

[243] Interview with Lt Gen. (Retd) H.S. Panag, 3 March 2017, Bangkok.

[244] Interview with Lt Gen. (Retd) Om Prakash, 27 September 2016, Gurgaon.

[245] Interview with Brig (Retd) Arun Sahgal, 4 November 2016, Bangkok.

Referring to how the Indian Army, led by him in 2000, pushed the Pakistani troops out of the Batalik sector one year after the two sides had fought a war in the Kargil sector, Gen. Panag wrote in 2016:

It was a bright sunny day after a week of bad weather and Pakistani troops were busy sunning themselves. On a code word, all hell broke loose. We engaged all posts, but the ones that were dominated by us received special attention. Surprise was total and the enemy troops were caught unaware in the open. In the critical first two minutes, substantial casualties were caused before the troops scurried for cover of the bunkers. We then focused on the bunkers, which, compared to ours, were in a poor state. The heavier L 70 air defence gun, which fires 330 rounds per minute, and 75/24 mountain gun wreaked havoc. The training and effort put in to haul them to the posts had paid dividends. Our fury lasted two hours, and in the ensuing lull, white flags came up on some posts for collecting casualties. We had destroyed 35 bunkers and approximately 25–30 were killed and wounded. Complete moral ascendency had been achieved and was maintained aggressively thereafter.[246]

Moral ascendency is not a function of psychology alone but of technological sophistication and surprise factor as well. Domination is not a static situation, but a continuous process and both forces try and gain that over the other, sometimes, surprising the other side with new technologies and weapon systems that the other side is not guarding against. Besides using standard battalion support weapons such as light machine guns, mortars, recoil-less rifles, anti-material rifles, and so on, sometimes other higher-grade weapons such as 105 mm mortars, 130 and 155 mm artillery guns, and anti-tank guided missiles to blow off the bunkers are brought in to dislodge the adversary.[247]

Relatively new weapon systems such as the UAVs often lead to CFVs. UAVs are widely used by both sides for reconnaissance purposes and they occasionally cross the LoC and IB, and when they do, they will be counted as a CFV.[248] An Indian Army brigadier posted in Rajouri pointed out that UAVs are sent for surveillance purposes every 10–15 days and the feed is

---

[246] Lt Gen. (Retd) H.S. Panag, 'How We Pushed Pak out of the Batalik Sector', *News Laundry*, 6 September 2016, available at https://www.newslaundry.com/2016/09/06/how-we-pushed-pak-out-of-the-batalik-sector, last accessed on 16 September 2016.

[247] Interview with Col Ajai Shukla, 6 September 2016, New Delhi.

[248] Interview with Lt Gen. (Retd) A.S. Nandal, 23 September 2016, New Delhi.

magnified to see if there is new construction of unusual troop formation on the other side.[249] Both Indian and Pakistani sides have started using UAVs extensively and have often shot down drones belonging to the other side.

Why is moral ascendency important, especially since the two sides are not fighting a pitched battle on a daily basis? For one, from an Indian point of view, Gen. Nandal explains:

> This prevents Pakistan from carrying out a task that is inimical to us. So, I am in control. He should not be able to harm me or facilitate infiltration to my side. I dominate him by observation and fire. He cannot move. There are posts on either side where you cannot move. Our vulnerable posts have been identified as sensitive. They may send their special forces, such as BAT, to come in and wreak harm.[250]

Moral ascendency can bring a certain amount of control over such things. If one side does not respond to the adversary's actions and eventually achieve moral ascendency, Gen. Panag argues, the other side will keep harassing.

Second, there is a long-term objective for constantly trying to achieve moral ascendency—to prepare for war. Gen. Bhatia stresses this point: 'Tomorrow, if there is a war, I am more confident that I can get hold of them and that is very important for a soldier. You know the intangibles are very important for a soldier.'[251] Gen. Om Prakash agrees to this long-term utility that once the troops are confident that they are superior to the other side, they would be able perform better when there is a combat. War, after all, is not just fought in the battlefields, but equally in the minds of men.

Sometimes these psychological games can go to unrealistic levels. Recall the popular Pakistani myth during the 1965 war that one Muslim soldier was 'worth ten Hindus'[252] and that the 'Hindu morale would not stand for more than a couple of hard blows delivered at the right time & the right place.'[253]

---

[249] Interview with Indian Army Officer 3, 14 May 2016, Poonch (J&K).

[250] Interview with Lt Gen. (Retd) A.S. Nandal, 23 September 2016, New Delhi.

[251] Interview with Lt Gen. (Retd) Vinod Bhatia, 19 September 2016, New Delhi.

[252] Cited in Dennis Kux, *India and the United States: Estranged Democracies, 1941–91* (New Delhi: Sage, 1994), 113.

[253] Cited in Peter Lavoy (ed.), *Assymetric Warfare in South Asia: The Causes and Consequences of the Kargil Conflict* (Cambridge: Cambridge University Press, 2009), 338.

In any case, the point is that 'such psychological and mind games can lead to CFVs'.[254] In an eyeball-to-eyeball confrontation in an unfriendly terrain, troops are trained to believe that they are better than the other side. Sometimes they take it upon themselves to prove it to the other side, and to themselves. The result is often relentless firing and casualties and deep-seated contempt for the 'inferior' other.

Moral ascendency is often an invitation to savagery since troops are trained to, as Gen. Afzal puts it, prove to the other side that they are better and stronger in 'professional competence and in savagery. All our lives, we as officers train our men to kill and this is not easy'.[255] The foregoing discussion shows how specific values and a system of self-beliefs, which typically form the military ethos, provide fuel for recurrent stand-offs and firing on the J&K borders.

Inadvertent CFVs

Accidental Firing and CFVs

> In June 2015, BSF troops were diffusing an unexploded shell in the Kakryal post in Jammu. When the diffusion caused a big noise, Rangers on the other side thought we were firing at them and started firing at us. And they had to respond.
>
> —Rakesh Sharma[256]

Another reason for CFVs is inadvertent actions, which include accidental firing, inadvertent crossing of civilians or even troops into the territory held by the other side, and unauthorized—though not inadvertent—crossing of civilians.

Let us examine the issue of accidental firing in some detail. Speculative firing at night, which happens due to a variety of reasons from closing the gaps between posts in sensitive areas or to target suspected movements or even to keep oneself awake,[257] could potentially invite response from the other side and lead to CFVs. Sometimes, there is a panic reaction from the troops guarding posts, leading to firing to which the other side would respond.[258]

[254] Interview with Indian Army Officer 5, 14 May 2016, Rajouri.
[255] Interview with Lt Gen. (Retd) Sikander Afzal, 16 April 2016, Bangkok.
[256] Interview with Rakesh Sharma, 15 September 2016, New Delhi.
[257] Interview with Lt Gen. (Retd) A.S. Nandal, 23 September 2016, New Delhi.
[258] Interview with Lt Gen. (Retd) Asif Yasin Malik, 15 April 2016, Bangkok.

Sometimes CFVs result from clear misunderstandings. A Jammu-based BSF officer narrated how once the Indian side had defused a shell on its side, which the Pakistani Rangers mistook for the initiation of fire by the BSF and responded. Since the Rangers fired at the BSF, the officer claimed, without clarifying, they had to return fire, which went on for some time. Another officer pointed out how animals get caught in the minefield at night and blow up. The blast sound could be mistaken by either side, leading to firing and CFVs.

Most accidental firing happens due to the 'speculative firing' that happens at night. Gen. Bhatia discusses how such accidental firing happens. A soldier standing on guard duty at night gets the feeling that someone is coming towards him. His response would be to fire at what he thinks is an infiltration. Such firing could go to the other side, at which the troops from the other side would fire back. Speculative firing in the gaps between posts is a standard practice used by the Indian troops on the LoC and IB in J&K. On the Pakistani side too, firing at night is something that happens routinely.[259] Serving officers on both sides did not comment on their own side engaging in speculative firing. Pakistani officers spoke of how the Indian side fires through the night.[260]

Gen. Sapru recalls from the early days of insurgency in the 1990s:

We were firing to counter infiltration in the sense that if there was a gap between two places, we'll fire in the nallah—maybe someone would be coming from there. So you fire at about 9 o'clock. Then fire at 9.10 p.m. ten yards away … then you fire at 9.40 p.m., then at 10 o'clock somewhere. It was speculative firing so that, if there is any infiltrator by chance somewhere, you might just get him. Such firing was not aimed at the adversary.[261]

Gen. Nandal agrees that CI firing was a SOP during the height of militancy in Kashmir: 'The lower-level officers would shoot throughout the night. There are gaps between posts and how do you dominate that? So CFVs are a means of domination and to prevent infiltration. And they

[259] Interview with Lt Gen. (Retd) Waheed Arshad, 15 April 2016, Bangkok.

[260] Interview with Gen. Azar Abbas, 13 December 2017, Murree; Interview with Brig. Akhtar Khan, 13 December 2017, Muzaffarabad.

[261] Interview with Lt Gen. (Retd) T.K. Sapru, 10 October 2016, Chandigarh.

fire back.'[262] Brig. Kanwal says that since troops cannot always distinguish the movements of animals from those of the infiltrators, they would fire at anything that moves. As a result, while one side may have shot an animal, the other side would fire back since 'he does not know that you have fired at an animal'. However, these days, troops using thermal imaging are able to distinguish between animals and humans and control their firing accordingly.

When troops are placed in an eyeball-to-eyeball situation, even if they are operating in a tightly controlled situation with clear SOPs, things could go wrong. The India–Pakistan border management, as discussed earlier, is ad hoc for the most part and the chances of things going wrong are real. Sometimes, accidents happen and CFVs follow; some other times, competitiveness and one-upmanship between local commanders posted on either side can lead to CFVs. The argument Gen. Panag makes in this context is pertinent:

When troops are eyeball to eyeball and are armed, there is always a game of one-upmanship that is played. Doctrines, rules, and international law, and so on.... These things are meaningless there, you do not bother about these. Incidents are triggered and it is never known to anybody, even journalists, what has happened on the ground. Let us say hypothetically, we do something and Pakistan responds, then there will be a hue and cry. But we will say that we did not do anything. Who will say? Even the government will promptly ask and we will say we did not do anything.[263]

Speculative firing at night, which may not be counted as a CFV at all,[264] since it is not aimed at the other side, however has every potential of escalating, especially if the general situation is one of tension.

Such reckless firing has an impact on the discipline of the forces too. Gen. Sapru points out: 'This trans-LoC firing has been the biggest problem for the Indian Army, because what is happening is that our boys are being very trigger-happy.'[265] Much of the firing that happens on the border, he stresses, is pointless:

[262] Interview with Lt. Gen (Retd) A.S. Nandal, 23 September 2016, Gurgaon.
[263] Interview with Lt Gen. (Retd) H.S. Panag, 19 September 2016, Chandigarh.
[264] Interview with Gen. Azar Abbas, 13 December 2017, Murree, Pakistan.
[265] Interview with Lt Gen. (Retd) T.K. Sapru, 10 October 2016, Chandigarh.

You are firing just in the air, at night, through the loophole towards Pakistan. You are not even firing at a bunker, because the bunker is 2,000 metres away. You are not firing at a post because that would be well protected, well bunkered, and all ... so you were firing in that direction just for the heck of it. You were not achieving any darn thing ... once a while, you'd get a kill ... if he is not careful.[266]

Brig. Sahgal testifies to it saying that sometimes troops fire for the sake of firing.

Unauthorized Crossing of Civilians

The crosser does not come with a placard saying 'I am an innocent man'.

—Lt Gen. (Retd) Vinod Bhatia[267]

Civilian crossings of either the LoC or IB are by themselves not a significant direct trigger of CFVs. However, the inability of the local authorities to properly handle the situation and the lack of jointly agreed upon SOPs could lead to crossings being a trigger for CFVs. When related CFVs do occur, they are usually during the crossing of the civilians itself, some of which could lead to major stand-offs between the forces.[268]

A serving army officer in Kashmir talked about how civilians coming from the Pakistani side to cut grass on the Indian side of the LoC could invite firing from the Indian troops because it is possible that there could be guides (to militants/infiltrators) in the garb of grazers: 'This might lead to return fire from Pakistani troops. On other occasions, animals stray to the other side, and if a villager goes across to take the animal back, the Pakistani side fires, leading, sometimes, to an Indian retaliation.'[269] Gen. Arshad says that unauthorized civilian crossing for purposes of grazing their cattle or cutting grass for the cattle has often led to CFVs.[270]

---

[266] Interview with Lt Gen. (Retd) T.K. Sapru, 10 October 2016, Chandigarh.

[267] Interview with Lt Gen. (Retd) Vinod Bhatia, 19 September 2016, New Delhi.

[268] Praveen Swami, 'Runaway Grandmother Sparked Savage Skirmish on LoC', *Hindu*, 10 January 2013, available at http://www.thehindu.com/news/national/runaway-grandmother-sparked-savage-skirmish-on-loc/article4291426.ece, last accessed on 23 July 2016.

[269] Interview with Indian Army Officer 5, 14 May 2016, Rajouri.

[270] Interview with Lt Gen. (Retd) Waheed Arshad, 15 April 2016, Bangkok.

Serving Pakistani army officers referred to how people living on the Pakistani side often run after their cattle who cross into the Indian side or who cross over to the Indian side to cut grass or fetch water. As Brig. Akhtar Khan of the Pakistan Army put it: 'Civilians do not recognize the LoC.'[271] They also argue that the Indian side fires at the civilians potentially leading to CFVs.

As Brig. Salik puts it: 'On the Pakistani side, the civilian population is right on the zero line and sometimes even ahead of the forward post. Sometimes people cross inadvertently—they might go after cattle that runs across. People would go across to attend marriages and come back. People familiar with the territory can easily bypass despite the difficult terrain.'[272] In one such major incident that happened in 2012, a grandmother who ran away to the Pakistani side from India's Charonda village triggered an action-reaction sequence of CFVs by the Pakistani and Indian soldiers.[273]

The number of civilians crossing from the Indian side has drastically come down since the Indian fence came up in 2001–2. Indian forces, according to Gen. Om Prakash, strictly prohibited Indian civilians from crossing over to the other side even before the fence came up: 'Today they are going for grass-cutting; tomorrow they will develop friendship with those guys; third time they will be guides to them. Therefore, no trans-LoC movement (is permitted).'[274]

However, as pointed out earlier, there are several villages located ahead of the Indian fence in the Kashmir LoC sector. There have been occasional cases of unauthorized civilian movements across the zero line, which have the potential to lead to CFVs. While the forces on the ground say that civilian interaction between the two sides is strictly prohibited, it is quite possible for the villagers to interact with the other side, especially in the absence of a fence, as this author witnessed during a field visit to some of those villages.

In places where there is no fence to stop civilian movement, what happens if the troops spot civilian movement at night? If crossing is

---

[271] Interview with Brig. Akhtar Khan, 13 December 2017, Muzaffarabad
[272] Interview with Brig. (Retd) Naeem Ahmad Salik, 13 April 2016, Bangkok.
[273] Swami, 'Runaway Grandmother Sparked Savage Skirmish on LoC'.
[274] Interview with Lt Gen. (Retd) Om Prakash, 27 September 2016, New Delhi.

detected, crossers are fired upon,[275] civilians or not, but even such risk of getting shot at does not prevent them from often attempting to cross over: 'Firing cannot stop a person from crossing. And if you stay there you know the topography, you know how the boulders are placed. That is how infiltration takes place. People who stay there or just behind the LOC ... Shepherds, porters, come up to the posts. These are the guys who guide the other side into infiltration.'[276] Others may not have bad intentions for crossing and yet risk getting shot at. As Gen. Bhatia recounts, sometimes it is not possible to distinguish between the good ones and the bad ones.

> The crosser does not come with a placard saying, 'I am an innocent man.' But because of experience out there, we come to know whether he is a terrorist. Sometimes, there are girls coming this side; sometimes there are old people coming this side; sometimes we get love birds coming or going to either side. All these things happen, so we have to use our common sense also.[277]

Daily life on the border areas on occasions requires civilians to cross back and forth and it used to be a regular feature before the fence came up in the early 2000s. A Pakistani general who did not want to be named described the plight of the locals in detail:

> Livestock of locals living near the LoC can move anywhere. Kids of age 12 and 14, and even elderly people of nearly 70, look after the goats grazing the grass. At times, an animal will move to the other side and the local shepherd will run after it because these livestock are the only livelihood for those communities. Now when the shepherd comes near the LoC chasing the animal, the Indians fire a warning shot, but the man is not going to stop because he wants to get hold of his animal as that is his source of livelihood. In the heat of the moment, CFVs happen. Both sides know of each other's position, so they immediately engage those positions to provide cover to the local shepherd so that

---

[275] Interview with Lt Gen. (Retd) Tariq Majid, 14 April 2016; Interview with Lt Gen. (Retd) A.S. Nandal, 23 September 2016, New Delhi; and Interview with Lt Gen. (Retd) Vinod Bhatia, 19 September 2016, New Delhi.

[276] Interview with Lt Gen. (Retd) A.S. Nandal, 23 September 2016, New Delhi.

[277] Interview with Lt Gen. (Retd) Vinod Bhatia, 19 September 2016, New Delhi.

they can retrieve their animal back, and in some cases, retrieve the wounded back and, even at times, retrieve the dead bodies back.[278]

In general, unauthorized crossing of civilians is handled routinely and without any untoward incident. Pakistani officers point out that when Pakistani soldiers sight Indian civilians crossing to the Pakistani side, their response depends on the circumstance in which the crossing takes place. Local commanders are instructed to immediately report to the chain of command and to contact the local commander on the Indian side to ascertain circumstances and the facts of the crossing.[279] Once the locals report an inadvertent crossing, the local commander reports it to the battalion headquarters and brigade headquarters, which in turn get in touch with their respective Indian counterparts. A background check is undertaken to ascertain bonafides. The issue is taken up at the next flag meeting. If not resolved there, the issue is sent up the chain of command.[280]

Gen. Ghazi agrees with this assessment and says that civilian activities often lead to CFVs and argues that there should be mechanisms to avoid them:

> There would also be shepherds whose flocks would cross over. In desperation, this man would come running towards the border, and his intentions being misconstrued, the other side would interfere with his movement. Then sometimes animals would be caught in minefields or even some of our own people. And that would lead to CFVs, because you need to recover that person or animal. Similarly, such civilian-related activities, especially on the Pakistan side, lead to frequent CFVs.[281]

Yet another cause of stand-offs and CFVs is when Kashmiris who had gone across to the other side decide to come back. Gen. Hasnain talks about such a scenario:

> Kashmiri migrants who went across in 1989–90 sometimes wish to come back and lack finances to do so. The routes are usually via Nepal or Dubai, and needs approximately rupees two lakh or so per individual; so that is mostly unaffordable. Such people take a taxi from Islamabad up to some known areas where guides exist. They manage to elude the

[278] Interview with Pakistani Official 4, 17 January 2017, Rawalpindi.
[279] Interview with Pakistani Official 3, 12 June 2016, Islamabad.
[280] Interview with Pakistani Official 2, 9 June 2016, Islamabad.
[281] Interview with Lt Gen. (Retd) Tariq Ghazi, 7 November 2016, Bangkok.

Pakistani authorities and reach the LoC with their families. According to our SOPs, we discourage crossing and force those attempting illegal crossings to return. In case a crossing is done undetected or under duress, the army calls the local police to handle the civilians. The police take them into custody, interrogate them, and do the further processing.[282]

Many times, however, such people who come over are turned back by the Indian forces. Gen. Nehra argued that such crossings are not encouraged by the forces:

> There were times when a message came through our sources at the flag meeting that some groups wanted to come and surrender with their weapons. I never entertained that; some people took that as an opportunity. There is a risk involved in that. What if a group of 20 comes with weapons and five among them vanish? They will create enough damage. This surrender policy has been announced for militants. I said, 'You went across to POK voluntarily, and if you want to surrender, then you come through diplomatic channels. If you cross the LoC, you have the risk of being shot.'[283]

So when disallowed, given how difficult it may be to officially return to the Indian side of the J&K, they would still continue to try their luck, and risk getting shot or triggering CFVs even though the J&K government has a sorrounder.

***

The findings of this chapter also indicate that even if terrorist infiltration into the Indian side of J&K ceases to exist, CFVs could potentially continue to take place leading to an escalation of tensions between the two sides. Data presented in this chapter clearly indicates that the CFA tends to hold during a result-oriented dialogue process between India and Pakistan on key disputes. This chapter also shows that the absence of a peace process alone is not the reason for the breakdown of the CFA nor can the occurrence of CFVs be solely explained by the presence of terrorist infiltration. Indeed, even in those years when terrorist infiltration into J&K, attempted or successful, was low, CFVs remained high.

Second, this chapter demolishes the well-established myth that the most significant reasons behind CFVs is terrorist infiltration from the Pakistani side. The chapter established that there are several types of CFVs, the most significant of which being the operational factors. The ability of operational factors to prompt CFVs directly speaks to the existence of AMFs that have a role to play in the India–Pakistan border stand-off.

Hence, there needs to be a lot more focus, both conceptually and empirically, on the role played by AMFs in determining the outbreak of CFVs in J&K. While Legro's attempt at addressing the specific military cultures of military organizations in explaining inadvertent escalation is a useful paradigm, it may not be very helpful in understanding the local-level AMFs and military subcultures that may not flow from the central military or national political cultural precepts. There is then a need to address the AMFs as a specific category and an independent variable.

Third, although the state of the relationship acts as a general enabling or disabling environment for CFVs to take place, it is the presence of the AMFs that has a clear impact on CFVs, an aspect that has not been given much attention to by analysts and the two governments. Going by this logic, then, resolving the bilateral disputes between India and Pakistan is the best way to prevent recurrent CFVs. But in the absence of such a comprehensive conflict resolution, especially in J&K, it would still be worthwhile to focus on reducing the impact of the autonomous factors that act as intervening variables in effecting CFVs. For instance, removing the ambiguity about defence construction could potentially remove a major cause of CFVs. From a policy perspective, then, while addressing the fundamental political causes of CFVs may be important, it would be equally important to focus on instituting measures on the ground, as identified earlier, to sustain the ceasefire of 2003.

Based on the previous discussion, we can arrive at several policy-relevant conclusions. First of all, the data on CFVs examined in this and in the previous chapters clearly show that constructive dialogue between the two sides and quiet along the J&K borders are strongly correlated. Between 2004 and 2007, when New Delhi and Islamabad engaged in a purposeful dialogue, particularly on Kashmir, CFVs dropped dramatically: in 2002, close to 5,800 CFVs were reported,

254 • Line on Fire

but in 2004, only four violations were reported. This positive trend continued until the 2008 terrorist attack on the Indian embassy in Kabul and thereafter the Mumbai attack. In short, terror attacks against India led to resumption of CFVs on the border. Since then, the numbers have risen steadily.

During times of bilateral tension, on the other hand, the CFA tends to break down and CFVs occur routinely. It is during those phases that the AMFs tend to have a dramatic influence on CFVs. This, of course, as pointed out in Chapter two, is mediated by the existing political permissibility. It is important to note that CFVs are usually not planned, directed, or cleared by higher military commands or political establishments, but are driven by dynamics on the ground as outlined previously in the book.

One question needs to be answered at this point. How is the randomness inherent in most of the AMFs described in the chapter checked/controlled when there is a peace process? For instance, an animal lands on a landmine at night and suddenly there is noise and the other side assumes that the enemy has fired, what would be its response?[284] During times of tension, there would be a tendency to assume that the other side has fired; however, during times of peace, they would check with the other side before reacting.

In sum, then, Indo-Pak rapprochement and talks on Kashmir provide for a quiet Indo-Pak border with many of the local-level military factors identified here having little or no influence. When tensions run high, on the other hand, CFVs become routine with AMFs having a dramatic influence.

---

[284] Grateful to Sadia Tasleem for bringing this to my attention.

6   Ceasefire Violations and Crisis Escalation
Analysing the Data

Across the line, we launched physical assaults, captured Pakistani posts—
there was one post near where the LoC starts in Munnawar Tawi, near the
Beas River—which took the Pakistanis by surprise. Indian troops attacked
a Pakistani post and killed 19 soldiers and got back a visitors' book in which
Musharraf had signed two weeks before the attack took place.

—Col (Retd) Ajai Shukla[1]

THIS CHAPTER ARGUES THAT THERE is an empirically evident linkage between CFVs in J&K and India–Pakistan escalation dynamics. While it might sound obvious, it needs to be examined in detail using empirical evidence precisely because the academic literature on South Asian escalation dynamics seems to, by and large, ignore the crucial links between CFVs and crisis escalation. Chapter 2 had highlighted how the linkage between CFVs and escalation has received little attention in the existing literature on South Asia.

Pakistani analysts and decision-makers, when referring to escalation dynamics in South Asia, tend to begin their analysis from the classical-conventional level (that is, conventional military mobilization by the Indian side to which Pakistan is forced to respond either conventionally or eventually using TNWs). In other words, such analysis conveniently, and for political reasons, sidesteps the causes behind such military aggression by India, that is, terror strikes on the Indian soil by Pak-based/sponsored terror outfits.

Indian analysts and policymakers, as does much of the academic literature on India–Pakistan escalation dynamics, focus on terror strikes

[1] Interview with Col Ajai Shukla, 6 September 2016, New Delhi.

as the trigger for the bilateral escalation dynamics. This chapter argues that while the Indian argument and that of the dominant literature on India–Pakistan escalation is an 'improvement' over Pakistan's narrower assessment of the causes of escalation, it is still analytically incomplete. The picture of the India–Pakistan escalation will remain incomplete until we link escalation with CFVs, as argued in this chapter.

One of the reasons why CFVs are not viewed as having the potential to trigger escalation between the two nuclear rivals is, one could argue, because not many analysts understand what a CFV entails or how serious it can be. I have argued earlier in the book that 'one CFV might be thousands of shots fired by a range of weapons from personal firearms to heavy artillery. The violation might include multiple exchanges of fire across multiple areas within a period of 24 hours in reaction to an initial violation.' Viewed from this angle, it becomes evident that CFVs constitute major incidents of firing across the border.

It is important to clarify at this stage that the relationship between CFVs and escalation is not purely unidirectional, that is, CFVs causing escalation.[2] While the intent here is to establish that CFVs leads to escalation (with CFVs being the independent variable and escalation being the dependent variable), it is also important to note that while CFVs do lead to escalation, during the process of crisis escalation, the latter leads to more CFVs. CFVs also have a cumulative snowballing effect: once they begin, several things could happen including political rhetoric, military posturing, and diplomatic stand-off, which can lead to more CFVs and even more escalation. In other words, the two are not mutually exclusive but feed into each other. Hence, the objective here is not to argue that the relationship is unidirectional (which it is not) but to show that CFVs *can* and *do* lead to escalation, and once the escalation process begins, CFVs and escalation feed off of each other.

This caveat does not take away from the fact that CFVs remain a major trigger for Indo-Pak escalation. Rather, it goes to strengthen the argument that CFVs play a significant role in the whole life cycle of a crisis escalation.

This chapter discusses eight cases to show how CFVs by themselves can lead to crisis escalation between India and Pakistan. In doing so, it juxtaposes quantitative data on CFVs and escalation during specific

---

[2] I am thankful to Fahd Humayun for prompting me to think about it.

periods to highlight how escalation has resulted from CFVs and how the two have fed off of each other.

A Practical Note on Escalation

A 2008 RAND Corporation study made a useful distinction between deliberate escalation ('escalation carried out for instrumental reasons'), inadvertent escalation ('the mechanism that engages when a combatant deliberately takes actions that it does not perceive to be escalatory but are interpreted that way by the enemy'), and accidental escalation ('escalation which occurs by accident').[3] All three categories are pertinent to our analysis here. Similarly, the RAND study also discusses different forms of escalation: vertical escalation, horizontal escalation, and political escalation.

This study, however, focuses on military (which comprises of vertical and horizontal escalation), diplomatic, and political escalation. Instead of viewing escalation as an actor-centric and actor-directed phenomenon, escalation data for this chapter is collected using Richard Smoke's 'phenomenal image' model, which is defined as a 'natural phenomenon of war, a process that seems to get started and keep going on its own, partially outside the control of any participant'. The difference here however is that the end point of the cases discussed here is not war; they stop well short of a shooting war.

Escalation has been generally studied in South Asia as an intended and calibrated action and generally as part of a 'bargaining strategy', not as unintended escalation. Unintended escalation though is often discussed in the context of accidental uses of battlefield nuclear weapons.[4] As a matter of fact, the Lahore Declaration of 1999, signed a year after their nuclear tests and months before the Kargil War between India and Pakistan, explicitly referred to it:

[3] Forrest E. Morgan, Karl P. Mueller, Evan S. Medeiros, Kevin L. Pollpeter, and Roger Cliff, *Dangerous Thresholds—Managing Escalation in the 21st Century* (Santa Monica, California: Project Air Force, RAND Corporation, 2008), available at https://www.rand.org/content/dam/rand/pubs/monographs/2008/RAND_MG614.sum.pdf, last accessed on 21 July 2017.

[4] See, for instance, Vipin Narang, 'Posturing for Peace,' *International Security* 34, no. 3 (Winter 2009–10): 38–78, https://www.belfercenter.org/sites/default/files/legacy/files/Narang.pdf, last accessed on 21 July 2017.

[The two sides] shall take immediate steps for reducing the risk of accidental or unauthorized use of nuclear weapons and discuss concepts and doctrines with a view to elaborating measures for confidence building in the nuclear and conventional fields, aimed at prevention of conflict.[5]

In sum then, a lion's share of the discussion on Indo-Pak crisis escalation is from the point of view of escalation stemming from terrorist attacks, accidental/unauthorized use of nuclear weapons, or hypothetical scenarios where conventional conflict leads up to nuclear exchanges, and so on. CFVs in this context are seen by the existing literature either as inconsequential to escalation or as the result of a crisis elsewhere: CFVs by themselves are hardly seen as a cause of crisis for escalation. This chapter seeks to correct this dominant 'misunderstanding'.

Using empirical data on escalation, this section of the chapter will problematize the two key expectations of the South Asian escalation literature: (*i*) Escalation is a rational, intended, and calibrated decision and action; and (*ii*) Terror strikes are the primary cause behind escalation to higher levels of the ladder.

In building a data set on political, diplomatic, and military escalation, the broad definitions of escalation given in Table 6.1 were used.

Table 6.1 Definitions of escalation

Political escalation	Military escalation	Diplomatic escalation
• Adverse statements from decision-making elites about the other country (not one-off statements but in a crisis context) • Cabinet meetings discussing the other country and calling for and deciding on reduced engagement	• Adverse statements by military leadership (about retaliation, nuclear signalling, and deployments, strategies) during times of crisis • Actual attacks (firing with heavy weapons, shelling, prolonged military stand-offs on the border with or without firing)	• Expelling embassy staff • Summoning high commissioner/deputy high commissioner by the host country's foreign ministry • Consular restrictions; demarche to ambassadors/diplomats

[5] 'Lahore Declaration', Ministry of External Affairs, Government of India, 21 February 1999; available at https://mea.gov.in/in-focus-article.htm?18997/Lahore+Declaration+February+1999, last accessed on 3 October 2018.

Political escalation	Military escalation	Diplomatic escalation
• Press conferences discussing the other country and calling for reduced engagement	• Exchange of small fire in a significant manner; sudden movement of troops close to LoC/IB	• Harassment of diplomats
• Statements blaming the other side for wrongdoing	• Military exercises during crises	• Criticizing other side at the UN forums
• Nuclear signalling by politicians	• Violations of air space during crises	• Cancellation of planned meetings between diplomats/ ministers and leaders
• Suspension or rollback of CBMs or threats to review existing agreements/treaties between two sides	• Cancellations of planned meetings between local commanders during crises	• Inclusion of critical language for the adversary in joint communiques with other countries

It is not possible to show which of these three types of escalation is more serious than the other two. But what is clear is that escalation in one sector (that is, political) can lead to escalation in another. So it might not be prudent to ignore escalation occurring in any of these three segments. Indeed, there could be more research on when escalation in one domain plays off in another, but that is outside the purview of this book.

Data on Escalation

This chapter uses three separate data sets—a consolidated data set of CFVs reported by India and Pakistan from 2002 to 2017, and two separate data sets for incidences of crisis escalation between India and Pakistan from 2002 to 2017. The three datasheets were then merged with the timelines matching chronologically.

The data sets offer a fortnightly analysis of the correspondence between CFVs and escalation of tensions between India and Pakistan. The instances of CFVs and escalations are quantified numerically and graphically represented here.

Relationship between CFVs and Escalation

The following graphical analysis of the data shows a strong relationship between the occurrence of CFVs and the escalation of tensions in the

India–Pakistan political, diplomatic, and military relations. I have taken eight cases wherein there is a strong relationship between CFVs and escalation from 2002 to 2017 to examine whether CFVs cause escalation and/or vice versa.

It is important to clarify at this point that the objective of this analysis is to pick out those instances where CFVs have been high, and in the corresponding period, the instances of major and moderate escalation reported by either/both India and Pakistan have also been high. This does not mean that there is no relationship between CFVs and minor incidences of escalation—there is. While I have broadly taken those incidents where CFVs lead to escalation of tensions in the bilateral relations, the inverse relationship, in some cases, also holds true—that is, escalation of tensions can lead to CFVs on the LoC or the IB.

The following eight cases contain three types of cases: one, where CFVs lead to crisis escalation; two, where CFVs contribute to worsening of an ongoing crisis and thereby spike the escalatory ladder; and three, where conventional military escalation gets played out on the front lines in the form of CFVs.

Case 6.1: 1 May 2002 to 30 June 2002

Let us refer to the data given in Figure 6.1 in order to analyse the relationship between escalation and CFVs between India and Pakistan from May 2002 to June 2002. Towards the end of the 2001–2 India–Pakistan military stand-off, CFVs played a crucial role in escalating the crisis. While it is true that CFVs did not begin the crisis—a terrorist attack did—the following description highlights how CFVs further escalated the crisis. It is also important to clarify that technically there was no ceasefire at that point of time (CFA was agreed to only in late 2003), but for practical purposes, we will call this instance of border firing as a CFV.

During the second phase of Operation Parakram, the Indian military preparations intended to retaliate against the terrorist attack on the Indian Parliament in the December of the previous year. The Indian Army troops and air force personnel began a scheduled military exercise on 2 May 2002 near the Pakistan border. On the same day, Pakistan reported several instances of CFVs at several places on the IB/WB and LoC (Chamb Jaurian [Gujarat], Bajwat, Bajragarhi, Charwa,

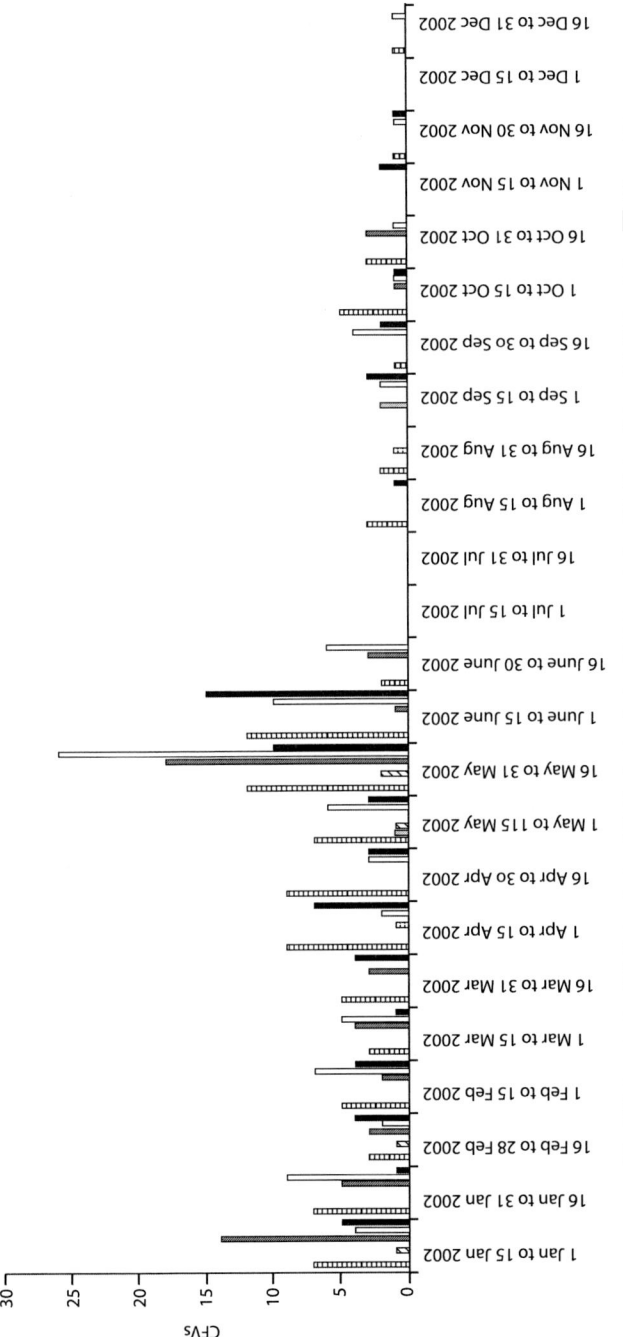

Figure 6.1 Fortnightly CFVs and escalation reported by India and by Pakistan in 2002

Source: Author.

Harpal, Chaprar, Sucheetgarh, Jammu, Akhnoor, Samba, Zafarwal, and Shakargarh–Narowal sectors). CFVs were reported as crossfire between Indian and Pakistani troops and continued till 5 May 2002 and then resumed on 13 May 2002.

This was followed by the audacious terrorist attack on 14 May 2002 in Kaluchak, Jammu wherein three Pakistani gunmen killed 30, including 10 children, in a Jammu army camp. The Indian defence minister held Pakistan directly responsible for the attack on the army base. This was followed by political and diplomatic rhetoric and several adverse statements.[6]

[6] New Delhi is not ready to pull back its troops from the border with Pakistan, Indian foreign minister Jaswant Singh told a visiting US state department official (*Times of India*, 'Rocca for Indo-Pak Status Quo', *Times of India*, 13 May 2002, available at https://timesofindia.indiatimes.com/india/ Rocca-for-Indo-Pak-status-quo/articleshow/9799105.cms, last accessed on 4 October 2018). Minister for Information Nisar A. Memon rejected claims that Pakistan was involved in the attacks in the Indian Occupied Kashmir (14 May 2002) (Pakistan Institute of International Affairs, 'Pakistan and the World', *Pakistan Horizon* 55(3) [April-June 2002]: 71–118.) India will find it difficult to show restraint in its military stand-off with Pakistan if attacks like the one at an Indian Army camp held near Jammu persist, said a junior minister, Omar Abdullah (Rediff News, 'Military Restraint May Not Last: Centre', *Rediff.com*, available at: http://www.rediff.com/news/2002/may/14jk7.htm, last accessed on 10 October 2018.) The government has sufficiently enhanced its military strength on borders to repulse any attack by the enemy, Information Minister Nisar Memon (15 May 2002). (Pakistan Institute of International Affairs, 'Pakistan and the World', 71–118.) The foreign office said that wild allegations of Pakistan's involvement in the Jammu incident and threats of retaliation by the Indian government were part of Delhi's plan to divert international attention from the genocide of the Muslim minority in Gujarat. In a statement, a foreign office spokesperson rejected the allegations levelled by Indian defence minister George Fernandes that Pakistan was behind the 14 May attack near Jammu (17 May 2002). (*Dawn*, 'Pakistan Rejects Indian Charge', *Dawn Newspaper- Weekly*, available at https://asianstudies.github.io/area-studies/SouthAsia/SAserials/ Dawn/2002/may182002.html, last accessed on 10 October 2018). The director-general of ISPR, Maj. Gen. Rashid Qureshi: 'Pakistan would not accept threats from India and was fully prepared to respond to any aggressive action' (18 May 2002). (*Dawn*, 'Pakistan Not to Accept Threats from India', *Dawn Newspaper-Weekly*, available at https://www.dawn.com/news/34886/pakistan-not-to-accept-threats-from-india, last accessed on 10 October 2018.)

CFVs spiked on 18 May 2002 and Pakistan reported that at least five people died and 37 others were injured on the Pakistani side of the LoC, which Pakistani authorities described as indiscriminate and unprovoked Indian shelling on the civilian population. Violations were reported from Chamb sector in the southernmost Bhimber district and then in the Chakothi sector and Neelum Valley in Muzaffarabad district, and in Forward Kahuta sector in Bagh district, during which the Indian troops reportedly used machine guns, mortars, and artillery.

On the diplomatic front, on 18 May 2002, Ashraf Jahangir Qazi, Pakistan's high commissioner to India, was recalled by Pakistan on the demand of the Indian government. Pakistan, in the meantime, kept the UN secretary-general abreast of 'India's warlike actions and on the ongoing heavy shelling'. The following day, on 19 May 2002, Pakistani media also reported that four villagers were killed and 40 others wounded by Indian firing. Political and diplomatic escalation continued till 1 July 2002. CFVs are reported from early May to mid-June 2002.

It may be noted that in this example, the crisis was not triggered by CFVs, even as it played a crucial role in further escalating the ongoing crisis. Moreover, since the Indian side knew well enough that despite making preparations for Operation Parakram, it would have been a costly affair to go to war with Pakistan, violence was conveniently shifted to the border, resulting in high levels of firing with high-calibre weapons. The evidence underlines the argument made in the chapter on the role played by CFVs during a crisis and escalating such a crisis.

This was also a case of CFVs contributing to a pre-existing military crisis leading to further military escalation, simultaneously fuelling diplomatic and political escalation.

Case 6.2: 16 April 2011 to 31 May 2011

Let us refer to the data given in Figure 6.2 in order to analyse the relationship between escalation and CFVs between India and Pakistan from mid-April 2011 to May 2011. On 16 April 2011, two BSF troopers Manoj Kumar and S.M. Patel were injured when an IED went off near the LoC in Sinagali area of Poonch district in J&K. This event triggered tensions between the two forces on the LoC with CFVs being reported on 22 and 24 April from the same district. As tension continued to rise, the Indian Army chief Gen. V.K. Singh said on 3 May 2011 that

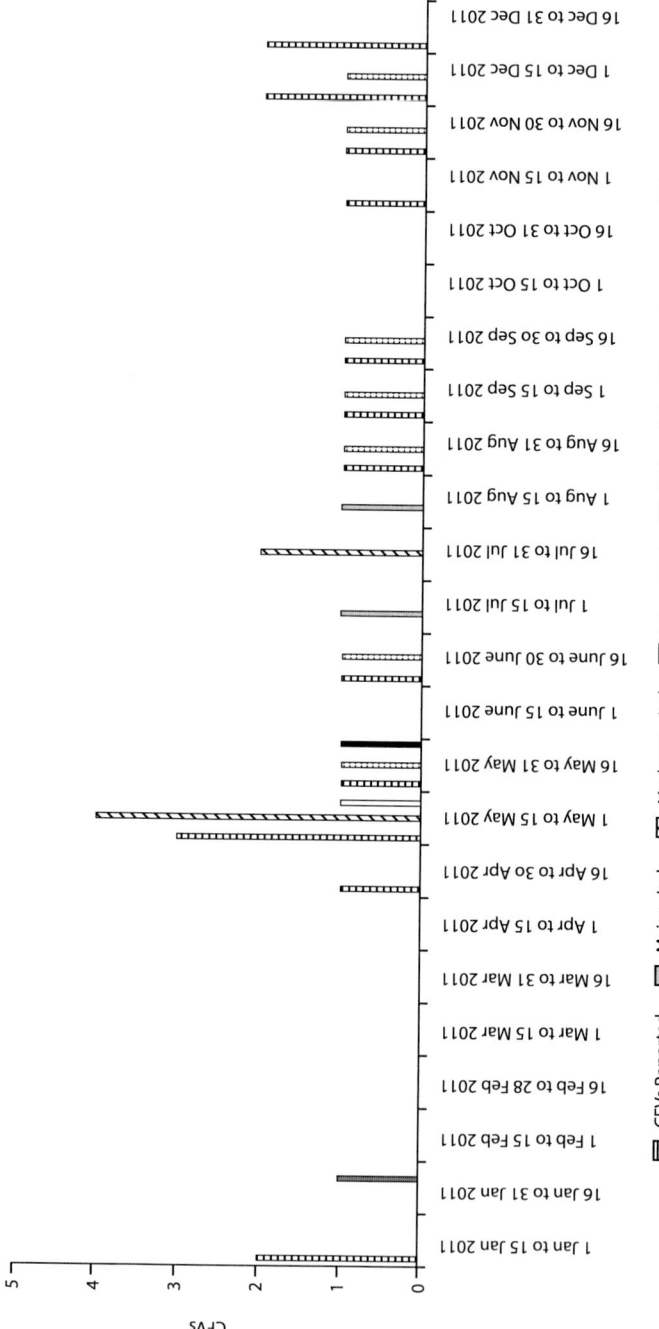

Figure 6.2 Fortnightly CFVs and escalation reported by India and by Pakistan in 2011

Source: Author.

the Indian armed forces were capable of carrying out surgical operations against terrorists similar to the one conducted by the US in Pakistan to kill al Qaeda chief Osama bin Laden, to which Pakistan's foreign secretary Salman Bashir reacted two days later by saying:

> Any other country that would ever act (similarly) on the assumption that it has the might ... will find it has made a basic miscalculation ... We see a lot of bravado in our region ... from the military, air force, which state that this can be repeated. We feel that sort of misadventure or miscalculation will result in a catastrophe'.[7]

The same day witnessed several more CFVs in Poonch.

On 8 May, the Indian MHA officials said that at least 700 militants are being trained across the LoC in Pakistan with over 100 of them waiting at 'launch pads' to infiltrate into J&K.[8] Two days later, the Indian military began 'Operation Vijayee Bhava', a month-long military exercise involving 50,000 Indian Army troops and the IAF in Bikaner and Suratgarh. On 14 and 15 May, Pakistan reported two CFVs in Sialkot. On 26 May 2011, Indian defence minister, A.K. Antony, stated at the Navy Commanders Conference that developments in Pakistan (including safety of Pakistan's nuclear weapons), especially the terror attack in Karachi (referring to the attack by Tehrik-i-Taliban Pakistan and Al Qaeda on PNS Mehran, the headquarters of the Pakistan Navy's Naval Air Arm on 22 May 2011), were of serious concern to India and that all three services were taking necessary precautions and 'closely monitoring' the situation.[9] More CFVs were reported on 30 May in Shakargarh. Pakistan reported indiscriminate firing by the Indian BSF causing panic among villagers of Shakargarh sector along the Sialkot WB.

[7] *Economic Times*, 'Osama bin Laden Dead: Pakistan Warns US, India against Covert Operations', *Economic Times*, 5 May 2011, available at http://economictimes.indiatimes.com/news/politics-and-nation/osama-bin-laden-dead-pakistan-warns-us-india-against-covert-operations/articleshow/8169040.cms, last accessed on 8 December 2016.

[8] *Indian Express*, 'Over 100 Militants Waiting at Launch Pads to Enter J-K', *Indian Express*, 8 May 2011, available at http://indianexpress.com/article/india/latest-news/over-100-militants-waiting-at-launch-pads-to-enter-jk/, last accessed on 8 December 2016.

[9] Special Correspondent, 'Pakistan Situation Worrisome', *Hindu*, 26 May 2011, available at http://www.thehindu.com/news/national/pakistan-situation-worrisome/article2048859.ece, last accessed on 8 December 2016.

This example goes to show two things: (*i*) that CFVs and the placing of IEDs on the LoC and IB/WB (even though the latter is not strictly CFV, they need to be viewed as part of the larger routine violence on the border) do lead to military and political stand-offs; (*ii*) general breakdowns in India–Pakistan relations have an immediate effect on the LoC and IB/WB in the form of CFVs; and (*iii*) CFVs are part of the India–Pakistan escalation dynamics.

Case 6.3: 1 July 2013 to end of October 2013

Let us refer to the data given in Figure 6.3 in order to analyse the relationship between escalation and CFVs between India and Pakistan from July 2013 to October 2013. A major escalation in August 2013 began with five Indian soldiers, four from the 21 Bihar Regiment and one from the Maratha Light Infantry, being killed in Poonch in an ambush by what the then Indian defence minister described as 'heavily armed terrorists along with persons dressed in Pakistan Army uniforms'.[10] While one is unsure whether this was conducted by the Pakistan Army or terrorists wearing army uniform, according to senior Indian Army officials, it was an ambush laid near the zero line by a BAT of the Pakistan Army's Mujahid Battalion.[11] However, it could potentially have been a 'surgical strike' organized by one of Pakistan's BATs. This led to a major crisis between the two sides. This crisis had its origins in a spate of CFVs that took place the previous month. Hence, the killing of the five Indian soldiers was a result of the previous month's violations and killings.

In July 2013, the Indian side had reported CFVs on 3, 8, 12, and 22 July.[12] On 27 July, Pakistan's ISPR stated that a Pakistani soldier was

[10] NDTV, 'Defence Minister AK Antony's Statement on Five Indians Being Killed by Pakistani Troops', *NDTV.com*, 6 August 2013, available at https://www.ndtv.com/india-news/read-defence-minister-ak-antonys-statement-on-five-indians-being-killed-by-pakistani-troops-530703, last accessed on 21 March 2017.

[11] Ahmed Ali Fayyaz, 'Five Indian Soldiers Killed near LoC', *Hindu*, 6 August 2013, available at http://www.thehindu.com/news/national/five-indian-soldiers-killed-near-loc/article4995032.ece, last accessed on 8 December 2017.

[12] *News18*, 'J&K: Pakistan Violates Ceasefire Twice in 10 Hours, one BSF Jawan Injured', *News18.com*, 27 July 2013, available at http://www.news18.com/news/india/jk-pakistan-violates-ceasefire-twice-in-10-hours-one-bsf-jawan-injured-627008.html, last accessed on 8 December 2017.

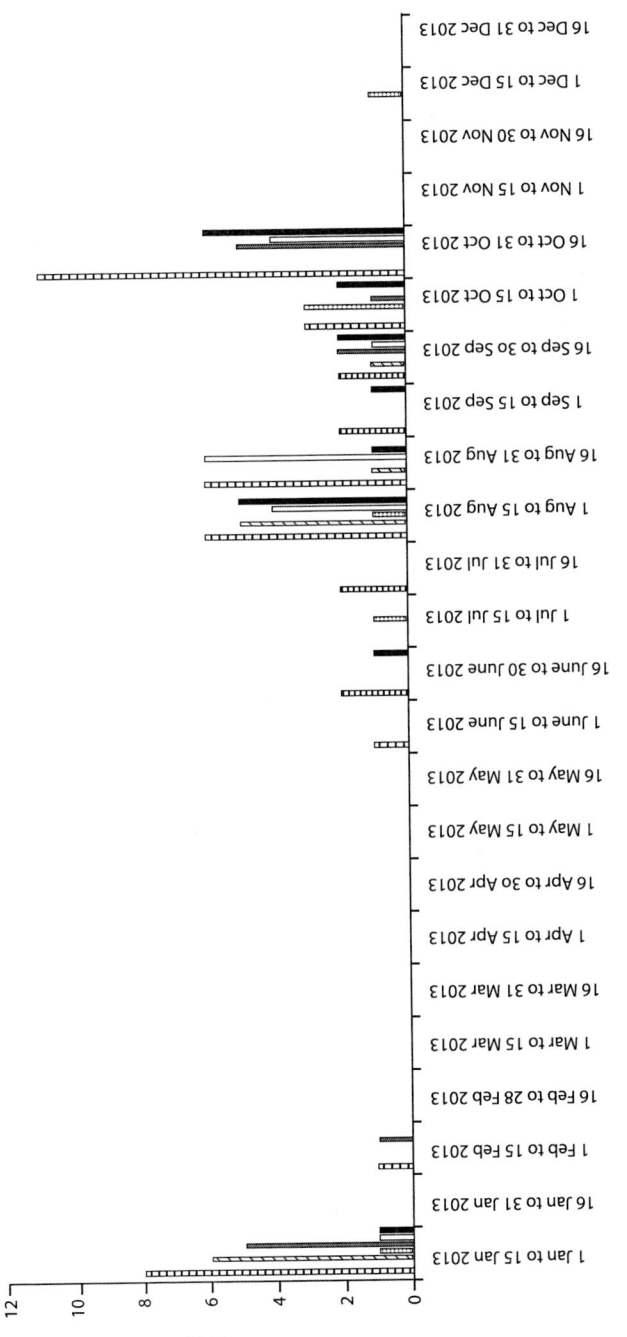

Figure 6.3 Fortnightly CFVs and escalation reported by India and by Pakistan in 2013

Source: Author.

killed in firing by Indian troops in Rawalakot's Nezapir sector on the LoC.[13] Praveen Swamy reported on 7 August, two days after the Indian soldiers were ambushed, that four Pakistanis (unclear whether they were innocent Pakistani civilians or infiltrators) were 'killed near Katwar Post, a forward position along the Line of Control in the Macchel sector, along the Neelam river, late on the night of 29 July' and that 'the alleged killings and skirmishes which followed it may have triggered off a cycle leading to the killings of five Indian troops in Poonch—sparking off the worst India–Pakistan crisis in months'.[14]

On the diplomatic front, Indian protesters gathered outside the Pakistan High Commission in New Delhi. Pakistan's deputy high commissioner was summoned by the MEA and a strong protest was lodged over the killings, and in return, Pakistan summoned India's deputy high commissioner in Islamabad over protests outside its high commission in New Delhi.

On 10 August, India asked Pakistan to take responsibility for killing of five of its soldiers on the LoC. On 12 August, Pakistan stated that the most-favoured nation (MFN) trading status for India was not under 'immediate consideration'. In the meantime, CFVs continued on the LoC (Poonch, Rajouri, Samba, Uri, and Battal) from 7 to 14 August. On 14 August, reports from Pakistan indicate that India gave a clear indication that killings would delay the secretary-level talks with Pakistan, saying that dialogue could only proceed in an environment free of violence and terror.

A political crisis also began to brew in the meantime. On 14 August, the Pakistan National Assembly passed a unanimous resolution condemning unprovoked aggression by the Indian Army across the LoC,[15] and a counter-resolution moved in India's Lok Sabha rejected Pakistan's

[13] Mubashir Zaidi, 'Pakistan Army Soldier Killed in Kashmir Border Firing: ISPR', *Dawn*, 27 July 2013, available at https://www.dawn.com/news/1032308, last accessed on 3 October 2018.

[14] Praveen Swami, 'Exclusive: Details of LoC Killings That Came before Poonch Ambush', *Firstpost*, available at http://www.firstpost.com/india/exclusive-details-of-loc-killings-that-came-before-poonch-ambush-1016785.html, last accessed on 8 December 2016.

[15] *Firstpost*, 'Full Text: Pakistan National Assembly Resolution against India', *Firstpost*, 14 August 2013, available at http://www.firstpost.com/world/full-text-pakistan-national-assembly-resolution-against-india-1032179.html, last accessed on 19 December 2016.

National Assembly resolution.[16] The then Indian prime minister Manmohan Singh, a votary of peace between India and Pakistan, warned Pakistan against 'anti-India activity' as tensions rose over the 5 August attack.

On the military front, the Indian Army chief Gen. Bikram Singh upped the ante the following day by asserting that India would retaliate if provoked further by Pakistan on the border. The chief said that Pakistani troops had 'pre-planned and pre-meditated' the action and asserted that India reserves the right to retaliate at a 'time and place of its choice'.[17]

Several CFVs were reported both on the LoC and IB/WB in Poonch, Jammu, Mendhar, Hamirpur, Balakote, Krishna Ghati, Kargil, Drass, Skardu, and so on from 14 to 26 August. On 23 August, with reports of two more Pakistani soldiers getting killed by Indian shelling, Islamabad proposed a meeting of senior diplomats and military officials to implement ceasefire on the LoC.

On 27 August, two more Pakistani soldiers were killed by Indian shelling even as Pakistan proposed to India that meetings of senior diplomats and military officials controlling CFVs be organized. No meetings were organized and CFVs continued till early September in Poonch, Mendhar, Balakote, and in Rajouri. On 24 September, the Indian Army launched a major CI operation in the Keran sector after a massive infiltration attempt from across the LoC into Jammu and Kashmir. The following day, on 25 September, two audacious terrorist attacks in Samba killed 10 people. India's home minister said that 'as per preliminary information, the terrorists came from across the border'.[18]

[16] 'Resolution Moved in Lok Sabha Rejects the Resolution Passed by the National Assembly of Pakistan', Ministry of External Affairs, Government of India, 15 March 2013, available at http://www.mea.gov.in/bilateral-documents. htm?dtl/21391/Resolution+moved+in+Lok+Sabha+rejects+the+resoluti on+passed+by+the+National+Assembly+of+Pakistan, last accessed on 19 December 2016.

[17] Vinay Kumar, 'We Will Retaliate if Provoked Further, Says Army Chief', *Hindu*, 14 August 2013, available at http://www.thehindu.com/news/national/ we-will-retaliate-if-provoked-further-says-army-chief/article4306810.ece, last accessed on 19 December 2016.

[18] *Times of India*, 'Army Operation Over in J&K's Samba, All Three Terrorists Gunned Down', *Times of India*, 26 September 2013, available at https://timesofindia.indiatimes.com/india/Army-operation-over-in-JKs-

BJP leaders, including the party's prime ministerial candidate Narendra Modi, questioned Prime Minister Singh for his plan to meet Pakistan's prime minister on the same day when militants dressed in Indian Army uniforms attacked a police station and an army base in Jammu and Kashmir.

The situation was temporarily de-escalated with a meeting between Prime Ministers Nawaz Sharif and Manmohan Singh on 29 September in New York on the sidelines of the UNGA meeting. The leaders agreed to ask the respective military officers to find 'effective means' to restore the 2003 ceasefire in Kashmir.

The meeting of the prime ministers and the agreement to get the senior military officials to talk to each other, however, did not put an end to the crisis. A fresh spell of CFVs was reported from Krishna Ghati and Mendhar sectors from 2 to 5 October with both Indian and Pakistani sides accusing each other of violating the CFA. Indian Army chief Gen. Bikram Singh told the media that the reason behind the spurt in violence was because of the uncertain Afghan situation and the upcoming winter: 'Will have to see what happens in Afghanistan in 2014. Pakistan want to push in many terrorists before winter.'[19] A few days later, the Pakistan Army chief Gen. Kayani responded to allegations about the Pakistan Army's involvement in pushing infiltrators into Kashmir saying that the 'Indian allegations against Pakistan Army and the Inter-Services Intelligence (ISI) were "unfortunate, unfounded and provocative"'.[20]

The escalation adversely affected the bilateral political dialogue as well. Indian external affairs minister Salman Khurshid said, 'But (as far as) the incidents at the LoC and border are concerned, they are upsetting.

Samba-all-three-terrorists-gunned-down/articleshow/23106927.cms, last accessed on 3 October 2018.

[19] *Reuters*, 'India Says Pakistan Army Backing Kashmir Incursions', *Reuters*, 8 October 2013, available at http://in.reuters.com/article/india-pakistan-incursion-kashmir/india-says-pakistan-army-backing-kashmir-incursions-idINDEE99707M20131008, last accessed on 19 December 2016.

[20] Kamran Yousaf, 'LoC Skirmishes: "Provocative" Indian Charges Anger Kayani', *The Express Tribune*, 12 October 2013, available at https://tribune.com.pk/story/617005/loc-skirmishes-provocative-indian-charges-anger-kayani/, last accessed on 3 October 2018.

The army is dealing with it and the defence minister is dealing with it, but I cannot say it is conducive to a faster movement in normalization.'[21] CFVs were reported again from mid-October to the end of the month from both the LoC and IB/WB sectors. On 17 October, Pakistan accused India of killing a Pakistan Rangers soldier in 'unprovoked firing' across the border in the eastern Punjab province. Recall that firing is unusual across the borders outside J&K. On 23 October, the two DGMOs talked on the hotline to ease the situation even as accusations flew back and forth. With no respite in sight, Manmohan Singh, on 25 October, accused 'Pakistan of breaking the 2003 ceasefire pact and blamed Prime Minister Nawaz Sharif for not reining in his men'.[22] Violence spread to Punjab with three alleged Pakistani drug smugglers being killed on the IB in Punjab. The crisis eventually petered out.

The above-mentioned example of a major escalation between the two sides was evidently a result of CFVs and killings on the India–Pakistan border in J&K. Alleged foiling of infiltration led to casualties of Pakistanis, leading to CFVs, and then cross-border operation by the Pakistani side killing five Indian soldiers. What took place on the border then quickly went up the escalation ladder and it soon became a political, diplomatic, and military crisis that went on for close to three months. The conclusion is straightforward: CFVs and related border violence have an escalatory effect on India–Pakistan political, military, and diplomatic relations.

Case 6.4: 1 June 2014 to 31 August 2014

Let us refer to the data given in Figure 6.4 in order to analyse the relationship between escalation and CFVs between India and Pakistan from June 2014 to August 2014. In the summer of 2014, several months before the J&K assembly elections, the LoC and the IB/WB started heating up again with CFVs beginning at the end of April and continuing

---

[21] *Indian Express*, 'India, Pakistan Not at "Resumed Talks" Stage: Salman Khurshid', *Indian Express*, 12 October 2013, available at http://archive. indianexpress.com/news/india-pakistan-not-at-resumed-talks-stage-salman-khurshid/1181709/, last accessed on 19 December 2016.

[22] *Dawn* 'Indian Premier Criticises Sharif over LoC Firing', *Dawn*, 25 October 2013, available at https://www.dawn.com/news/1051623, last accessed on 20 December 2016.

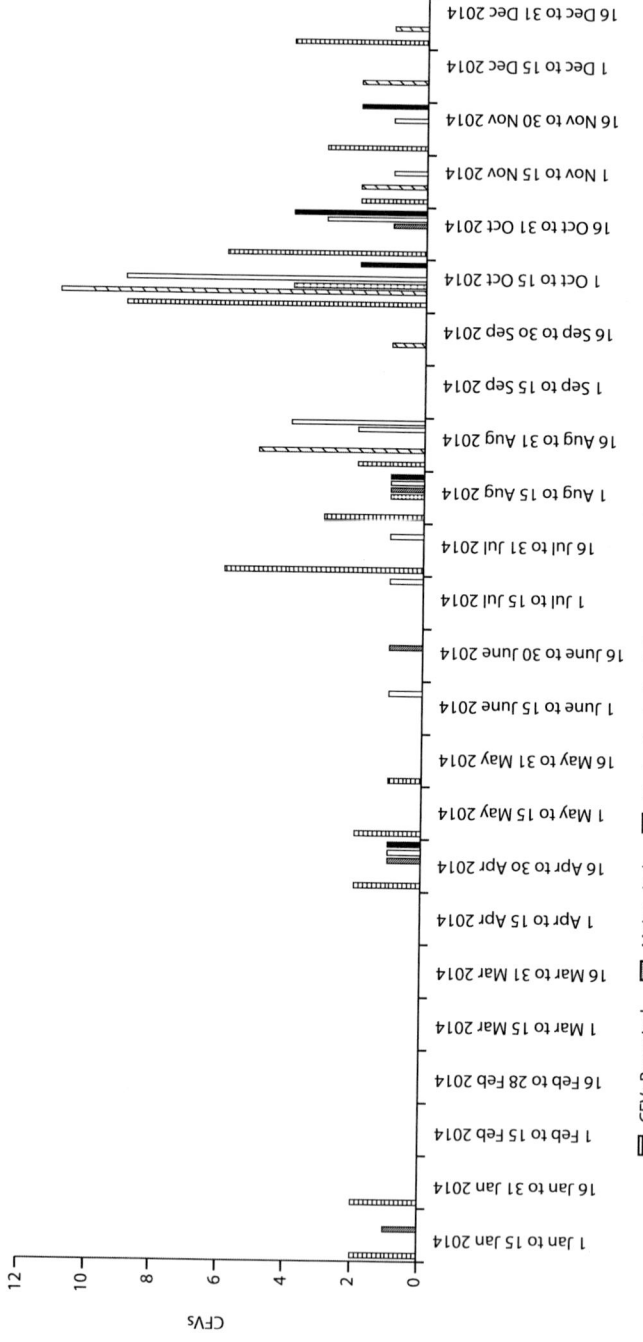

Figure 6.4 Fortnightly CFVs and escalation reported by India and by Pakistan in 2014

Source: Author.

into May and June. Midway through June, one month after the hardline leader Narendra Modi was sworn in as India's new prime minister, there seemed to be no let-up and New Delhi made it clear to Islamabad that there could be no progress in India–Pakistan talks if Pakistan continued to violate the CFA. CFVs continued into July and August, even though Pakistan handed over to India as a goodwill gesture a BSF soldier who was swept across the border in Jammu and Kashmir by the Chenab River.

By mid-August, closer to the independence days of both the countries, the two militaries continued to fire, and on 12 August, the deputy high commissioner of India in Islamabad was summoned to the foreign office and was handed over a protest after firing by Indian forces along the WB killed a Pakistani woman.[23] Firing went on even as the two countries celebrated their independence days.

In the third week of August, Pakistani high commissioner to India, Abdul Basit, extended invitations to Kashmiri separatist leaders to consult them before the foreign secretary–level talks to be held in Islamabad. This was not taken kindly by the new government, and on 18 August, it called off foreign secretary–level talks with Pakistan with just a few days to go, indicating unhappiness over Pakistan envoy's engagement with Kashmiri separatist leaders.

According to the Indian government's statement:

> The invitation to so-called leaders of the Hurriyat by Pakistan's High Commissioner does indeed raise questions about Pakistan's sincerity, and shows that its negative approaches and attempts to interfere in India's internal affairs continue unabated … Under the present circumstances, it is felt that no useful purpose will be served by the Indian Foreign Secretary going to Islamabad next week.[24]

Basit's invitation to Kashmiri separatist leadership and the cancellation of foreign secretary–level talks came amid a spurt of violations of the ceasefire along the LoC as well as IB. CFVs eventually petered out

---

[23] *Dawn*, 'Woman Killed by Indian Firing', *Dawn*, 12 August 2014, available at https://www.dawn.com/news/1124787, last accessed on 19 December 2016.

[24] Suhasini Haidar, 'India–Pak. Talks Are Off', *Hindu*, 18 August 2014, available at http://www.thehindu.com/news/national/india-calls-off-foreign-secretarylevel-talks-with-pakistan/article6329082.ece, last accessed on 19 December 2016.

by late August. This is yet another instance of CVs prompting escalation of tensions, primarily diplomatic, between the two sides.

Case 6.5: 1 October 2014 to 31 December 2014

In early October 2014, during the newly elected Indian prime minister Modi's visit to Washington, CFVs started spiking again. On 2 October, the joint statement issued by the United States and India committed to work together to dismantle Al Qaeda, LeT, and their affiliates. The statement also urged Pakistan to bring the perpetrators of the 2008 Mumbai terrorist attack to justice. Back in the subcontinent, from 2 October to 14 October, CFVs were being reported from several locations in the valley: Sabjian, Mandi, Hamirpur, Arnia, R.S. Pura, Pargwal, Ganjansoo, Kanachak, and Samba. On 2 November 2014, the Pakistan Taliban issued a direct threat to Indian Prime Minister Modi (via Twitter) and vowed revenge against him. On 3 November, a suicide bombing at Wagah border killed at least 55 and injured over 200 persons.

Politicians jumped into the fray as well. On 7 October 2014, a powerful BJP leader and a Modi confidante, Amit Shah, who later went to become India's ruling party's president, told the media that Pakistan is begging for a flag meeting, and that India said that there would be no flag meeting until the firing stopped. In response, Pakistani leader Bilawal Bhutto tweeted: 'Another attack on LOC. Seems India adopting Israel model vs Pakistan. Modi must realize we can retaliate unlike his victims from Gujarat.'[25]

On 8 October, the Indian MHA called for a high-level meeting as violence along the LoC started escalating. On 10 October, Pakistan's PM Nawaz Sharif chaired a meeting of the National Security Committee to discuss the CFVs along the LoC.

During the escalation, there were also attempts at subtle but clear nuclear signalling. Pakistan defence minister Khawaja Asif stated: 'Pakistan has the ability to reply to Indian aggression. We do not want

---

[25] *Hindustan Times*, 'India Adopting Israel Model against Pakistan: Bilawal', *Hindustan Times*, 9 October 2014; available at https://www.hindustantimes.com/india/india-adopting-israel-model-against-pakistan-bilawal/story-W2raAQWFKPCYrd1GqAaO3I.html, last accessed on 3 October 2018.

the situation on the borders of two nuclear neighbours to escalate into confrontation', and its federal minister for states and frontier regions Lt Gen. Abdul Qadir Baloch (Retd) said war is not the solution to any issue but 'India should realise the fact that Pakistan is a nuclear power'.[26]

The vertical escalation and the heavy weapons used in the long stand-off caused a great deal of damage to the villages around the IB/WB in the Jammu/Sialkot sector. Nearly 30,000 people were displaced from 113 border villages along the 192 km long IB in the Jammu, Samba, and Kathua districts. Around eight people died and 80 others, including nine security men, have been injured since 1 October. By 10 October, around 12 Pakistani villagers were killed in the Indian firing, 70,000 villagers have been affected, and 20,000 were displaced.[27]

Media reports indicated that 'Indian forces have been given a free hand to deal with the situation appropriately and reject talks until all firing from Pakistan stops'.[28] One report claimed that 'Islamabad may not be awed, but it certainly is shocked by the ferocity and volume of the Indian response to ceasefire violations along the International Border in Jammu and Kashmir'.[29]

Recall our discussion in the previous chapter about BSF's 2014 pro-active operations in the Jammu sector. It is useful to bring back some

[26] Mail Today Bureau, 'Pakistan Issues 'Nuclear Warning' to India, 10 October 2014, *India Today* [wensite], available at https://www.indiatoday.in/world/pakistan/story/pakistan-issues-nuclear-warning-to-india-209346-2014-10-10 last accessed on 3 October 2018.

[27] *Express Tribune*, 'Unprovoked Firing: Deaths Mount as BSF Shells Pak Villages,' *Express Tribune*, 10 October, 2014, available at https://tribune.com.pk/story/773176/unprovoked-firing-deaths-mount-as-bsf-shells-pak-villages/, last accessed on 25 December 2014.

[28] Nitin Gokhale, 'India Warns Pakistan it's Not Afraid of Escalating Fire: Sources', NDTV, 8 October 2014, available at https://www.ndtv.com/cheat-sheet/india-warns-pakistan-its-not-afraid-of-escalating-fire-sources-676560, last accessed on 25 December 2016.

[29] Abhishek Bhalla and Gautam Datt, 'Islamabad Shocked as Indian Army Launches "Massive" Retaliation to Border Firing ... and Confident PM Modi Promises "Everything will be All Right Soon"', *MailOnlineIndia*, 9 October 2014, available at http://www.dailymail.co.uk/indiahome/indianews/article-2785698/Islamabad-shocked-Indian-Army-launches-massive-retaliation-border-firing-confident-PM-Modi-promises-right-soon.html, last accessed on 25 December 2016.

important aspects of that discussion here. Early on during the escalation, BSF higher-ups decided to graduate the retaliatory firing from small arms to shelling. As part of a major plan, BSF moved over 100 high-calibre guns (for shelling) from Punjab and Kashmir sectors to Jammu. They were used on the 192 km Jammu border with Pakistan in a coordinated manner, pulverizing the Pakistani posts.

In Sharma's own words, 'from July 2014 onwards, till October 2015, there was very little small-arm fire, and in major cross-border firing, heavy mortar was used'.[30] On 10 October 2014, India's MEA spokesperson Syed Akbaruddin said that 'it is for Pakistan to end its adventurism … de-escalation is entirely in Pakistan's hands'.[31] He warns Pakistan of an 'appropriate response' from India for whatever it chose to do. In response, on 14 October, Pakistan's ambassador to the UN, Masood Khan, delivered Pakistan national security adviser Sartaj Aziz's letter addressed to the secretary-general on the deteriorating security situation along the LoC in Kashmir at the UN's chief office in New York. The war of words then was matched by more action on the front lines as CFVs continued through October.

In early December, as the crisis persisted, India warned Pakistan on 2 December of a 'strong response' in response to its policy of aiding and abetting cross-border terrorism, a week after four militant strikes killed 11 security personnel and two civilians in J&K. India's defence minister Manohar Parrikar during his visit to J&K said, 'I feel that there has to be some strong response which will once and for all reduce these blatant attempts. It is an open secret that they (militants) came from Pakistan … You will see the developments in the next six months … We have to ultimately teach those who are rogue a proper lesson.'[32]

---

[30] Interview with Rakesh Sharma, 15 September 2016, New Delhi.

[31] *Times of India*, 'Border Tension: Onus on Pakistan to De-escalate, India Says', *Times of India*, 11 October 2014; available at http://timesofindia.india-times.com/articleshow/44779226.cms?utm_source=contentofinterest&utm_medium=text&utm_campaign=cppst, last accessed on 3 October 2018.

[32] *Times of India*, '"Strong Action" against Pakistan in 6 Months: Parrikar', *Times of India*, 13 December 2014, available at http://timesofindia.indiatimes.com/india/Strong-action-against-Pakistan-in-6-months-Parrikar/articleshow/45500932.cms, last accessed on 26 December 2016.

On 13 December 2014, Pakistan reacted to Manohar Parrikar's 'provocative' statement and underlined that it was fully capable to defend itself against any Indian aggression.[33]

Soon thereafter, in early January 2015, Pakistani firing kills one BSF soldier on the IB in Samba and four Rangers die in the BSF retaliation.[34] The CFVs petered out in mid-January only to resume the following month. Once again, CFVs, in the absence of terror attacks, led to political and military escalation in this case.

Case 6.6: 1 July 2015 to 30 September 2015

Let us refer to the data given in Figure 6.5 in order to analyse the relationship between escalation and CFVs between India and Pakistan from July 2015 to September 2015. The period from July to September 2015 witnessed CFVs and resultant bilateral crisis escalation. From 1 July till 15 July 2015, both India and Pakistan reported CFVs from Jammu, Nowgam, Uri, and other places on the LoC. Reports from Pakistan on 6 July indicated that several houses were damaged in the heavy shelling on Pakistani villages in the Charwah sector along the Sialkot WB. At a *Geo TV* talk show on 8 July, Pakistan defence minister Khawaja Muhammad Asif stated that use of nuclear weapons was always an option as they were not kept merely for show but as deterrents.

A temporary halt in the firing was achieved when, on 10 July, the prime ministers of Pakistan and India met on the sidelines of the SCO summit in Ufa. The two countries agreed to resume the bilateral dialogue. However, the rapprochement did not last long and firing resumed on 16 July with the Pakistan Army shooting down an Indian UAV allegedly on a 'spy mission' near the LoC, prompting the Pakistan Foreign Office to summon the Indian high commissioner to lodge a protest over the incident.

---

[33] Mateen Haider, 'Pakistan Warns India against Issuing "Provocative" Statements', *Dawn*, 13 December 2014, available at https://www.dawn.com/news/1150648, last accessed on 16 December 2016.

[34] *India*, 'BSF Jawan Killed in Pakistan Shelling along International Border in Samba', *India*, 5 January 2015, available at http://www.india.com/news/india/bsf-jawan-killed-in-pakistan-shelling-along-international-border-in-samba-239519/, last accessed on 25 December 2016.

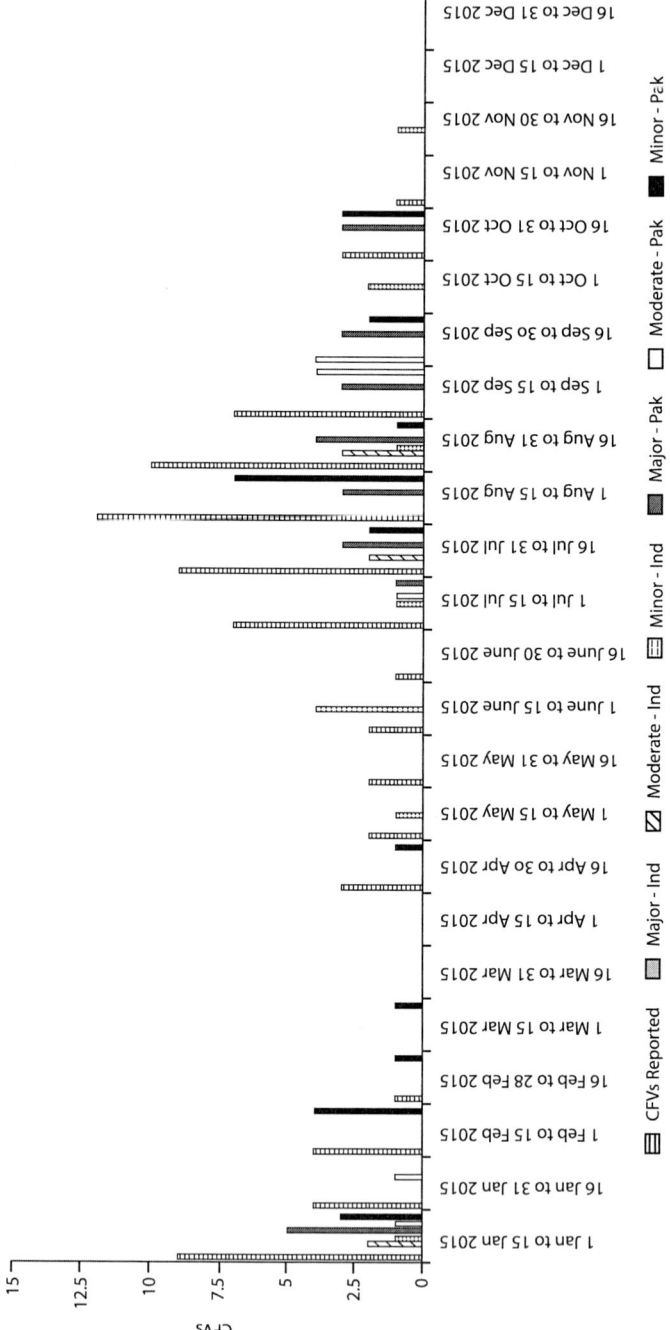

Figure 6.5 Fortnightly CFVs and escalation reported by India and by Pakistan in 2015

Source: Author.

The following day, Pakistan lodged a complaint against India with the UNMOGIP for 'CFVs', claiming that four Pakistani citizens were killed in the firing. Tensions also escalated diplomatically with the India–Pakistan visa row: the two sides accused each other of not issuing visas to their diplomats. India maintains that Pakistan refused to issue visas to its 12 officials, including a naval attaché, a charge Pakistan has denied.[35]

After another temporary halt, the two sides resumed firing on 1 August with around 12 violations being reported by the two sides. Senior Pakistani official Sartaj Aziz informed the National Assembly on 1 August 2015 that the Pakistan government was considering to raise the issue of RAW's interference in the country at the UNGA session in September.

Around mid-August onwards, 10 more CFVs were reported by India and Pakistan. On 22 August, Pakistan called off the National Security Advisor (NSA)-level talks saying, 'The scheduled NSA-level talks cannot be held on the basis of the preconditions set by India' (referring to the conditions laid down by the Indian foreign minister that the meeting would only discuss terrorism and that the talks would be strictly bilateral—Sushma Swaraj had given a deadline till midnight to respond to Indian conditions).[36]

Pakistan, responding to the Indian demands, accused India of 'concocting terror incidents and keeping the LoC hot'. India accused Pakistan of using CFVs and terror attacks to 'run away from the talks'.

On 28 August, Pakistani military officials told the members of the Senate body during a visit to the Joint Staff (JS) headquarters that 'India was the only external military threat to Pakistan'.[37] Pakistan's minister for interior Chaudhry Nisar Ali Khan accused the Indian government of trying to sabotage efforts for peace.

[35] NDTV, 'After Border Tension, India and Pakistan in Visa Row: Report', NDTV, 17 July 2015, available at https://www.ndtv.com/india-news/after-border-tension-india-and-pakistan-in-visa-row-report-782526, last accessed on 5 January 2017.

[36] Suhasini Haidar, 'As Sparring Worsens, NSA Talks Are Off', Hindu, 22 August 2015, available at http://www.thehindu.com/news/international/south-asia/indiapakistan-national-security-advisorlevel-talks-called-off/article7569679.ece, accessed on 6 January 2017.

[37] Dawn, 'India Is the Only External Threat, Says Military', Dawn, 28 August 2015, available at https://www.dawn.com/news/1203329, last accessed on 7 January 2017.

CFVs continued into the following month with both sides reporting violations by the other side. On 1 September, India's army chief Gen. Dalbir Singh, referring to the frequent CFVs along the J&K borders, said that 'India was prepared to face offensive military action at its borders should the need arise'.[38]

On 3 September 2015, Prime Minister Nawaz Sharif of Pakistan said that 'the hearts of Pakistanis beat in unison with Kashmiris and warned that the incidents of firing across the Line of Control (LoC) were a threat to international peace'.[39] The following day, Prime Minister Chaudhry Abdul Majeed of Pakistan-controlled Kashmir 'called upon the international community to take notice of growing incidents of unprovoked firing by Indian troops in areas along the Line of Control (LoC) and the Working Boundary. Otherwise, he cautioned, the situation could lead to confrontation'.[40] As CFVs continued, on 5 September, Islamabad urged the United Nations Security Council to take notice of provocative Indian actions along the Line of Control and the Working Boundary.[41]

On 7 September, Pakistan's army chief Gen. Raheel Sharif, responding to the Indian Army chief's statement, said that his forces were fully ready to defend against external aggression and that '[the] armed forces of Pakistan are fully capable of dealing with all types of internal and external threats, may it be conventional or sub-conventional; whether it is cold start or hot start. We are ready!'[42]

[38] National Bureau, 'India Prepared for Military Action, Says Army Chief', *Hindu*, 1 September 2015, http://www.thehindu.com/news/national/india-needs-to-be-prepared-for-military-action-says-army-chief-dalbir-singh/article7603623.ece, last accessed on 8 January 2017.

[39] *Dawn*, 'LoC Firing Threat to International Peace, Says PM', *Dawn*, 3 September 2015, available at https://www.dawn.com/news/1204629, last accessed on 8 January 2017.

[40] *Dawn*, 'World Community Urged to Take Notice of Indian Firing at LoC', *Dawn*, 4 September 2015, available at https://www.dawn.com/news/1204837, last accessed on 8 January 2017.

[41] *Dawn*, 'Pakistan Takes Issue of Ceasefire Violations to UN Security Council', *Dawn*, 5 September 2015, available at https://www.dawn.com/news/1205099, last accessed on 8 January 2017.

[42] Fayyaz Hussain, '"Cold or Hot Start", Pakistan Army Is Ready for Anything: General Raheel Sharif, *Daily Pakistan*, 6 September 2016, available

Both sides reported more violations through the month of September. On 17 September, the Pakistan Foreign Office summoned an Indian diplomat to lodge a protest over the death of a Pakistani soldier in a skirmish on the LoC in Kashmir, an act that was repeated two days later, this time due to the death of two civilians. Frequent violations continued in October and November. Two Indian soldiers were killed in the firing in early November.[43] Situation remained tense till late December, till Indian prime minister Narendra Modi paid a surprise visit to Lahore to meet his Pakistani counterpart Nawaz Sharif.

This case highlights how CFVs have in the past led to military, political, and diplomatic crises. We also saw how even meetings by the two political leaderships sometimes fail to de-escalate the escalation on the frontlines.

Case 6.7: 28 April 2017 to 6 May 2017

On 28 April, Indian and Pakistani media reported an unprecedented meeting between Pakistan prime minister Nawaz Sharif and an Indian business tycoon reportedly close to the Indian prime minister Narendra Modi, Sajjan Jindal. The meeting was held at a time when relations between the two countries were severely strained due to a series of CFVs. One would have thought that the meeting would bring about a much-needed thaw. However, two days later, on 30 April, Pakistan's COAS Gen. Qamar Javed Bajwa visited the Haji Pir sector on the LoC and stated Pakistan's support for the Kashmiris...rightful political struggle for right to self-determination'.[44] An ISPR statement quoted Bajwa that 'India had unleashed its aggression and frustration on the people of India–held Kashmir as well as Pakistani villages along the LoC and Working Boundary'.[45]

---

at https://en.dailypakistan.com.pk/headline/we-are-mindful-of-our-enemies-nefarious-designs-army-chief-gen-raheel-sharif/, last accessed on 10 January 2017.

[43] *BBC*, 'Kashmir: Indian Soldiers Killed in "Pakistan Firing"', *BBC*, 3 November 2015, available at http://www.bbc.com/news/world-asia-india-34707217, last accessed on 19 December 2016.

[44] Tariq Naqash, 'COAS Visits LoC: "Violence in IHK by Indian Forces Is State-Sponsored Terrorism"', *Dawn*, 30 April 2017, available at https://www.dawn.com/news/1330214, last accessed on 25 December 2017.

[45] Naqash, 'COAS Visits LoC'.

Whether the visit of Bajwa to forward locations on the LoC was to offset the Jindal–Sharif meeting is a matter of speculation. But CFVs resumed the following day in the Krishna Ghati–Poonch sector. On 1 May, the Indian Army put out a statement accusing the Pakistan Army of carrying out 'unprovoked rocket and mortar firing on two forward posts on the Line of Control in Krishna Ghati Sector (in Poonch district)'.... 'Simultaneously, a BAT (Border Action Team) action was launched on a patrol operating in between the two posts'.... 'In an unsoldierly act by the Pakistani Army, the bodies of two of our soldiers in the patrol were mutilated'.... 'Such a despicable act of the Pakistan Army will be appropriately responded to'.[46] The Indian DGMO stated that 'such a dastardly and inhuman act is beyond any norms of civility and merits unequivocal condemnation and response'.[47]

Tensions began to build up with calls for retaliation and cross-border action. Media played up the incident and asked for retaliation, some even suggesting how the retaliation can be carried out.[48]

In response to a frenzied campaign for retaliation, the vice-chief of the Indian Army staff, Sarath Chand, in early May, promised action but said, 'I do not want to say what we will do. Instead of speaking, we will focus on our action at a time and place of our choosing. They will have to take responsibility and face consequences for it.'[49]

[46] *Deccan Herald*, 'Pak Army "Laid Death Trap" 250 mts Inside J&K, Beheaded 2 Indian Jawans', *Deccan Chronicle*, 2 May 2017, https://www. deccanchronicle.com/nation/current-affairs/010517/pak-forces-sneaked-into-jk-beheaded-2-indian-soldiers-senior-army-officer.html, last accessed on 25 December 2017.

[47] *Times of India*, 'We will Respond to Pakistan at a Time and Place of our Choosing: Army', *Times of India*, 2 May 2017, available at https:// timesofindia.indiatimes.com/india/we-will-respond-to-pakistan-at-time-and-place-of-our-choosing-army/articleshow/58481334.cms, last accessed on 25 December 2017.

[48] *News18*, 'Five Ways India Can Avenge Mutilation of Its Soldiers by Pakistan', *News18*, 2 May 2017, available at https://www.news18.com/news/india/five-ways-india-can-avenge-pakistan-mutilation-of-soldiers-1388951. html, last accessed on 25 December 2017.

[49] *Economic Times*, 'Will Respond to Pakistan at Time and Place of Our Choosing: Indian Army', 12 July 2018, *Economic Times*, //economictimes. indiatimes.com/articleshow/58481470.cms?utm_source=contentof

At the political level, the Indian defence minister Arun Jaitley also promised retaliation: 'Such acts do not take place even during war. It is an extreme form of barbarism. The whole country has full faith in our armed forces, which will react appropriately. The sacrifice of these soldiers will not go in vain.'[50] Home Minister Rajnath Singh chaired a meeting of senior security and intelligence officials to assess the situation. BJP parliamentarian R.K. Singh, also a former union home secretary, stated: 'Pakistan understands only one language and, therefore, we need to kill more Pakistani soldiers and give them the same treatment.'[51] Former army chief Gen. Bikram Singh stated: 'We did surgical strikes and then we did not push it through. We will have to bleed Pakistan ... even economically.'[52]

In response to the Indian statements, Pakistan's DGMO Maj Gen. Sahir Shamshad Mirza in a hotline conversation with his Indian counterpart Lt Gen. A.K. Bhatt 'warned India against "misadventure"'.[53] Pakistan complained that the Indian forces were targeting civilians and said that 'continuity of such action would invite appropriate response.'[54]

On the diplomatic front, Foreign Secretary S. Jaishankar summoned the Pakistan high commissioner Abdul Basit and conveyed 'India's outrage at the killing and the barbaric act of mutilation of the bodies of the two Indian soldiers.'[55] The MEA termed the incident as a 'strong act

---

interest&utm_medium=text&utm_campaign=cppst, last accessed on 3 October 2018.

[50] Yusuf Jameel and Sanjib K.R. Baruah, 'Pakistani Forces Kill, Mutilate 2 Soldiers; India Retaliates', *Asian Age*, 2 May 2017, available at http://www.asianage.com/india/all-india/020517/pak-forces-kill-mutilate-2-soldiers-india-retaliates.html, last accessed on 25 December 2017.

[51] Jameel and Baruah, 'Pakistani Forces Kill, Mutilate 2 Soldiers'.

[52] *News18*, 'Five Ways India Can Avenge Mutilation of Its Soldiers by Pakistan', *News18*, available at https://www.news18.com/news/india/five-ways-india-can-avenge-pakistan-mutilation-of-soldiers-1388951.html, last accessed on 25 December 2017.

[53] Baqir Sajjad Syed, 'New Delhi Warned against "Misadventure"', *Dawn*, 3 May 2017, available at https://www.dawn.com/news/1330767, last accessed on 25 December 2017.

[54] Syed, 'New Delhi Warned against "Misadventure"'.

[55] *Scroll*, 'Blood Trails Show Those Who Mutilated Soldiers' Bodies Were from Pakistan, India Tells Abdul Basit', *Scroll*, 3 May 2017; https://scroll.

of provocation' and claimed that evidences on the ground confirm the attackers came from Pakistan. Pakistan's Foreign Office responded by saying that the 'Pakistan Army did not commit any ceasefire violation on LoC as alleged by India. Indian blame of mutilating Indian soldiers is also false.'[56]

In the meantime, CFVs continued to rise on the LoC. On 3 May, 'amid the raucous call for retaliation',[57] the Indian Army chief said that 'we do not talk about future plans beforehand; we share details after execution'.[58] These statements led to speculation of potential 'surgical strikes' that were carried out the previous year under orders of the same army chief.

On 8 May, right in the middle of the stand-off, the Pakistan International Airlines (PIA) suspended the Karachi-Mumbai route. Though PIA had claimed that it was due to commercial reasons, the timing of the announcement led to speculation about the reason. Pakistan also decided not to participate in the South Asian Satellite launched by India. CFVs continued throughout the month of May and eventually petered out. During April–May 2017, India reported (no data available for Pakistan for this period) 107 CFVs.[59]

---

in/latest/836443/mea-summons-pakistan-envoy-over-mutilation-of-indian-soldiers-along-the-loc, last accessed on 3 October 2018.

[56] Ravi Krishnan Khajuria, 'Pakistan's latest Barbaric Act: Bodies of Two Indian Soldiers Mutilated, Army Vows appropriate Response,' *Hindustan Times*, 28 May 2017, available at https://www.hindustantimes.com/india-news/pakistan-mutilates-bodies-of-two-indian-soldiers-army-vows-revenge/story-MuI5fTZdmRyavJNnAqwlPI.html, last accessed on 25 December 2017.

[57] Anindita Sanyal, '"We Share Details after Execution": Army Chief Rawat on Call for Action', NDTV, 4 May 2017, available at https://www.ndtv.com/india-news/we-share-details-after-execution-army-chief-rawat-on-call-for-action-1689479, last accessed on 25 December 2017.

[58] *DNA*, 'Soldiers Mutilation: Indian Army Retaliating to Pakistani Aggression, Says Army Chief Bipin Rawat', *DNA*, 4 May 2017, available at http://www.dnaindia.com/india/report-soldiers-mutilation-we-don-t-talk-about-future-plans-beforehand-says-army-chief-on-possible-action-2427200, last accessed on 25 December 2017.

[59] Press Information Bureau, 'Casualties in Firing by Pakistan Army', Ministry of Defence, Government of India, 25 July 2017, available at http://pib.nic.in/newsite/PrintRelease.aspx?relid=168967, last accessed on 28 August 2017.

During the entire phase of this stand-off, there were no terrorist attacks nor were any terrorists intercepted along the LoC trying to sneak in. But CFVs and related killings escalated tensions through the month. Thanks to the media coverage of the incidents, passionate and angry calls for retaliation were made, leading to a military and diplomatic crisis between the two sides.

Case 6.8: June 2017 to July 2017

CFVs in May 2017 spilt over into June and then to July after a short interval. While there is a certain continuity between this case and the previous one, it might be useful to view this as a different case for analytical purposes. CFVs at several locations on the LoC were reported in the first week of June: Nowshera, Krishna Ghati, Bhimber (Rajouri), and Poonch sectors on the Indian side, and Battal, Jandrot, Hotspring, Nezapir, and Tatta Pani sectors on the Pakistani side. The Pakistani DGMO and his Indian counterpart made an unscheduled hotline contact to discuss the ongoing CFVs that resulted in the deaths of several civilians on the Pakistani side.[60]

After the hotline conversation, an ISPR statement said that 'any Indian misadventure from across/along LoC in any form shall be responded with full force at the time and place of our choosing with onus of responsibility on Indian aggressive behaviour'.[61] It further fuelled the crisis by releasing 'video clips showing destruction of Indian posts due to retaliatory fire by Pakistani forces'. Indian side, on its part, put out a statement saying that the Indian DGMO had warned his counterpart that 'if Pak Army continues to abet infiltrations and cause trans-LoC firings, the Indian Army will take appropriate retaliatory actions'.[62]

These statements by the senior military leadership could be read as communicating redlines/threats during periods of tensions. Tensions began to rise once again.

Infiltration and CFVs continued unabated. Several infiltrators were killed by the Indian forces along the LoC. Between 10 and 14 June, CFVs

---

[60] Baqir Sajjad Syed, 'Threats of Retaliation Traded with India', *Dawn*, 6 June 2017, available at https://www.dawn.com/news/1337734, last accessed on 25 December 2017.

[61] Syed, 'Threats of Retaliation Traded with India'.

[62] Syed, 'Threats of Retaliation Traded with India'.

were reported from the same sectors with rising casualties, injuries, and damage to civilian habitats. CFVs were not even stopped by the brief meeting of the Indian and Pakistani prime ministers in Astana, Kazakhstan. On 9 June, even as the two leaders met in Astana, Pakistan's Foreign Office spokesperson Nafees Zakaria said, 'We have cautioned India from making any strategic miscalculation. It appears that India is seeking conflict with Pakistan.'[63] The Pakistani warning to India about 'strategic miscalculation' came in the middle of escalating tension along LoC.

In the meantime, COAS Gen. Qamar Javed Bajwa made a visit to forward positions along the LoC in Muzaffarabad and discussed with officers posted there the 'operational situation, Indian cease fire violations and response by Pakistani troops' and stated that 'no Indian misadventure shall go without a befitting response.'[64] Earlier, the Indian Army chief had stated that the 'Indian Army is fully ready for a two-and-a-half-front war.'[65] It was almost as if the two sides were mirroring each other's statements.

CFVs continued through the month of June, slowing down in the second half of the month and then picked up again in early July. CFVs were reported from Rajouri, Poonch, and Uri on the Indian side and Nakyal and Bhimber sectors on the Pakistani side. The Pakistani press reported that civilians were being targeted by the Indian Army. Pakistani DGMO called his counterpart to lodge a protest about it to which the Indian DGMO reportedly said, 'If Pakistan Army continues to abet infiltrations and cause trans-LoC firings, the Indian Army will take appropriate retaliatory actions.'[66]

Express Tribune, 'FO's Weekly Briefing: India's Belligerence Threat to Regional Peace', *Express Tribune*, 8 June 2017, available at https://tribune.com.pk/story/1430469/pakistan-warns-india-strategic-miscalculation/, last accessed on 26 December 2017.

Sajjad Hussain, 'Pak Forces Capable of Defeating All Threats Irrespective of', Outlook India, 10 June 2017, https://www.outlookindia.com/newsscroll/pak-forces-capable-of-defeating-all-threats-irrespective-of/1072415, last accessed on 3 October 2018.

Dawn, 'Army Reiterates Support for Right to Self Determination for Kashmiris across LOC', *Dawn*, 10 June 2017, available at https://www.dawn.com/news/1338673, last accessed on 26 December 2017.

Dinakar Peri and Mubashir Zaidi, 'India, Pakistan DGMOs Discuss Situation along LoC', *Hindu*, 5 June 2017, available at http://www.thehindu.

Despite the DGMO contact, CFVs and casualties contained to rise. On 9 July, the director general for South Asia in Pakistan's Foreign Office, Mohammad Faisal, summoned Indian deputy high commissioner in Islamabad J.P. Singh and 'condemned fresh unprovoked ceasefire violations by the Indian forces in Chirikot and Satwal sectors on July 8, resulting in the killing of three women and injuries to another.'[67]

In the middle of the month, tensions resumed again when Pakistan accused India of initiating CFVs resulting 'in the death of four Pakistani soldiers and a civilian in the Athmuqam Sector.'[68] The following day, Pakistan threatened India 'that it could consider choking India's supply lines near the Line of Control (LoC) if the latter did not "rein in" its troops committing ceasefire violations.'[69] Civilian and military casualties were reported on the Indian side as well. Cross-LoC trade was suspended as India accused Pakistani trucks of carrying drugs into India. On 24 July, 'Indian Deputy High Commissioner (DHC) J.P. Singh was summoned by the Foreign Office (FO) once again on Monday over "unprovoked" ceasefire violations by Indian forces along the Line of Control (LoC) on July 21, which had resulted in the death of a 12-year-old boy and injuries to three others.'[70]

Politicians chipped in as well. Indian union minister M. Venkaiah Naidu said Pakistan 'should understand that aiding and abetting terror will not help them. They had an experience in 1971, they should

---

com/news/national/india-pakistan-dgmos-discuss-situation-along-loc/article18722580.ece, last accessed on 26 December 2017.

[67] Syed Irfan Raza, 'Indian Official Summoned again over LoC Violation', *Dawn*, 10 July 2017, available at https://www.dawn.com/news/1344293, last accessed on 26 December 2017.

[68] Dinakar Peri, 'Will Retaliate on LoC, says India', *Hindu*, 17 July 2017, available at http://www.thehindu.com/news/national/dgmo-speak-pakistan-accuses-india-of-targeting-its-troops/article19295370.ece, last accessed on 27 December 2017.'

[69] Baqir Sajjad Syed and Tariq Naqash, 'Pakistan Threatens to Choke Indian Supply Lines near LoC', *Dawn*, 18 July 2017, available at https://www.dawn.com/news/1346009, last accessed on 27 December 2017.

[70] *Dawn*, 'Indian Deputy High Commissioner Summoned for Third Time This Month over Ceasefire Violations', *Dawn*, 24 July 2017, available at https://www.dawn.com/news/1347368, last accessed on 27 December 2017.

remember that experience and focus on creating peace and prosperity for their people.[71] Damage to civilian habitats was particularly intense with locals having to be relocated from the LoC/IB. The bus service between Poonch in India and Rawalakot in Pakistan was also suspended due to tensions.[72]

CFVs continued through the month of July and then reduced.

This is yet another instance of rising tensions and crisis escalation between India and Pakistan as a direct result of CFVs in the absence of a terror angle.

**

Using painstakingly put together empirical data on escalation and CFVs from 2002 to 2016, this chapter examined the linkage between CFVs and escalation based on which it can be concluded that there exists a strong relationship between CFVs on the India–Pakistan border in J&K and crisis escalation between the two countries. The eight examples presented in this chapter examined three types of cases: one, where CFVs lead to crisis escalation; two, where CFVs contribute to worsening an ongoing crisis and thereby spiking the escalatory ladder, and three; where conventional military escalation gets played out in the front lines in the form of CFVs, either because it is nearly impossible to go to war and so focus gets shifted to the border, or because firing on the border, however severe, is not viewed as risky.

Using these different types of examples on CFVs and escalation, we can affirm that escalation is not always a pre-determined, rational, intended, and calibrated decision or action; and, that terror strikes are not the only cause behind escalation to higher levels of the ladder. In fact, there are several more instances when CFVs have led to escalation than

---

[71] Special Correspondent, 'Remember 1971, Venkaiah Tells Pakistan', *Hindu*, 23 July 2017, available at http://www.thehindu.com/news/national/remember-1971-venkaiah-tells-pakistan/article19337957.ece, last accessed on 27 December 2017.

[72] *Firstpost*, 'Ceasefire Violation along LoC: India-Pakistan Bus Services Halted from Poonch as Tension Escalates', *Firstpost*, 10 July 2017, available at https://www.firstpost.com/india/ceasefire-violation-along-loc-india-pakistan-bus-services-halted-from-poonch-as-tension-escalates-3796803.html,   last accessed on 27 December 2017.

have terror strikes. Moreover, not all terror attacks have led to escalation either.

In doing so, this chapter has attempted to correct a major theme in the literature on South Asian escalation dynamics: that CFVs are hardly a cause of crisis escalation. If so, then it would not be appropriate to view CFVs as inconsequential to escalation or as the result of a crisis elsewhere: CFVs, on their own, form a major causative factor in the India–Pakistan escalatory dynamics.

7   Implications for Theory and Practice

THE PRINCIPAL PURPOSE OF THIS BOOK has been to explain the causes of CFVs on the India–Pakistan border in J&K. Besides explaining the causes of CFVs within the larger historical context of India–Pakistan border negotiations, the book has nuanced and problematized the existing notions about the escalatory dynamics between the two South Asian nuclear rivals. Further, this book has established a significant relationship, often causative, between CFVs in J&K and India–Pakistan escalation dynamics.

The previous chapters, especially Chapters five and six, have established a clear linkage between CFVs and India–Pakistan escalation dynamics. They have also shown how AMFs routinely trigger CFVs leading to bilateral escalation. This chapter reflects on the theoretical and practical implications of the arguments made in this book.

The central argument that this book makes about the relationship between CFVs and escalation dynamics between the two South Asian nuclear powers not only departs from the existing policy and scholarly narratives about the causes and dynamics of India–Pakistan crisis escalation, but more pertinently, poses several theoretical challenges to the traditional understanding of escalation dynamics. Moreover, the ability of AMFs to trigger local-level escalation leading to a snowball escalatory impact at higher levels further complicates the 'clean picture' of escalation that exists in the contemporary theoretical imagination about the India–Pakistan escalation dynamics.

Traditional theorization on South Asian escalation (borrowed from the dominant Cold War literature on escalation) heavily invests in linking the role of terror strikes against India by Pak-based terror groups and the Indian conventional retaliation against Pakistan. It also emphasizes the role of central decision-makers in making escalatory decisions. There is also a strand of this literature that focuses on inadvertent escalation but even that begins at the level of terror attacks or conventional operations. In short, the traditional escalatory imagination focuses on spectacular events, and centralized decisions on whether or not to escalate, how much to escalate, and when to climb down from the escalatory ladder and negotiate peace with the adversary.

Let us break down the assumptions of such a 'too-neat-to-be-true' theoretical model: events that have the potential to cause escalation are clearly identifiable; near perfect civil-military communication on the various rungs of the escalation dynamics; straightforward decision-making about what kind of weapon systems to be introduced at what point and how much fire power to be used in general; and finally, the ability of the central decision-makers to calibrate escalation based on a rational calculation of the costs and benefits of escalating, backing down, or negotiating.

Such a theorization clearly does not expect the possibility of: (*i*) AMFs triggering severe CFVs; (*ii*) CFVs triggering escalation; and, (*iii*) to some extent, accidental/inadvertent escalation. The absence of such expectations would further cement the already strong belief that escalation is controllable, especially due to the existence of a general context of nuclear deterrence-induced stability. As discussed in Chapter two, escalation is usually understood in the context of war, and anything short of war is usually not taken seriously enough. 'We have been there before and so we know how to handle that' would be the refrain when faced with lower-level crisis escalation.

The rather relaxed definition of escalation adopted in this book—'escalation as a sudden intensification of political, military, and diplomatic tensions between countries in a general atmosphere of adversarial relations that may or may not lead to a war'—however, would help us view escalation occurring in a not so tightly controlled atmosphere, but as a result of local military factors, that is, AMFs.

Theoretical Implications

This book, which focuses on the ability of AMFs to trigger crisis escalation, often without the clearance of the central leadership of either side breaks new ground in several ways. AMFs as a non-traditional explanation for India–Pakistan escalation dynamics makes this book uniquely different from the existing empirical literature and theoretical explanations for crisis escalation between India and Pakistan. Moreover, while the traditional explanation gives us a rather uncluttered model to understand crisis escalation, the explanation in this book makes the traditional explanation far more positively complicated.

The argument here is not that the traditional explanations for escalation in South Asia are redundant or untenable but that this book adds an entirely new dimension to our understanding of South Asian escalation dynamics. In that sense, the arguments made in this book add to the already existing literature on India–Pakistan crisis escalation.

Let us now examine some of the conceptual and theoretical implications of the arguments that have been made in this book.

A Complex Picture of Indo-Pak Escalation Dynamics

A key contribution of this book is to highlight the complex picture of the India–Pakistan escalation dynamics. Traditional explanations about Indo-Pak escalation dynamics would have us believe that there is a neat and uncluttered escalation ladder (as discussed in Chapter 2), but the findings of this book clearly indicate that the picture is far more complex than that. The reason why the existing explanation conveys a partial picture of escalation is because it does not include CFVs as a cause for escalation, let alone account for AMFs causing CFVs and thereby escalation. A complex picture of escalation, which this book offers, is useful in thinking about policies that can control escalation. More so, it helps complete the imperfect picture of the India–Pakistan escalation dynamics.

Risk-Taking under Nuclear Conditions

India and Pakistan are often engaged in a game of brinkmanship and risk-taking under nuclear conditions. Given that Pakistan has claimed that it would lower the nuclear threshold to offset Indian conventional aggression underlines the fact that there is a nuclear dimension to the India–Pakistan military stand-off. The traditional understanding paints an escalation ladder that begins with a terror attack and escalates to the nuclear level. This book shows that the point of initiation is inadequately conceived: the first rung of the ladder could also be major CFVs on the LoC or the IB/WB in J&K; just as terror attacks could set off the escalation dynamics, so could serious CFVs. In that sense, the book has merely added one more rung to the existing understanding of escalation dynamics. However, in doing so, the book has enhanced the scope of ongoing debates on risk-taking under nuclear conditions in South Asia.

While it is debatable what kind of a conventional punitive action India would undertake against Pakistan in the wake of a terror attack, if any at all, and how Pakistan would respond to that, if at all it decides to, what is evident is that CFVs can, by their own accord or in combination with terror attacks and mounting media pressure during times of domestic political considerations such as elections, escalate bilateral tension and aggravate the escalation dynamics.

It is understandable why the impact of CFVs are viewed differently from that of terror attacks. Given the politically charged rhetoric on terrorism in India in the aftermath of December 2001 and Mumbai 2008, the response time for any Indian government would be short after another major terrorist attack. However, the fear of quick escalation and the attention it receives is quite disproportionate. On the other hand, CFVs have a different dimension. The very fact that there is a lot of secrecy, ignorance, and under-reported cases of CFVs among the general public in some ways can diminish the pressure over the political leadership to act quickly.[1] However, the new media attention on CFVs and the politics surrounding it could potentially change the way politicians view CFVs in future.

The argument here is not that CFVs would lead to nuclear exchanges—to argue that would be highly overstating the point. But then, even terror attacks need not each and every time, and they have not in the past, led to conventional exchanges either, let alone to nuclear exchanges. The point basically is that it adds another rung to the existing escalation ladder that exists under nuclear conditions.

From a theoretical point of view then, what is noteworthy is that the two sides have internalized the robustness of a stable environment of deterrence between themselves and have intuitively used that to engage in risk-taking behaviour under nuclear conditions: there is a firm belief, especially on the Indian side, that there is a lot of space available for quick operations aimed at limited war aims under the nuclear threshold. Nuclear risk-taking is neither new nor pertaining specifically to CFVs.

---

[1] I thank Sadia Tasleem for highlighting this point.

Bilateral military, political, and diplomatic stand-offs have taken place under nuclear conditions in the past, which have not led to an outbreak of war. The years 2001–2 and the resultant stand-off and the Mumbai terror attack and after are examples of that.

However, what needs to be noted here is that such risky behaviour was also taking place in the backdrop of CFVs, which were not even recognized as risky. A 'revisionist' reading of India–Pakistan risk-taking under nuclear conditions, wherein the CFV rung is introduced at the bottom of the ladder, should then lead us to several interesting conclusions about the South Asian escalatory dynamics, not least of which is the possibility of inadvertent escalation that could begin due to deeply entrenched military cultural factors.

Surgical Strikes and Escalation Dynamics

As discussed in Chapter two, the Indian Army carried out a 'surgical strike' across the LoC on the Pakistani side in September 2016. Surgical strikes may be understood as pre-planned high-intensity cross-LoC operations to extract tactical advantages by one side. What made the 2016 surgical strikes stand out is that it was a declared one and has clear strategic rationale behind it. Be that as it may, we need to focus on two issues for conceptual clarity and theoretical understanding. First of all, it could be argued that the surgical strikes have altered the India–Pakistan strategic calculus: surgical strikes put the 'initiative to escalate' dilemma on Pakistan with Islamabad having to choose between risking escalation by retaliating or accepting the status quo by not doing so.

The second related question is how Pakistan would respond should there be a future strike. Would Pakistan continue to respect the new status quo or would it respond risking potential escalation? Would India be able to ensure that the strike is carefully calibrated so as not to cross Pakistan's redlines?

While it could then be argued that the strikes may have altered the strategic balance in India's favour, to what extent has it addressed India's original concern—that is, Pakistan's support for sub-conventional actors? Evidence shows that infiltration has only increased, which means that despite the 'success' of the surgical strikes, New Delhi has failed to dissuade Pakistan from giving support to sub-conventional elements.

Abdication of Political Responsibility

This book has demonstrated that escalatory danger emanating from CFVs triggered by AMFs cannot be ruled out. Indeed, there have been several cases where such escalation has happened. Have the political class in New Delhi and the politico-military class in Pakistan recognized the danger? Or have they let the local factors play out? Has there, more pertinently, been an alarming abdication of responsibility by the politico-military classes in India and Pakistan with regard to the dynamics on the LoC and IB?

One of the challenges of a more conceptual nature that I have tried to bring out in this book is the abdication of political responsibility at several levels by the leadership in both the countries in the management of their borders. Politicians and civilian bureaucrats seem to be content with letting things continue the way they do. Managing India's complicated and contentious borders, particularly in J&K, requires a lot of expertise, patient negotiations, and strategic overview, which seem to be missing at the political and bureaucratic levels. Moreover, it also requires a lot of patience and willingness to deal with a rather 'messy' set of issues. This again does not seem to interest the rather short attention span of the political class and bureaucrats. The result of the absence of political will is obvious: political leadership is content to give 'complete autonomy' to the forces to manage the borders with the easy excuse that they would not like to 'politicize' national security issues.

With regard to the question of political responsibility, several more issues could be flagged. On the one hand, there is a seeming lack of political interest in what happens on the borders despite their apparent implications. There is a certain belief within the political class (including within the bureaucracy) that 'these things happen on the border and let them continue'. This traditionally used to be the reaction of the political class about CFVs as well.

On the other hand, however, there is an emergent situation wherein the political class utilizes what happens on the LoC/IB for its partisan political benefit. First of all, there is today a clearly visible linkage between recurrent violence on the LoC/IB and domestic politics in India (not so much in Pakistan as is the case in India). Thanks to the vibrant and sensationalist media, violations on the border and related casualties have become a major point of discussion in India's domestic politics. This narrative has been further strengthened by the September 2016 'surgical strikes' by the Indian Army across the LoC, sanctioned by the government in New Delhi. With the LoC stand-off being played out in elections in India, the potential of CFVs escalating—as either side would not want to be seen as being hit hard by the other side—and more fire assaults being sanctioned by the government will only rise.

In that sense, then, governments have strong political incentives for creating a permissive political environment for perceived political gains. This is without precedent as violations in the past—say in the 1990s or the 2000s—had very little domestic impact nor were they calibrated for domestic political gains.

Political classes also often 'let things play out' in order to offset domestic criticism against the apparent inaction from their side against the adversary's firing. This becomes even more important as the media claims, unquestionably accepting the official narrative, that their own side only fires in retaliation and is never the initiator. Political leaders often claim that they 'have given complete autonomy' to the armed forces to carry out operations on the LoC. The popular narrative on CFVs swings between 'innocent victim' and 'extracting revenge'.

One direct implication of 'such autonomy' or even the abdication of responsibility by the political class is that the armed forces have started asserting themselves and 'going public' with their views on how to manage the LoC or how to respond to the adversary even to the extent of educating the political class. For the Indian armed forces, this is an unprecedented opportunity to bask under some much-awaited glory. While there is not yet any evidence to suggest that this has any implications for civil-military relations in the county, there is no taking away from the fact that 'giving armed forces autonomy' and the armed forces 'asserting themselves' and 'going public' with their version are certainly unhealthy in a democracy.

Finally, there is yet another important reason why there is a willingness by the political class to 'abdicate their responsibility' when it comes to dealing with the LoC/IB—there is an acute lack of knowledge among the bureaucrats and political classes on what happens on the border, especially the details regarding the various reasons for the outbreak of CFVs. The public also seems to favour the 'professional military' to the 'uninformed politician' to manage the borders.

But for our purposes, we must be concerned about what it means for escalation. In a politically charged environment where the politico-bureaucratic establishment abdicates its responsibility or shoots from the shoulders of the armed forces for political gains, and the armed forces using this new-found autonomy to their advantage, one could argue that the ability of local factors to quickly climb the escalatory ladder increases manifold.

An argument could be made that perhaps 'CFVs have a stabilizing effect in the overall Indo-Pak crises dynamics, allowing both governments to escape audience cost by involving in cheap and less risky military action to assuage domestic pressures for kinetic action. If both parties merely exchange munitions across the LoC without actually changing their ground position—does that pose an escalatory threat as volume of munitions can be matched, nullifying the need to undertake risky and costly escalation?'[2]

The related argument is that one should not make too much out of these things (CFVs) and let them boil at a 'sub-critical' level as a steam-venting mechanism, and that these things play out at the local level and do not have any implications for the larger stability. But such an argument is deeply problematic.

For one, evidence shows that CFVs are not always contained at the local level anymore—they often spiral up; second, false optimism about stability in nuclear environments can be dangerous (the argument, as stressed earlier, is *not* that CFVs would lead to nuclear confrontation but that CFVs do often trigger an escalatory dynamics the end result of which is at best unclear); third, and most importantly, allowing the 'steam-venting mechanism' to continue at the local level instead of engaging in conflict resolution makes a future military rapprochement all the more difficult, especially at the local levels, for, after all, militaries operate on the basis of honour and memory: the more we let things boil, the more intractable conflicts get, making it so much more difficult to resolve them. Recall how units that faced each other during the Kargil conflict continue to fire at each other when they get posted in counterpart locations on the LoC.

Fourth, the argument that 'volume of munitions can be matched nullifying the need to undertake risky and costly escalation' is a sound one and has worked in the past, when there was not too much focus on the action happening on the borders. However, there is an increasing

---

[2] Email correspondence with Deep Jyoti Barman, 14 April 2018.

politicization of violence on the border today and that might complicate the utility of cheap strategies at maintaining an ugly stability.

Finally, when it comes to inadvertent escalation, pre-meditated and deliberate military action has a lower chance of escalating to undesired levels, even though such escalation cannot be ruled out, than unsanctioned lower level tactical action. In other words, what is more difficult to handle and constrain are the spillover effects of CFVs triggered by factors relating to military subculture than deliberate military action causing CFVs. Decision-makers expect a push back when they deliberately choose to use force and are hence prepared to deal with it and calibrate it.

This point about 'deliberate military operations' can be further nuanced. When stand-down orders are issued to the two militaries from the two political bosses, would they abide by them? Indian forces are likely to, but what about the Pakistan Army? Given the enormous autonomy that it enjoys in the Pakistani scheme of things, would it stand down? We cannot be sure. More so, recall earlier discussions about how the forces would continue to fire at will till they get a 'kill' on the other side for a casualty they suffered, and how commanders would permit that. While this is a general point whose applicability is constant, the argument is that the more the two countries wait and let things boil, the more difficult it would get the two militaries to give up their local stakes and associated interests, with lesser incentive for the Pakistan Army to do so.

Tactical Gain, Strategic Loss

Another issue identified in the preceding chapters of this book is the Indian and Pakistani preoccupations with extremely tactical considerations on the front lines of the border and how such exceptionally minor, often frivolous, considerations, but pursued with vigour and determination, can have larger strategic implications. What the preceding discussion about the role of local military factors on the border in bilateral escalation highlights is that tactical considerations, often negligible such as objecting to the improvement being made to an existing bunker and so on and the consequent challenging fire leading to CFVs, have routinely and frequently escalated to full-blown military, political, and diplomatic crises between the two sides.

Deterrence theorists have long argued that one of the essential prerequisites of stable deterrence is the willingness to accept a certain amount of mutual vulnerability. In other words, the search for absolute guarantees of security can drive states towards an unhealthy arms race, leading to heightened levels of security-dilemma-induced insecurity. If so, the idea is to let a little mutually accepted vulnerability exist in a dyadic conflictual relationship so as to maintain healthy stability. Let us examine this insight in the India–Pakistan context.

The Indian and Pakistani militaries often fight on for weeks on end to gain a minor advantage on the ground vis-à-vis the adversary. What is troubling in such situations is that neither side is willing to accept even the slightest tactical vulnerability, even though what is at stake is tiny (geographically speaking) or the issue in question is 'dominance' and 'honour' rather than serious substantive national interest that might demand some acceptance of mutual vulnerability at the tactical level, just as deterrence demands vulnerability at the strategic level.[3] In a sense, then, the inability of the two sides to resolve minor issues at the tactical level is also reflective of the state of deterrence stability at higher levels. It is true that the considerations that go into decision-making at the strategic level are very different from those at the tactical level. And yet the desire for invulnerability is seen both at the strategic and tactical levels.

Regime Type and Escalation Dynamics

Is there a relationship between regime type and AMFs (and CFVs, by extension)? There are two types of regimes in question here: the civilian government in New Delhi willfully giving autonomy to the military or the former not being fully in the know of what the latter does due to technical reasons; and the political class in Islamabad being hardly in control of what the Pakistan military does. Let us unpack these two types to examine their respective implications.

In the case of India, it is clear from the discussion in Chapter 5 that the existence and functioning of AMFs are not always known to the political-bureaucratic establishment in New Delhi, or they are not always under the control of the political establishment. Under such circumstances, it is possible for the AMFs to act unconstrained, leading to escalation. New Delhi could be caught unawares and would be dictated by a fait accompli. This does not sit well with stability.

At the same time, given the nature of civil-military dynamics in India, New Delhi would be in a position to clamp down on the military brass

---

[3] I am grateful to John H. (Jack) Gill for flagging this insight with me.

to climb down and fall in line with the larger political objectives without much resistance from the latter. In other words, the democratic set-up in New Delhi allows for inadvertent escalation and the possibility of AMFs leading to higher levels of escalation with the political leadership being dictated by a certain fait accompli. And yet, as and when the political class in New Delhi desires to assert control, it would be in a position to do so. Military subcultures in this case would become subservient to the larger political commands in the larger scheme of things. Military subcultures in this case have no relevance outside its immediate spatio-temporal environs.

The situation is more complex in Pakistan where there are three levels of control, that is, the political establishment in Islamabad, the army high command in Rawalpindi, and the lower echelons of the army in operational environments on the border. The ability of the AMFs to assert themselves is relatively less in Pakistan, given that the army top brass is not ignorant of what happens on the ground and therefore has greater control over AMFs. This, however, does not rule out the existence of AMFs or their ability to cause CFVs and escalation, as we saw in Chapter five. In other words, Rawalpindi's ability to calibrate CFVs on the LoC/IB is far higher than New Delhi's ability to do so. While the Indian Army might be equally well placed to do so vis-à-vis its troops on the ground, it has very little capability to calibrate such firing as and when it wants to, given that it is accountable to the political class in New Delhi.

However, on the Pakistan side, the ability of the army leadership to calibrate CFVs is almost unconstrained, and that poses a key challenge. The Pakistani civilian government's efforts at conflict resolution with India may or may not be in keeping with the Pakistan Army's world view at a given time. It is then possible that the political establishment in Islamabad and the military brass in Rawalpindi may have differing preferences on the CFV question, and in such a contest, Rawalpindi would be in a position to overrule Islamabad. This makes a dialogue process between India and Pakistan to gain control over escalation or to arrive at CBMs less successful. If the Pakistan Army is not keen on negotiating them, it would be in a position to veto them by initiating CFVs on the border. The army–civilian disharmony in Pakistan further complicates conflict resolution in the India–Pakistan context. The reason why both India and Pakistan were on board the peace process between 2004 and 2008 and there were hardly any CFVs during this period is because there was perfect congruence between Islamabad and Rawalpindi, given that the country's president was also its army chief.

What this means then is that regime type and a combination thereof matters when it comes to CFVs and crisis escalation. To sum up, while AMFs exist in both India and Pakistan, in Pakistan's case, AMFs are controlled and calibrated by the Pakistan Army due to better line of communication between the 'central authority' in Pakistan and its lower commanders. In the case of India, given the inability of the political establishment to grasp the existence and functioning of AMFs, the latter have a lot more autonomy. However, given the political incongruence between Islamabad and Rawalpindi, India–Pakistan negotiations on CFVs or CFV-related CBMs could fall prey to such dissonance.

In any case, it is therefore important to examine the relevance of organizational subcultures both in India and Pakistan in order to understand AMFs and CFVs better.

False Optimism about Central Control

There exists a strong belief in India and Pakistan that the respective establishments are in complete control of what happens on the ground on the border and that local friction or CFVs can be easily controlled at higher levels. It is also widely believed that 'some venting' at the local level would not pose any strategic problems. After all, they have been firing at each other all these years but nothing has gone out of control as a result of CFVs, goes the argument. However, the entrenched belief that escalation can be managed at the higher levels is worrisome given the close linkage CFVs today have with domestic politics, electoral dynamics, and the media attention. While it is true that a decade or two ago, what took place on the border remained there, it may not be the case anymore.

In any case, the belief in the respective establishments that 'we are in control' poses a major challenge for sub-regional stability in the region. A deeply entrenched (false) optimism about being in control would be deeply problematic for escalation control in the region. What makes the situation more challenging is the fact that the two sides may not even have a shared understanding of the fact that CFVs could result from AMFs. If their understanding of the causes and consequences of CFVs drastically differ, their approach to escalation control and conflict de-escalation would also differ as also their expectations of each other.

The anatomy of a future crisis between India and Pakistan on the border is likely to involve the following ingredients: AMFs triggering CFVs between the two forces; resultant injuries and casualties; sensationalist media on either side provocatively covering and editorializing the violations and how the other side needs to be taught a lesson; domestic implications depending on the election cycle (India has periodic state assembly elections); political establishment thereby pressurized into vowing to retaliate; and militaries retaliating with high-calibre weapon systems. If these violations coincide with small-scale or spectacular terrorist attacks, they would act as force multipliers in the escalation dynamics.

In such a situation, the ability of the political class to climb down or de-escalate would be very difficult and not without serious political costs. When CFVs and domestic political calculations run into each other, leaders are likely to exhibit extreme 'loss aversion'—a 'tendency to strongly prefer avoiding losses over acquiring gains'. What situations such as this show is that the sense of control by central decision-makers can be misplaced.

Crisis Learning and Escalation[4]

Notwithstanding the dangers of CFV-induced escalation, past behaviour by India and Pakistan indicates that they have learnt that a bilateral escalatory ladder is rife with uncertainties and pitfalls. The 2001–2

---

[4] This is drawn from Happymon Jacob, 'Conceptualizing Nuclear Learning: A Study of the Indian Experience', in *Nuclear Learning in South Asia: The Next Decade, Naval Postgraduate School*, Feroz Hassan Khan, Ryan Jacobs, and Emily Burke, eds. (Monterey: Center on Contemporary Conflict, 2014), available at https://my.nps.edu/documents/104111744/106151936/2+Nuclear+Lear ning_Jacob.pdf/3ef50dc6-eca0-44f1-836e-9d9d419e64b6, last accessed on 2 January 2017.

On nuclear learning, see Joseph S. Nye, 'Nuclear Learning and U.S.-Soviet Security Regimes', *International Organization* 41, no. 3 (Summer 1987): 371-402; Philip E. Tetlock, 'Learning in U.S. and Soviet Foreign Policy: In Search of an Elusive Concept', in *Learning in U.S. and Soviet Foreign Policy*, George W. Breslauer and Philip E. Tetlock, eds. (New York: Westview Press, 1991); Jeffery W. Knopf, 'The Concept of Nuclear Learning', *Nonproliferation Review* 19, no. 1 (March 2012): 79–93; and Karthika Sasikumar, 'Learning to Play the Game: Strategic Culture and Nuclear Learning', in *Does India Think Strategically? Institutions, Strategic Culture, and Security Policies*, Happymon Jacob, ed. (New Delhi: Manohar Publications, 2014).

standoff and 2008 Mumbai crisis had a clear lesson for India: waging a war against Pakistan is not an option under the nuclear shadow and that regional crises have international implications when nuclear weapons are involved. Pakistan is perhaps 'playing' the nuclear madman in the subcontinent by signalling to India that even limited conventional aggression against Pakistan would invite nuclear retaliation. Pakistan might well be bluffing, but India is not prepared to call this bluff. Certainly not at the level of conventional warfighting.

What then would happen if there is a repeat of the Mumbai attack? New Delhi will continue to find it tough to carry out any punitive military action in response to an attack such as Mumbai; rather, it is likely to lead to further international isolation of Pakistan. This is something India has learnt from Mumbai: while you cannot physically attack Pakistan, you can always shame Pakistan, and the international community will happily join the chorus.

Kargil also clearly taught the two sides that the LoC and the IB are sacrosanct: if Pakistan uses force to change the status quo, it will not be tolerated by India, a la Kargil. In other words, India and Pakistan have learnt from Kargil, and other crises thereafter, what is acceptable or unacceptable to each other and to the international community. However, the surgical strikes of 2016 and the Pakistani non-response to it may have led India to believe that punitive strikes, without land capture, across the LoC in J&K might not meet with the same resistance as elsewhere on the IB.

While this is true of escalation in general, what needs to be noted is that the assumption here is that escalation would be a decision taken by central decision-makers and that they would be able to calibrate the use of violence and force. CFVs, as this book has argued, fall outside this framework and trigger escalation, even though the 'lessons learnt' about escalation might force the two sides to call it quits before it leads to a general war.

Policy Implications and Recommendations[5]

In highlighting the importance of AMFs in triggering CFVs, which have the potential for triggering Indo-Pak crisis escalation, this book

[5] Some of the recommendations mentioned in this section also appear in an earlier report publication of the author: Happymon Jacob, 'Ceasefire Violations in Jammu and Kashmir: A Line on Fire', *Peaceworks*, 15 September 2017, United States Institute of Peace, Washington, DC.

has implicitly argued that there is a need to institute mechanisms for escalation control. Evidence brought together in this book vividly shows that wrong diagnosis by India and Pakistan about the causes of CFVs has led to the adoption of wrong policies by the two governments to deal with the recurrent violations of the ceasefire.

The excessive focus in India on terrorist infiltration triggering CFVs has led to policies aimed at preventing terrorism but have not addressed the other causes, as described in this book, that lead to violations. Findings of this book suggest that even if terrorist infiltration ceases to exist, CFVs could potentially continue to take place, leading to an escalation of tensions between the two sides. The Pakistani argument about unprovoked firing at civilians also does not account for the alternative explanations examined in the book. Hence, policymaking on escalation control in South Asia is likely to be suboptimal and misleading due to the wrong diagnosis of CFVs.

In the light of the non-traditional arguments made in this book about the causes of CFVs, I will now briefly outline what could be done in order to control CFVs and escalation.

Importance of Looking beyond the Capitals for Answers

First of all, there is a need to look beyond the two capitals for answers to reduce violations and escalation. This book has argued that local military factors on the India–Pakistan border are a major factor behind the recurrent breakdown of the 2003 CFA. That is, CFVs are generally not planned, directed, or cleared by higher military commands or political establishments, but are instead driven by the dynamics on the front lines. If indeed that is the case, there is an urgent requirement to focus on the front lines of the India–Pakistan border in J&K.

Importance of Agreements

One of the concrete results of political disinterestedness, as discussed earlier, is the absence of meaningful conflict resolution relating to the border. It is indeed reflective of the sorry state of affairs that the various civilian ministries and the political leaderships in India and Pakistan have not managed to finalize the 1961 ground rules agreement to guard the India–Pakistan border from Gujarat to Jammu, something they have been negotiating since the 1970s. The unwillingness to finalize the mechanisms is particularly evident in the Indian context. While the forces guarding the border have repeatedly asked the government to finalize the ground rules, not only have there been no initiatives to finalize these rules but also, more ironically, there is a perception within the government that there is perhaps no urgency in finalizing those rules. The same applies to the CFA of 2003. There is neither any appetite nor a recognition about the need to formalize the unwritten CFA of 2003. The chapters in this book have identified several such aspects where political will is sorely lacking.

A clear and detailed written agreement that clarifies the dos, don'ts, rules, guidelines, and principles would enable the two sides to better manage the border and significantly reduce the ad hoc nature of the current arrangements. Both serving and retired officers support this idea. Accepting the Karachi Agreement would be politically impossible for New Delhi, but adopting some of its salient features into a new agreement would send a strong signal of willingness to compromise and cooperate to Islamabad. This is especially important because the Simla Agreement of 1972, which superseded the Karachi Agreement of 1948, has no provisions relating to the management of the LoC, unlike the Karachi Agreement which discusses such issues in great detail.

Second, the two governments should also take steps to finalize the India–Pakistan Ground Rules Agreement of 1961, which could help manage the Jammu-Sialkot border. The CFA, when finalized, would also apply to this boundary since this territory lies in J&K. Serving and retired officers tend to support the idea of written down agreements. A senior serving army officer in the valley told this author that the 2003 ceasefire should be formalized and regularized since it is important to have a written CFA for better managing the border with Pakistan.[6] Brig. Kanwal and several others on the Indian side say they would welcome such a step.

Pakistani officials interviewed for this study concurred that 'the agreement should be formalized', even though they do not think that this alone would reduce CFVs 'because, political environment and other factors determine if CFVs take place or not'.[7] They believe that the 2003

---

[6] Interview with Indian Army Officer 3, 14 May 2016, Poonch (J&K).

[7] Interview with Pakistan Army Officer 1, 7 June 2016, Islamabad; Interview with Pakistan Army Officer 2, 9 June 2016, Islamabad; and Interview with Pakistan Army Officer 3, 12 June 2017, Islamabad.

agreement has not been formalized primarily due to lack of political will.[8] Interestingly, they also argued that militaries have concluded a CFA and they are holding it to some extent. Now, it is up to the political leaderships to move forward and look for ways to formalize it in the long term. They recommend that while formalizing a new CFA, both the 2003 agreement and the Karachi Agreement need to be taken together to implement the ceasefire.[9]

Gen. Tariq Majid, when asked whether Pakistan would accept a written down CFA since they have not accepted the finality of the LoC and IB, pointed out, 'It's not an issue. This would still not mean that a final boundary line is being drawn. They would agree to an arrangement that helps prevent escalation.'[10]

In sum, then, it is clear that there is widespread agreement on the ground that the 2003 CFA is inadequate to bring about stability on the India–Pakistan LoC. Moreover, there is also a need, as pointed out earlier, to take urgent steps to finalize the 1961 Border Ground Rules Agreement, which happens to be in force in the Jammu IB/WB.

Third, India and Pakistan could also explore the possibility of developing joint SOPs on a number of issues such as managing villagers living close to the zero line, return of inadvertent crossers, tackling movements at night, and accidental firing, among others. More pertinently, the two sides could also explore the possibility of starting simultaneous coordinated patrolling of small stretches of land, as it is practiced along the IB in Punjab, for instance. The more agreements and joint SOPs there are, the more the chances of CFVs reduce.

Finally, the two sides should consider instituting ad hoc mechanisms for greater clarity on the ground alignment of the 'notional line' in the Kashmir (LoC) sector. Pakistan should consider accepting the BPs in the Jammu-Sialkot sector as the temporary border until the final settlement of the J&K dispute, considering the extent of firing taking place on the IB/WB sector. Clearly demarcating the zero line could potentially avoid at least some of the incidents now likely along the LoC and IB.

---

[8] Interview with Pakistan Army Official 2, 9 June 2016, Islamabad; and Interview with Pakistan Army Official 3, 12 June 2016, Islamabad.

[9] Interview with Pakistan Army Officer 2, 9 June 2016, Islamabad; and Interview with Pakistan Army Officer 3, 12 June 2016, Islamabad.

[10] Interview with Lt Gen. (Retd) Tariq Majid, 14 April 2016, Bangkok.

Defence Construction

Defence construction is one of the most prominent causes of CFVs in LoC and IB/WB. Previous bans on defence construction along the zero line have clearly been ineffective, a matter of lip service and looking the other way. The two sides should formulate a new agreement to clarify and itemize the conditions under which fresh construction, repair works, and extensions are permitted. The current practice of paying lip service to 'no new construction' and yet building when the other side is not looking is only creating more problems. One option is to allow new construction since, legally, the Simla Agreement does not prohibit it. Such flexibility, however, could end up becoming too flexible and lead to more violations. However, they could consider keeping the limit within which new facilities may be built as 150 yards from the LoC. They could also consider agreeing not to build anything new within the restricted area but to allow maintenance and improvement of existing construction. In any case, all of the above requires a great deal of bilateral negotiations.

Focus on Military Subcultures

This book has identified that AMFs trigger CFVs, leading to crisis escalation between the two countries. It might then be useful to focus on such military subcultures while framing policy measures to reduce CFVs and control escalation.

With regard to local military factors triggering violations, more structured communication could be put in place between the two forces, given the drop in violations when meetings between officers of the BSF and the Rangers take place and when the DGMOs meet. More designated flag meeting points should be established beyond the current four in Uri, Tangdhar, Chakan da Bagh, and Mendhar. It might be a good idea for the DGMOs to meet for at least two days in Islamabad or Delhi or even Lahore or Amritsar rather than Wagah. As Syed Ata Hasnain says, 'DGMO meetings should not become glorified flag meetings at the higher level.'[11]

More local meetings would also be helpful. Brig. Kanwal of the Indian Army argues that there should be more regular flag meetings on

---

[11] Interview with Lt Gen. (Retd) Syed Ata Hasnain, 5 June 2015, New Delhi.

the LoC. He also supports the idea of military-to-military CBMs, which could include more meetings, exchanges, and visits, among other things.

Pakistani officers suggest that greater interaction between company commanders will bring about greater situational awareness on both sides, especially in sectors where the local population lives close to the LoC. In such places, interaction between company commanders will help create confidence and reduce tension.[12]

Senior retired officers also recommend exchanges of military delegations and participation in each other's military seminars so as to build more confidence between the two sides. They could contemplate an agreement to facilitate visits at the institutional level between the two staff colleges and National Defence Colleges to promote discussion, cooperation, and collaboration on military thinking and national security perspectives. Such measures could go a long way in fostering understanding and trust.

The two forces could agree not to trade fire on their respective independence days and other religious or national festivals. Such a practice is more or less in place at the Attari-Wagah border, of exchanging sweets on such days. Extending this concept to Indian and Pakistani battalion-level formations could potentially reduce the possibility of CFVs at least on those days. It could also help build confidence among those in the forward areas.

Focus on Escalation Control[13]

Mechanisms for escalation control need to be instituted at various local levels in order to control escalation triggered by CFVs. Gen. Arshad talks about an unwritten agreement that no helicopters would be shot down. This could be formalized. The two forces could consider an understanding on the use of UAVs since their increasing use would become a flashpoint. Indeed, there is today a need to think of including UAVs in the existing CBM on airspace violation.

---

[12] Interview with Pakistan Army Officer 1, 7 June 2016, Islamabad; and Interview with Pakistan Army Officer 2, 9 June 2016, Islamabad.

[13] Participation in the Ottawa track-two dialogue discussions have helped me in gaining insights on what could be done by the two militaries to control escalation.

India and Pakistan could also consider jointly identifying sensitive sectors so that the specific issues concerning those sectors can be properly understood and resolved at senior levels of the two military leaderships. Indeed, the two sides could also consider organizing joint coordinated patrolling of small stretches of land on the LoC and IB to build confidence between the forces.

There is also a need to increase the number of structured flag meetings between local commanders. For instance, brigade commanders' flag meetings could be organized once in three months/six months; divisional commanders could meet once in six months at formation-level flag meetings; flag meeting points could be increased; immediate response should be provided to flag meeting requests; and, hotlines between important divisional headquarters should be established.

Given the increase in the calibre of weapons used by the two forces on the J&K border, it might be a good idea to withdraw the heavy weapons from the front lines. During interactions with serving and retired officers, one got the feeling that it may be a good idea to pull back heavy weapons from the LoC and IB/WB as a general CBM as well as to control escalation. Withdrawing weapon systems such as long-range artillery guns, heavy mortars, medium guns, and so on to 30–50 km behind the zero line, so that they are not placed in direct firing distance from each other's territory, would help reduce the escalatory potential of CFVs. Since CFVs usually begin with small arms and graduate to heavy weapons, removing heavy weapons from the site of action could provide an opportunity for both the sides to contain CFVS before they escalate further.

In order to further control escalation, the two sides could also establish the following procedures to follow in case of a local CFV: Immediately report matter to the other side at local level using existing HLM links or casual meeting, if possible. Immediately inform respective formation/army headquarter on both sides. Each side should carry out own investigation. Institute a joint investigation and visit of locations. And, share report with each other and/or discuss during DGMO HLC.

Need for Civilian-Centric Measures

Civilian movement along the border often leads to CFVs. While both sides have their own SOPS to deal with unauthorized or accidental crossing of civilians, they do not have jointly agreed upon SOPs to deal with such issues. Issues relating to civilians are dealt with in an ad hoc manner by both sides. Some officers are cautious while others believe in more humane ways of dealing with the issue. An elaborate set of SOPs to deter, engage, and repatriate civilians should be developed by the two sides. The two sides need to outline a system for handling the movement of civilians who are residents of the area. Moreover, those Kashmiris who want to return to their homes in the Indian J&K are another possible provocation for the LOC stand-off. There should a working understanding by the two sides on the modalities of such homecoming.

Need for Dialogue on Contentious Issues

Evidence brought out in this book clearly suggests that the 2003 agreement tends to hold when a dialogue process is under way between India and Pakistan on key disputes; local factors seeming to have little or no influence under such a positive environment. During times of bilateral tension, however, as has been the case since 2009, the agreement tends to break down and CFVs are routine. During such phases, local factors tend to have a dramatic influence on CFVs. What this means then is that there should be a meaningful dialogue between India and Pakistan on their outstanding issues in order for CFVs to be reduced and escalation controlled.

It is clear that the larger political conflict of J&K acts as a primary cause for the CFVs in J&K. As Gen. (Retd) Azhar Ali Shah asserts, CFVs should not be taken in isolation since they are only the tip of the iceberg:'The whole gambit of policy, strategy, and the grand strategy must be kept in mind while analysing its causes as well as finding its solutions.'[14]

Terrorism

Just like, for Pakistan, Kashmir constitutes a major issue in the bilateral relationship, terrorism emanating from the Pakistani soil is the key reason New Delhi finds it hard to sustain a dialogue with Pakistan. Without making a moral equivalence between these two issues, it needs to be said that both these issues need to be addressed. The Pakistani side also needs to meaningfully address the issue of infiltration into Kashmir.

[14] Interview with Gen. (Retd) Azhar Ali Shah, 4 April 2016, Lahore.

Even though this book argues that infiltration is not the most prominent cause for CFVs, it remains a significant cause, and hence, it needs to be addressed.

Finally, at the expense of repeating what has already been stated, let me say that there is a need to address issues relating to instability at lower levels of the conflict, since it is not just the major war efforts that could drive the two states into a fight but equally or more importantly, the escalation from the lower levels. The two states need to institute joint mechanisms to arrest the escalation process at lower levels, where it is easier and politically less costly to control the escalation dynamics. Several of these measures are mentioned earlier. The exercise of ensuring stability in the subcontinent lies in routine and mundane measures, not in the sublime and the grandest of moves.

Appendices

Appendix 1

List of Interviewees and Field Visits

Interviewees

(Several Indian and Pakistani active and retired officers whose interviews are used in this book spoke on condition of anonymity.)

Indian Military Officers (Retired)

Bhatia, Vinod. Indian Army. Lieutenant General, retired. DGMO 2012–2014. Currently the director of the Centre for Joint Warfare Studies, New Delhi, India. Interviewed 19 September 2016.

Hasnain, Syed Ata. Indian Army. Lieutenant General, retired. Military Secretary at headquarters in New Delhi, 2012–2017. Formerly commanded the 15 Corps in Kashmir. Interviewed 5 June 2015.

Kanwal, Gurmeet. Indian Army. Brigadier General, retired. Commanded infantry brigade in the Gurez Sector in northern Kashmir on the Line of Control during Operation Parakram in 2001 and 2002. Leading Military Scholar. Interviewed 4 May 2016.

Nanavatty, Rustom K. Indian Army. Lieutenant General, retired. Commander-in-Chief of the army's Northern Command. Interviewed 6 December 2017.

Nandal, A.S. Indian Army. Lieutenant General, retired. Commanded 16 Corps, Commandant of Army Infantry School, Dr. Ambedkar Nagar. Interviewed 23 September 2016.

Nehra, JP. Indian Army. Lieutenant General, retired. Interviewed 3 December 2016.

Panag, Harcharanjit Singh. Indian Army. Lieutenant General, retired. Commanded two of India's key army commands, Central and Northern. Leading Commentator on Strategic Issues. Interviewed 3 March 2017.

Prakash, Om. Indian Army. Lieutenant General, retired. Commanded 25 Infantry Division along the Line of Control in Kashmir. Later Commander of 15 Corps in Srinagar. Interviewed 27 September 2016.

Roy, Rameshwar. Indian Army. Lieutenant General, retired. Commander 16 Corps. Interviewed 22 September 2016.

Sahgal, Arun. Indian Army. Brigadier, retired. Executive Director, Forum for Strategic Initiative, New Delhi, India. Former Founding Director of Net Assessment, Indian Integrated Defense Staff (IDS). Interviewed 4 November 2016.

Sapru, Tej Kumar. Indian Army. Lieutenant General, retired. Commander 16 Corps, Indian Army. Later Commander, Northern Army. Interviewed 10 October 2016.

Shukla, Ajai. Indian Army. Colonel, retired. War Correspondent and Prime Time News Anchor for New Delhi Television (NDTV). Currently Consulting Editor on Strategic Affairs with Business Standard. Interviewed 6 September 2016.

Indian Military Officers (Serving)

(Names withheld on request)

Army Officer 1. 25 Infantry Battalion, Rajouri. Interviewed 18 May 2016.

Army Officer 2. Northern Army Command. Interviewed 13 May 2016.

Army Officer 3. 25 Infantry Division. Interviewed 14 May 2016.

Army Officer 4. Hamirpur Battalion. Interviewed 15 May 2016.

Army Officer 5. 25 Infantry Division. Interviewed 14 May 2016.

Army Officer 6. 28 Infantry Division. Interviewed 15 May 2016.

Army Officer 7. 104 Infantry Brigade, Tangdhar. Interviewed 16 May 2016.

Border Security Force Officers (Retired)

Sharma, Rakesh. Indian Border Security Force. Inspector General, retired. Jammu Frontier. Interviewed 15 September 2016.

Border Security Force Officers (Serving)

(Names withheld on request)

Jammu

BSF Officer 1. Jammu Frontier. Interviewed 2 June 2016.

BSF Officer 2. Border Out Post, Pittal. Interviewed 2 June 2016.

BSF Officer 3. Octroi Post, Jammu. Interviewed 2 June 2016.

BSF Officer 4. 89 Battalion. Interviewed 3 June 2016.

BSF Officer 5. Jammu Frontier. Interviewed 3 June 2016.

BSF Officer 6. 97 Battalion. Interviewed 4 June 2016.

BSF Officer 7. Samba. Interviewed 4 June 2016.

Punjab

BSF Officer 8. Gurdaspur Sector. Interviewed 5 June 2016.

BSF Officer 9. Gurdaspur Sector. Interviewed 5 June 2016.

BSF Officer 10. Gurdaspur Sector. Interviewed 5 June 2016.

BSF Officer 11. Gurdaspur Sector. Interviewed 5 June 2016.

BSF Officer 12. Amritsar Sector. Interviewed 6 June 2016.

BSF Officer 13. Ferozepur Sector. Interviewed 7 June 2016.

Rajasthan

BSF Officer 14. Jodhpur Sector. Interviewed 10 June 2016.

BSF Officer 15. Jaisalmer Sector. Interviewed 10 June 2016.

BSF Officer 16. Jaisalmer Sector. Interviewed 11 June 2016.

BSF Officer 17. Jaisalmer Sector. Interviewed 11 June 2016.

318 • Appendix 1

Gujarat

BSF Officer 18. Sector HQ, Bhuj. Interviewed 14 June 2016.

BSF Officer 19. Bhuj Sector. Interviewed 14 June 2016.

BSF Officer 20. 157 Battalion. Bhuj Sector. Interviewed 16 June 2016.

New Delhi

BSF Officer 21. BSF Headquarters, New Delhi. Interviewed 16 September 2016.

Pakistani Military Officers (Retired)

Afzal, Sikander. Pakistan Army. Lieutenant General, retired. Director General (Analysis) in Inter-Services Intelligence. Later commander of 2 Corps. Interviewed 16 April 2016.

Ali, Ghazanfar. Pakistan Army. Brigadier, retired. Defence Analyst. Interviewed 11 April 2016.

Arshad, Waheed. Pakistan Army. Lieutenant General, retired. Director at Military Operations Directorate at time of 2003 CFA. Retired as Army Chief of General Staff. Interviewed 15 April 2016.

Ghazi, Tariq Waseem. Pakistan Army. Lieutenant General, retired. Commanded Army Corps based in Sindh, 2001–2004. Later appointed Defense Secretary, Pakistan, 2005–2007. Interviewed 7 November 2016.

Majid, Tariq. Pakistan Army. General, retired. Director-General of Military Intelligence, Chief of General Staff, Commander of 10 Corps, Chairman Joint Chiefs of Staff Committee. Interviewed 14 April 2016.

Malik, Asif Yasin. Pakistan Army. Lieutenant General, retired. Director General Joint Intelligence, Commander 11 Corps, Secretary at Ministry of Defence. Interviewed 15 April 2016.

Salik, Naeem Ahmad. Pakistani Army. Brigadier General, retired. Former Director, Arms Control and Disarmament Affairs at the Strategic Plans Division within Pakistan's Nuclear Command Authority. Leading Scholar on Pakistani nuclear policy and doctrine. Interviewed 13 April 2016.

Shah, Azhar Ali. Pakistan Army. General, retired. Interviewed 4 April 2016.

Shuaib, Amjad. Pakistan Army. Lieutenant General, retired. Adjutant General, Pakistan Army in 2000. Interviewed 18 December 2016.

Pakistani Military Officers and Rangers (Serving)

(Some names withheld on request)

Pakistani Official 1. Interviewed 7 June 2016.

Pakistani Official 2. Interviewed 9 June 2016.

Pakistani Official 3. Interviewed 12 June 2016.

Pakistani Official 4. Interviewed 17 January 2017.

Pakistan Army Officer 5. Interviewed 13 December 2017.

Pakistan Army Officer 6. Interviewed 14 December, 2017.

Pakistan Army Officer 7. Interviewed 13 December 2017.

Pakistan Army Officer 8. Interviewed 13 December 2017.

Pakistan Army Officer 9. Interviewed 14 December 2017.

Pakistan Army Officer 10, Rawalapindi, 15 December 2017.

Maj. Gen. Azar Abbas, GOC 12 Infantry Division. Interviewed 13 December 2017.

Brig. Akhtar Khan, Commander, 1 AK Brigade, Muzaffarabad. Interviewed 13 December 2017.

Brig. Noor, Commander, 2 AK Brigade, Rawalakot. Interviewed 14 December 2017.

Lt. Gen. Bilal Akbar, Chief of General Staff, Pakistan Army, GHQ, Rawalpindi. Interviewed 15 December 2017.

Deputy Chief of General Staff, Pakistan army, GHQ, Rawalpindi. Interviewed 15 December 2017.

Pakistani Civilian Officers

Pakistan Civilian Officer 1. Interviewed 13/14 December 2017.

Pakistan Civilian Officer 2. Interviewed 13 December 2017.

Pakistan Civilian Officer 3. Interviewed 13/14 December 2017.

Pakistani traders, Muzaffarabad. Interviewed 13 December 2017.
Pakistani villagers, Rawalakot. Interviewed 14 December 2017.

Indian Diplomats (Retired)

Chandra, Satish. Ambassador. Former High Commissioner to Pakistan. Permanent representative to the UN. Interviewed 14 September 2016.

Katju, Vivek. Ambassador. Former Joint Secretary (Pakistan, Iran, Afghanistan), Additional Secretary and Special Secretary (political and international organisations) in Ministry of External Affairs. Interviewed 6 September 2016.

Raghavan, TCA. Ambassador. Former Indian High Commissioner to Pakistan. Interviewed 8 September 2016.

Pakistani Diplomats (Retired)

Bashir, Salman. Ambassador. Former High Commissioner to India. Additional Foreign Secretary in Ministry of Foreign Affairs. Interviewed 4 November, 2016.

Khan, Aziz Ahmed. Ambassador. Former High Commissioner to India. Director, South Asia Division in Ministry of Foreign Affairs. Honorary Vice President at Jinnah Institute, Islamabad. Interviewed 15 December 2016.

Khokhar, Riaz Hussain. Ambassador. Former High Commissioner to India. Later Foreign Secretary of Pakistan. Interviewed 15 December 2016.

Other Officials

Pillai, GK. Former Indian Home Secretary. Indian Administrative Service. Interviewed 21 September, 2016.

UNMOGIP Officials

UNMOGIP Official 1 – Rawalakot, Pakistan. Interviewed 15 December 2017.

UNMOGIP Official 2 – New Delhi, India. Interviewed 25 July 2016.

Field Visits

INDIA

Kashmir (Rajouri, Tangdhar, Udhampur, Hamirpur)
13–16 May 2016

Jammu (BOP Pittal, Jammu Frontier, Samba)
4–6 June 2016

Punjab (Gurdaspur Sector, Hussainiwala, Amritsar Sector, Ferozepur Sector)
5–7 June 2016

Rajasthan (Jodhpur Sector, Jaisalmer Sector)
10–13 June 2016

Gujarat (Bhuj Sector, Sir Creek, Rann of Kutch)
14–16 June 2016

PAKISTAN

December 2017

Murree Divisional HQ 12 Division

Muzaffarabad AK-1 Brigade

    o Travel and Trade Facilitation Centre, Chakothi

Rawlakot AK-2 Brigade

    o Villages on the LoC
    o Travel and Trade Facilitation Centre, Rawlakot

General Headquarters of the Pakistan Army in Rawalpindi

Round Tables/Conferences/Track-twos on CFVs from which the Author Benefited

1. Round Table on CFVs
   + Date and Venue: 3 March 2018, Jawaharlal Nehru University, New Delhi
   + Topic: Chaophraya Dialogue Policy Roundtable on Ceasefire Violations in J&K; and launch of website—Indo Pak Conflict Monitor

- Chair: Ambassador Vivek Katju
- Speakers: Lt Gen (Retd) Ata Hasnain, Ms Nirupama Subramanian and Dr Happymon Jacob

2. Lecture at the Observer Research Foundation
   - Date and Venue: 27 February 2018, Observer Research Foundation, Mumbai
   - Topic: Ceasefire Violations and the Current State of India Pakistan Relations
   - Chair: Sudheendra Kulkarni

3. Track-II Dialogues
   (i) Chaophraya Dialogue
      - 8–9 December 2017, Bangkok
      - 23–4 March 2018, Bangkok
   (ii) Ottawa Dialogue
      - 16–17 October 2013, Bangkok
      - 19–20 February 2014, Colombo
      - 5–6 November 2014, Bangkok
      - 15–16 April 2015, Bangkok
      - 15–16 April 2016, Bangkok
      - 5–6 November 2016, Bangkok
      - 27–8 May, 2017 Bangkok
      - 25–6 October 2017, Bangkok
      - 5–8 March 2018, Bangkok

4. Seminar at the Institute of Peace and Conflict Studies, New Delhi
   - Date and Venue: 1 December 2017, Institute of Peace and Conflict Studies, New Delhi
   - Topic: Ceasefire Violations in J&K - A Line on Fire
   - Speaker: Dr Happymon Jacob
   - Panel discussants: Lt Gen (Retd) Vinod Bhatia, Former Director General Military Operations (DGMO); Col (Retd) Ajai Shukla, Columnist, Business Standard; and SPS Sandhu, Commandant, Western Theatre Headquarters, Border Security Force (BSF).

Appendix 2

Agreement Relating to Cease-fire Line in J&K

July 27, 1949

AGREEMENT BETWEEN MILITARY REPRESENTATIVES
OF INDIA AND PAKISTAN REGARDING THE
ESTABLISHMENT OF CEASE-FIRE LINE IN THE STATE
OF JAMMU AND KASHMIR

Karachi, 27 July 1949

I

INTRODUCTION

A. The military representatives of India and Pakistan met together in Karachi from 18 July to 27 JULY 1949 under the auspices of the Truce Sub-committee of the United Nations Commission for India and Pakistan.

B. The members of the Indian Delegation were:

1. Lt.-Gen. S.M. Shrinagesh
2. Maj.-Gen. K.S. Thimaya
3. Brig. S.H.F.J. Manekshaw

As observers:

1. Mr. H.M. Patel
2. Mr. V. Sahay C.

The members of the Pakistan Delegation were:

1. Maj.-Gen. W.J. Cawthorn
2. Maj.-Gen. Nazir Ahmad
3. Brig. M. Sher Khan

As observers:

1. Mr. M. Ayub
2. Mr. A.A. Khan.

D. The members of the Truce Sub-committee of the United Nations Commission for India and Pakistan were:

1. Chairman, Mr. Hernando Samper (Colombia)
2. Mr. William L.S. Williams (United States)
3. Lt.-Gen. Maurice Delvoie (Military Adviser)
4. Mr. Miguel A. Marin (Legal Adviser).

II

AGREEMENT

A. Considering:

1. That the United Nations Commission for India and Pakistan, in its letter dated 2 July 1949, invited the Governments of India and Pakistan to send fully authorised military representatives to meet jointly in Karachi under the auspices of the Commission's Truce Sub-committee to establish a cease-fire line in the State of Jammu and Kashmir, mutually agreed upon by the Governments of India and Pakistan;

2. That the United Nations Commission for India and Pakistan in its letter stated that "The meetings will be for military purposes; political issues will not be considered", and that "They will be conducted without prejudice to negotiations concerning the Truce Agreement";

3. That in the same letter the United Nations Commission for India and Pakistan further stated that: "The cease-fire line is a complement of the suspension of hostilities, which falls within the provisions of Part I of the Resolution of 13 August 1948, and can be considered separately from the questions relating to Part II of the same Resolution";

4. That the Governments of India and Pakistan, in their letters dated 7 July 1949 to the Chairman of the Commission, accepted the Commission's invitation to the military conference in Karachi;

5. The Delegations of India and Pakistan, duly authorized, have reached the following agreement:

   I. Under the provisions of Part I of the Resolution of 13 August 1948, and as a complement of the suspension of hostilities in the State of Jammu and Kashmir on 1 January 1949, a cease-fire line is established.

   II. The cease-fire line runs from MANAWAR in the south, north to KERAN and from KERAN east to the glacier area, as follows:

1. The line from MANAWAR to the south bank of the JHELUM River at URUSA (inclusive to India) is the fine now defined by the factual positions about which there is agreement between both parties. Where there has hitherto not been agreement, the line shall be as follows:

   I. In PATRANA area: KOEL (inclusive to Pakistan) north along the KHUWALA KAS Nullah up to point 2276 (inclusive to India), thence to KIRNI (inclusive to India).

   II. KHAMBHA, PIR SATWAN, point 3150 and Point 3606 are inclusive to India, thence the line runs to the factual position at BAGLA GALA, thence to the factual position at Point 3300.

   III. In the area south of URI the positions of PIR KANTHI and LED! GAL! are inclusive to Pakistan.

1. From the north bank of the JHELUM River the line runs from a point opposite the village of URUSA (NL 972109), thence north following the BALLASETH DA NAR Nullah (inclusive to Pakistan), up to NL 973140, thence northeast to CHOTA KAZINAG (Point 10657, inclusive to India), thence to NM 010180, thence to NM 037210, thence to Point 11825 (NM 025354, inclusive to Pakistan), thence to TUTUMARI GALI (to be shared by both sides, posts to be established 500 yds. on either side of the GALI), thence to the northwest through the first "R" of BURST NAR to north of GABDORI, thence straight west to just north of Point 9870, thence along the black line north of BIJILDHAR to north of BATARASI, thence to just south of SUDPURA, thence due north to the KATHAKAZINAG Nullah, thence along the Nullah to its junction

with the GRANGNAR Nullah, thence along the latter Nullah to KAJNWALA PATHRA (inclusive to India), thence across the DHANNA ridge (following the factual positions) to RICHMAR GALI (inclusive to India), thence north to THANDA KATHA Nullah, thence north to the KISHANGANGA River. The line then follows the KISHANGANGA River up to a point situated between JARGT and TARBAN, thence (all inclusive to Pakistan) to BANKORAN, thence northeast to KHORI, thence to the hill feature 8930 (in Square 9053), thence straight north to Point 10164 (in Square 9057), thence to Point 10323 (in Square 9161), thence northeast straight to GUTHUR, thence to BHUTPATHRA, thence to NL 980707, thence following the BUGINA Nullah to the junction with the KISHANGANGA River at Point 4739. Thereafter the line follows the KISHANGANGA to KERAN and onwards to Point 4996 (NL 975818).

2. From Point 4996 the line follows (all inclusive to Pakistan) the JAMGAR Nullah eastward to Point 12124, to KATWARE, to Point 6678, thence to the northeast to SARIAN (Point 11279), to Point 11837, to Point 13090, to Point 12641, thence east again to Point 11142, thence to DHAKKI, thence to Point 11415, thence to Point 10301, thence to Point 7507, thence to Point 10685, thence to Point 8388, thence southeast to Point 11812. Thence the line runs (all inclusive to India) to Point 13220, thence across the River to the east to Point 13449 (DURMAT), thence to Point 14586 (ANZBARI), thence to Point 13554, thence to Milestone 45 on the BURZIL Nullah, thence to the east to ZIANKAL (Point 12909), thence to the southeast to Point 11114, thence to Point 12216, thence to Point 12867, thence to the east to Point 11264, thence to KARO (Point 14985), thence to Point 14014, thence to Point 12089, thence following the track to Point 12879. From there the line runs to Point 13647 (KAROBAL GALI, to be shared by both sides). The cease-fire line runs thence through RETAGAH CHHISH (Point 15316), thence through Point 15889, thence through Point 17392, thence through Point 16458, thence to MARIOLA (to be shared by both sides), thence through Point 17561, thence through Point 17352, thence through Point 18400, thence through Point 16760, thence to (inclusive to India), DALUNANG.

3. From DALUNANG eastwards the cease-fire line will follow the general line Point 15495, ISHMAN, MANUS, GANGAM, GUNDERMAN, Point 13620, JUNKAR (Point 17628), MARMAK, NATSARA, SHANGRUTH (Point 17531), CHORBAT LA (Point 15700), CHALUNKA (on the SHYOK River), KHOR, thence north to the glaciers. This portion of the cease-fire line shall be demarcated in detail on the basis of the factual position as of 27 July 1949 by the local commanders, assisted by United Nations Military Observers.

4. The cease-fire line described above shall be drawn on a one inch map (where available) and then be verified mutually on the ground by local commanders on each side with the assistance of the United Nations Military Observers, so as to eliminate any no-man's land. In the event that the local commanders are unable to reach agreement, the matter shall be referred to the Commission's Military Adviser, whose decision shall be final. After this verification, the Military Adviser will issue to each High Command a map on which will be marked the definitive cease-fire line.

5. No troops shall be stationed or operate in the area of the BURZIL Nullah from south of MINIMARG to the cease-fire line. This area is bounded on the west by the Ridge leading northeast from DUDGAI KAL to Point 13071, to Point 9447, to Point 13466, to Point 13463, and on the east by the Ridge running from Point 12470, to Point 11608, to Point 13004, to Point 13976, to Point 13450. Pakistan may, however, post troops on the western of the above ridges to cover the approaches to KHAMBRI Baipass.

6. In any dispositions that may be adopted in consequence of the present agreement troops will remain, at least 500 yards from the cease-fire line except where the KTSHANGANGA River constitutes the line. Points which have been shown as inclusive to one party may be occupied by that party, but the troops of the other party shall remain at a distance of 500 yards.

7. Both sides shall be free to adjust their defensive positions behind the cease-fire line as determined in paragraphs A to E inclusive above, subject to no wire or mines being used when new bunkers and defences are constructed. There shall be no increase of forces or strengthening of defences in areas where no major adjustments are involved by the determination of the cease-fire line.

8. The action permitted by paragraph F above shall not be accompanied or accomplished by the introduction of additional military potential by either side into the State of Jammu and Kashmir.

9. Except as modified by Paragraphs II-A to II-G, inclusive, above, the military agreements between the two High Commands relating to the cease-fire of 1 January 1949 shall continue to remain operative. I. The United Nations Commission for India and Pakistan will station Observers where it deems necessary.

10. The Delegations shall refer this Agreement to their respective Governments for ratification. The documents of ratification shall be deposited with the United Nations Commission for India and Pakistan not later than 31 July 1949.

11. A period of 30 days from the date of ratification shall be allowed to each side to vacate the areas at present occupied by them beyond the cease-fire line as now determined. Before the expiration of this 30-day period their shall be no forward movement into areas to be taken over by either side pursuant to this agreement, except by mutual agreement between local commanders.

IN FAITH WHEREOF the undersigned sign this document in three original copies.

DONE in Karachi on 27 July 1949

For the Government of India:

(Signed) S.M. SHRINAGESH

For the Government of Pakistan:

(Signed) W.J. CAWTHORN

For the United Nations Commission for India and Pakistan:

(Signed) HERNANDO SAMPER

(Signed) MAURICE DELVOIE.

Source: 'Agreement relating to Cease-fire Line in J&K', Ministry of External Affairs, Government of India, available at https://mea.gov.in/bilateral-documents.htm?dtl/5252/Agreement+relating+to+Ceasefire+Line+in+JampK, last accessed on 22 October 2018.

Appendix 3

Agreement Regarding Procedures to End Border Disputes (W. Pakistan)

January 11, 1960

AGREEMENT BETWEEN GOVERNMENTS OF INDIA AND
PAKISTAN REGARDING PROCEDURES TO END DISPUTES
AND INCIDENTS ALONG THE INDO-WEST PAKISTAN
BORDER AREAS

New Delhi

1. West Pakistan-Punjab border—Of the total of 325 miles of the border in this sector, demarcation has been completed along about 252 miles. About 73 miles of the border has not yet been demarcated due to differences between the Governments of India and Pakistan regarding interpretation of the decision and Award of the Punjab Boundary Commission presented by Sir Cyril Radcliffe as Chairman of the Commission. These differences have been settled along the lines given below in a spirit of accommodation

    I. The Sarja Marja, Rakh Hardit Singh and Pathanke (Amritsar-Lahore border)—The Governments of India and Pakistan agre6 that the boundary between West Pakistan and India in this region should follow the boundary between the Tehsils of Lahore and Kasur as laid down under Punjab Government Notification No. 2183-E, dated 2nd June 1939. These three villages will in consequence fall within the territorial jurisdiction of the Government of Pakistan.

II. Chak Ladheke (Amritsar-Lahore border)—The Governments of India and Pakistan agree that the delineation of the boundary will be as shown in the map of the Kasur Tehsil by Sir Cyril Radcliffe and Chak Ladheke will in consequence fall within the territorial jurisdiction of the Government of India.

III. Ferozepur (Lahore-Ferozepore border)—The Governments of India and Pakistan agree that the West Pakistan-Punjab (India) boundary in this region is along the district boundaries of these districts and not along the actual course of the river Sutlej.

IV. Suleimanke (Ferozepur-Montngoamgerreye border)—The Governments of India and Pakistan agree to adjust the district boundaries in this region as specified in the attached, and as shown in the map appended thereto as Annexure

2. West Pakistan-Bombay border-Exploratory discussions regarding the boundary dispute in the Kutch-Sind region showed that the differences between the Governments of India and Pakistan could not be settled. Both Governments have decided to study the relevant material and hold discussions later with a view to arriving at a settlement of this dispute.

3. Detailed Ground Rules for the guidance of the Border Security forces along the Indo-West Pakistan frontier) prepared as a result of the deliberations of the Conference (Annexure 11) will be put into force by both sides immediately. These Rules will be reviewed and brought up-to-date after the boundary has been finally demarcated and the return of areas in adverse possession of either country has, been effected in the West Pakistan-Punjab (India) sector. Similar action will be taken in respect of the other two sectors in due course.

The Governments of India and Pakistan agree to give top priority to completion of demarcation along the West Pakistan-Punjab (India) sector in accordance with the settlements arrived at during this conference. Both Governments will direct their Surveyors General to complete the demarcation and the fixing of pillars in this sector by the end of April, 1960. Return of areas held in adverse possession by either country in this sector will be completed by 15th October, 1960. Necessary preparatory work to this end should be undertaken immediately by all concerned.

(Sd.) M.J. DESAI,

Commonwealth Secretary Ministry of External Affairs, Government of India.

(Sd) J.G. KHARAS,

Joint Secretary Ministry of Foreign Affairs and Commonwealth Relations, Government of Pakistan.

New Delhi:

January 11, 1960.

SCHEDULE: REFERRED TO IN PARA 1 (iv)

1. The boundary between Pakistan and India in the vicinity of Suleimanke headworks will be along the line marked A B C D E F G H I J K L M in the map at Annexure 1. The points A and M represent the junction of this section of the boundary with the boundary between Ferozepur and Montgomery districts. The portion A B C D E F will follow the boundary of the original area acquired for the Suleimanke Headworks subject to the modification in respect of the reach D to F as specified in para 2. From F to G it will follow the alignment of the existing Left Marginal Bund. From G to H it will follow the dotted straight line shown in the map as closely as practicable subject to such adjustments in alignment at site as may be required from technical considerations to be decided mutually after carrying out necessary surveys. From H to K viz. RD 47,500, the boundary will follow the alignment of the existing marginal bund. From K to L it will follow the alignment of the existing new Hasta bund. From L it will run in a straight line to the apex point of the bulge in the district boundary, as shown on the map.

2. The boundary will run at a distance of 50 feet from the outer toe of the existing Left Marginal Bund in all the reaches where the boundary as defined in para I above runs along it, i.e. from D to G and from H to K. In the reach from G to H it would similarly be placed 50 feet from the outer toe of the proposed bund. In the reach K to L, the boundary will run at a distance of 100 feet from the eastern toe of the existing new Hasta bund.

3. The two parties recognise that they have common and mutual interest in the proper upkeep and maintenance of the Left Marginal

Bund at Suleimanke, and to that end, they declare their intention to co-operate by mutual agreement to the fullest possible extent. In particular,

1. Each party will maintain in its territory according to the following specifications the portion of the Left Marginal Bund that will lie in Pakistan or continue to be in India

    I. Top width - 25 feet

    II. Side slope on the River side - 3 to 1

    III. Outer slope - 2 to I

    IV. Free Board above the highest flood level on record as on 10-1-1960 -5 feet minimum

2. Each party will carry out annual river survey in its own territory upto the conventional distance upstream of the Barrage at Suleimanke, and exchange it with the other party.

The representatives of either party will be allowed to inspect the Left Marginal Bund in the territory of the other party at regular intervals that may be mutually fixed or at any time when either party makes a special request. Such inspections will be made jointly by the representatives of both parties, and each party will afford all necessary facilities to the other party.

(Sd.) S.N. RAVIKANT, 10-1-1960 C.E. Irrigation, Punjab (India)

(Sd.) M.J. DESAI.

(Sd.) M. MAHBOOB, 10-1-1960 Chief Engineer, Irrigation West Pakistan.

(Sd.) J.G. KHARAS

ANNEXURE I

(Not Printed)

ANNEXURE

GROUND RULES FOR BORDER GUARDS

In pursuance of the directive given to the sub-committee these ground rules were formulated by Lt Gen. P.N. Thapar, GOC-in-C, Western Command (India) and Lt Gen. Bakhtiar Rana, SQA, MC Corps, Commander, Pakistan. In their deliberations they were assisted from the Pakistan side by Brig. Said-ud-Din, Director-General, West Pakistan

Rangers, Brig. Tikka Khan and Mr M.S. Koreishi, PFS, Under Secretary, Ministry of Foreign Affairs, and on the Indian side by Shri Bhagwan Singh Rosha, IPS, DIG, PAP., Brig. Gurbakhsh Singh, Shri Govardhan, IPS, IG. Rajasthan, Shri V.G. Kanetkar, IP., DIG., Bombay and Shri M.M. Sen, I.C.S., Deputy Secretary, Ministry of Defence. The ground rules formulated in this paper are applicable to the West Pakistan-Punjab (India), West Pakistan-Rajasthan and West Pakistan-Bombay border.

On this border the security forces of both the countries are located at some places in close proximity to each other, and to avoid any untoward incident and resulting tension, it is necessary that pending

Pakistan Border Issues (W. Pak.) I I Jan. 1960 305 the determination of the final boundary and the exchange of the Witorie, in adverse possession of the two Governments, the security forces of the two respective countries should observe the ground rules as laid down hereinafter..

On this frontier the de facto boundary is generally known to the security forces of both sides and the local population. In case of disputes arising in any sector, regarding the de facto boundary the status quo will be maintained by the local post commanders and a working boundary in the areas under dispute, should be decided upon by the officers mentioned in paragraph 4 below and jointly recorded in a descriptive manner and clearly identified on the ground.

This working boundary will be decided upon by the undermentioned assisted by appropriate Civil Officers:

(i) West Pakistan/Punjab (1) Border between the Director-General,

West Pakistan Rangers/rep. and the D.T.G., P-.A.P, Punjab (India)/rep.

West Pakistan/Rajasthan Border between the Director-General,

West Pakistan Rangers/rep. and D.I.G., RAC/rep.

(iii) West Pakistan/Bombay Border between the Director- General,

West Pakistan Rangers/rep. DIG., (HQ)/rep.

The de facto boundary may or may not coincide with the dejure international boundary and the observance of the de facto boundary by both sides will not commit the two Governments in any manner in respect of their dejure claim.

Neither side will have any permanent or temporary border security forces or any other armed personnel within 150 yards on either side of this de facto boundary and no picket forward posts or observation posts will be established within this area.

Notwithstanding the provisions of paragraph 6 above, both sides may

1. go right up to the de facto boundary in hot pursuit of an offender; (b) send patrols within the zone specified above upto the de facto boundary, provided :
   The each side will inform the other about the actual patrol beat or any changes thereto if it falls within 50 yards of the boundary
2. patrols are small in numbers, i.e. not exceeding a section of one and ten; (iii) patrols invariably move with flags; and
   (iv) only personal weapons are carried by the patrols (no L.M.Gs. will be carried);
3. retain such pickets, forward posts and observation posts as are already established until the de jure boundary is finalised and return of territories under adverse possession takes place. A list of such posts on both sides will be exchanged by 1-2-60. New posts within the 150 yards belt on either side will only be established by mutual agreement.

Defensive works existing within 150 yards on either side of the de facto/ working boundary not included in the list mentioned in para 7(c) above must be destroyed or filled up by 15-3-1960 and reports to this effect will be exchanged by both sides.

Notwithstanding the provisions of paragraph 6 to 8 above, in areas regarding which disputes of title are already pending with the respective Governments for a decision, the status quo inclusive of defence and security measures will be strictly maintained until such time as the de jure boundary is finalised and the return of territories in adverse possession of the two countries takes place.

It will be the duty of the border security forces on either side to prevent armed civilians entering the 300 yards stretch of the border (150 yards on either side of the working boundary).

Border security forces of both sides are charged with the responsibility of preventing smuggling in their respective areas. Therefore, it is incumbent upon them to arrest smugglers of any nationality, whether armed or unarmed, and to deal with them under the law of the land.

In the case of local population, inadvertent crossings are likely to take place along with border. The border security forces, after satisfying themselves that the crossing was done inadvertently, shall immediately return the persons concerned to the opposite commanders at officers level.

Whenever the personnel of the border forces of either country inadvertently stray across the border line information about it should be immediately conveyed to the nearest post of the other side and the personnel must be handed back without delay to their nearest post along with their arms and ammunition etc. if any, through Gazetted Officers/Upper Subordinates of both sides.

Bonafide governmental bodies e.g. survey parties, etc., whilst operating in the border area shall not be interfered with. The programme of such parties will be notified to both sides by the Government concerned-at least a month ahead. Such parties will report to the nearest post of their own country before starting the work.

Whenever any cattle are alleged to have been lifted across the border a report, to be lodged with the opposite border post commander to whom the details such as the tracks of the cattle and of the criminals involved will be handed over. The Border Post Commanders concerned will acknowledge receipt of the report and then inform the nearest Police Station in their own country who will make all efforts to recover the cattle. After recovery the cattle must be handed back immediately to the Police Officers on the opposite side.

Grazing of unattended cattle on the border shall be discouraged. In the case of stray cattle these will be returned immediately by the Border Post Commanders to their opposite numbers after having satisfied themselves that the cattle have in actual fact strayed from across the border.

The SPs of Border Districts will also attend where necessary the monthly border meetings for the purpose of exchange of cattle and discussing border crimes.

The duties of the Sub-centres/Wing Commanders/SPs and lower Commanders in their respective areas of responsibility shall be as under:

1. They will maintain close liaison with their opposite numbers.
2. They will, by frequent visits, make themselves known to the Border Security Forces of the opposite side.
3. They will receive all complaints regarding border violation/ tension. They will immediately hold a joint enquiry not later than 24 hours of the information report. Where this is not possible due to long distances and difficulties of communications, the joint enquiry should be held as soon as possible.
4. Where two border posts are situated in close proximity to each other and it is possible for them to communicate by flags, any commander who wishes to meet his counterpart, will wave a flag of the specifications given in paragraph 23 below and will proceed to the border unarmed without any escort to a pre-arranged place. The opposite commander or the senior officer on seeing the flag, will acknowledge the signal and proceed to the place of meeting also with a flag unarmed and without escort. The use of flags shall be introduced by 15-2-1960.

   Where the posts are separated by a long distance, contact will be established in the following manner:

   A party consisting of I and 6 armed with their personal weapons for their own protection and carrying the appropriate flag will proceed to the post of the other side. On arrival within 300 yards of this post, they will establish a temporary base and send forward two men unarmed with the appropriate flags to make necessary contact.
5. Nationals of both the countries, while cultivating land upto the de facto boundary of the country concerned shall not be interfered with by the border security forces of the other side.
6. If a national of one country lays a fresh claim to land across the de facto border and takes any step in furtherance of that claim which is objected to by the other side, the two commanders will hold a joint enquiry on the spot and restrain the person from enforcing his claim until the matter is settled.

Where, due to the change in the course of a river, territory of one country is thrown on the other side, such change will NOT affect either the dejure or de facto position of the territory.

It is felt that the tension on the borders will be greatly minimised if there is close personal touch between commanders of the two border security forces and therefore the following periodic meetings are recommended:

1. Wing Comdrs Rangers (Pak)/ Monthly at the S.Ps of PAP/RAC (India) border. Special Reserve Police, Bombay, (India).
2. Officers mentioned in para 4 As required above or their representatives shall also meet. These officers will be authorised by their respective Governments to settle the disputes on the spot as far as possible.

The military commanders shall also meet as and when the situation demands and whenever they consider it necessary.

If unfortunately, in spite of this, firing occurs, the other side shall refrain from replying. The local commanders will get in touch with each other by telephone and will meet with a view to bringing about a cease-fire forthwith. After every firing incident, it is necessary for both sides to carry out a joint investigation, fix responsibility and submit their respective reports for information of their higher authorities.

In order to maintain close liaison between the border forces of the two countries, it is essential that adequate telephone and other communications are provided at various levels.

All pickets and patrols on both sides will have flags of the follow] rig description

Pickets

Pole Cloth Size 7 ft 4 × 3 feet

Colours India .... Orange

Patrols

Pole cloth 3 feet 2 × 2l/2 ft

Pakistan Blue.

I At night flags will be substituted by light signals (two red/verey 'ghts) or signal by torches as mutually arranged between the post commanders.

The areas:

Whenever there is a joint enquiry by DCs or Commissioners on the two sides, the respective commanders of security forces I of shall also attend the meeting and submit for the information of the respective higher commanders their assessment of the situation created by the particular incident.

Finally, we recommend

1. that the press on both sides should be persuaded to exercise restraint and not to publish exaggerated reports or material which is likely to inflame the feelings of the population on both sides. Should incorrect reports be published, contradictions at a governmental level should be issued at the earliest opportunity;
2. that after the dejure boundary has been finalised and the return of territories in adverse possession has been effected these ground rules should be reviewed in order to bring them up-to-date.

Lt Gen. BSADKH-TIAR RANA,
S-Q.A., M.C., Corps Commander, West Pakistan.
New Delhi, 9th January, 1960.

P.N. THAPAR,
Lt Gen. Sd/- G.O.C.-in-C, Western Command, India.
New Delhi, 9th January, 1960.

Source: 'Agreement Regarding Procedures to End Border Disputes (W. Pakistan)', Ministry of External Affairs, Government of India, available at http://mea.gov.in/bilateral-documents.htm?dtl/6316/Agreement+regarding+Procedures+to+End+Border+Disputes+W+Pakistan, last accessed on 22 October 2018.

Appendix 4

Simla Agreement July 2, 1972

July 02, 1972

The Simla Agreement signed by Prime Minister Indira Gandhi and President Zulfikar Ali Bhutto of Pakistan on 2nd July 1972 was much more than a peace treaty seeking to reverse the consequences of the 1971 war (i.e. to bring about withdrawals of troops and an exchange of PoWs). It was a comprehensive blue print for good neighbourly relations between India and Pakistan. Under the Simla Agreement both countries undertook to abjure conflict and confrontation which had marred relations in the past, and to work towards the establishment of durable peace, friendship and cooperation.

The Simla Agreement contains a set of guiding principles, mutually agreed to by India and Pakistan, which both sides would adhere to while managing relations with each other. These emphasize: respect for each other's territorial integrity and sovereignty; non-interference in each other's internal affairs; respect for each other's unity, political independence; sovereign equality; and abjuring hostile propaganda. The following principles of the Agreement are, however, particularly noteworthy:

+ A mutual commitment to the peaceful resolution of all issues through direct bilateral approaches.
+ To build the foundations of a cooperative relationship with special focus on people to people contacts.

✦ To uphold the inviolability of the Line of Control in Jammu and Kashmir, which is a most important CBM between India and Pakistan, and a key to durable peace.

India has faithfully observed the Simla Agreement in the conduct of its relations with Pakistan.

SIMLA AGREEMENT

Agreement on Bilateral Relations between the Government of India and the Government of Pakistan

1. The Government of India and the Government of Pakistan are resolved that the two countries put an end to the conflict and confrontation that have hitherto marred their relations and work for the promotion of a friendly and harmonious relationship and the establishment of durable peace in the sub-continent, so that both countries may henceforth devote their resources and energies to the pressing talk of advancing the welfare of their peoples. In order to achieve this objective, the Government of India and the Government of Pakistan have agreed as follows:-

   o That the principles and purposes of the Charter of the United Nations shall govern the relations between the two countries;

   o That the two countries are resolved to settle their differences by peaceful means through bilateral negotiations or by any other peaceful means mutually agreed upon between them. Pending the final settlement of any of the problems between the two countries, neither side shall unilaterally alter the situation and both shall prevent the organization, assistance or encouragement of any acts detrimental to the maintenance of peaceful and harmonious relations;

   o That the pre-requisite for reconciliation, good neighbourliness and durable peace between them is a commitment by both the countries to peaceful co-existence, respect for each other's territorial integrity and sovereignty and non-interference in each other's internal affairs, on the basis of equality and mutual benefit;

   o That the basic issues and causes of conflict which have bedevilled the relations between the two countries for the last 25 years shall be resolved by peaceful means;

   o That they shall always respect each other's national unity, territorial integrity, political independence and sovereign equality;

o That in accordance with the Charter of the United Nations they will refrain from the threat or use of force against the territorial integrity or political independence of each other.

2. Both Governments will take all steps within their power to prevent hostile propaganda directed against each other. Both countries will encourage the dissemination of such information as would promote the development of friendly relations between them.

3. In order progressively to restore and normalize relations between the two countries step by step, it was agreed that;

o Steps shall be taken to resume communications, postal, telegraphic, sea, land including border posts, and air links including overflights.

o Appropriate steps shall be taken to promote travel facilities for the nationals of the other country.

o Trade and co-operation in economic and other agreed fields will be resumed as far as possible.

o Exchange in the fields of science and culture will be promoted.

In this connection delegations from the two countries will meet from time to time to work out the necessary details.

4. In order to initiate the process of the establishment of durable peace, both the Governments agree that:

o Indian and Pakistani forces shall be withdrawn to their side of the international border.

o In Jammu and Kashmir, the line of control resulting from the cease-fire of December 17, 1971 shall be respected by both sides without prejudice to the recognized position of either side. Neither side shall seek to alter it unilaterally, irrespective of mutual differences and legal interpretations. Both sides further undertake to refrain from the threat or the use of force in violation of this Line.

The withdrawals shall commence upon entry into force of this Agreement and shall be completed within a period of 30 days thereof.

5. This Agreement will be subject to ratification by both countries in accordance with their respective constitutional procedures, and will come into force with effect from the date on which the Instruments of Ratification are exchanged.

6. Both Governments agree that their respective Heads will meet again at a mutually convenient time in the future and that, in the

meanwhile, the representatives of the two sides will meet to discuss further the modalities and arrangements for the establishment of durable peace and normalization of relations, including the questions of repatriation of prisoners of war and civilian internees, a final settlement of Jammu and Kashmir and the resumption of diplomatic relations.

Sd/-
(Indira Gandhi)
Prime Minister
Republic of India

Sd/-
(Zulfikar Ali Bhutto)
President
Islamic Republic of Pakistan

Simla, the 2nd July, 1972

Source: 'Simla Agreement July 2, 1972', UN Doc. No. 31419, United Nations Treaty Collection, available at https://treaties.un.org/doc/publication/unts/volume%201843/volume-1843-i-31419-english.pdf, last accessed on 22 October 2018.

Appendix 5

Clarifications on LoC

July 02, 1972

Delineation of the Line of Control in Jammu and Kashmir resulting from the Cease fire on 17 December 1971 in accordance with the Simla Agreement of 02 July 1972

General

1. The representatives of the Chiefs of Army Staff of India and Pakistan held a series of meetings alternately at Suchetgarh, on the Indian side and Wagah Check Post, on the Pakistan side, to delineate the Line of Control in Jammu and Kashmir resulting from the cease fire of 17 December 1971 in accordance with Paragraph 4 (ii) of the Simla Agreement signed between the Govt of India and the Govt of Pakistan on 02 July 1972.

2. A copy of the relevant extracts of Simla Agreement is at Appendix A attached.

   Schedule of Various Meetings

3. The delineation of the Line of Control was effected during nine meetings as follows:-

	Dates	Venue
(a) First Meeting	10–12 August 1972	Suchetgarh
(b) Second Meeting	21–22 August 1972	Wagah
(c) Third Meeting	28–29 August 1972	Suchetgarh
(d) Fourth Meeting	03–15 Sept. 1972	Wagah
(e) Fifth Meeting	18 Sept. – 01 Oct. 1972	Suchetgarh
(f) Sixth Meeting	07–08 October 1972	Wagah
(g) Seventh Meeting	14–22 October 1972	Suchetgarh
(h) Eighth Meeting	07–09 November 1972	Wagah
(i) Ninth and Final Meeting	11 December 1972	Suchetgarh

Composition of Indian and Pakistani Delegations

4. The composition of the two delegations were as under:-

Indian Delegation	Pakistan Delegation
Lt Gen PS Bhagat, PVSM, VC	Lt Gen Abdul Hameed Khan, S Pk, SQA
Maj Gen MR Rajwade, VSM, MC	Brig SM Abbasi
Maj Gen IS Gill, PVSM, MC	Col Mahmud Shaukat
Col CM Sahni	Col Syed Refaqat, TQA
Lt Col MS Chahal, VSM	Lt Col MM Afzal Khan
Lt Col BM Tewari	Lt Col Ahmad Saeed

Methodology of Delineation

5. The Line of Control was reproduced on two sets of maps prepared by each side, each set consisting of 27 map sheets formed into 19 mosaics. Each individual mosaic of all four sets of maps with the Line of Control marked on them has been signed by the representatives of the Chiefs of Army Staff of India and Pakistan and each side has exchanged one set of signed mosaics as required under the joint statement by the representative of Govt of India and Pakistan signed at Delhi on 29 August 1972.

6. A copy of the document is being displayed for perusal.

Evidence to disprove Pakistan's contention that the Line of Control is not delineated

7. Jointly Attested Mosaics of the Line of Control: Mosaics of the Line of Control duly signed by Lt Gen Abdul Hameed Khan, S Pk, SQA of the Pakistan Army and Lt Gen PS Bhagat, PVSM, VC of the Indian Army are held by both sides. The original copies of the Mosaics are displayed and a miniaturised copy of one such Mosaic is attached as Appendix B for perusal.

8. Delineation of the Line of Control on a Pakistani Map: A Pakistan Map, Scale 1,50,000. Sheet No. 43 N/15, First Edition published under the direction of Major General Anis Ali Syed St(M), afwc, B.Sc (C.E) HONS, M.Sc. M.A.S.C.E., F.I.E., Surveyor General of Pakistan, with the Line of Control duly printed, recovered from one of the recaptured positions is displayed.

9. Satellite Imagery/Air Photographs: A Satellite Imagery of the area of instant operations, taken during October 1998, reveals that there was no military activity in the area also on intrusion. The Satellite Imagery is being displayed. Air Photographs of the area also highlight the Regular Posts on both sides of the Line of Control, thus substantiating the fact that the troops on ground were aware of the alignment of Line of Control. Relevant Air Photographs are being displayed for perusal. Pakistan in the last 27 years, has never disputed the delineation jointly ratified by the two representatives of the Chiefs of Army Staff of India and Pakistan. As such, this is a deliberate attempt to mislead and cover up the armed intrusion across the Line of Control by Pakistan Army.

Line of Control in Jammu and Kashmir A Part of Simla Agreement

It is a bit surprising to read in newspapers that some people in Pakistan have expressed a doubt that the Line of Control in Kashmir is vague. These statements indicate complete innocence about the meticulous care and thoroughness with which this Line was discussed, surveyed where necessary, identified on ground and delineated on maps giving detailed grid references and description of land marks. These were checked and re-checked before representatives of the two countries signed the documents pertaining to this Line and which were thereafter approved both Governments of India and Pakistan. It is necessary to describe the whole process for those who are not aware of how this crucial matter was handled.

The Simla Agreement stipulated that in Jammu & Kashmir, the Line of Control separating the two Armies on the day of cease-fire will be delineated. India and Pakistan very carefully selected senior military commanders to shoulder this historic responsibility. On the Indian side the team captain was the well known, highly respected, gallant soldier scholar, Lt Gen PS Bhagat, PVSM, Victoria Cross and on Pakistan side the highly respected veteran and a man of sterling character Lt Gen Hameed Khan, S Pk, SQA. It was a fortunate coincidence that Bhagat and Hameed knew each other since their days in the Indian Military Academy, Dehradun. Consequently they worked on the difficult, time consuming and laborious mission with trust, utter frankness and mutual regard and respect. General Bhagat's team included the then Director Military Operations, Maj Gen IS Gill, PVSM, MC. known in the Indian Army as a man of 24-carat-gold for his sterling qualities. Similarly, on the Pakistani side was the then Director Military Operations, Brig. SM Abbasi, scion of the princely family of Bahawalpur. Included in the teams were also Deputy Directors of Survey of India and Pakistan with adequate number of trained survey personnel and survey equipment. The senior military commanders of the two sides were assisted by three sector commanders along the entire length of 740 Km of Line of Control which was divided in three segments namely the Southern Sector, the Central Sector and the Northern Sector. In turn, sector commanders were assisted by sub sector commanders to do the ground work on the entire Line of Control. For Example, in the Northern Sector were included the four Sub Sector Commanders of Partapur Sub Sector, Kargil Sub Sector (including Batalik), Shingo (Kaksar) Sub Sector and Drass Sub Sector which are the areas of current conflict. Sector and Sub Sector commanders of the two countries worked in close co-operation.

A total of nine meetings were held between the senior military commanders of the two countries and their teams between 10 Aug 72 and 11 Dec 72, alternatively at Suchetgarh near Jammu, and Wagah near Amritsar. At each meeting the inputs of sub sectors were discussed, the sticky points resolved and where necessary, a joint survey was ordered to ensure that nothing was left vague or uncertain. It is pertinent to add that there were some issues which had to be resolved by the Army Chiefs of

India and Pakistan and for these both the meetings were held at Lahore in Nov and Dec 72 between Field Marshal Sam Manekshaw and General Tikka Khan. All issues were amicably resolved.

In the whole exercise two sets of maps each comprising of 27 maps were prepared. These marked maps were joined and 19 mosaics were prepared, thus clearly delineating the entire stretch of Line of Control running through 740 Km starting from Sangam and ending at Pt NJ-9842. Besides the maps, there were 19 Annexures consisting of 40 pages, giving the details of every feature, landmark and coordinates of the Line of Control. The delineated Line of Control was jointly prepared and signed by two senior military commanders, Lt Gen PS Bhagat and Lt Gen Hameed Khan. These documents were jointly signed and exchanged by the two senior military commanders on 11 Dec 72 at Suchetgarh.

Immediately after signing of the delineation maps and documents at the final meeting of senior military commanders on 11 Dec 72, the DMO flew to New Delhi and reported to the COAS along with copies of the signed delineation proceedings and one copy of the signed maps at 1500 hours 11 Dec 72. The COAS presented these at a meeting of the Political Affairs Committee of the Cabinet at 16 hours the same day. At 1620 hours a message was received from Mr Aziz Ahmed, Special Assistant to the President of Pakistan for Mr PN Haksar, Principal Secretary to the Prime Minister, informing him that the Government of Pakistan had accorded its approval to the Joint Recommendations submitted by the senior military commanders of Pakistan and India on that day in regard to delineation of the Line of Control in Jammu and Kashmir. This message was passed to the COAS at Parliament House and at 1747 hours the DMO informed the DMO Pakistan Army on the telephone that the Government of India had accorded its approval to the Joint Recommendations in regard to the delineation proceedings.

At 0700 hours on 17 Dec 72 the mutually agreed statement was released in New Delhi and Islamabad. At 2100 hours on 20 Dec 72, a joint statement by the Indian and Pakistan Governments was released to the media regarding withdrawal of troops to the International Border and delineation in conformity with the Line of Control in Jammu and Kashmir.

In view of the facts explained above, there should be absolutely no reason for any reservation in anyone's mind in India or Pakistan that there is anything vague or uncertain about the Line of Control in Jammu and Kashmir. It is pertinent to add that for a period of over 27 years, the Line of Control in Jammu and Kashmir has stood the test of time. There have been frequent clashes as well as exchange of fire which were invariably discussed and resolved in flag meetings of the two sides. The authenticity of the Line of Control was never questioned. It is worthwhile adding that each flag meeting invariably developed into a competition in hospitality!

It is also appropriate to take a close look on the wording of Paragraph dealing with the sanctity of the Line of Control of the Simla Agreement which reads as under:-

'In order to initiate the process of the establishment of durable peace. Both the Governments agree that: In Jammu and Kashmir, the Line of Control resulting from cease fire on 17th December, 1971 shall be respected by both sides without prejudice to the recognised position of either side. **Neither side shall seek to alter it unilaterally, irrespective of mutual differences and legal interpretations. Both sides undertake to refrain from threat of use of force in violation of this Line.'**

[The Writer Lt Gen (Dr) ML Chibber, was Deputy Director of Military Operations after 1971 War and later C-in-C Northern Command when Pakistan was prevented from occupying Soltero Ridge and Siachen Glacier]

Extract of Simla Agreement Pertaining to Line of Control

4. In order to initiate the process of the establishment of durable peace, both the Governments agree that:
    (i) Indian and Pakistani forces shall be withdrawn to their side of the international border.
    (ii) In Jammu and Kashmir, the line of control resulting from the cease-fire of December 17, 1971, shall be respected by both sides without prejudice to the recognised position of either side. Neither side shall seek to alter it unilaterally, irrespective of mutual differences and legal interpretations. Both sides further undertake to refrain from the threat or the use of force in violation of this line.

(iii) The withdrawals shall commence upon entry into force of this agreement and shall be completed within a period of 30 days thereof.

5. This agreement will be subject to ratification by both countries in accordance with their respective constitutional procedures, and will come into force with effect from the date on which the instruments of ratification are exchanged.

6. Both Governments agree that their respective heads will meet again at a mutually convenient time in the future and that, in the meanwhile the representatives of the two sides will meet to discuss further the modalities and arrangements for the establishment of durable peace and normalisation of relations including the questions of repatriation of prisoners of war and civilian internees, a final settlement of Jammu and Kashmir and the resumption of diplomatic relations.

(INDIRA GANDHI)
Prime Minister Republic of India

(ZULFIKAR ALI BHUTTO)
President Islamic Republic of Pakistan.

Simla, the 22nd of July, 1972

Source: 'Clarifications on LoC', Ministry of External Affairs, Government of India, availaible at https://mea.gov.in/in-focus-article.htm?19004/Clarifications+on+LoC, last accessed on 22 October 2018.

Appendix 6

Agreement between India and Pakistan on Air Space Violations

No. 31419

INDIA
and
PAKISTAN

Agreement on prevention of air space violations and for permitting over flights and landings by military aircraft (with appendix). Signed at New Delhi on 6 April 1991

Authentic text: English.
Registered by India on 15 December 1994.

INDE
et
PAKISTAN

Accord relatif a la prevention de violations de l' espace aerien et a la permission de survols et d'atterrissages par des avions militaires (avec appendice). Signe a New Delhi le 6 avril 1991

Texte authentique : anglais.
Enregistre par I'Inde le 15 decembre 1994.

AGREEMENT[1] BETWEEN INDIA AND PAKISTAN ON PREVENTION OF AIR SPACE VIOLATIONS AND FOR PERMITTING OVER FLIGHTS AND LANDINGS BY MILITARY AIRCRAFT

PREAMBLE

States parties to the present Air Agreement, Recognising the fact that both the Indian Air Force (IAF) and the Pakistan Air Force (PAF) aircraft operate near each other's airspace.

Aware that despite best efforts by both sides, violations of each other's airspace have occurred from time to time-

Desirous of promoting good neighbourly relations between the two countries. Conscious of the fact that renewed efforts should be made to avoid unnecessary alarm.

Have agreed to enter into the following Air Agreement.

AIR VIOLATIONS

Article - 1

Henceforth, both sides will take adequate measures to ensure, that air violations of each other's airspace do not take place. However, if any inadvertant violation cc=s take place, the incident will be promptly investigated and the Headquarters (HQ) of the other Air Force informed of the results without delay, through diplomatic channels.

Article - 2

Subject to Articles 3, 4 and 6, the following restrictions are to be observed by military aircraft of both the forces:-

a. Combat aircraft (to include fighter, bomber, reconnaissance, jet military trainer and armed helicopter aircraft) will not fly within 10 kms of each other's airspace including ADIZ. No aircraft of any side will enter the airspace over the territorial waters of the ether country, except by prior permission.

b. Unarmed transport and logistics aircraft including unarmed helicopters, and Air Observation Post (AOP) aircraft, will be

[1] Came into force on 19 August 1992 by the exchange of the instruments of ratification, which took place at New Delhi, in accordance with article 9.

permitted upto 1000 metres from each other's airspace including ADIZ.

Article-3

Aerial Survey, Supply Dropping, Mercy and Rescue Missions

In the event of a country having to undertake flights less than 1000 metres from the other's airspace including ADIZ, for purposes such as aerial survey, supply dropping for mercy missions and aerial rescue missions, the country concerned will give the following information in advance to their own Air Advisors for notification to the Air HQ of the other country:-

a. Type of aircraft/helicopter.

b. Height of flight within Plus/Minus 1000 ft.

c. Block No. of days (normally not to exceed seven days) when flights are proposed to be undertaken.

d. Proposed timing of flight, where possible.

e. Area involved (in latitude and longitude).

No formal clearance would be required as the flights are being undertaken within own territory.

AIR EXERCISES NEAR BORDER

Article-4

In order to avoid any tension being created, prior notice be given with regard to air exercises, or any special air activity proposed to be undertaken close to each other's airspace including ADIZ, even though the limits as laid down in Article 2 are not likely to be infringed.

COMMUNICATION BETWEEN IAF AND PAF

Article - 5

In matters of safety and any air operations in emergency situations, the authorities designated by the respective Governments should contact each other by the quickest means of communications available. The Air Advisor shall be kept informed of such contacts. Matters of flight safety and urgent air operations should promptly be brought to the notice of the other side through the authorities designated by using the telephone line established between the Army Headquarters of the two countries.

OPERATIONS FROM AIR FIELDS CLOSE TO THE BORDERS

Article - 6

Combat aircraft (as defined in Article 2 a. above) operating from the air bases specified below will maintain a distance of 5 kms from each other's airspace:-

a. Indian Side
    (1) Jammu.
    (2) Pathankot.
    (3) Amritsar.
    (4) Suratgarh.

b. Pakistan Side
    (1) Pasrur.
    (2) Lahore.
    (3) Vehari.
    (4) Rahim Yar Khan.

FLIGHTS OF MILITARY AIRCRAFT THROUGH EACH OTHER'S AIR SPACE

Article-7

Military aircraft may fly through each other's airspace with the prior permission of the other country and subject to conditions specified in Appendix A to this Agreement.

Notwithstandinc paragraph 1 of this Article, each country has the sovereign right to specify further conditions/ at short notice, for flights of military aircraft through its airspace.

VALIDITY OF AGREEMENT

Article - 8

This Agreement supersedes all previous understandings in so far as air space violations and over flights and landings by military aircraft ore concerned.

Article - 9

This Agreement is subject to ratification. It shall come into force with effect from the date on which the Instruments of Ratification are exchanged.

Article - 10

Done at New Delhi on this Sixth day of April 1991.

For the Government of
the Republic of India:
MUCHKUND DUBEY

Foreign Secretary

For the Government of
theIslamic Republic of Pakistan:
SHAHARYAR M. KHAN

Foreign Secretary

APPENDIX A

CONDITIONS FOR GRANT OF FLIGHT CLEARANCE FOR
MILITARY AIRCRAFT OF BOTH COUNTRIES

1. The side requesting permission for their military aircraft to fly
through the air space of the other country or for landing(s) by such
aircraft at airfield(s) in the other country, will approach the respective
Air HQ, through their Air Advisor for clearance to undertake the
flight, at least seven days before the scheduled date(s) of the flight(s).
If, due to unforeseen circumstances, this notice is less than seven
days, the other country would, as far as possible, make all efforts to
accommodate the request. The following details of each flight will be
intimated to the concerned Air Headquarters:-
   a. Aircraft type.
   b. Aircraft registration number.
   c. Aircraft call sign.
   d. Name of the Captain of the Aircraft.
   e. Number of the crew.
   f. Cruising level.
   g. General nature of cargo carried and number of passengers who
   are on board the Aircraft.
   h. Purpose of the flight.
   j. Standby aircraft number and call sign.
   k. Name of standby Captain and air crew.
   l. Flight plan for outbound and return legs Including air route,
   Flight Information Region (FIR) entry/exit points and times.
   Expected Time of Arrival (ETAs)/ Expected Time of Departure
   (ETDs) and flight levels etc.
   m. Type and quality of fuel required at various air fields landing.

2. All flights approved will be valid for 3 days within plus/minus three hours of the given time schedule of each day provided flight details remain unchanged. Any subsequent changes of the flight plan will require fresh clearance from Air HO, for which advance notice of 72 hours will be essential.

3. Routes to be followed by aircraft will be specified by respective countries at the time of requesting flight clearance. If the route proposed by the originator country is, for any reason, not acceptable to the other country, the latter would, if possible, suggest a viable alternative route at the earliest.

4. The aircraft will not fly below 8000 ft or over 40,000 ft Above Ground Level (AGL).

5. The concerned Flight Information Centre of the other country will be contacted by the transiting aircraft during the flight before entering the airspace of the other country.

6. Flights across each other's airspace will normally be completed between sun rise and sun set. Over-flights by night may be permitted, on specific request, under special c1rcumstances.

7. No war-like material e.g. arms, ammunition, explosives, (except escape aid explosives), pyrotechnics (except emergency very light pistol signal cartridges), nuclear/fissionable material, Nuclear Biological and Chemical (NBC) materials, photographic material (whether or not installed), electronic devices other than required for the normal operation of the aircraft, may be carried in the aircraft.

8. Non-professional cameras belonging to the passengers and which are not capable of aerial photography, may however be carried but photography at Airports or of defence installations, bridges and industries etc is not permitted.

9. Normally, both countries shall permit over flights to transit across the other's airspace along approved international Air Traffic Services (ATS) routes without the aircraft having to make a technical halt. However, each country has the sovereign right to insist on such a halt if the country being overflown so desires.

10. Special care is to be exercised by the transiting aircraft to stay within the ATS routes and not to stray outside the limits of the route.

11. Visas for the crew and passengers will be issued by the respective Embassy with utmost promptness.

Source: 'Agreement on Prevention of Air Space Violations and for Permitting Over Flights and Landings by Military Aircraft (with appendix). Signed at New Delhi on 6 April 1991', Un Doc No. 31419, United Nations Treaty Collection, available at https://treaties.un.org/doc/publication/unts/volume%201843/volume-1843-i-31419-english.pdf, last accessed on 22 October 2018.

Appendix 7

Joint Statement, Second Round of Expert Level Talks between India and Pakistan on Conventional Confidence Building Measures

August 08, 2005

1. The Second Round of Expert Level Talks between India and Pakistan on Conventional Confidence Building Measures was held in New Delhi on 08 August 2005. Mr Dilip Sinha, Joint Secretary, Ministry of External Affairs, led the Indian side. Mr Tariq Osman Hyder, Additional Secretary (UN&EC), Ministry of Foreign Affairs, led the Pakistan delegation,

2. The talks between the two delegations were held in a cordial and constructive atmosphere.

3. Both sides exchanged views on their respective security concepts.

4. The two sides exchanged views on various proposals and agreed on the following CBMs:

   I. Reaffirmed their commitment to uphold the ongoing ceasefire.

   II. To implement the 1991 Agreement between Pakistan and India on Air Space Violations in letter and spirit.

   III. Upgrade the existing hotline between the two DGMOs by end September 2005.

   IV. Not to develop any new posts and defence works along the LOC.

V. Hold monthly Flag Meetings, between local commanders, at Kargil/ Olding, Uri/ Chakothi, Naushera/ Sadabad and Jammu/ Sialkot Sectors.

VI. Speedy return of inadvertent Line crossers, and to work out a comprehensive framework to that end.

VII. Periodically review the existing CBMs.

5. The two sides also agreed to report the progress made in the present round of talks to the respective Foreign Secretaries, who will decide on the date and venue of the next Expert Level meeting on Conventional CBMs.

New Delhi
August 08, 2005

Source: 'Joint Statement, Second Round of Expert Level Talks between India and Pakistan on Conventional Confidence Building Measures', Ministry of External Affairs, Government of India, available at https://mea.gov.in/bilateral-documents.htm?dtl/6845/Joint+Statement+Second+Round+of+Expert+Level+Talks+between+India+and+Pakistan+on+Conventional+Confidence+Building+Measures, last accessed on 22 October 2018.

Appendix 8

Joint Statement, 3rd Round of Pakistan-India Expert Level Dialogue on Conventional CBMs

April 27, 2006

The third round of Pakistan-India Expert Level Dialogue on Conventional Confidence Building Measures (CBMs) was held in Islamabad on 27 April 2006. The Pakistan delegation was led by Mr. Tariq Osman Hyder, Additional Secretary (United Nations), Ministry of Foreign Affairs, and Mr. Dilip Sinha, Joint Secretary, Ministry of External Affairs, led the Indian delegation to the talks.

The two sides held discussions on Conventional CBMs in a cordial and constructive atmosphere.

As mandated by Foreign Secretaries the two sides continued consultations on security concepts to develop measures for confidence building in the conventional field aimed at avoidance of conflict.

As indicated in the Joint Statement of 18 January 2006, the Pakistan side presented a draft Agreement to the Indian side on the Prevention of Incidents at Sea in order to ensure safety of navigation by naval vessels, and aircraft belonging to the two sides.

The two sides agreed on the following CBMs aimed at avoidance of conflict:

1. Finalisation of Border Ground Rules for implementation along the international border.
2. Modalities for holding quarterly flag meetings, and on needs basis, at sector level commanders in already agreed sectors. Modalities for communication in this context would be further discussed.
3. Elaborating, consistent with its intent, the agreement reached on no development of new posts and defence works along the LoC.
4. Finalisation of an agreement on speedy return of inadvertent line crosser(s).

Both sides agreed to periodically discuss further CBMs and to review and monitor the implementation of existing Conventional CBMs as called for in the Lahore MoU of 1999 and as mandated by the Foreign Secretaries in the Composite Dialogue process. They also agreed to report the progress made in the present round of the talks to the respective Foreign Secretaries who will decide on the date and venue of the next Expert Level meeting on Conventional CBMs.

Islamabad
April 27, 2006

Source: 'Joint Statement, 3rd Round of Pakistan-India Expert Level Dialogue on Conventional CBMs', Ministry of External Affairs, Government of India, available at https://mea.gov.in/bilateral-documents.htm?dtl/6113/joint+statem ent+3rd+round+of+pakistanindia, last accessed on 22 October 2018.

Appendix 9

Joint Press Statement on Biannual Talks between Director Generals of BSF and Pakistan Rangers Held at New Delhi from 9–12 September 2015

Press Information Bureau
Government of India
Ministry of Home Affairs
12-September-2015 17:11 IST
Joint Press Statement on Bi-Annual talks-2015 between Director
Generals of BSF and Pakistan Rangers held at New Delhi
from 9th to 12th Sept 2015

During the Home Secretary Level Talks held at Islamabad, Pakistan in May 1989, in it was decided that officials of the Border Security Force (BSF) and Pakistan Rangers would hold Bi-Annual talks and review the implementation of the agreed norms of cooperation between the two Border Guarding Forces. It was envisaged that the top leadership of both the Border Guarding Forces will meet periodically and discuss issues of relevance to both the forces. Issues requiring coordinated efforts like dealing with Drug menace, smuggling, simultaneous coordinated patrolling, timely exchange of information etc. were to form the core of discussions.

The Pakistan Rangers are on a 4 day visit to India from 9th to 12th Sept 2015. Formal talks between the Border Security Force and Pakistan

Rangers this year began on 10th September at BSF headquarters, New Delhi. Major General Umar Farooq Burki, Director General, Pakistan Rangers (Punjab) led a 16 members Pakistani delegation to India. The 23 members' Indian delegation was led by Shri D K Pathak, IPS, DG BSF. Both the delegations also had 2 representatives from respective home & foreign ministries along with officers from narcotics control & survey department.

The talks were held in a constructive atmosphere. The need for cooperation to maintain the sanctity of the borders was stressed upon. The meeting took up specific issues of concern. Incidents of firing at the borders, smuggling of narcotics, infiltration attempts and defence construction activities were discussed. The issue of inadvertent crossing over by border population and on how to facilitate their return on both the sides was also discussed. The security of the border population being a primary concern of the both sides, it was felt that utmost caution and care would be taken to deal with the civilians. The need for confidence building measures including timely exchange of information, at the field level and mobile communication, simultaneous coordinated patrolling, and sporting events etc. were also discussed.

The Joint Record of Discussion charting a future route map of cooperation between the two Border Guarding Forces was signed earlier in the day today at 1100 hrs on September 12, 2015. It was mutually agreed to hold the next talks in the first half of 2016 in Pakistan. The talks ended on an optimistic note with both sides agreeing on constant endeavour to maintain peaceful and tranquil borders.

Source: 'Joint Statement, Second Round of Expert Level Talks between India and Pakistan on Conventional Confidence Building Measures', Ministry of External Affairs, Government of India, available at https://mea.gov.in/bilateral-documents.htm?dtl/6845/Joint+Statement+Second+Round+of+Expert+Level+Talks+between+India+and+Pakistan+on+Conventional+Confidence+Building+Measures, last accessed on 22 October 2018.

Bibliography

Abbas, S.S. "'India Violated Ceasefire Agreement More than 90 Times This Year', FO Claims'. *Dawn* (Online). 17 October 2016. Available at https://www.dawn.com/news/1290533 (accessed on 1 March 2017).

Allison, Graham T. *Essence of Decision: Explaining the Cuban Missile Crisis.* Boston: Little, Brown and Company, 1971.

Ansari, J. 'Ghatak Surgical Strikes Not First of its Kind, India Carried Several Similar Strikes in Last 10 years'. *India Today* (Online). 3 October 2016. Available at http://indiatoday.intoday.in/story/surgical-strikes-india-pakistan-loc-pok-indian-army-government/1/779426.html (accessed on 11 March 2017).

Ashiq, P. 'More IED Blasts in India than in Afghanistan, Syria: Report'. *Hindustan Times* (Online). 7 May 2015. Available at http://www.hindustantimes.com/india/more-ied-blasts-in-india-than-in-afghanistan-syria-report/story-a6OHsxDdjrmvvgL1R0YJvN.html (accessed on 10 June 2016).

Aziz, Sartaj. *Between Dreams and Realities: Some Milestones in Pakistan's History.* Karachi: Oxford University Press, 2009.

Bajwa, Farooq Naseem. *From Kutch to Tashkent: The Indo-Pakistan War of 1965.* London: Oxford University Press, 1965.

Bammi, Y.M. 'Revisiting the 1965 War'. *Journal of Defence Studies* 10, no. 2 (2016): 121–37.

Bangash, Y.K. 'Constructing the State: Constitutional Integration of the Princely States of Pakistan'. In *State and Nation-Building in Pakistan: Beyond Islam and Security*, edited by Roger D. Long, Gurharpal Singh, Yunas Samad, Ian Talbot. New York: Routledge, 2016.

Baruah, Amit and Sandeep Dikshit. 'India, Pak. Ceasefire Comes into Being'. *Hindu* (Online). 25 November 2003. Available at http://www.thehindu.com/2003/11/26/stories/2003112604940100.htm (accessed on 1 February 2017).

Bass, G.J. *The Blood Telegram: Nixon, Kissinger, and a Forgotten Genocide.* London: Hurst & Co, 2014.

BBC. '1971: Pakistan Intensifies Air Raids on India' (Online). 3 December 1971. Available at http://news.bbc.co.uk/onthisday/hi/dates/stories/december/3/newsid_2519000/2519133.stm (accessed on 5 January 2017).

———. 'How the Kashmir Crisis Began' (Online). 26 October 2007. Available at http://news.bbc.co.uk/2/hi/south_asia/7057694.stm (accessed on 21 June 2017).

———. 'India Says Dialogue under Stress' (Online). 21 July 2008. Available at http://news.bbc.co.uk/2/hi/south_asia/7517840.stm (accessed on 3 March 2017).

———. 'Kashmir: Indian Soldiers Killed in Pakistan Firing' (Online). 3 November 2015. Available at http://www.bbc.com/news/world-asia-india-34707217 (accessed on 19 December 2016).

Berry, Jeffrey M. 'Validity and Reliability Issues in Elite Interviewing'. *Political Science and Politics* 35, no. 4 (December 2002): 680.

Bhalla, A. 'Fratricide, Suicide Cases in the Army on the Rise'. *DNA* (Online). 19 July 2017. Available at http://www.dnaindia.com/india/report-fratricide-suicide-cases-in-the-army-on-the-rise-2506532 (accessed on 11 September 2017).

Bhalla, A. and Gautam Dutt. 'Islamabad Shocked as Indian Army Launches "Massive" Retaliation to Border Firing... and Confident PM Modi Promises "Everything will be all Right Soon"'. *Daily Mail* (Online). 9 October 2014. Available at http://www.dailymail.co.uk/indiahome/indianews/article-2785698/Islamabad-shocked-Indian-Army-launches-massive-retaliation-border-firing-confident-PM-Modi-promises-right-soon.html (accessed on 3 January 2017).

Bhasin, A.S. *India Pakistan Relations 1947–2011: A Documentary Study*. New Delhi: Geetika Publishers, 2012.

Bose, S. 'The Question of Genocide and the Quest for Justice in the 1971 War'. *Journal of Genocide Research* 13, no. 4 (2011): 393–419.

Brecher, M. *Crises in World Politics: Theory and Reality*. Oxford: Pergamon Press, 1993.

Brodie, B. *Escalation and the Nuclear Option*. New Jersey: Princeton University Press, 1996.

Bukhari, S. 2009. 'Senior BSF Officer Killed in Jammu Mine Blast'. *Hindu*(Online). 17 November 2009. Available at http://www.thehindu.com/news/national/Senior-BSF-officer-killed-in-Jammu-mine-blast/article16892528.ece (accessed on 11 March 2017).

———. 'Deathtraps along the Border'. *Friday Times*. (Online). 10 April 2015. Available at http://www.thefridaytimes.com/tft/deathtraps-along-the-border/ (accessed on 10 June 2016).

Carlson, L.J. 'A Theory of Escalation and International Conflict'. *Journal of Conflict Resolution* 39, no. 3 (1995): 511–34.

Center for Nonproliferation Studies. 'Lahore Declaration, 21 February 1999'. Nuclear Threat Initiative (Online). n.d. Available at http://www.nti.org/media/pdfs/aptlahore.pdf (accessed on 30 August 2017).

Chakravorty, B.C. *History of the Indo-Pak War, 1965*. New Delhi: History Division, Ministry of Defence, Government of India, 1992.

Chakravorty, P.K. '1965 War: Pakistan's Strategic Blunder'. Indian Army (Online). 2015. Available at https://indianarmy.nic.in/writereaddata/documents/Articles1965/PKChakravorty230915.pdf (accessed on 2 April 2017).

Chari, P.R. 'Kargil, LoC and the Simla Agreement'. Institute of Peace & Conflict Studies. (Online). 1999. Available at http://www.ipcs.org/article/indo-pak/kargil-loc-and-the-simla-agreement-210.html (accessed on 2 June 2017).

———. 'Nuclear Restraint, Nuclear Risk Reduction, and the Stability/Instability Paradox in South Asia'. In *The Stability/Instability Paradox: Nuclear Weapons and Brinksmanship in South Asia*, edited by Michael Krepon and Chris Gagne. Washington, DC: Henry L. Stimson Center, 2001.

Chaulia, S. 'Ceasefire Violation: How India Is Misreading the "Suicidal Logic" of Pakistani Army'. *Economic Times* (Online). 12 October 2014. Available at http://articles.economictimes.indiatimes.com/2014-10-12/news/54928928_1_pakistan-army-nawaz-sharif-pakistani (accessed on 12 October 2014).

Cheema, Pervez Iqbal. 'The Politics of the Punjab Boundary Award'. Heidelberg Paper no.1, South Asia Institute, Heidelberg Papers in South Asian and Comparative Politics, 2000.

Chester, L. *Borders and Conflict in South Asia: The Radcliffe Boundary Commission and the Partition of Punjab*. Manchester: Manchester University Press, 2009.

Cordera, S. 'India's Response to the 1971 East Pakistan Crisis: Hidden and Open Reasons for Intervention'. *Journal of Genocide Research* 17, no. 1 (2015): 45–62.

Dalton, T. and George Perkovich. 'India's Nuclear Options and Escalation Dominance'. Carnegie Endowment (Online). 2016. Available at http://carnegieendowment.org/2016/05/19/india-s-nuclear-options-and-escalation-dominance/iydh (accessed on 20 July 2017).

Daniyal, S. 'Role Reversal: When India Proposed a Plebiscite to Solve Kashmir—and Pakistan Rejected It'. *Scroll* (Online). 22 September 2016. Available at https://scroll.in/article/816661/role-reversal-when-india-proposed-a-plebiscite-to-solve-kashmir-and-pakistan-rejected-it (accessed on 22 September 2016).

Das, B.K. 'Pathankot Fallout: Laser Walls for Riverine Areas of Indo-Pak Border Soon'. *India Today* (Online). 30 November 1999. Available at http://

indiatoday.intoday.in/story/laser-walls-for-riverine-areas-of-indo-pak-border-soon/1/572478.html/ (accessed on 22 September 2017).

Das, P. 'Issues in the Management of the India–Pakistan International Border'. *Strategic Analysis* 38, no. 3 (2014): 307–24.

Dasgupta, C. *War and Diplomacy, 1947–48*. New Delhi: SAGE Publications, 2002.

Datta, R. 'Pak Planning Kargil Dobaara?' *Daily Pioneer*. (Online). 17 August 2013. Available at http://www.dailypioneer.com/todays-newspaper/pak-planning-kargil-dobaara.html (accessed on 11 March 2017).

Dawn. 'Pakistan Not to Accept Threats from India (Online). 17 May 2002. Available at https://www.dawn.com/news/34886/pakistan-not-to-accept-threats-from-india (accessed on 10 October 2018).

———. '1970 Polls: When Election Results created a Storm' (Online). 8 January 2012. Available at http://www.dawn.com/news/686541 (accessed on 5 January 2017).

———. 'Indian Premier Criticises Sharif over LoC Firing' (Online). 25 October 2013. Available at https://www.dawn.com/news/1051623 (accessed on 20 December 2016).

———. 'Woman Killed by Indian Firing' (Online). 12 August 2014. Available at https://www.dawn.com/news/1124787 (accessed on 19 December 2016).

———. 'India Kills 2 Troops Invited to Meeting' (Online). 1 January 2015. Available at https://www.dawn.com/news/1154352 (accessed on 10 June 2016).

———. 'India Is the only External Threat, Says Military' (Online). 28 August 2015. Available at https://www.dawn.com/news/1203329 (accessed on 7 January 2017).

———. 'LoC Firing Threat to International Peace, Says PM' (Online). 3 September 2015. Available at https://www.dawn.com/news/1204629 (accessed on 8 January 2017).

———. 'World Community Urged to Take Notice of Indian Firing at LoC' (Online). 4 September 2015. Available at https://www.dawn.com/news/1204837 (accessed on 8 January 2017).

———. 'Pakistan takes Issue of Ceasefire Violations to UN Security Council' (Online). 5 September 2015. Available at https://www.dawn.com/news/1205099 (accessed on 8 January 2017).

———. 'Freedom Fighters' Fighting in Kashmir, not Terrorists, Says Musharraf' (Online). 9 December 2015. Available at http://www.dawn.com/news/1225049 (accessed on 18 July 2017).

———. 'Army Reiterates Support for Right to Self Determination for Kashmiris across LOC' (Online). 10 June 2017. Available at https://www.dawn.com/news/1338673 (accessed on 26 December 2017).

————. 'Indian Deputy High Commissioner Summoned for Third Time this Month over Ceasefire Violations' (Online). 24 July 2017. Available at https://www.dawn.com/news/1347368 (accessed on 27 December 2017).

Dawn Wire Service. 'Pakistan Rejects Indian Charge' (Online). 2002. Available at https://asianstudies.github.io/area-studies/SouthAsia/SAserials/Dawn/2002/may182002.html (accessed on 10 October 2018).

Dawson, P. *The United Nations Military Observer Group in India and Pakistan (UNMOGIP) 1948–1965.* Bombay: Popular Prakashan, 1995.

Deccan Chronicle. 'Modi's J&K Rhetoric meant for Elections' (Online). 14 August 2014. Available at http://www.deccanchronicle.com/140814/commentary-op-ed/article/modi%E2%80%99s-jk-rhetoric-meant-elections (accessed on 3 January 2017).

————. 'Hours before Modi's Visit to J&K, Pak Violates Ceasefire, BSF Retaliates' (Online). 19 April 2016. Available at http://www.deccanchronicle.com/nation/current-affairs/190416/hours-before-modi-s-visit-to-j-k-pak-violates-ceasefire-bsf-retaliates.html (accessed on 3 January 2017).

————. 'No Comments, Says MEA on Foreign Secy's Remark on Surgical Strike' (Online). 20 October 2016. Available at http://www.deccanchronicle.com/nation/current-affairs/201016/no-comments-says-mea-on-foreign-secys-remark-on-surgical-strike.html?fromNewsdog=1 (accessed on 11 March 2017).

————. 'Army Jawan Killed in Pak Sniper Firing in Kashmir' (Online). 9 November 2016. Available at http://www.deccanchronicle.com/nation/current-affairs/091116/army-jawan-killed-in-pak-sniper-firing-in-kashmir.html (accessed on 21 September 2017).

————. 'Pak Army "Laid Death Trap" 250 mts Inside J&K, Beheaded 2 Indian Jawans' (Online). 1 May 2017. Available at https://www.deccanchronicle.com/nation/current-affairs/010517/pak-forces-sneaked-into-jk-beheaded-2-indian-soldiers-senior-army-officer.html (accessed on 25 December 2017).

Dikshit, S. 'Sir Creek Dispute: India, Pakistan for Early Resolution'. *Hindu* (Online). 8 August 2004. Available at http://www.thehindu.com/2004/08/08/stories/2004080806920100.htm (accessed on 8 August 2004).

Dixit, J.N. *India-Pakistan in War and Peace.* London: Routledge, 2002.

DNA. 'Even as India Lodges Protest, Pakistan Targets Border Villages with Mortar Bombs' (Online). 16 July 2015. Available at http://www.dnaindia.com/india/report-even-as-india-lodges-protest-pakistan-targets-border-villages-with-mortar-bombs-2105047 (accessed on 11 March 2017).

————. 'Ceasefire Violations: Pak Envoy Abdul Basit Blames India even as Firing Continues' (Online). 16 August 2015. Available at http://www.dnaindia.

com/india/report-ceasefire-violations-pak-envoy-abdul-basit-blames-india-even-as-firing-continues-2115049 (accessed on 22 December 2017).

DNA. 'Pakistan Provokes India again, Kills Labourer on International Border' (Online). 24 October 2015. Available at http://www.dnaindia.com/india/report-pakistan-provokes-india-again-kills-labourer-on-international-border-2137893 (accessed on 3 April 2016).

———. 'Surgical Strikes also Carried out under Manmohan Singh, We Never Publicised It: Congress' (Online). 2 October 2016. Available at http://www.dnaindia.com/india/report-surgical-strikes-als-carried-out-under-manmohan-singh-we-never-pubilcised-it-congress-2260658 (accessed on 11 March 2017).

———. 'Soldiers Mutilation: Indian Army Retaliating to Pakistani Aggression, Says Army Chief Bipin Rawat'. 4 May 2017. Available at http://www.dnaindia.com/india/report-soldiers-mutilation-we-don-t-talk-about-future-plans-beforehand-says-army-chief-on-possible-action-2427200 (accessed on 25 December 2017).

Dogar, B. and R. Roy. 'Kashmir Solution just a Signature Away: Kasuri'. Aman Ki Asha (Online). n.d. Available at www.amankiasha.com (accessed on 2 April 2017).

Dulat, A.S. and A. Sinha. *Kashmir: The Vajpayee Years*. New Delhi: Harper Collins, 2015.

Dutta, S. '"DNA" Exclusive: Uri Commander's Forceful Retaliation led to Beheadings?' DNA (Online). 10 January 2013. Available at http://www.dnaindia.com/india/report-dna-exclusive-uri-commander-s-forceful-retaliation-led-to-beheadings-1787448 (accessed on 5 December 2017).

Economic Times. 'Osama bin Laden Dead: Pakistan Warns US, India against Covert Operations' (Online). 5 May 2011. Available at http://economictimes.indiatimes.com/news/politics-and-nation/osama-bin-laden-dead-pakistan-warns-us-india-against-covert-operations/articleshow/8169040.cms (accessed on 8 December 2016).

———. 'Pakistan Targets 15 Border Outposts, Shells Villages in Jammu' (Online). 20 July 2014. Available at http://articles.economictimes.indiatimes.com/2014-07-20/news/51780181_1_pakistan-rangers-ceasefire-violation-s-pura (accessed on 11 March 2017).

———. 'Kargil "Misadventure", was "Stab" in Atal Vajpayee's Back: Nawaz Sharif' (Online). 18 February 2016. Available at http://economictimes.indiatimes.com/news/defence/kargil-misadventure-was-stab-in-atal-vajpayees-back-nawaz-sharif/articleshow/51035959.cms (accessed on 15 January 2017).

———. 'BSF may be Withdrawn from LoC, Deployed to Secure Indo-Pak International Border' (Online). 15 March 2016. Available at http://

economictimes.indiatimes.com/news/defence/bsf-may-be-withdrawn-from-loc-deployed-to-secure-indo-pak-international-border/articleshow/51416201.cms (accessed on 25 June 2017).

———. 'India–Pakistan Border to soon have Smart Fencing: Kiren Rijiju' (Online). 2017. Available at http://economictimes.indiatimes.com/news/defence/india-pakistan-border-to-soon-have-smart-fencing-kiren-rijiju/articleshow/56940473.cms (accessed on 22 September 2017).

———. 'Will Continue Giving Befitting Reply: Army Vice Chief on Ceasefire Violation by Pakistan' (Online). 5 February 2018. Available at https://economictimes.indiatimes.com/news/defence/will-continue-giving-befitting-reply-army-vice-chief-on-ceasefire-violation-by-pakistan/articleshow/62787673.cms (accessed on 6 February 2018).

Express Tribune. 'Unprovoked Firing: Deaths Mount as BSF Shells Pak Villages' (Online). 10 October 2014. Available at https://tribune.com.pk/story/773176/unprovoked-firing-deaths-mount-as-bsf-shells-pak-villages/ (accessed on 25 December 2014)

———. 'FO's Weekly Briefing: India's Belligerence Threat to Regional Peace' (Online). 8 June 2017. Available at https://tribune.com.pk/story/1430469/pakistan-warns-india-strategic-miscalculation/ (accessed on 26 December 2017).

Farrell, B.R. 'The Security Council and Kashmir'. *Transnational Law & Contemporary Problems* 22 (2013): 343.

Fayyaz, A.A. 'Five Indian Soldiers Killed near LoC'. *Hindu* (Online). 6 August 2013. Available at http://www.thehindu.com/news/national/five-indian-soldiers-killed-near-loc/article4995032.ece (accessed on 8 December 2017).

Financial Express. 'One Year of Surgical Strikes: Indian Army Says It Will Cross LoC Again if Required' (Online). 7 September 2017. Available at http://www.financialexpress.com/india-news/big-blow-for-pakistan-indian-army-threatens-more-surgical-strikes-says-will-cross-loc-if-required/844925/ (accessed on 23 October 2017).

Firstpost. 'Full Text: Pakistan National Assembly Resolution against India' (Online). 14 August 2013. Available at http://www.firstpost.com/world/full-text-pakistan-national-assembly-resolution-against-india-1032179.html (accessed on 19 December 2016).

———. 'Ceasefire Violation along LoC: India–Pakistan Bus Services Halted from Poonch as Tension Escalates' (Online). 10 July 2017. Available at https://www.firstpost.com/india/ceasefire-violation-along-loc-india-pakistan-bus-services-halted-from-poonch-as-tension-escalates-3796803.html (accessed on 27 December 2017).

Frontline. 'Ceasefire Violations' (Online). 2013. Available at http://www.frontline. in/the-nation/ceasefire-violations/article5037702.ece (accessed on 12 January 2017).

Ganguly, S. 'Indo-Pakistani Nuclear Issues and the Stability/Instability Paradox'. *Studies in Conflict and Terrorism* 18, no. 4 (October–December 1995).

———. 'Conflict and Crisis in South and Southwest Asia'. In *The International Dimensions of Internal Conflict*, edited by Michael E. Brown. Cambridge, MA: MIT Press, 1996.

———. 'Nuclear Stability in South Asia'. *International Security* 33, no. 2 (2008): 45–70.

———. *Deadly Impasse: Indo-Pakistani Relations at the Dawn of a New Century*, Cambridge: Cambridge University Press, 2016.

George, Varghese K. 'Battlefield Nuke Deployment by Pakistan Raises Risk: U.S'. *Hindu.* 30 March 2016.

Ghose, D. 'Why Is Pakistan Violating Ceasefire along LoC? Because it Needs to Prop up India as External Enemy, Say Experts'. Firstpost (Online). 18 August 2015. Available at http://www.firstpost.com/india/why-is-pakistan-violating-ceasefire-along-loc-because-it-needs-to-prop-up-india-as-external-enemy-say-experts-2396422.html (accessed on 3 January 2017).

Gill, John H. 'Military Operations in the Kargil Conflict'. In *Asymmetric Warfare in South Asia: The Causes and Consequences of the Kargil Conflict*, edited by Peter R. Lavoy. New Delhi: Cambridge University Press, 2009, 95.

Gokhale, N. 'Blog: Suicides in Army – A Comprehensive Review Needed'. NDTV (Online). 11 August 2012. Available at http://www.ndtv.com/india-news/blog-suicides-in-army-a-comprehensive-review-needed-496357 (accessed on 11 March 2017).

———. 'India Warns Pakistan it's Not Afraid of Escalating Fire: Sources' NDTV (Online). 8 October 2014. Available at https://www.ndtv.com/cheat-sheet/india-warns-pakistan-its-not-afraid-of-escalating-fire-sources-676560 (accessed on 25 December 2016).

Government of India. *Official History of the 1971 War*. New Delhi: History Division, Ministry of Defence.

Guardian. 'US Embassy Cables: India "Unlikely" to Deploy Cold Start against Pakistan' (Online). 16 February 2010. Available at http://www.theguardian.com/world/us-embassy-cables-documents/248971 (accessed on 17 July 2017).

Guha, R. *India after Gandhi: The History of the World's Largest Democracy*. New Delhi: Picador, 2007.

Gupta, S. 'Provoked? A Look at the Indo-Pak Relationship'. *Hindustan Times* (Online). 13 January 2013. Available at http://www.hindustantimes.

com/delhi/provoked-a-look-at-the-indo-pak-relationship/story-uq3orbhbUCFhu9ztmpVsBJ.html (accessed on 11 March 2017).

Haidar, S. 'India–Pak. Talks Are Off'. *Hindu* (Online). 18 August 2014. Available at http://www.thehindu.com/news/national/india-calls-off-foreign-secretarylevel-talks-with-pakistan/article6329082.ece (accessed on 19 December 2016).

———. 'As Sparring Worsens, NSA Talks Are Off'. *Hindu* (Online). 22 August 2015. Available at http://www.thehindu.com/news/international/south-asia/indiapakistan-national-security-advisorlevel-talks-called-off/article7569679.ece (accessed on 6 January 2017).

———. 'India, Pakistan nearly Agreed on Siachen Three Times: Shyam Saran'. *Hindu* (Online). 6 September 2017. Available at http://www.thehindu.com/news/national/india-pakistan-nearly-agreed-on-siachen-three-times-shyam-saran/article19631457.ece?homepage=true (accessed on 5 January 2017).

Haider, M. 'Pakistan Warns India against Issuing "Provocative" Statements'. *Dawn* (Online). 13 December 2014. Available at https://www.dawn.com/news/1150648 (accessed on 16 December 2016).

Hasnain, S. A. 'Meeting Point'. *Indian Express* (Online). 9 January 2014. Available at http://indianexpress.com/article/opinion/columns/meeting-point-4/ (accessed on 10 June 2016).

———. 'Looking beyond a Tattered Truce'. *Hindu* (Online). 1 September 2014. Available at http://www.thehindu.com/opinion/op-ed/looking-beyond-a-tattered-truce/article6367256.ece (accessed on 21 March 2017).

———. 'The LoC/IB and Fire Assaults: What's this all About?' *Daily Excelsior* (Online). 2 November 2016. Available at http://www.dailyexcelsior.com/locib-fire-assaults-whats/ (accessed on 3 September 2017).

Hindu. 'Pakistan Situation Worrisome' (Online). 26 May 2011. Available at http://www.thehindu.com/news/national/pakistan-situation-worrisome/article2048859.ece (accessed on 8 December 2016).

———. 'UN Mission in Kashmir Can Be Terminated Only by UNSC' (Online). 23 January 2013. Available at http://www.thehindu.com/news/national/un-mission-in-kashmir-can-be-terminated-only-by-unsc/article4335377.ece (accessed on 23 January 2016).

———. 'Pakistan Violates Ceasefire, Objects to Construction on Indian Side' (Online). 30 November 2014. Available at http://www.thehindu.com/news/national/pakistan-violates-ceasefire-objects-to-construction-on-indian-side/article6648688.ece (accessed on 23 March 2017).

———. 'Woman Killed as Pak Rangers Violate Ceasefire' (Online). 15 July 2015. Available at http://www.thehindu.com/news/national/bsf-jawan-injured-in-firing-by-pakistan-rangers/article7424706.ece (accessed on 21 September 2017).

Hindu. 'India Prepared for Military Action, Says Army Chief' (Online). 1 September 2015. Available at http://www.thehindu.com/news/national/india-needs-to-be-prepared-for-military-action-says-army-chief-dalbir-singh/article7603623.ece (accessed on 8 January 2017).

———. 'India Responds to Nawaz Sharif's U.N. Speech' (Online). 1 October 2015. Available at http://www.thehindu.com/news/national/india-responds-to-nawaz-sharifs-speech-at-un/article7710260.ece (accessed on 3 March 2017).

———. 'Remember 1971, Venkaiah Tells Pakistan' (Online). 23 July 2017. Available at http://www.thehindu.com/news/national/remember-1971-venkaiah-tells-pakistan/article19337957.ece (accessed on 27 December 2017).

Hindustan Times. 'BSF, Pak Rangers Reach Consensus during Meeting in Lahore: MEA' (Online). 28 July 2016. Available at http://www.hindustantimes.com/india-news/bsf-pak-rangers-reach-consensus-during-meeting-in-lahore-mea/story-jceTV9lb66rIZlVSkDDvVN.html (accessed on 10 June 2017).

———. 'Soldier Inadvertently Crossed LoC, Pak Has Been Informed: Indian Army Source' (Online). 30 September 2016. Available at http://www.hindustantimes.com/india-news/soldier-inadvertently-crosses-loc-pak-has-been-informed-indian-army-source/story-XlTFmHzcPSRbTa1UytmNtN.html (accessed on 1 December 2016).

Holsti, O.R. *Crisis, Escalation, War.* Montreal: McGill-Queens University Press, 1972.

Hussain, A. 'India Wants to Discuss Only Terrorism, NA Body Told'. Business Recorder (Online). 2017. Available at http://epaper.brecorder.com/m/2015/10/28/11-page/538022-news.html (accessed 22 December 2017).

Hussain, F. '"Cold or Hot Start", Pakistan Army Is Ready for Anything: General Raheel Sharif'. *Daily Pakistan* (Online). 6 September 2016. Available at https://en.dailypakistan.com.pk/headline/we-are-mindful-of-our-enemies-nefarious-designs-army-chief-gen-raheel-sharif/ (accessed on 10 January 2017).

Hussain, S. 'Pak Forces Capable of Defeating All Threats Irrespective of', *Outlook* (Online). 10 June 2017. Available at https://www.outlookindia.com/newsscroll/pak-forces-capable-of-defeating-all-threats-irrespective-of/1072415 (accessed on 3 October 2018).

Ilahi, Shereen. 'The Radcliffe Boundary Commission and the Fate of Kashmir'. *India Review* 2, no. 1 (2003): 77–102.

'India and Pakistan: Agreement on Cease-Fire in Rann of Kutch'. *International Legal Materials* 4, no. 5 (1965): 921–3.

India. 'BSF Jawan Killed in Pakistan Shelling along International Border in Samba' (Online). 5 January 2015. Available at http://www.india.com/news/india/bsf-jawan-killed-in-pakistan-shelling-along-international-border-in-samba-239519/ (accessed on 25 December 2016).

Indian Express. 'Over 100 Militants Waiting at Launch Pads to Enter J-K' (Online). 8 May 2011. Available at http://indianexpress.com/article/india/latest-news/over-100-militants-waiting-at-launch-pads-to-enter-jk/ (accessed on 8 December 2016).

———. 'India, Pakistan Not at "Resumed Talks" Stage: Salman Khurshid (Online). 12 October 2013. Available at http://archive.indianexpress.com/news/india-pakistan-Not-at-resumed-talks-stage-salman-khurshid/1181709/ (accessed on 19 December 2016).

———. 'Pakistan Rangers not Accepting Protest Notes over Ceasefire: BSF' (Online). 6 January 2015. Available at http://indianexpress.com/article/india/india-others/pakistan-rangers-not-accepting-protest-notes-over-ceasefire-bsf/ (accessed on 6 January 2015).

———. 'Surgical Strikes: Full Text of Indian Army DGMO Lt Gen Ranbir Singh's Press Conference' (Online). 29 September 2016. Available at http://indianexpress.com/article/india/india-news-india/pakistan-infiltration-attempts-indian-army-surgical-strikes-line-of-control-jammu-and-kashmir-uri-poonch-pok-3055874/ (accessed on 11 March 2017).

———. 'Soldier Chandu Chavan, Who Inadvertently Strayed across LoC in 2016, Handed over to India' (Online). 21 January 2017. Available at http://indianexpress.com/article/india/pakistan-army-announces-return-of-indian-soldier-who-crossed-over-loc-accidentally-4485043/ (accessed on 16 September 2016).

———. 'Mutilating of Jawans "Pre-planned Operation by Pakistan Army"' (Online). 1 May 2017. Available at http://indianexpress.com/article/india/mutilating-of-jawans-pre-planned-operation-by-pakistan-army/ (accessed on 12 August 2017).

———. 'India Retaliating Appropriately to Pak Ceasefire Violations: Nirmala Sitharaman' (Online). 5 March 2018. Available at http://indianexpress.com/article/india/india-retaliating-appropriately-to-pak-ceasefire-violations-nirmala-sitharaman-5087242/ (last accessed on 5 March 2018).

'Indian Independence Act 1947' (Online). 1947. Available at http://www.legislation.gov.uk/ukpga/1947/30/pdfs/ukpga_19470030_en.pdf (accessed on 25 February 2017).

India Today. 'JCO Killed in Sniper Fire from Pakistan at LoC' (Online). 25 August 2015. Available at http://indiatoday.intoday.in/story/jco-killed-in-sniper-fire-from-pakistan-at-loc/1/460916.html (accessed on 21 September 2017).

India TV. 'Army Jawan Injured in Mine Blast along LoC in Jammu and Kashmir' (Online). 14 December 2014. Available at http://www.indiatvnews.com/news/india/army-jawan-injured-in-mine-blast-along-loc-in-jammu-and-kashmir-45221.html (accessed on 10 June 2016).

Institute of Defence Studies and Analyses. 'Ask an Expert, "Abhinav Upadhyay asked: In the backdrop of recent skirmishes along the LoC, how can India create strong disincentives for such hostile actions by Pakistan?"' (Online). n.d. Available at http://www.idsa.in/askanexpert/recentskirmishesalongtheLoC (accessed on 22 December 2016).

Inter-Services Public Relations. 'PR-94/2011-ISPR' (Online). 2011. Available at https://www.ispr.gov.pk/front/main.asp?o=t-press_release&id=1721 (accessed on 6 February 2016).

———. 'Press Release "No PR-211/2013-ISPR"' (Online). 2017. Available at https://www.ispr.gov.pk/front/t-press_release.asp?date=2013/12/24 &print=1 (accessed on 10 March 2017).

Jacob, Happymon. 'Conceptualizing Nuclear Learning: A Study of the Indian Experience'. In *Nuclear Learning in South Asia: The Next Decade*, edited by Feroz Hassan Khan, Ryan Jacobs, and Emily Burke. Monterey: Naval Postgraduate School, 2014.

———. 'A Peaceful Way out of Siachen'. *Hindu* (Online). 11 February 2016. Available at http://www.thehindu.com/opinion/lead/A-peaceful-way-out-on-Siachen/article15617657.ece (accessed on 11 February 2016).

———. 'The Pathankot Paradigm'. *Hindu* (Online). 2 April 2016. Available at http://www.thehindu.com/opinion/lead/The-Pathankot-paradigm/article14213873.ece (accessed on 1 July 2017).

———. 'A Year of Living Dangerously'. *Hindu* (Online). 22 December 2016. Available at http://www.thehindu.com/opinion/lead/A-year-of-living-dangerously/article16919538.ece/ucbrowser/?hbt=uc (accessed on 1 December 2017)

———. 'A Christmas Course Correction'. *Hindu* (Online). 29 December 2016. Available at http://www.thehindu.com/todays-paper/tp-opinion/a-christmas-course-correction/article8038253.ece (accessed on 1 July 2017).

———. *Ceasefire Violations in Jammu and Kashmir: A Line on Fire, Peaceworks.* Washington, DC: United States Institute of Peace, 2017.

———. 'Diary of a Very Long Year'. *Hindu.* 26 September 2017.

———. 'Time to Consider a Trilateral Asian ABM Treat'. Stimson (Online). 2017. Available at https://www.stimson.org/sites/default/files/file-attachments/Happymon%20Jacob_Off%20Ramps%20Essay-FINAL.pdf (accessed on 1 December 2017).

———. 'The India Pakistan Nuclear Dyad: Strategic Stability and Cross-Domain Deterrence'. In *The End of Strategic Stability? Nuclear Weapons and the Challenge of Regional Rivalries*, edited by Lawrence Rubin and Adam Stulberg. Washington, DC: Georgetown University Press, 2018.

———. 'The Strategy of Conflict'. *Hindu* (Online). 16 March 2018. Available at http://www.thehindu.com/opinion/lead/the-strategy-of-conflict/article23264085.ece?homepage=true (accessed on 20 March 2018).

———. 'Data Exposes what India & Pakistan Don't Reveal about the Constant "Ceasefire Violations"'. *Print* (Online). 3 April 2018. Available at https://theprint.in/opinion/india-pakistan-constant-ceasefire-violations/46434/ (accessed on 3 April 2018).

Jacobs, Frank. 'Peacocks at Sunset'. *New York Times* (Online). 3 July 2012. Available at https://opinionator.blogs.nytimes.com/2012/07/03/peacocks-at-sunset (accessed on 3 July 2012).

Jameel, Yusuf and Sanjib K.R. Baruah. 'Pakistani Forces Kill, Mutilate 2 Soldiers; India Retaliates'. *Asian Age*. 2 May 2017. Available at http://www.asianage.com/india/all-india/020517/pak-forces-kill-mutilate-2-soldiers-india-retaliates.html (accessed on 25 December 2017).

Jammu-Kashmir Now. 'Kargil War Briefing: Live from Kargil War Memorial'. YouTube (video). 2014. Available at https://www.youtube.com/watch?v=nfGST9O2vA0 (accessed on 10 October 2017).

Jose, B. 'All Options against Pakistan Open, Says Army Chief General Bipin Rawat'. *India Today* (Online). 6 June 2017. Available at http://indiatoday.intoday.in/story/general-bipin-rawat-pakistan-ceasefire-violations-terror/1/971780.html (accessed on 5 August 2017).

Joshi, M. 'Why India Insists on Keeping Gilgit Baltistan Firmly in the Kashmir Equation'. *Wire* (Online). 2 June 2015. Available at https://thewire.in/3018/why-india-is-bringing-gilgit-baltistan-back-into-the-kashmir-equation/ (accessed on 2 June 2015).

Joshi, S. 'India's Military Instrument: A Doctrine Stillborn'. *Journal of Strategic Studies* 36, no. 4 (2013): 512–40.

Joshua, A. 'Non-papers Exchanged on Sir Creek Issue'. *Hindu* (Online). 21 May 2011. Available at http://www.thehindu.com/news/national/nonpapers-exchanged-on-sir-creek issue/article2037946.ece (accessed on 21 May 2011).

Kahn, H. *On Escalation: Metaphors and Scenarios*. New York: Praeger, 1965.

Kakakhel, I. 'Lower House Blasts India over Ceasefire Violations at LoC'. *Daily Times* (Online). 19 November 2016. Available at http://dailytimes.com.pk/pakistan/19-Nov-16/lower-house-blasts-india-over-ceasefire-violations-at-loc (accessed on 22 March 2017).

Kanwal, G. 'Pakistan's Strategic Blunder at Kargil'. *CLAWS Journal* 1 (Summer 2009): 55. Available at http://www.claws.in/images/journals_doc/1400824835Gurmeet%20Kanwal%20CJ%20SSummer%202009.pdf (accessed on 15 September 2015).

———. 'Worst-Case Scenarios: What Would Happen if Indo-Pak War Breaks Out?' *Hindustan Times* (Online). 8 October 2015. Available at http://www.hindustantimes.com/analysis/indo-pak-tensions-a-fictional-nuclear-war-scenario/story-gundIhC1iC0amJjMFYo3AN.html (accessed on 29 July 2017).

Kapur, S.P. 'India and Pakistan's Unstable Peace: Why Nuclear South Asia Is Not Like Cold War Europe'. *International Security* 30, no. 2 (2005): 127–52.

Karl, D.J. 'Lessons for Proliferation Scholarship in South Asia: The Buddha Smiles Again'. *Asian Survey* 41, no. 6 (2001): 1002–22.

Kasuri, K.M. *Neither a Hawk nor a Dove: An Insider's Account of Pakistan's Foreign Policy.* Oxford: Oxford University Press, 2015.

Kaufman, W. 'Limited War'. In *Military Policy and National Security*, edited by William Kaufman. Princeton, NJ: Princeton University Press, 1956.

Khajuria, Amit 'Shelling Spreads along Entire IB'. *Tribune* (Online). 23 May 2018. Available at https://www.tribuneindia.com/news/jammu-kashmir/shelling-spreads-along-entire-ib/593607.html (accessed on 25 May 2018).

Khajuria, Amit and Arteev Sharma '5 Killed, 90,000 Displaced along IB'. *Tribune* (Online). 24 May 2018. Available at https://www.tribuneindia.com/news/jammu-kashmir/5-killed-90-000-displaced-along-ib/594110.html (accessed on 25 May 2018).

Khajuria, R.K. 'Pakistan's latest Barbaric Act: Bodies of Two Indian Soldiers Mutilated, Army Vows Appropriate Response'. *Hindustan Times* (Online). 28 May 2017. Available at http://www.hindustantimes.com/india-news/pakistan-mutilates-bodies-of-two-indian-soldiers-army-vows-revenge/story-MuI5fTZdmRyavJNnAqwlPI.html (accessed on 28 May 2017).

Khan, F. 'The Rann of Kutch Dispute'. *Pakistan Horizon* 18, no. 4 (1965): 374–84.

———. 'The Rann of Kutch Award'. *Pakistan Horizon* 21, no. 2 (1968): 123–33.

Khan, F.H. 'South Asian Stability Workshop, A Crisis Simulation Exercise' (Online). 2013. Available at https://calhoun.nps.edu/bitstream/handle/10945/37069/2013%20008%20South%20Asian%20Stability%20Workshop.pdf;sequence=4 (accessed on 29 July 2017).

'Khalid Kidwai: Nuclear Risks in South Asia' [online video]. 2015. Available at https://pugwash.org/2015/11/02/video-gen-kidwai-on-nuclear-risks-in-south-asia-nagasaki-conference/ (accessed on 8 August 2016).

Knopf, J.W. 'Recasting the Proliferation Optimism-Pessimism Debate'. *Security Studies* 12, no. 1 (2002): 41–96.

———. 'The Concept of Nuclear Learning'. *Nonproliferation Review* 19, no. 1 (2012): 79–93.

Krepon, M. 'The Stability-Instability Paradox, Misperception and Escalation Control in South Asia'. Stimson (Online). 2003. Available at https://www.stimson.org/sites/default/files/file-attachments/stability-instability-paradox-south-asia.pdf (accessed on 4 September 2016).

Krepon, Michael, Rodney W. Jones, and Ziad Haider, eds. *Escalation Control and the Nuclear Option in South Asia*. Washington, DC: Henry L. Stimson Center, 2004.

Kulkarni, T. and Happymon Jacob. 'Sir Creek: A Disputed Yet Well Managed Border', BSF's Borderman, 2017.

Kumar V. 'We will Retaliate if Provoked further, Says Army Chief'. *Hindu* (Online). 14 January 2013. Available at http://www.thehindu.com/news/national/we-will-retaliate-if-provoked-further-says-army-chief/article4306810.ece (accessed on 19 December 2016).

Kumar, P. 'Sir Creek Row Began Over Pile Firewood'. *Asian Age* 10 November (1998).

Kux, Dennis. *India and the United States: Estranged Democracies, 1941–91*. New Delhi: Sage, 1994.

Kyndiah, P.R. '"Landmine Casualty", Lok Sabha, Unstarred Question' (Online). 2002. Available at http://pib.nic.in/newsite/erelcontent.aspx?relid=6008 (accessed on 14 May 2017).

Ladwig III, W.C. 'A Cold Start for Hot Wars? The Indian Army's New Limited War Doctrine'. *International Security* 32, no. 3 (2008): 158–90.

Lakshmi, R. 'India's Border Fence Extended to Kashmir'. *Washington Post* (Online). 30 July 2003. Available at https://www.washingtonpost.com/archive/politics/2003/07/30/indias-border-fence-extended-to-kashmir/39e3e816-9704-4a3b-8d6c-fd46123ce005/?utm_term=.390d52c3e317 (accessed on 10 June 2016).

Lavoy, P., ed. *Asymmetric Warfare in South Asia: The Causes and Consequences of the Kargil Conflict*. Cambridge: Cambridge University Press, 2009.

Legro, J.W. 'Military Culture and Inadvertent Escalation in World War II'. *International Security* 18, no. 4 (1994): 108–42.

Leng, Russell J. 'Competing Perspectives and Empirical Evidence'. *International Studies Review* 6, no. 4 (December 2004): 56.

Malhotra, Inder. 'The Collapse of the Shimla Accord'. *Indian Express* (Online). 9 June 2014. Available at http://indianexpress.com/article/opinion/columns/the-collapse-of-the-shimla-accord/ (accessed on 9 June 2014).

Malik, V.P. 'Limited War and Escalation Control – I' (Online). 2004. Available at http://www.ipcs.org/article/nuclear/limited-war-and-escalation-control-i-1570.html (accessed on 17 July 2017).

———. *Kargil-From Surprise to Victory*. New Delhi: Harper Collins, 2010.

Mann, S.S. '"Ban on Landmines"'. Lok Sabha, Unstarred Question 2599' (Online). 2002. Available at http://mea.gov.in/lok-sabha.htm?dtl/13427/Q+2599Ban+on+Landmines (accessed on 4 June 2017).

Mehta, A.K. 'A Line without Ceasefires'. *Hindu* (Online). 18 October 2014. Available at http://www.thehindu.com/opinion/lead/a-line-without-cease fires/article6512297.ece (accessed on 22 December 2016).

Mehta, P.B. 'Reluctant India: India and the Politics of Democracy Promotion'. *Journal of Democracy* 22, no. 4 (2011): 97–109.

Menon, S. *Choices: Inside the Making of Indian Foreign Policy*. New Delhi: Penguin Random House India, 2016.

Ministry of Defence. *Annual Report 2014–15*. New Delhi: Government of India, n.d. Available at http://ddpmod.gov.in/sites/default/files/Annual%20report%202014-2015.pdf (accessed on 27 June 2017)

———. *Annual Report 2015–16*. New Delhi: Government of India, n.d. Available at http://ddpmod.gov.in/sites/default/files/Annual%20Report%20MOD_2016.pdf (accessed on 27 June 2017).

———. *Annual Report 2016–17*. New Delhi: Government of India, n.d. Available at http://www.mod.nic.in/writereaddata/AnnualReport1617.pdf (accessed on 27 June 2017).

Ministry of External Affairs. *Annual Report 2015–16*. New Delhi: Government of India, n.d. Available at https://www.mea.gov.in/Uploads/PublicationDocs/26525_26525_External_Affairs_English_AR_2015-16_Final_compressed.pdf (accessed on 27 June 2017).

———. 'Agreement between Military Representatives of India and Pakistan Regarding the Establishment of Cease-Fire Line in the State of Jammu and Kashmir' (Online). 1949. Available at http://mea.gov.in/bilateral-documents.htm?dtl/5252/Agreement+relating+to+Ceasefire+Line+in+JampK (accessed on 21 June 2017).

———. 'Agreed Minutes of the Meeting on Border Incidents and Shrines' (Online). 1955. Available at http://mea.gov.in/bilateral-documents.htm?dtl/7714/Agreed+Minutes+of+the+Meeting+on+Border+Incidents+and+Shrines (accessed on 8 July 2017).

———. 'Agreement between Governments of India and Pakistan Regarding Procedures to End Disputes and Incidents Along the Indo-East Pakistan

Border Areas' (Online). 1959. Available at http://mea.gov.in/bilateral-documents.htm?dtl/6179/Agreement+regarding+Procedures+to+End+Border+Disputes+E+Pakistan (accessed on 11 August 2016).

———. 'Shri U. N. Chakravarty's Letter to Security Council on Kashmir' (Online). 1964. Available at http://mealib.nic.in/?pdf2552?000 (accessed on 12 September 2016).

———. 'Defence Minister, Shri Y. B. Chavan's Statement in Parliament on August 16, 1965' (Online). 1965. Available at http://mealib.nic.in/?pdf2553?000 (accessed on 25 June 2017).

———. 'Tashkent Declaration Signed by Prime Minister of India and President of Pakistan, 10 January 1966' (Online). 1966. Available at http://mea.gov.in/bilateral-documents.htm?dtl/5993/Tashkent+Declaration (accessed on 21 June 2017).

———. 'Note Verbale from the Swiss Embassy in New Delhi to the Ministry of External Affairs Conveying a Message from the Government of Pakistan' (Online). 1971. Available at http://mea.gov.in/Images/pdf/India-Pakistan-std.pdf (accessed on 11 January 2017).

———. 'Clarifications on the LOC' (Online). 1972. Available at http://mea.gov.in/in-focus-article.htm?19004/Clarifications+on+LoC (accessed on 5 January 2017).

———. 'Simla Agreement, 2 July 1972' (Online). 1972. Available at http://mea.gov.in/in-focus-article.htm?19005/Simla+Agreement+July+2+1972 (accessed on 25 January 2017).

———. 'Shri B. N. Chakravarty's Letter to the President of Security Council on Kashmir' (Online). 1995. Available at http://mealib.nic.in/?pdf2552?000 (accessed on 22 June 2017).

———. 'Statement in the Lok Sabha on May 12, 1972 by the Minister of Defence, Shri Jagjivan Ram' (Online). 1995. Available at http://mealib.nic.in/?pdf2560?000 (accessed on 25 June 2017).

———. 'Joint Statement, India–Pakistan Discussions on Opening of Crossing Points across the LoC, October 29, 2005' (Online). 2005. Available at http://bit.ly/2aVmVYN (accessed on 4 June 2017)

———. 'Joint Press Statement, India–Pakistan talks on Sir Creek, May 26, 2006' (Online). 2006. Available at http://mea.gov.in/bilateral-documents.htm?dtl/6165/Joint+Press+Statement+IndiaPakistan+talks+on+Sir+Creek (accessed on 21 June 2017).

———. 'Joint Statement, 3rd Round of Pakistan-India Expert Level Dialogue on Conventional CBMs' (Online). 2006. Available at http://www.mea.gov.in/Speeches-Statements.htm?dtl/2176/joint+statement+3rd+round+of+pakistanindia+expert+level+dialogue+on+conventional+cbms (accessed on 27 April 2006).

Ministry of External Affairs. 'On India–Pakistan Foreign Secretary Level Talks in New Delhi' (Online). 2006. Available at http://www.mea.gov.in/media-briefings.htm?dtl/2730/On+IndiaPakistan+Foreign+Secretary+level+tal ks+in+New+Delhi (accessed on 2 September 2016).

———. 'Briefing by Foreign Secretary after India–Pakistan Foreign Secretary-Level Talks' (Online). 2008. Available at http://www.mea.gov.in/media-briefings.htm?dtl/3202/Briefing+by+Foreign+Secretary+after+IndiaPaki stan+Foreign+Secretary+level+talks (accessed on 2 April 2017).

———. 'Resolution moved in Lok Sabha Rejects the Resolution Passed by the National Assembly of Pakistan' (Online). 2013. Available at http://www. mea.gov.in/bilateral-documents.htm?dtl/21391/Resolution+moved+in+L ok+Sabha+rejects+the+resolution+passed+by+the+National+Assembly +of+Pakistan (accessed on 19 December 2016).

Misra, A. 'The Sir Creek Boundary Dispute: A Victim of India–Pakistan Linkage Politics'. *Boundary and Security Bulletin* 8, no. 4 (2001): 91–6.

Morgan, Forrest E., Karl P. Mueller, Evan S. Medeiros, Kevin L. Pollpeter, and Roger Cliff. *Dangerous Thresholds—Managing Escalation in the 21st Century*. Santa Monica, CA: Project Air Force, RAND Corporation, 2008. Available at https://www.rand.org/content/dam/rand/pubs/monographs/2008/ RAND_MG614.sum.pdf (accessed on 21 July 2017).

Murphy, E. *The Making of Terrorism in Pakistan: Historical and Social Roots of Extremism*. Oxon: Routledge, 2013.

Mustafa, Z. 'The Kashmir Dispute and the Simla Agreement'. *Pakistan Horizon* 25, no. 3 (1972): 38–52.

Nair, P. 'Skirmishing on the Line of Control'. *Economic and Political Weekly* 48, no. 4 (2013). Available at https://www.epw.in/journal/2013/04/web-exclusives/skirmishing-line-control.html (accessed on 29 October 2018).

Naqash, T. 'Pakistan Aware of Designs behind Ceasefire Violations: COAS'. *Dawn* (Online). 22 February 2017. Available at https://www.dawn.com/ news/1316231 (accessed on 22 March 2017).

Narang, V. 'Posturing for Peace'. *International Security* 34, no. 3 (Winter 2009–10): 38–78, https://www.belfercenter.org/sites/default/files/legacy/files/ Narang.pdf (accessed on 2 March 2017)

———. 'Plenary: Beyond the Nuclear Threshold: Causes and Consequences of First Use' (Online). 2017. Available at https://fbfy83yid9j1dqsev3zq0w8n-wpengine.netdna-ssl.com/wp-content/uploads/2013/08/Vipin-Narang-Remarks-Carnegie-Nukefest-2017.pdf (accessed on 20 March 2017).

NDTV. 'After Border Tension, India and Pakistan in Visa Row: Report'. (Online). 17 July 2015. Available at https://www.ndtv.com/india-news/ after-border-tension-india-and-pakistan-in-visa-row-report-782526 (accessed on 5 January 2017).

———. 'Formalise 2003 India–Pakistan Ceasefire Agreement: Abdul Basit' (Online). 30 October 2015. Available at http://www.ndtv.com/india-news/ formalise-2003-india-pakistan-ceasefire-agreement-abdul-basit-1238292 (accessed on 2 March 2017).

———. 'Every Claim of India About 26/11 Backed By Man Who Headed Pak Probe' (Online). 4 August 2015. Available at http://www.ndtv.com/india-news/mumbai-attacks-launched-from-pakistan-soil-says-former-pak-investigator-in-article-1203702 (accessed on 18 July 2017).

———. 'Defence Minister AK Antony's Statement on Five Indians Being Killed by Pakistani Troops' (Online). 6 August 2013. Available at https://www. ndtv.com/india-news/read-defence-minister-ak-antonys-statement-on-five-indians-being-killed-by-pakistani-troops-530703 (accessed on 21 March 2017).

News. 'India Kills Pakistani Soldier for Inadvertently Crossing LoC' (Online). 16 February 2013. Available at https://www.thenews.com.pk/archive/ print/628648-india-kills-pakistani-soldier-for-inadvertently-crossing-loc (accessed on 3 January 2017).

News18. 'Musharraf Planned Kargil, Nawaz Didn't Know: Ex-Pak Gen' (Online). 3 June 2008. Available at https://www.news18.com/news/india/ musharraf-planned-kargil-nawaz-didnt-know-ex-pak-gen-290441.html (accessed on 15 September 2017).

———. 'J&K: Pakistan Violates Ceasefire Twice in 10 Hours, One BSF Jawan Injured' (Online). 27 July 2013. Available at http://www.news18.com/ news/india/jk-pakistan-violates-ceasefire-twice-in-10-hours-one-bsf-jawan-injured-627008.html (accessed on 8 December 2017).

——— 'Five Ways India Can Avenge Mutilation of Its Soldiers by Pakistan' (Online). 2 May 2017. Available at https://www.news18.com/news/india/ five-ways-india-can-avenge-pakistan-mutilation-of-soldiers-1388951.html (accessed on 25 December 2017).

New York Times. 'Statement by Yahya Khan' (Online). 18 December 1971. Available at http://www.nytimes.com/1971/12/18/archives/statement-by-yahya-khan.html (accessed on 5 January 2017).

Noorani, A.G. 'CBMs for the Siachen Glacier, Sir Creek and Wular Barrage'. In *Crisis Prevention, Confidence Building and Reconciliation in South Asia*, edited by Michael Krepon and Amit Sevak. New York: St. Martin's Press, 1995.

———. 'Can't "Disappear" this Body' (Online). 9 February 2013. Available at http://www.thehindu.com/opinion/lead/cant-disappear-this-body/ article4394238.ece (accessed on 12 March 2017).

———. 'History as Prison'. *Frontline* (Online). 2005. Available at http://www. frontline.in/static/html/fl2219/stories/20050923000507700.htm (accessed on 20 April 2017).

Noorani, A.G. 'The Siachen Impasse' (Online). 2017. Available at http://www.frontline.in/static/html/fl1923/stories/20021122000207000.htm (accessed on 5 January 2017).

Nye, J.S. 'Nuclear Learning and US–Soviet Security Regimes'. *International Organization* 41, no. 3 (1987): 371–402.

Outlook. 'Jawan's Suicide Led to Unrest among Troops in Samba' (Online). 3 September 2012. Available at http://www.outlookindia.com/newswire/story/jawans-suicide-led-to-unrest-among-troops-in-samba/774029 (accessed on 11 March 2017).

Pakistan Horizon, 'Documents', 26, no. 1 (1973): 107.

Pakistan Institute of International Affairs. 'Pakistan and the World'. *Pakistan Horizon* 55(3) (Chronology: April-June 2002): 71-118.

Panag, H.S. 'How We Pushed Pak out of the Batalik Sector' (Online). 6 September 2016. Available at https://www.newslaundry.com/2016/09/06/how-we-pushed-pak-out-of-the-batalik-sector (accessed on 16 September 2016).

———. 'The "Lost" Operation against Pakistan in Chorbat-la' (Online). 14 September 2016. Available at https://www.newslaundry.com/2016/09/14/the-lost-operation-against-pakistan-in-chorbat-la (accessed on 14 September 2016).

Pande, Aparna. *Explaining Pakistan's Foreign Policy: Escaping India*. New York: Routledge, 2011.

Pandit, R. 'Government Gives Army Free Hand to Avenge Pakistan's Mutilation Act: Sources'. *Times of India* (Online). 2007. Available at http://timesofindia.indiatimes.com/india/government-gives-army-free-hand-to-avenge-pakistans-mutilation-act-sources/articleshow/58464264.cms (accessed on 15 May 2017).

———. 'Pak Fire Goes Beyond LoC, Hits Kargil after 10 Years'. *Times of India* (Online). 17 August 2013. Available at http://epaper.timesofindia.com/Repository/getFiles.asp?Style=OliveXLib:LowLevelEntityToPrint_TOINEW&Type=text/html&Locale=english-skin-custom&Path=TOIM/2013/08/17&ID=Ar00106 (accessed on 11 March 2017).

———. '597 Military Personnel Have Committed Suicide in Last 5 years, Government Says'. *Times of India* (Online). 22 July 2014. Available at http://timesofindia.indiatimes.com/india/597-military-personnel-have-committed-suicide-in-last-5-years-government-says/articleshow/38873826.cms (accessed on 11 March 2017).

Parthasarathy, G. 'Missed Opportunities from Simla to Agra'. *Tribune* (Online). 7 March 2004. Available at http://www.tribuneindia.com/2004/20040307/spectrum/book4.htm (accessed on 23 April 2017).

Peri, Dinakar. 'Will Retaliate on LoC, Says India'. *Hindu* (Online). 17 July 2017. Available at http://www.thehindu.com/news/national/dgmo-speak-pakistan-accuses-india-of-targeting-its-troops/article19295370.ece (accessed on 27 December 2017).

Peri, Dinakar and Mubashir Zaidi. 'India, Pakistan DGMOs Discuss Situation along LoC'. *Hindu* (Online). 5 June 2017. Available at http://www.thehindu.com/news/national/india-pakistan-dgmos-discuss-situation-along-loc/article18722580.ece (accessed on 26 December 2017).

Perkovich, G. and Toby Dalton. *Not War Not Peace: Motivating Pakistan to Prevent Cross-Border Terrorism.* New York: Oxford University Press, 2016.

Pioneer. 'Escalating the Proxy War' (Online). 30 November 2015. Available at http://www.dailypioneer.com/columnists/edit/escalating-the-proxy-war.html (Accessed on 1 December 2016).

Posen, B.R. 'Inadvertent Nuclear War?: Escalation and NATO's Northern Flank'. *International Security* 7, no. 2 (1982): 28–54.

———. *The Sources of Military Doctrine: France, Britain, and Germany between the World Wars.* Ithaca: Cornell University Press, 1984.

———. *Inadvertent Escalation: Conventional War and Nuclear Risks.* New York: Cornell University Press, 1991.

Press Information Bureau. 'Planting of Landmines by Pakistan' (Online). 11 March 2013. Available at http://pib.nic.in/newsite/PrintRelease.aspx?relid=93392 (accessed on 5 July 2016).

———. 'Commanders Flag Meetings' (Online). 17 December 2013. Available at http://pib.nic.in/newsite/PrintRelease.aspx?relid=101910 (accessed on 22 June 2017).

———. 'Exodus of People from J&K after Ceasefire Violation by Pakistan' (Online). 3 December 2014. Available at http://pib.nic.in/newsite/PrintRelease.aspx?relid=112489 (accessed on 22 June 2016).

———. 'Fencing of International Border' (Online). 5 December 2014. Available at http://pib.nic.in/newsite/PrintRelease.aspx?relid=112676 (accessed on 23 July 2017).

———. 'Ceasefire Violations' (Online). 11 December 2015. Available at http://pib.nic.in/newsite/PrintRelease.aspx?relid=133036 (accessed on 22 July 201).

———. 'Vacating Loonda Post in LoC, Kashmir' (Online). 2016. Available at http://pib.nic.in/archive/releases98/lyr2002/rdec2002/04122002/r041220024.html (accessed on 5 July 2016).

———. 'Casualties in Firing by Pakistan Army' (Online). 25 July 2017. Available at http://pib.nic.in/newsite/PrintRelease.aspx?relid=168967 (accessed on 28 August 2017).

Pruitt, Dean and Jeffrey Z. Rubin. *Social Conflict: Escalation, Stalemate, and Settlement.* New York: Random House, 1994.

PTI. 'Military Restraint May Not Last: Centre' (Online). 2002. Available at http://www.rediff.com/news/2002/may/14jk7.htm (accessed on 10 October 2018).

———. 'Cross-LoC Strikes Happened in Past Too: FS Contradicts Parrikar' (Online). 19 October 2016. Available at https://www.rediff.com/news/report/cross-loc-strikes-happened-in-past-too/20161018.htm (accessed on 19 November 2018).

Pugwash International Conferences on Science and World Affairs. 'Lt Gen. Kidwai on Nuclear Risks in South Asia, Nagasaki Conference'. YouTube (video). 2015. Available at https://pugwash.org/2015/11/02/video-gen-kidwai-on-nuclear-risks-in-south-asia-nagasaki-conference/ (accessed on 8 August 2016).

Puri, B. *Kashmir, Insurgency and After.* New Delhi: Orient Longman, 2008.

Puri, L. '30 Killed in Jammu Suicide Attack'. *Hindu* (Online). 15 May 2002. Available at http://www.thehindu.com/2002/05/15/stories/2002051503030100.htm (accessed on 1 February 2017).

Purushotham, S. 'Internal Violence: The "Police Action" in Hyderabad'. *Comparative Studies in Society and History* 57, no. 2 (2015): 435–66.

Raghavan, S. *1971: A Global History of the Creation of Bangladesh.* Cambridge, MA: Harvard University Press, 2013.

———. 'The Boundary Dispute with China' (Online). 2017. Available at http://www.india-seminar.com/2008/584/584_srinath_raghavan.htm (accessed on 3 January 2017).

Rao, B.R. 'Sir Creek: Ripe Fruit That's Hanging Low'. *Times of India* (Online). 4 January 2013. Available at http://timesofindia.indiatimes.com/edit-page/Sir-Creek-Ripe-fruit-thats-hanging-low/articleshow/17877109.cms (accessed on 4 January 2013).

Rasler, K.A. and W.R. Thompson. 'Contested Territory, Strategic Rivalries, and Conflict Escalation'. *International Studies Quarterly* 50, no. 1 (2006): 145–67.

Rather, Z.A. and Deepika Gupta. 'Ceasefire Violation—Pakistan's Transgression on the Line of Control, A Situation Growing more Serious'. *International Research Journal of Social Sciences* 3, no. 1 (2014): 38–44.

Ray, Jayanta Kumar. *Aspects of India's International Relations, 1700 to 2000: South Asia and the World.* New Delhi: Pearson Longman, 2007.

Raza, Syed Irfan. 'Indian Official Summoned again over LoC Violation'. *Dawn* (Online). 10 July 2017. Available at https://www.dawn.com/news/1344293 (accessed on 26 December 2017).

Reddy, B.M. 'Jaish behind Parliament Attack: ex-ISI Chief'. *Hindu* (Online). 7 March 2004. Available at http://www.thehindu.com/2004/03/07/stories/2004030703320900.htm (accessed on 4 January 2017).

Rediff. 'Pak shows White Flags but doesn't Turn Up for Flag Meet' (Online). 28 October 2013. Available at http://www.rediff.com/news/report/pak-shows-white-flags-but-doesnt-turn-up-for-flag-meet/20131028.htm,m (accessed on 10 June 2016).

Reidel, B. *Avoiding Armageddon: America, India, and Pakistan to the Brink and Back*. Washington, DC: Brooking Institution Press, 2013.

Reuters. 'India Says Pakistan Army Backing Kashmir Incursions' (Online). 8 October 2013. Available at http://in.reuters.com/article/india-pakistan-incursion-kashmir/india-says-pakistan-army-backing-kashmir-incursions-idINDEE99707M20131008 (accessed on 19 December 2016).

Roy, S. '"No Relevance", Centre Asks UN Mission to Vacate Delhi Office'. *Indian Express* (Online). 8 July 2014. Available at http://indianexpress.com/article/india/india-others/no-relevance-centre-asks-un-mission-to-vacate-delhi-office/ (accessed on 7 July 2017).

Sadiq, I. 'Two Pakistani Minors Killed in Shakargarh Cross-Border Firing: DCO'. *Dawn* (Online). 26 October 2015. Available at https://www.dawn.com/news/1215495 (accessed on 3 January 2017).

Sagan, S., ed. *Inside Nuclear South Asia*. Stanford, CA: Stanford University Press, 2009.

Sagar, P.R. 'Pakistan's SSG Commandoes Targetting Indian Soldiers along LoC'. *New Indian Express* (Online). 31 October 2016. Available at http://www.newindianexpress.com/nation/2016/oct/31/pakistans-ssg-commandoes-targetting-indian-soldiers-along-loc-1533561.html (accessed on 11 March 2017).

———. 'Army Losing Sniper Edge over Pakistan on LoC'. *New Indian Express* (Online). 12 February 2017. Available at http://www.newindianexpress.com/thesundaystandard/2017/feb/12/army-losing-sniper-edge-over-pakistan-on-loc-1569609.html (accessed on 11 March 2017).

Sankaran, J. 'The Enduring Power of Bad Ideas: "Cold Start" and Battlefield Nuclear Weapons in South Asia' (Online). 2014. Available at https://www.armscontrol.org/ACT/201_11/Features/Cold-Start-and-Battlefield-Nuclear-Weapons-in-South-Asia (accessed on 25 August 2017).

Sanyal, A. 'Pakistan Using Heavy Shells—a First Since Ceasefire Agreement: Sources'. NDTV (Online). 16 August 2015. Available at http://www.ndtv.com/india-news/pakistan-using-heavy-shells-a-first-since-ceasefire-agreement-sources-1207926 (accessed on 3 January 2017).

Sanyal, A. '"We Share Details after Execution": Army Chief Rawat On Call For Action'. NDTV (Online). 4 May 2017. Available at https://www.ndtv.com/india-news/we-share-details-after-execution-army-chief-rawat-on-call-for-action-1689479 (accessed on 25 December 2017).

Sasikumar, K. 'Learning to Play the Game: Strategic Culture and Nuclear Learning'. In *Does India Think Strategically? Institutions, Strategic Culture, and Security Policies*, edited by Happymon Jacob. New Delhi: Manohar Publications, 2014.

Sawhney, P. 'At the Crossroad' (Online). 2014. Available at http://force newsmagazine.blogspot.de/2014/01/at-crossroad.html (accessed on 21 September 2017).

Schelling, T.C. *The Strategy of Conflict*. Cambridge, MA: Harvard University Press, 1960.

Schofield, Julian and Reeta Tremblay. 'Renewing UNMOGIP: The Persisting Problem of Kashmir'. *Peacekeeping and International Relations* 27, no. 6 (1990): 14–16.

Scott, D. 'Sino-Indian Territorial Issues: The "Razor's Edge"?'. In *The Rise of China: Implications for India*, edited by Harsh Pant. New Delhi: Cambridge University Press, 2011.

Sears, Stephen W. *The British Empire*. New World City: Horizon, 2014.

Seitz, Sam. 'On a Knife's Edge: Conventional and Nuclear Deterrence in South Asia'. *Politics in Theory and Practice* (blog). 30 September 2016. Available at https://politicstheorypractice.wordpress.com/2016/09/30/on-a-knifes-edge-conventional-and-nuclear-deterrence-in-south-asia/ (accessed on 29 July 2017).

Sen, S.R. 'Ceasefire Violation on the Eve of India–Pakistan Talks, BSF Jawan Killed'. NDTV (Online). 9 July 2015. Available at http://www.ndtv.com/india-news/bsf-jawan-killed-in-firing-by-pak-troops-from-across-the-border-in-jammu-and-kashmir-779863 (accessed on 3 January 2017).

Shah, S.A. 'River Boundary Delimitation and the Resolution of the Sir Creek Dispute between Pakistan and India'. *Vermont Law Review* 34, no. 357 (2009): 357–413.

Shanker, Mahesh and T.V. Paul. 'Nuclear Doctrines and Stable Strategic Relationships: The Case of South Asia'. *International Affairs* 92, no. 1 (2016). Available at https://www.chathamhouse.org/sites/files/chathamhouse/publications/ia/INTA92_1_01_ShankarPaul.pdf (accessed on 5 November 2017).

Sharma, A. 'BSF Dominates Talks with Pakistan Rangers, Has Its Way on Major Points'. *Economic Times* (Online). 14 September 2015. Available at http://economictimes.indiatimes.com/news/defence/bsf-dominates-talks-with-pakistan-rangers-has-its-way-on-major-points/articleshow/48949576.cms (accessed on 10 June 2016).

Sharma, B. 'Why India Needs to Read Nawaz Sharif's UNGA Speech More Closely' Huffpost (Online). 1 October 2015. Available at http://www. huffingtonpost.in/2015/10/01/nawaz-sharif_n_8225782.html?m=false (accessed on 3 April 2017).

Shukla, A. 'Army Weighs Retaliation for Beheading of Two Soldiers'. *Broadsword* (blog). 3 May 2017. Available at http://ajaishukla.blogspot.de/2017/05/army-weighs-retaliation-for-beheading.html (accessed on 11 September 2017).

Singh, J. *In Service of Emergent India: A Call to Honor.* Bloomington: Indiana University Press, 2007.

Singh, M. 'The War Begins'. *India Today* (Online). 29 October 2001. Available at http://indiatoday.intoday.in/story/an-imaginary-scenario-of-india-launching-military-strikes-at-pakistan-run-terror-camps/1/231558.html (accessed on 21 September 2017).

Singh, Rahul. 'Soldier Inadvertently Crossed LoC, Pak Has Been Informed: Indian Army Source'. *Hindustan Times* (Online). 30 September 2016. Available at http://www.hindustantimes.com/india-news/soldier-inadvertently-crosses-loc-pak-has-been-informed-indian-army-source/story-XlTFm HzcPSRbTa1UytmNtN.html (accessed on 1 December 2016).

Singh, V. 'Sunday Anchor: Home Is Where the Border Is'. *Hindu* (Online). 6 September 2015. Available at http://www.thehindu.com/sunday-anchor/home-is-where-the-border-is/article7620260.ece (accessed on 5 April 2017).

———. 'Govt. Junks Border Wall Plan'. *Hindu* (Online). 18 February 2017. Available at http://www.thehindu.com/news/national/govt-junks-border-wall-plan/article17322150.ece (accessed on 22 September 2017).

Smith, Stephen A. 'Assessing the Risk of Inadvertent Nuclear War between India and Pakistan'. Calhoun: The NPS Institutional Archive DSpace Repository (Online). 2002. Available at https://calhoun. nps.edu/bitstream/handle/10945/3272/02Dec_Smith_Stephen. pdf?sequence=1&isAllowed=y (accessed on 29 July 2017).

Smoke, R. *War: Controlling Escalation.* Cambridge, MA: Harvard University Press, 1977.

Snedden, C. *Understanding Kashmir and Kashmiris.* London: Oxford University Press, 2015.

Snyder, G.H. 'Crisis Bargaining'. In *International Crises: Insights from Behavioural Research*, edited by Charles F. Hermann. New York: Free Press, 1972.

South Asia Terrorism Portal. 'Responses to India's Offer of Cease-fire' (Online). n.d. Available at http://www.satp.org/satporgtp/countries/india/states/jandk/documents/papers/Response_Ceasefire.htm (accessed on 21 March 2017)

Srinath Raghavan, S. *War and Peace in Modern India: A Strategic History of Nehru Years*. Ranikhet: Permanent Black, 2010.

Subramaniam, A. 'From Kargil to Parakram, A Lesson in Forceful Persuasion'. *Hindu* (Online). 27 July 2012. Available at http://www.thehindu.com/opinion/op-ed/from-kargil-to-parakram-a-lesson-in-forceful-persuasion/article3687855.ece (accessed on 21 September 2017).

Swami, P. 'Border Barrier'. *Frontline* 18, no. 9 (15–28 September 2001). Available at http://www.frontline.in/static/html/fl1819/18191290.htm (accessed on 25 June 2017).

————. 'A Message Loud and Clear'. *Frontline* 20, no. 16 (August 2003). Available at http://www.frontline.in/static/html/fl2016/stories/200308 15003503600.htm (accessed on 1 February 2017).

————. 'Runaway Grandmother Sparked Savage Skirmish on LoC'. *Hindu* (Online). 10 January 2013. Available at http://www.thehindu.com/news/national/runaway-grandmother-sparked-savage-skirmish-on-loc/article4291126.ece (accessed on 22 December 2016).

————. 'Exclusive: Details of LoC Killings That Came before Poonch Ambush'. Firstpost (Online). 7 August 2013. Available at http://www.firstpost.com/india/exclusive-details-of-loc-killings-that-came-before-poonch-ambush-1016785.html (accessed on 8 December 2016).

————. 'Shooting Ourselves in the Foot'. *Hindu* (Online). 21 October 2014. Available at http://indianexpress.com/article/opinion/columns/shooting-ourselves-in-the-foot/99/ (accessed on 22 December 2016).

————. 'The Abyss Ahead of the Line of Control'. *Indian Express* (Online). 24 November 2016. Available at http://indianexpress.com/article/explained/india-pakistan-relation-army-jammu-kashmir-terrorism-4392082/ (accessed on 10 June 2017).

————. 'Pakistan Army Brass Ordered Attack to Avenge Losses on Line of Control'. *Indian Express* (Online). 2017. Available at http://indianexpress.com/article/india/pakistan-army-brass-ordered-attack-to-avenge-losses-on-line-of-control-4638185/ (accessed on 14 September 2017).

Syed, B.S. 'Ceasefire Violations by India Threaten Stability, Warns Army'. *Dawn* (Online). 9 February 2017. Available at https://www.dawn.com/news/1313677 (accessed on 8 August 2017).

————. 'New Delhi Warned against "Misadventure"'. *Dawn* (Online). 3 May 2017. Available at https://www.dawn.com/news/1330767 (accessed on 25 December 2017).

————. 'Threats of Retaliation Traded with India'. *Dawn* (Online). 6 June 2017. Available at https://www.dawn.com/news/1337734 (accessed on 25 December 2017).

Syed, Baqir Sajjad and Tariq Naqash. 'Pakistan Threatens to Choke Indian Supply Lines near LoC'. *Dawn* (Online). 18 July 2017. Available at https://www.dawn.com/news/1346009 (accessed on 27 December 2017).

Tetlock, P.E. 'Learning in U.S. and Soviet Foreign Policy: In Search of an Elusive Concept'. In *Learning in U.S. and Soviet Foreign Policy*, edited by George W. Breslauer and Philip E. Tetlock. New York: Westview Press, 1991.

Times of India. 'One BSF Jawan Dead, Three Injured in Pak Firing' (Online). 16 July 2014. Available at http://timesofindia.indiatimes.com/india/One-BSF-jawan-dead-three-injured-in-Pak-firing/articleshow/38478589.cms (accessed on 11 March 2017).

———. 'Strong Action' Against Pakistan in 6 Months: Parrikar' (Online). 13 December 2014. Available at http://timesofindia.indiatimes.com/india/Strong-action-against-Pakistan-in-6-months-Parrikar/articleshow/45500932.cms (accessed on 26 December 2016).

———. 'US Snubs Pakistan's Bogus Complaint about Indian Interference in Balochistan' (Online). 22 October 2015. Available at http://timesofindia.indiatimes.com/india/US-snubs-Pakistans-bogus-complaint-about-Indian-interference-in-Balochistan/articleshow/49489193.cms (accessed on 19 July 2017).

———. 'Army used Artillery Guns to "Destroy" Pakistani Posts across LoC' (Online). 4 November 2016. Available at http://timesofindia.indiatimes.com/india/Army-used-artillery-guns-to-destroy-Pakistani-posts-across-LoC/articleshow/55250508.cms (accessed on 2 December 2017).

———. 'Patrol-Free, Multi-layer Smart Fence along Pakistan, Bangladesh Border by End of 2017: BSF' (Online). 30 November 2016. Available at http://timesofindia.indiatimes.com/india/Patrol-free-multi-layered-smart-fence-along-Pakistan-Bangladesh-border-by-late-2017-BSF/articleshow/55708888.cms (accessed on 22 September 2017).

Thompson, J. 'The Dynamics of Violence along the Kashmir Divide, 2003–2015'. Stimson (Online). 2008. Available at https://www.stimson.org/sites/default/files/dynamics-violence-kashmir-divide.pdf (accessed on 7 February 2016).

TNN. 'Rocca for Indo-Pak Status Quo'. (Online). 2002. Available at https://timesofindia.indiatimes.com/india/Rocca-for-Indo-Pak-status-quo/articleshow/9799105.cms (accessed on 4 October 2018).

Tribune. 'India, Pak Armies Decide to Defuse Tensions on LoC at Flag Meeting' (Online). 21 September 2015. Available at http://www.tribuneindia.com/news/jammu-kashmir/india-pak-armies-decide-to-defuse-tensions-on-loc-at-flag-meeting/135932.html (accessed on 10 June 2016).

United Nations. 'United Nations Security Council Resolution 307 (1971)' (Online). Available at http://www.un.org/en/ga/search/view_doc.asp? symbol=S/RES/307(1971) (accessed on 21 March 2017).

———. 'India–Pakistan Background' (Online). 2017. Available at http://www. un.org/en/peacekeeping/missions/past/unipombackgr.html (accessed on 3 January 2017).

Untawale, M.G. 'The Kutch-Sindh Dispute: A Case Study in International Arbitration'. *The International and Comparative Law Quarterly* 23, no. 4 (1974): 818–39.

Vasquez, J.A. *The War Puzzle*. Cambridge: Cambridge University Press, 1993.

Verghese, B.G. 'A J&K Primer: From Myth to Reality'. Working paper, Centre for Policy Research, New Delhi, 2007.

Wani, F. 'Amid Ceasefire Violations by Pakistan Troops, Army Chief Asks Soldiers to Be Aggressive in Approach'. *New Indian Express* (Online). 15 November 2016. Available at http://www.newindianexpress.com/ nation/2016/nov/15/amid-ceasefire-violations-by-pakistan-troops--army-chief-asks-soldiers-to-be-aggressive-in-approach-1538903.html (accessed on 6 December 2017).

Wirsing, R. 'War Or Peace on the Line of Control?: The India–Pakistan Dispute Over Kashmir Turns Fifty'. *Boundary and Territorial Briefing: International Boundaries Research Unit, University of Durham* 2, no. 5 (1998): 1–39.

Yusuf, M. 'An India–Pakistan Crisis: Should We Care?' (Online). 2016. Available at https://warontherocks.com/2016/11/an-indian-pakistan-crisis-should-we-care/ (accessed on 15 July 2017).

Yusuf, Moeed. *Brokering Peace in Nuclear Environments U.S. Crisis Management in South Asia*. Stanford, CA: Stanford University Press, 2018.

Unpublished Interviews

Abbas, Azar. Unpublished interview conducted by Happymon Jacob, 14 December 2017.

Afzal, S. Unpublished interview conducted by Happymon Jacob, 16 April 2016.

Ali, G. Unpublished interview conducted by Happymon Jacob, 11 April 2016.

Akbar, Bilal. Unpublished interview conducted by Happymon Jacob, 15 December 2017.

Arshad, W. Unpublished interview conducted by Happymon Jacob, 15 April 2016.

Bhatia, V. Unpublished interview conducted by Happymon Jacob, 19 September 2016.

BSF IG, BSF DIG, and other senior BSF officials. Unpublished interview conducted by Happymon Jacob, 25 April 2016.

BSF Officer 1. Unpublished interview conducted by Happymon Jacob, 2 June 2016.

BSF Officer 2. Unpublished interview conducted by Happymon Jacob, 2 June 2016.

BSF Officer 3. Unpublished interview conducted by Happymon Jacob, 2 June 2016.

BSF Officer 4. Unpublished interview conducted by Happymon Jacob, 3 June 2016.

BSF Officer 5. Unpublished interview conducted by Happymon Jacob, 3 June 2016.

BSF Officer 6. Unpublished interview conducted by Happymon Jacob, 4 June 2016.

BSF Officer 7. Unpublished interview conducted by Happymon Jacob, 4 June 2016.

BSF Officer 8. Unpublished interview conducted by Happymon Jacob, 5 June 2016.

BSF Officer 9. Unpublished interview conducted by Happymon Jacob, 5 June 2016.

BSF Officer 10. Unpublished interview conducted by Happymon Jacob, 5 June 2016.

BSF Officer 11. Unpublished interview conducted by Happymon Jacob, 5 June 2016.

BSF Officer 12. Unpublished interview conducted by Happymon Jacob, 6 June 2016.

BSF Officer 13. Unpublished interview conducted by Happymon Jacob, 7 June 2016.

BSF Officer 14. Unpublished interview conducted by Happymon Jacob, 10 June 2016.

BSF Officer 15. Unpublished interview conducted by Happymon Jacob, 8 June 2016.

BSF Officer 16. Unpublished interview conducted by Happymon Jacob, 11 June 2016.

BSF Officer 17. Unpublished interview conducted by Happymon Jacob, 11 June 2016.

BSF Officer 18. Unpublished interview conducted by Happymon Jacob and Tanvi Kulkarni, 14 June 2016.

BSF Officer 19. Unpublished interview conducted by Happymon Jacob and Tanvi Kulkarni, 14 June 2016.

BSF Officer 20. Unpublished interview conducted by Happymon Jacob and Tanvi Kulkarni, 16 June 2016.

BSF Officer 21. Unpublished interview conducted by Happymon Jacob, 16 September 2016.

Chandra, Satish. Unpublished interview conducted by Happymon Jacob, 14 September 2016.

Ghazi, T. Unpublished interview conducted by Happymon Jacob, 7 November 2016.

Ghazi, T. Unpublished interview conducted by Happymon Jacob, 29 May 2017.

Ghazi, T. Unpublished interview conducted by Happymon Jacob, 6 March 2018.

GOC, 12 Division, Pakistan Army. Unpublished interview conducted by Happymon Jacob, 13 December 2017.

Hasnain, S.A. Unpublished interview conducted by Happymon Jacob, 5 June 2015.

Hasnain, S.A. Unpublished interview conducted by Happymon Jacob, 5 June 2016.

Indian Army Colonel (name withheld). Unpublished interviewed conducted by Happymon Jacob, 16 June 2016.

Indian Army Officer 1. Unpublished interview conducted by Happymon Jacob, 18 May 2016.

Indian Army Officer 2. Unpublished interview conducted by Happymon Jacob, 13 May 2016.

Indian Army Officer 3. Unpublished interview conducted by Happymon Jacob, 14 May 2016.

Indian Army Officer 4. Unpublished interview conducted by Happymon Jacob, 15 May 2016.

Indian Army Officer 5. Unpublished interview conducted by Happymon Jacob, 14 May 2016.

Indian Army Officer 6. Unpublished interview conducted by Happymon Jacob, 15 May 2016.

Indian Army Officer 7. Unpublished interview conducted by Happymon Jacob, 16 May 2016.

Kanwal, G. Unpublished interview conducted by Happymon Jacob, 4 May 2016.

Khan, Aziz Ahmed. Unpublished interview conducted by Happymon Jacob, 30 May 2016.

Khan, Aziz Ahmed. Unpublished interview conducted by Happymon Jacob, 13 December 2016.

Khan, Aziz Ahmed. Unpublished interview conducted by Happymon Jacob, 15 December 2016.

Majid, T. Unpublished interview conducted by Happymon Jacob, 14 April 2016.

Malik, A.Y. Unpublished interview conducted by Happymon Jacob, 15 April 2016.

Nanavatty, Rustom K. Unpublished interview conducted by Happymon Jacob, 6 December 2017.

Nandal, A.S. Unpublished interview conducted by Happymon Jacob, 23 September 2016.

Nehra, J.P. Unpublished interview conducted by Tanvi Kulkarni, 3 December 2016.

Brigadier Noor. Unpublished interview conducted by Happymon Jacob, 14 December 2017.

Pakistani Officials 1 and 2. Unpublished interview conducted by M. Faizal, 2016.

Pakistani Officials 2 and 3. Unpublished interview conducted by M. Faizal, 2016.

Pakistani Officials 1, 2, and 3. Unpublished interview conducted by M. Faizal, 2016

Pakistan Official 4. Unpublished interview conducted by M. Faisal, 17 January 2017.

Pakistani Army Officers 1 and 2. Unpublished interview conducted by M. Faizal, 2017.

Pakistani Army Officers 1, 2 and 3. Unpublished interview conducted by M. Faizal, 2017.

Pakistani Army Officer 2. Unpublished interview conducted by M Faisal, 9 June 2016.

Pakistani Army Officers 2 and 3. Unpublished interview conducted by M. Faizal, 2017.

Pakistani Army Officer 3. Unpublished interview conducted by M. Faisal, 12 June 2016.

Brig. Khan, Pakistani Army Officers 5, 6, and 7. Unpublished interview conducted by Happymon Jacob, 2017.

Panag, H.S. Unpublished interview conducted by Tanvi Kulkarni, 19 September 2016.

Panag, H.S. Unpublished interview conducted by Happymon Jacob, 3 March 2017.

Pillai, G.K. Unpublished interview conducted by Happymon Jacob, 21 September 2016.

Prakash, O. Unpublished interview conducted by Happymon Jacob, 27 September 2016.

Raghavan, T.C.A. Unpublished interview conducted by Happymon Jacob, 8 September 2016.

Rajagopalan, Rajesh. Email correspondence with the author. 12 December 2017.

Retired Pakistani General (name withheld on request). Unpublished interview conducted by Happymon Jacob, April 2016.

Retired Pakistani Lt. General. Unpublished interview conducted by Happymon Jacob on condition of anonymity, 2016.

Sahgal, A. Unpublished interview conducted by Happymon Jacob, 4 November 2016.

Salik, N. Unpublished interview published by Happymon Jacob, 13 April 2016.

Sapru, T.K. Unpublished interview conducted by Tanvi Kulkarni, 10 October 2016.

Senior BSF Officer. Unpublished interview conducted by Happymon Jacob, 16 September 2016.

Senior BSF official. Unpublished interview conducted by Happymon Jacob, 2016.

Senior retired Indian army official. Unpublished interview conducted by Happymon Jacob, 22 January 2016.

Shah, A.A. Unpublished interviewed conducted by Happymon Jacob, 4 April 2016.

Sharma, R. Unpublished interview conducted by Happymon Jacob, 15 September 2016.

Shuaib, A. Unpublished interview conducted by M. Faisal, 18 December 2016.

Shukla, A. Unpublished interview conducted by Happymon Jacob, 6 September 2016.

UNMOGIP officials. Unpublished interview conducted by Happymon Jacob, 25 July 2016.

Unnamed officials in J&K. Unpublished interview conducted by Happymon Jacob, 2016.

Index